INTRODUCING AFFORDABLE HOUSING

By
Stephen Harriott and Lesley Matthews
(with Paul Grainger)

Chartered Institute of Housing Practice Studies
in collaboration
with the Housing Studies Association

The Chartered Institute of Housing

The Chartered Institute of Housing (CIH) is the professional body for people involved in housing and communities. We are a registered charity and not-for-profit organisation. We have a diverse and growing membership of over 21,000 people – both in the public and private sectors – living and working in over 20 countries on five continents across the world. We exist to maximise the contribution that housing professionals make to the wellbeing of communities. Our vision is to be the first point of contact for – and the credible voice of – anyone involved or interested in housing.

Chartered Institute of Housing
Octavia House, Westwood Way, Coventry CV4 8JP
Tel: 024 7685 1700
Email: customer.services@cih.org
Website: www.cih.org

The Housing Studies Association

The Housing Studies Association promotes the study of housing by bringing together housing researchers with others interested in housing research in the housing policy and practitioner communities. It acts as a voice for housing research by organising conferences and seminars, lobbying government and other agencies and providing services to members.

The CIH Housing Practice Studies are published in collaboration with the Housing Studies Association and aims to provide important and valuable material and insights for housing managers, staff, students, trainers and policy-makers. Books in the series are designed to promote debate, but the contents do not necessarily reflect the views of the CIH or the HSA. The Editorial Team for the series is: General Editors: Dr. Peter Williams, John Perry and Professor Peter Malpass, and Production Editor: Alan Dearling.

Cover photographs: top left – Handihelp is part of the Ridgeway Care & Repair service. Care & Repair assist older people and those with learning difficulties remain living independently in their own homes by making adaptations and undertaking small repairs and maintenance tasks. Photographer: Dave Pratt Photography, Bristol; top right – Mixed tenure development of 35 apartments in Southampton. Photographer: Jason Allen, Hook; bottom left – Maurice Bryan, Sarsen resident and published poet. Photographer: Dave Pratt Photography, Bristol; bottom right – Aster resident with her new kitchen. Photographer: Andy Cahill, Photoworks, Bournemouth.

ISBN: 978-1-905018-63-5

Introducing affordable housing
Stephen Harriott and Lesley Matthews (with Paul Grainger)
Published by the Chartered Institute of Housing

Printed on FSC stock from sustainable sources by the Hobbs the Printers Ltd, Totton, Hampshire SO40 3WX

Contents

Foreword

I don't believe that you can underestimate the importance of high standards in social housing in contributing to the social fabric of our society. To achieve that quality it is essential that we have housing professionals who have the skills and expertise to bring together a wide range of services and to be innovative and enterprising in developing new solutions and approaches in the challenging environment in which we operate.

Not surprisingly, in my career of over 30 years in the profession, I have seen much change. The range of organisations providing affordable homes is now much more diverse, with the growth in housing associations and groups, arms length management organisations and private companies. I believe that the more variety we have, with organisations building expertise and offering different approaches, the more likely we are to continue to raise standards. We also have a more diverse range of clients, with areas such as care and support or low-cost home ownership now being part of the portfolio of services provided by housing organisations.

The links between inadequate housing and low standards in education, poor health and difficulties in maintaining employment are now recognised; partly as a result of this, in recent years we have seen much higher levels of financial investment in social housing. But we still have a long way to go before we can say that we are proud of all our homes and neighbourhoods – and the housing profession has the key role in achieving that.

Introducing affordable housing plays an important part in equipping all who work in the sector with the knowledge to enable us to make a significant contribution to creating homes and communities where people choose to live. It is invaluable for new students and experienced practitioners alike.

This book not only offers a comprehensive guide to the fundamentals of housing management, it also provides an understanding of the importance of housing in the quality of people's lives. Most importantly, it has the potential to stimulate ideas about how the service can be developed for the future.

Aster Group's vision is '*Passion for excellence, pride in performance*', reflecting our commitment to delivering to high standards – and we welcome the opportunity to be associated with a book that provides the platform from which those aspirations can be realised.

Introducing affordable housing will continue to play an important role in helping equip all who work in housing to both raise and meet our clients' expectations.

Richard Kitson
Group Chief Executive
Aster Group

About the authors

Stephen Harriott is Managing Director of Living Excellence Ltd, a management consultancy specialising in social housing. He has held senior positions in housing as Group Chief Executive of AmicusHorizon Group, Amicus Group, Origin Group, Chief Executive at St Pancras & Humanist Housing Association and Managing Director with English Churches Housing Group. He was previously a senior lecturer in housing at Northumbria University, is a former Chair of the Northern Region Branch of the Chartered Institute of Housing, and has served as an External Examiner at the University of Greenwich.

Lesley Matthews is Associate Dean (Academic Programmes) in the School of the Built Environment at Northumbria University, which offers both undergraduate and postgraduate programmes accredited by the Chartered Institute of Housing (CIH) as well as the Royal Institute of Chartered Surveyors (RICS). She has contributed to the development of a variety of professional housing courses over many years, and teaches both full and part-time students with an interest in housing. Her academic interests include housing economics and housing finance, and she is currently responsible for both quality assurance and the enhancement of learning and teaching in the School.

Paul Grainger wrote large parts of Chapter 2. He is an experienced housing manager who has held a number of senior positions in local authority housing departments. He is currently a senior lecturer and programme leader in housing at Northumbria University.

All authors are Fellows of the Chartered Institute of Housing.

Acknowledgements

Many people have contributed, both intentionally and unintentionally, to the revised edition of this book, not least many students on professional housing courses at Northumbria University as well as our colleagues in housing throughout the UK.

A special thanks to John Perry at the CIH who offered us invaluable advice, assistance and suggestions from his home in Nicaragua.

Our thanks are also offered to those who have so generously and freely given permission to publish their work, especially to Edwin Trotter for permission to use his design drawings of Turnbull Street and other material, and George Kennedy of G R Kennedy, Chartered Architects of Dunoon, Scotland, for supplying a range of materials relating to the redevelopment of Commercial Buildings. Policy Press gave permission to publish the Vacancy Matrix taken from Smith and Merrett (1988) *The Challenge of Empty Housing,* and Homes for Northumberland kindly supplied the example of a Repairs Receipt (shown in Figure 6.16) and the Repairs Satisfaction Questionnaire (in Figure 6.17).

Any opinions expressed in the text are, of course, entirely our own, and we remain responsible for these as well as any unintended errors.

List of Abbreviations

ABC	Acceptable Behaviour Contract.
ACG	Annual capital guideline. The government's former limit for each local authority's capital spending programme; now replaced by supported capital expenditure (SCE).
ADP	Approved development programme. This was the Housing Corporation's annual capital programme for England. Replaced by the NAHP.
AEF	Aggregate External Finance. Amount paid annually to councils by government grants and from business rates.
AHIP	Affordable Housing Investment Programme, the Scottish version of the NAHP.
AHS	Annual Housing Strategy; housing strategy of the NIHE.
AI	Architect's instruction. This is an instruction to a contractor in relation to a building contract.
ALMO	Arms length management organisation. A separate organisation set up to manage council housing by a local authority.
AMRA	Asset Management Revenue Account, used to manage debt repayments by English councils.
APD	Agreed Programme Developer, status needed to bid for SHG in Wales.
ASB	Anti-social behaviour.
ASBO	Anti-Social Behaviour Order.
BPSA	Business Plan Statistical Appendix (a CLG publication of data from local authorities).
BRE	Building Research Establishment.
BREEAM	Building Research Establishment Environmental Assessment Method.
BRMA	Broad rental market areas; areas used to determine the LHA.
CAD	Computer-aided design.
CCT	Compulsory Competitive Tendering. A government initiative which required local authorities to submit the delivery of parts of their services to competition. Introduced into housing in 1995 but replaced by Best Value in 1999.

CCTV	Closed circuit television.
CDM	Construction (Design and Management) Regulations. Introduced by the Health and Safety Executive, placing obligations on clients in relation to health and safety. In particular, they require most construction projects to have a CDM co-ordinator appointed.
CFCR	Contributions from current revenue; revenue contributions to capital spending by Scottish councils, the Scottish equivalent of RCCOs.
CIH	Chartered Institute of Housing, the professional body for housing managers.
CIPFA	Chartered Institute of Public Finance and Accountancy.
CLG	Department for Communities and Local Government.
CLT	Community Land Trust.
CML	Council of Mortgage Lenders.
CRE	Commission for Racial Equality.
CSH	Code for Sustainable Homes.
CTB	Council tax benefit. A subsidy paid to low-income households to reduce their council tax liability.
DEA	Domestic energy assessor; accredits EPCs.
DETR	Department of the Environment, Transport and the Regions.
DHS	Decent Homes Standard.
DoE	Department of the Environment; largely superseded by the ODPM, then later CLG.
DPDs	Development Plan Documents (England).
DSD	Department for Social Development (Northern Ireland).
DWP	Department for Work and Pensions, responsible for Housing Benefit.
EMB	Estate Management Boards. These refer to organisations which are established to manage facilities and housing within a geographical area, typically between 100 and 1,500 homes with logical boundaries and common interests. The governing body will comprise elected tenants, the landlord, and co-opted persons (e.g. owner-occupiers in the area).
EPBD	Energy Performance of Buildings Directive.

EPC	Energy Performance Certificate; operates alongside CSH and is part of the Home Information Pack.
EU	European Union.
EUV	Existing use value, used as the capital value element for formula rent calculations (under rent restructuring).
EUV-SH	Existing use value for social housing: method by which stock is valued for resource accounting purposes.
FSS	Formula spending share, used to distribute RSG according to LA needs.
GB	Great Britain.
GNP	Gross national product. The annual value of output of the United Kingdom economy.
HA	Housing association.
HAG	Housing Association Grant. A capital grant from the Housing and Regeneration Directorate of the Scottish Government; equivalent to SHG in England and Wales.
HARR	Housing association repairs and re-improvement indicator.
HB	Housing benefit; the main means-tested benefit towards meeting the rented housing costs of low-income households.
HC	Housing Corporation, now absorbed into the HCA.
HCA	Homes and Communities Agency.
HHSRS	Housing Health and Safety Rating System.
HIP	Housing Investment Programme; English local authorities' former annual bids for capital resources for housing from the government.
	OR
HIP	Home Information Pack, required to be produced by all sellers and landlords for prospective buyers or renters in England.
HNF	Housing needs formula. The HCA's index of housing need used in resource allocation decisions.
HQI	Housing Quality Indicator
HRA	Housing revenue account. This is the revenue account which all housing authorities have to establish for their council housing activities.
HSG	Housing support grant, HRA subsidy in Scotland.

HSOP	Housing Strategy and Operational Programme in Wales.
HSSA	Housing Strategy Statistical Appendix (a CLG statistical publication).
JCT	Joint Contracts Tribunal. A professional body which issues draft building contracts reflecting the needs of client and contractors.
KLOEs	Key Lines of Enquiry; council housing performance indicators used by the Housing Inspectorate of the Audit Commission.
LA	Local authority.
LASCI	Local authority stock condition indicator.
LDF	Local Development Framework (England).
LDP	Local Development Plan (Wales).
LHA	Local housing allowance; the HB for most private sector tenants.
LIBOR	London Interbank Offered Rate.
LSVT	Large scale voluntary transfer. This refers to the transfer of council owned stock to a housing association, normally one which has been set up specifically to receive the council housing stock. The resulting associations have become known as LSVT associations.
MINCS	Mixed income new communities.
MMC	Modern methods of construction.
MRA	Major Repairs Allowance, paid as part of the HRA subsidy in England.
NAHP	National Affordable Housing Programme; the HCA's resources for affordable housing.
NEC	New engineering contract.
NI	Northern Ireland.
NICHA	Northern Ireland Co-ownership Housing Association.
NIHE	Northern Ireland Housing Executive. The NIHE provides 'council' housing in Northern Ireland, rather than the local authorities.
ODPM	Office of the Deputy Prime Minister. Most responsibilities for housing have since moved to the CLG.
OSM	Off-site manufacturing.
PFI	Private finance initiative. A government scheme designed to encourage private finance into public sector capital projects.

PPBS	Planning, Programming Budgeting Systems. A method of budget setting which focuses on objectives and alternative ways of meeting them.
PPS	Planning Policy Statement (England and NI).
PPW	Planning Policy Wales.
PRS	Private rented sector.
PSSCI	Private sector stock condition indicator.
QS	Quantity surveyor.
RCCOs	Revenue contributions to capital outlays. These are amounts of money set aside in the housing revenue account in England and Wales to pay for capital improvements to council housing out of rental revenue income; called CFCRs in Scotland.
RDS	Regional Development Strategy (NI).
RHP	Regional housing pot; capital funding determined by the CLG and distributed to RSLs by the HCA.
RSL	Registered social landlord. In England, this term will gradually be replaced by 'registered provider' following the Housing and Regeneration Act 2008.
RSG	Revenue support grant. The annual sum of money made available by the government to subsidise a local authority's General Fund revenue spending.
RSS	Regional Spatial Strategy (England).
RTB	Right to buy. Introduced in the 1980 Housing Act which enables qualifying tenants to buy their property at a discount.
SCE	Supported Capital Expenditure; amount of council borrowing which the government will support through the subsidy system.
SHG	Social Housing Grant in England and Wales; HAG in Scotland.
SHIP	Strategic Housing Investment Plan in Scotland; equivalent to English HIP.
SHQS	Scottish Housing Quality Standard.
SMI	Support for Mortgage Interest, available to those on most means-tested benefits.
SSA	Standard spending assessment. A government assessment of necessary revenue expenditure by each local authority on individual services. It is

	used in the determination of the revenue support grant.
SSCI	Scottish Sustainable Communities Initiative.
SSHA	Scottish Special Housing Association, whose stock was transferred to Scottish Homes and later, Communities Scotland.
TAN	Technical Advice Note (Wales).
THFC	The Housing Finance Corporation. A body set up to obtain private loans for a number of smaller housing associations who might find it difficult or more expensive to arrange loans on their own behalf.
TMO	A Tenant Management Organisation is an independent legal body controlled by tenants which enters into a legal management agreement with the landlord to manage housing on the landlords behalf. Often created under the Right to Manage legislation.
TMV	Tenanted market value. The assumed market value of an estate which takes account of the predicted net income of the stock.
TPAS	Tenant Participation Advisory Service. A consultancy set up to promote tenant participation. Used extensively by local authorities and housing associations.
TSA	Tenant Services Authority, is currently the regulatory body for housing associations and private sector social housing providers in England. LAs and ALMOS are likely to be included in the TSA regulation in 2010.
UK	United Kingdom.
US	United States (of America).
WAG	Welsh Assembly Government.
WHQS	Welsh Housing Quality Standard.

CHAPTER 1: What is affordable housing?

1. Introduction

Previously called *Introducing Social Housing*, the title of the new edition of this basic text now refers to *affordable* housing, reflecting recent changes in government policy. Although most of the book does in fact continue to deal with 'social' housing, it also now covers an additional category of housing for people whose needs are not met by the open market. This is what is now often called 'intermediate' housing. These two types are now embraced by the term 'affordable' housing. However, 'traditional' social housing remains by far the most important part of the wider affordable housing sector.

Despite the massive changes which have taken place in housing over the last 20 years or so, social housing – that is, housing managed mainly by councils, arms length management organisations or by housing associations – still has a major role. It provides homes for more than one-fifth of the UK population. It is a major item on the government's policy agenda. It is a crucial issue in English regional policy – and also for the devolved governments in Scotland, Wales and Northern Ireland. The way it is managed is a significant factor in tackling crime and anti-social behaviour. For these and other reasons, the government has been increasing housing investment in recent years. This makes an understanding of social housing policy and practice of prime importance not only for those studying or practicing in housing itself, but also for those interested in wider social and public policy.

This book is primarily directed to students of housing who wish to learn about the nature of *social* housing in the UK, the key features of its management, and its place in the UK housing system. It has been written particularly for those pursuing (or interested in) a career in social housing, and for individuals new to the profession, since it reflects the academic requirements for membership of the Chartered Institute of Housing. It is, therefore, particularly suited to courses of study such as the Edexcel Higher National Certificate in Housing Studies, Certificated courses for the CIH, Foundation Degrees in Housing as well as undergraduate degrees in Housing Studies. However, this text will also be useful to anyone with an interest in social housing, such as those taking a wide range of courses in social policy, public administration, estate management, building management, architecture, housing development or surveying.

This first chapter, *What is affordable housing?* introduces the concept of affordable and social housing, initially by considering what is meant by social housing in the context of the UK and then tracing its historical development and the reasons for (and nature of) the involvement of the public sector in housing provision. It then identifies the types of organisations which provide affordable and social housing in the UK today, and considers how they vary in size and location. Finally, there is a brief examination of what is involved in the *management* of social housing provision by these organisations, which is the primary focus for much of the rest of the text.

Chapter 2: *What is the context of affordable housing?* considers the wider context within which affordable housing is provided by housing organisations, examining the place of affordable housing in the UK housing system. Most housing in the UK is provided within a market system, which essentially means that it is allocated according to the ability to pay. Affordable housing is different in this key respect. This chapter explores the significance of the different *tenures*, each distinguished by differing legal rights and obligations attached to occupation. Tenures exhibit many differences, in terms of influences on their provision, their changing size and importance, the types of households they attract, the types of property they contain and the condition of those properties. These differences are explored in some detail, as well as the ways in which different tenures interact with each other. The social context in which the housing system operates is considered, with a discussion of issues such as the polarisation of tenures, with social housing increasingly housing poorer people with wealthier households moving into owner-occupation. The concept of social housing as a residual – or form of welfare or safety-net housing – is discussed alongside wider issues of social exclusion, poverty and disadvantage. Other factors affecting the quality of life, such as crime and anti-social behaviour are examined, along with the government's policy initiatives for dealing with many of these issues through the regeneration of neighbourhoods and measures designed to create sustainable communities.

Chapter 3: *Who runs affordable housing?* moves on to explore the delivery of affordable housing services by examining different possible approaches to *running a social housing business.* It looks at the role of local authorities, housing associations, arms length management organisations and private sector managers in delivering social housing. It considers the different ways in which the delivery of the key tasks can be structured in social housing organisations, and the reasons for this. In recent years, there have been a number of important influences on service delivery which have resulted in many different approaches. These include the growth of different forms of *tenant participation* in the management process, the *decentralisation* (and re-centralisation) of some key management tasks, and the introduction of the inspection regime for the management of social housing. The role of the new Homes and Communities Agency in England is discussed alongside its counterparts in Scotland, Wales and Northern Ireland, and together with new developments in social housing regulation and inspection.

Chapter 4: *How is affordable housing funded?* examines the financial framework within which social housing providers operate. It begins by exploring the significant influence of the *economic context* for public housing finance, before moving on to examine the specific financial frameworks which govern the provision of finance to different social housing organisations. This is examined not just in the context of differences applicable to different social tenures, but also in the context of increasing government emphasis on the *targeting* of financial subsidy to those most in need, via means-tested housing benefit payments. It also examines other ways in which public finance for housing has been re-directed in recent years, and the reasons for these changed priorities. The chapter also looks in some detail at how housing organisations finance their day-to-day, operational activities and includes an exploration of the Housing Revenue Account in local authorities and ALMOs and the income and expenditure accounts in housing associations.

As the next step in the achievement of a social housing scheme, Chapter 5: *How is affordable housing developed?* turns to the *process* by which new affordable housing is *provided* in the UK, with a detailed examination of the steps which are essential to achieving a social housing development or refurbishment. It identifies the roles of different professionals in the traditional approach to the development process, and considers the requirements of the various stages in development, from a management perspective. It identifies key aspects which will influence the likely success and sustainability of the constructed scheme, both for its occupiers and for those who must manage it. The chapter includes a detailed account of how social housing organisations obtain funding for the development of new homes, and concludes by exploring the reasons for the more recent emphasis on 'partnering' approaches to the process and examines what is meant by 'partnering'.

Having achieved the development of a new social or affordable housing scheme, Chapter 6: *How is affordable housing managed?* examines the tasks which are conventionally viewed as 'housing management', identifying the key roles of social housing managers in allocating social housing, setting and collecting the rents, and ensuring that homes are adequately maintained. The chapter also examines the role of the housing manager in dealing with anti-social behaviour. These are the 'front-line' tasks of housing managers, the activities which will most directly affect tenants and hence their satisfaction with the service provided. Approaches to these key tasks are explored in some detail, and issues of 'best practice' identified.

The final chapter: *Meeting the challenges* concludes with a review of the challenges facing housing managers towards the end of the first decade of the 21st century and the recognition that these challenges will require housing professionals to have a good understanding of the past in order to inform their future actions.

2. Defining affordable and social housing

The term *affordable housing* mainly consists of social housing (see below) but, as explained above, it also includes a small proportion (less than three per cent) of 'intermediate' housing. This new category itself consists of two types of housing whose price is less than what would be charged in the open market. It includes (a) *intermediate renting*, which is housing rented at levels above social rents, but still below the full market level, and (b) various kinds of *low-cost home ownership*. These different affordable housing 'products' are described in detail in Chapter 4. They are developed by the same agencies that provide social housing (although not all social housing providers are involved in doing so). The rest of this chapter deals with the major part of the affordable housing sector, which is social housing.

The term *social housing* means housing provided and managed by local authorities and arms length management organisations (ALMOs) – commonly called *council housing* – as well as by housing associations and other organisations regulated by government. The essential characteristic of social housing is that it is provided by organisations which do not make a profit for their owners in the way that a company in the private sector would aim to do.

Social housing organisations generally provide homes for those households which find it difficult to obtain a home of an appropriate size or quality in private housing markets. This may result from low incomes, which mean that private rents and prices are not *affordable*, or there may be other reasons why access to suitable housing is difficult, for example, for some households or individuals with special needs. The involvement of the public sector in the provision of housing was intended to help to meet these housing needs, to ensure that every household (regardless of income) could attain a decent home. Affordable housing can mean both housing for rent and shared ownership where the social housing landlord owns some of the equity on a property and the remainder is owned by the leaseholder (with the assistance of a mortgage) who can eventually buy more equity and eventually own the property outright. In some models of shared ownership the share owned by the landlord is rented by the shared owner and in other models an equity loan is given. However, in all cases the principle of shared ownership is that the combination of rent and mortgage payments is less than the costs of a full mortgage on the property.

Since affordable housing providers exist to ensure that homes are available to households in *housing need*, the process of obtaining access to affordable housing is very different to the private tenures. In the private rented sector, or in owner-occupied markets, the ability to obtain a home depends very heavily on the *ability to pay* for it. In general (unless there is discrimination), if households have sufficient income they can obtain a property of the type they want. Their *demand* for housing – the desire for housing, backed by the ability to pay for it – will, ultimately, be met by a private housing provider.

In contrast, in the social tenures the ability to pay is *not* a criterion. In the absence of any *supply constraints* – a shortage of available properties to let – social housing organisations could permit anyone who wanted a home to occupy, and pay rent for, one of their properties. However, in most areas of the UK, there are insufficient homes in the social housing sector to meet the requirements of everyone who might want properties. For this reason, social housing organisations must identify (and publish) the criteria by which they will determine which households gain access and which do not. These are known as *allocations or lettings policies*, and a range of traditional approaches, together with the move to using more consumer-focused or 'choice-based' lettings systems are examined in detail in Chapter 6.

In addition to providing homes, local authorities are also an important vehicle through which the government provides various types of financial subsidy to the housing costs of individual households, including those in social housing. For example, most households with low incomes may obtain *housing benefit*, which pays some or all of the property's rental costs. Indeed, a very large proportion of social housing tenants is in receipt of housing benefit, and this is examined in greater detail in Chapter 4.

The nature of the housing provided by local authorities and other social landlords varies considerably, in part reflecting differences in the housing needs which different organisations attempt to meet. A number of housing associations exist primarily to provide housing for one particular type of housing need, such as the elderly, so their properties will reflect this specialism. Until recently, local authorities were more likely to provide homes for general, family needs, so they tend to have higher proportions of houses than housing associations. However, some local authorities, particularly large urban authorities, have considerable numbers of flats in tower blocks; in Glasgow, for example, the Glasgow Housing Association, when it became the new owner of the city's former council housing, had over 20,000 flats in tower blocks. The largest estates have been built by local authorities, some of them extremely large and typically located on the outskirts of large cities. In contrast, housing association developments have in the past tended to be small, and may only consist of a single building, such as a hostel, or two or three properties in a small rural scheme. Hence, there is no *typical* profile for the housing stock of different providers. Social housing is provided in all varieties of building and in a huge range of locations.

3. How has affordable housing evolved in the UK?

Prior to the advent of social housing provision in the UK, households with low incomes were unable to afford the private, market rents which were demanded for decent housing. They were forced to make do with whatever they could afford, which meant either renting sub-standard, *slum* housing and/or living in very cramped, overcrowded conditions. By the mid-19th century, these problems had become particularly acute in the rapidly expanding urban areas of the UK. It was concerns about the impact of these overcrowded conditions on public health and the environment which first led to government involvement in housing issues.

3.1: Regulation: 19th and early 20th century public intervention

In 1846, the *Nuisances Removal Act* permitted local authorities to take action against acute public health problems, such as the *middens* which provided working class sanitary facilities. The *Public Health Act* of 1848 permitted the setting up of local Health Boards, intended to address problems of sanitation and tackle the epidemics of cholera and typhoid, which regularly swept through the overcrowded dwellings in urban areas. Later, the *Torrens Act* of 1868 permitted local authorities to demolish properties which were *unfit for human habitation*, and an attempt was made to address the problems of poor quality building standards with the 1875 *Public Health Act*, which encouraged local 'bye laws' for minimum standards of construction. Shortly after, the *Cross Act* (Artisans' and Labourers' Dwellings Improvement Act) of 1875 extended the powers of *clearance* – demolition – to entire slum areas.

These acts marked the beginning of attempts to *regulate* the private provision of housing, but the view of most politicians at that time was that housing provision, and its finance, were private sector concerns. In general, the acts gave *enabling powers* to local authorities rather than statutory *duties*, and since local authorities' incomes were raised from their local populations, local voters were reluctant to take on any unnecessary obligations which would raise their taxes. These voters were also likely to be the landlords of the overcrowded properties. The result was that, when the *Shaftesbury Acts* (the *Labouring Classes' Lodging Houses Act* and the *Common Lodging Houses Act*) were passed in 1851, local authorities largely ignored their new powers to build housing.

The *Housing of the Working Classes Act* of 1890, which largely consolidated and amended earlier acts, again permitted local authorities to provide council housing; but since no government subsidy was available and the finance had to be found by the local authorities themselves, few councils engaged in housing provision or slum clearance.

Around this time, however, a number of private benefactors, appalled by the housing conditions in which many households lived, set up charitable trusts to provide private finance for decent rented housing – individuals such as Peabody, Guinness and Rothschild – but the scope of the problem was such that they made little impact; and, due to the quality of the dwellings provided, the rents were relatively high, affordable only by skilled workers.

Octavia Hill (1838-1912), viewed by some as the founder of modern housing management, took a somewhat different approach, focusing on the improved management of existing properties and their tenants. She effectively combined improved housing management with social work, and

> *...was able to show that, by an authoritarian, labour-intensive system of management, using trained middle class women managers and rent collectors, it was possible to make profits out of housing the poor in decent conditions* (Malpass and Murie, 1999, p36).

The extent to which social housing management should reflect a 'social work' dimension remains, to this day, a topic for debate amongst social housing managers. Malpass and Murie (1999, p37) argue that the later municipalisation of working class housing resulted in the re-definition of housing management as a '*bureaucratic-administrative activity done by men*', with few elements of the Octavia Hill approach.

In the early 20th century, the government first intervened more directly in housing markets with the introduction of *rent controls* in 1915, in response to rapidly rising rents at the start of the First World War. This fixed private rents at pre-war levels, effectively forcing private landlords to subsidise the housing costs of their tenants. Some form of rent control – latterly known as 'fair rents' – largely existed from then until their abolition (for new tenancies) in the 1988 Housing Act. By reducing the returns available to private landlords, rent controls undoubtedly contributed to the decline of the private rented sector in the UK since 1915.

3.2: 20th century: the emergence of council provision in the inter-war years

The first significant involvement of the public sector in the *provision* of housing followed the end of the First World War. There were chronic housing shortages, and council house building was viewed as the best and quickest way to respond effectively to the situation. With the *Housing and Planning Act* (the Addison Act) of 1919, the government encouraged councils to build new homes by, for the first time, offering significant subsidies. The *Tudor Walters Report* of 1918 changed perceptions about house design, so that the preferred home changed from the tightly packed, 'high density' form of 19th century terraced housing for the working classes to more spacious environments of homes with a garden and inside amenities (baths and WCs). Many council homes were built to a 'garden village' layout in the 1920s, when the quality of council housing was high but rents, too, were beyond the reach of the poorest. The later *Wheatley Act* (Housing (Financial Provisions) Act) of 1924 improved the subsidy arrangements, so that by 1939, over a million council homes had been produced, representing around ten per cent of the total housing stock (Malpass and Murie, 1999).

In 1930, the *Greenwood Act* changed the emphasis of housing policy from simply expanding housing supply to *slum clearance*, encouraging councils to demolish sub-standard dwellings and provide new council homes for their occupiers. This was intended to supplement the provisions of the Wheatley Act, but by the early thirties, the government was under pressure to reduce public spending. As a result, the Housing (Financial Provisions) Act of 1933 repealed the Wheatley Act, so that subsidy was now available *only* to build new housing for households from slum clearance areas. Local authorities did succeed in re-housing large numbers of households – over a quarter of a million homes were demolished between 1931 and 1939 – but the quality of new council homes declined during this period, and councils now had new problems, with large numbers of much poorer tenants from the demolished slums.

Until 1935, the financial accounts of new council estates were effectively separated, depending on the act (the subsidy system) under which they had been provided. This meant that tenants in properties built with lower subsidies had to pay higher rents. Partly as a way of helping councils to introduce *rebates* on rents for poor tenants, a new unified *Housing Revenue Account* was introduced by the 1935 Housing Act, so that subsidies could be transferred between schemes. Much later, this would permit councils to cross-subsidise newer schemes from the rents of older schemes.

3.3: Expansion of council housing and owner-occupation following World War Two

The Second World War created new and acute housing shortages. During the war, there was very little construction or repair, and, in contrast to the First World War, around 400,000 homes were destroyed by bombing. Public sector attention was, therefore, directed once again to expanding the supply of housing, and for a time, slum clearance virtually ceased. The Housing (Financial and Miscellaneous Provisions) Act of 1946 introduced new subsidies, and in response to shortages, a system of building licences ensured that construction activity was undertaken largely by councils. This was also the period in which new, *system-built* techniques of construction were first introduced, employing factory produced components in an attempt to reduce the need for skilled labour.

By the early 1950s, there was a new Conservative government, which wished to encourage greater private sector provision. Building licences were phased out, and as council house building declined (except for slum clearance), there was a boom in the construction of properties for owner-occupation. As subsidies were progressively reduced during the fifties and early sixties, councils were encouraged to build high-density developments, including high-rise and medium-rise blocks of flats (which attracted higher levels of subsidy from 1956 to 1967). Many of the system-built developments proved to be particularly problematic in management terms, due both to poor design and poor standards of construction, and large numbers have since been demolished.

The Rent Act 1957 removed rent controls from better quality private rented properties, with decontrol of the remainder as they became vacant. This was intended to revive the private rented sector, but probably had the reverse effect, by permitting landlords to sell their newly decontrolled dwellings for owner-occupation. A further boost to owner-occupation was provided in 1963, when the government abolished Schedule A income taxation – a tax on the *imputed* rent income which owner-occupiers chose to forego. In effect, owner-occupiers were choosing to take this income 'in kind', by occupying the property themselves, instead of renting it out. (This is similar to being taxed on the value of services received from, say, a company car – it is a benefit in kind, which nevertheless has value to the recipient and so is effectively another source of income.) The abolition of Schedule A taxation therefore represented a significant tax advantage to owner-occupiers.

The Housing Act of 1961 provided the first significant public funding for housing associations in England, with £25 million available as loans from the *National Federation of Housing Societies* to provide homes at *cost-rents*. The 1964 Housing Act set up the *Housing Corporation* to regulate and finance housing associations, extending their interests into co-ownership schemes. However, at this time, two-thirds of any finance had to be raised from the private sector – usually building societies – which is similar to the present system of housing association finance (examined in Chapter 4).

The Labour government elected in 1964 promised a huge expansion of council house building, with a target of half a million homes a year. Rent controls were re-introduced for the private sector with the 1965 Rent Act; these were called *Fair Rents*, and assessed by a Rent Officer (employed by the Civil Service). The 1967 Housing Subsidies Act increased the subsidies available to local authorities, and new minimum (and very generous) space standards were introduced as a result of the *Parker Morris* report.

3.4: Policies for social housing in the 1970s

By the late sixties, general economic problems had caused a reduction in council house building and slum clearance, and instead, there was a new policy emphasis on the rehabilitation of the existing, private sector stock. For example, in England and Wales the 1969 Housing Act introduced *General Improvement Areas,* followed in the 1974 Housing Act by *Housing Action Areas*. Similar legislation was passed for Scotland and Northern Ireland. These acts encouraged local authorities to identify areas for systematic improvement, and more generous improvement grants were made available to private owners.

The *Cullingworth Report* of 1969 reflected a growing view that local authorities took too narrow a view of their responsibilities for housing. This recommended that all restrictions on the letting of local authority housing should be lifted, and in particular, that local authorities should look after the most vulnerable households in their area. A new requirement in the 1970s, that local authorities produce *housing strategies* for their areas (see Chapter 4), was intended to force authorities to adopt a wider, more strategic role in housing. However, it was not until 1977 that, for the first time, local authorities were given a statutory duty to provide housing for some categories of homeless households, in the *Housing (Homeless Persons) Act*.

By the early 1970s, housing *finance* had become a key policy issue. The 1972 Housing Finance Act introduced, for the first time, a *mandatory* (compulsory) rent rebate scheme for council tenants. This was necessary because rent controls – *fair rents* – were also introduced for council tenants, with the intention of increasing council rents to private sector levels and removing their connection with the cost of provision. As a result, the housing revenue account – the rent income account – could now generate a surplus; rents could be higher than the amount required to repay debt interest and the costs of management and maintenance. Fair rents were later abandoned (for council housing) by the 1975 Housing Rents and Subsidies Act, because this was widely perceived as unfair to council tenants.

The 1974 Housing Act also extended the role of the Housing Corporation, by introducing *Housing Association Grant* for housing associations. Similar provisions applied to Scotland and Northern Ireland. This was a very generous grant system, no longer requiring that associations obtain private finance. This marked the beginning of the considerable, recent expansion of housing association provision of social housing, albeit on a very small scale in comparison with local authorities.

3.5: Housing policy under the Conservative government from 1979-97

The election of the Conservative government in 1979, under Margaret Thatcher, marked a turning point in the provision of social housing in the UK. In pursuit of a 'property-owning democracy', the expansion of owner-occupation now became the central goal of housing policy. The Housing Act 1980 (and the Housing (Tenants' Rights etc.) Scotland Act 1980) introduced the right of most council tenants to purchase their council home at a discount – the right to buy policy – as well as new public sector tenancies with new rights.

The right to buy led to a massive transfer of housing from local authority ownership into owner-occupation as council tenants exercised the right and purchased their home, often with a large discount. From 1980 to 2007 a total of 2.29 million homes were sold under the right to buy in Great Britain (Wilcox, 2008), though the pattern of sales had been variable. In the period 1980 to 1985, 607,318 homes were sold and there were further peaks in sales in 1988 (160,569) and in 1989 (181,370). However, in 2007 only 21,675 homes were sold under the right to buy, due largely to rising house prices throughout the early 2000s.

The *Building Societies Act* of 1986 deregulated the provision of housing finance for owner-occupation, bringing 'high street' banks into the market, so that a great deal more finance was available, and many more households became eligible for mortgages.

As part of a substantial policy shift in favour of individual subsidies, the rent rebate system was reformed in 1982, to provide a new *housing benefit*. The results of this new policy shift were to influence housing in the UK throughout the 1980s, with policies which would continue to affect social housing provision to the current time.

3.6: Large-scale stock transfers

The 1988 Housing Act enabled the voluntary transfer of stock by local authorities and the first council to transfer was Chiltern District Council in Buckinghamshire which transferred its 4,650 homes to a new housing association it had set up following a successful ballot of tenants.

> *This started a quiet revolution in social housing which spread over the next two years to other places in the South East, then expanded across England. Confined initially to the leafy suburbs, in 1996 stock transfer arrived in inner city estates (Walsall and Manchester) and now looks likely to result in the disposal of the whole council housing stock in cities such as Coventry, Birmingham and Sunderland* (John Perry, JRF, 2000).

In fact the transfers in Coventry and Sunderland were able to achieve the support of tenants but the transfer in Birmingham was surprisingly rejected in 2002.

The main driving force behind stock transfer since 1988 has been the conflicting need to finance the necessary backlog of improvements and repair in the council housing stock and the government's need to restrain public borrowing. As public expenditure on housing counts as government borrowing, it has often been subject to severe restrictions by successive governments. In contrast, while the grants made to housing associations in the form of Social Housing Grant count as part of public expenditure, any private finance which they borrow does not. If council stock is transferred to a housing association, as part of a large scale voluntary transfer, for example, then the borrowed funds used to finance this lie beyond central government control.

3.7: Housing policy under the Labour government since 1997

The election of the Labour government in 1997 resulted in a number of key developments in the governance of the UK. The most fundamental of these was a change in the way in which housing policy is developed and implemented, following the devolution of aspects of government in Scotland, Wales and Northern Ireland.

With the creation of the Scottish parliament and Scottish Executive (now called the Scottish Government), and assemblies in Wales and Northern Ireland, the government delegated responsibilities for housing issues to those new bodies. The differences in powers devolved to the different parts of the UK, and implications of these changes for the processes of providing, managing and regulating social housing, are considered in subsequent chapters of the book.

A further development of housing policy saw the government focus on partnership working as a fundamental tool in governing and monitoring the increasingly diverse social housing sector, and in tackling the key issues of community safety, social exclusion, the regeneration of neighbourhoods, and the creation of sustainable communities. Government policies have also stressed increased *choice*. This was seen, for example, through discounted home ownership schemes and the continued encouragement of stock transfers. Choice in terms of the individual's access to a home and its location have been supported through changes in the law relating to housing allocations through the *Homelessness Act 2002* in England, and the emphasis on choice-based lettings. Developing approaches to the governance of housing associations, and particularly the local housing company model adopted for many stock transfers, has seen much greater representation of tenants on governing bodies.

The publication of the *Sustainable Communities Plan* in 2003 heralded a major increase in resources for housing with a commitment to build at least 200,000 new homes in designated growth areas, funding for market renewal in areas of low demand and a commitment to bring existing social housing up to a decent standard. This injection of resources in housing was also accompanied by an increasing use of inspection as a means of regulating social landlords. In addition, the government continued to emphasise its desire to reduce the role of local authorities as social housing providers by requiring all local housing authorities with housing stock to consider alternatives such as stock transfer, arms length management organisations or the use of the private finance initiative to bring the stock up to the Decent Homes Standard.

In Scotland, stock transfer as an option for tacking the decent homes shortfall has been much less popular than in England, with Berwickshire the first transfer followed later by the Scottish Borders and Dumfries and Galloway (in 2003), with Glasgow City (the largest LSVT to date) also adding around 90,000 dwellings to the transfer total during 2003. In Wales it was also the case that stock transfer took place much more slowly than in England, but in response to the challenge of meeting the Welsh Housing Quality Standard, transfers here became more common and by 2008 almost a third of Welsh councils had transferred their stock.

3.8: Recent developments in affordable housing

In 2007 there were a number of significant policy developments, which are examined in some detail later in the book. The first was the Cave Review of social housing regulation which was commissioned by the government in order to take a fresh look at how the social housing was regulated. Unsurprisingly Professor Cave identified that there was not a '...*level playing field*' in relation to regulation and he proposed the separation of the combined duties of the Housing Corporation as both regulator and funder of housing associations in England. As a result the government agreed to establish a new regulator (The Office for Tenants and Social Landlords – The Tenant Services Agency) and a new investment agency bringing together English Partnerships and the Housing Corporation – the new Homes and Communities Agency. Both new organisations came into operation in December 2008. In addition, the government commissioned Professor John Hills to look at the future of social housing in England and his views are reviewed in the later chapters of this book.

In the summer of 2007 the government published a green paper called *Homes for the future; more sustainable, more affordable* (CLG, 2007). The green paper set out the government's vision which was:

> *We want everyone to have access to a decent home at a price they can afford, in a place where they want to live and work. Good quality, affordable housing enables stable and secure family lives: we are all healthier, happier and wealthier when we have decent homes close to schools, healthcare and transport links.*

The green paper indicated that the government would raise its new housing target for 2016 of 240,000 additional homes a year to meet the growing demand and address affordability issues. It indicated that this level of housing supply needed to increase over time towards this target and it said that it believed that a total of three million new homes were needed by 2020, two million of them by 2016. These would include:

- *1.6 million homes already in existing plans including around 650,000 homes in Growth Areas* with support from the 2003 Sustainable Communities Plan (e.g. Thames Gateway and Milton Keynes/South Midlands).
- *150,000-200,000 additional homes in the new round of regional plans under consideration*, including many smaller sites and urban area schemes.
- *100,000 extra homes in 45 existing towns and cities.*
- *5 new eco-town schemes*, with the entire community designed to be able to reach zero-carbon standards. Each scheme could provide between 5,000 and 20,000 new homes giving a total of some *25-100,000 homes.*

In relation to affordable housing the government said it planned an *£8.4 billion programme for affordable housing* over the period 2008-11, a £3 billion increase compared to the previous three years. The full programme was designed to deliver at least 155,000 new affordable homes over the following three years, almost double the number of affordable homes compared to 2006-08. More than 100,000 of these would be for affordable rent, and more than 50,000 for affordable sale through the

Government's HomeBuy initiatives. The programme was to involve £12 billion of private borrowing to more than match the £8.4 billion of Housing Corporation funding.

In 2008, parliament passed the Housing and Regeneration Act which established the Homes and Communities Agency, set up the Tenant Services Authority and made a number of other important changes to housing policy. These are explored in some detail in subsequent chapters.

4. Markets and affordable housing

As identified previously, affordable housing is intended for households in housing need. This housing need is generated usually by their inability to purchase or rent a property in the private market. In economic terms a market refers to a situation in which prices for goods or services are determined by the interaction of supply (the goods or services offered by the sellers) and demand (the willingness and ability of customers to purchase or pay rent). In private housing markets, you can observe the way that changes in demand and supply affect prices most easily in owner-occupied markets. When the demand for owner-occupied homes falls (perhaps due to increased interest rates causing an increase in the monthly loan repayments, or rising unemployment causing falling household incomes), prices will be driven down. For example, this happened particularly in parts of England from the early 1990s to 1995 (depending on the region), as Table 1.1 shows. Prices had risen fastest in London and the south of England in the late 1980s, so the market collapse occurred earlier there and with a greater effect on prices.

Conversely, when very many people are keen to buy, prices are pushed up – as we saw in the UK during the housing 'booms' of the mid to late 1980s and then, later,

Table 1.1: Average regional house prices (£s), selected years 1991-95

Region	1991	1992	1993	1995
England:				
North	46,005	45,589	49,337	47,060
North West	51,178	56,508	55,885	56,533
Greater London	85,742	74,049	81,332	89,528
South East	79,042	74,783	76,029	80,939
South West	65,346	61,654	61,319	65,096
Wales	48,989	49,551	52,465	52,978
Scotland	48,772	50,010	49,568	53,143
Northern Ireland	35,392	38,287	38,880	42,810

Source: Wilcox, 2008.

Table 1.2: Average regional house prices (£s), selected years 1998-2007

Region	1998	2000	2003	2006	2007
England:					
North	57,776	65,145	101,561	143,097	154,761
North West	65,514	78,415	115,447	157,947	170,203
Greater London	114,783	163,577	241,864	305,544	342,122
South East	103,797	137,354	211,056	251,400	271,981
South West	80,203	104,233	174,482	213,586	230,885
Wales	60,902	72,285	109,661	157,457	169,848
Scotland	63,585	69,961	103,641	137,192	158,798
Northern Ireland	59,376	72,514	95,217	169,259	229,701

Source: Wilcox, 2008.

from the late 1990s to around 2006-07, as is indicated in Table 1.2. However, the credit crunch of 2007 led to a rapid decline in house prices from 2008 onwards as a combination of a lack of availability of mortgage finance and recession took their toll on the housing market and sales.

When landlords let properties in private rented housing markets, assuming that there are no rent controls (price ceilings set by the government), a similar process operates. As identified above, rents must offer a reasonable return on the investment made by the landlord. If private market rents fall to levels which do not provide a sufficient return to landlords, they will withdraw from renting, causing the supply to fall. This will, ultimately cause rents to rise again, until the supply from landlords prepared to stay in the market just equals the demand at the market rent.

At market rent levels, there are likely to be many households who wish to rent, but who cannot afford the price. They may have a need for housing, but cannot turn this need into a demand for housing. This is the case in many parts of the UK; there is a shortage of decent homes available at rents that many people can afford. So, rents, like house purchase prices, are expensive; unless landlords receive a reasonable return, they will not let property.

Before the public sector became involved in the provision of housing, families with low incomes were forced to live in very overcrowded, poor quality properties, often sharing with a number of other families. The government first became committed to the provision of finance for house building after the end of the First World War, when it provided capital subsidies toward the cost of building council homes. Much later, councils were urged to introduce rent subsidy schemes, in the form of rent rebates. Public finance was now to be used not simply to provide lower-cost homes, via *capital* subsidies, but also directly to reduce weekly housing costs for households, via *revenue* subsidies. The current provision of public finance for housing still has these two distinct elements – capital investment and revenue subsidy – which we look at in more detail in Chapter 4.

5. Who provides social housing in the UK?

5.1: Tenure in the UK

Although owner-occupation is the predominant form of housing in the UK, the social housing sector remains an important and sizeable tenure. In Great Britain the two key providers of social housing are local housing authorities and housing associations. Northern Ireland has the *Northern Ireland Housing Executive*, with roles and responsibilities in relation to social housing which are similar to local authorities in the rest of the UK. The table below sets out the dwelling stock by tenure in the United Kingdom as at March 2006 (Wilcox, 2008).

Table 1.3: Tenure in the UK as at March 2006 in 000s (with %)

	England	Wales	Scotland	Northern Ireland	United Kingdom
Owner-occupiers	15,442 70.23%	955 72.68%	1,614 67.05%	511 72.79%	18,522 70.13%
Privately rented	2,611 11.87%	137 10.43%	178 7.40%	69 9.83%	2,995 11.34%
Housing association	1,850 8.41%	66 5.02%	252 10.47%	23 3.28%	2,191 8.30%
Local authority	2,086 9.49%	156 11.87%	363 15.08%	99 14.10%	2,704 10.24%
All dwellings	**21,989**	**1,314**	**2,407**	**702**	**26,412**

Source: Wilcox, 2008.

The tenure distribution across the United Kingdom is very similar with the exception of Scotland where there is a much lower level of owner-occupation at 67.05 per cent and higher levels of social housing (at almost 26 per cent) compared to 18 per cent in England.

5.2: Tenure in England

The table and chart show a very significant increase in owner-occupation in England since 1976 from 55.7 per cent to over 70 per cent in March 2006. The most significant reason for this change has been the reduction in social housing largely caused by the right to buy introduced in 1980 with local authority tenure reducing

Figure 1.1: Tenure as a % of all dwellings in England

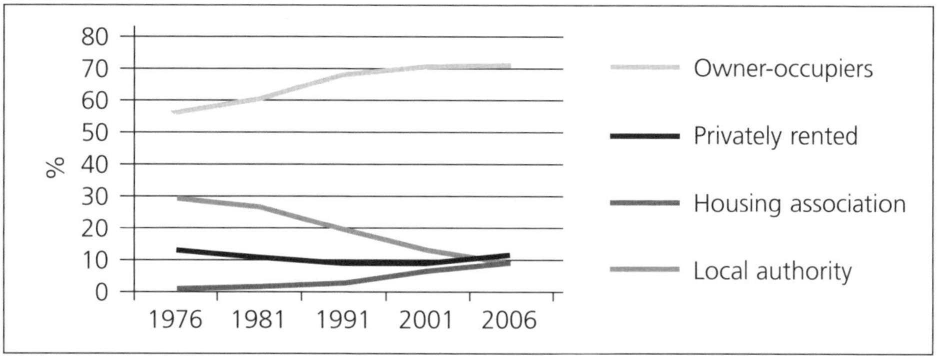

Table 1.4: Tenure as a % of all dwellings in England

	1976	1981	1991	2001	2006
Owner-occupiers	55.7	59.8	67.3	69.9	70.2
Privately rented	13.6	11.3	9.8	10.1	11.9
Housing association	1.6	2.3	3.1	6.7	8.4
Local authority	29	26.6	19.8	13.3	9.5

Source: Table 1.4 and Figure 1.1 adapted from Wilcox, 2008.

from 29 per cent in 1976 to just 9.5 per cent in 2006 and stock transfer from local authorities to housing associations. The combined social housing sector (local authority plus housing association) has decreased by 30.6 per cent in 1976 to just under 18 per cent in 2006.

5.3: Tenure in Wales

As in England there has been a significant increase in owner-occupation in Wales from 62 per cent in 1981 to 73 per cent in 2006. This has been accompanied by a drop in social housing from 28.6 per cent in 1981 to 16.9 per cent in 2006. As in England much of the transfer of homes from social housing to owner-occupation has been as a result of the right to buy.

5.4: Tenure in Scotland

The picture however in Scotland is significantly different with a massive expansion in the percentage of homes which are owner-occupied from only 36.4 per cent in 1981

Figure 1.2: Tenure as a % of all dwellings in Wales

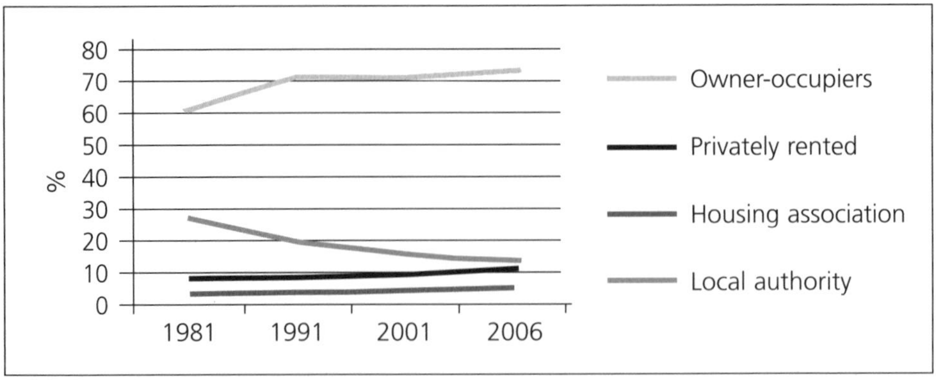

Table 1.5: Tenure as a % of all dwellings in Wales

	1981	1991	2001	2006
Owner-occupiers	61.9	70.7	71.0	72.7
Privately rented	9.6	8.2	10.0	10.4
Housing association	2.2	2.4	4.3	5.0
Local authority	26.4	18.8	14.7	11.9

Source: Table 1.5 and Figure 1.2 adapted from Wilcox, 2008.

to over 67 per cent in 2006. This has been accompanied by a similarly massive reduction in social housing from 53.9 per cent in 1981 down to 25.6 per cent in 2006; again linked to the right to buy.

5.5: Local authorities

Although in recent years the government has attempted to reduce the role of local authorities as social housing *landlords* they nonetheless still remain the main provider of social housing in Britain. However, not all local authorities have housing responsibilities. For example, shire county councils in England only play a minor role in the provision of housing services.

For housing authorities in England and Wales most of their legal duties are set out in the 1985 Housing Act which was a consolidating piece of legislation, bringing together a plethora of housing laws contained in earlier acts of parliament. In Scotland the responsibilities of housing authorities are laid down in the Housing (Scotland) Act 1987 and the Housing (Scotland) Act 2001.

Figure 1.3: Tenure as a % of all dwellings in Scotland

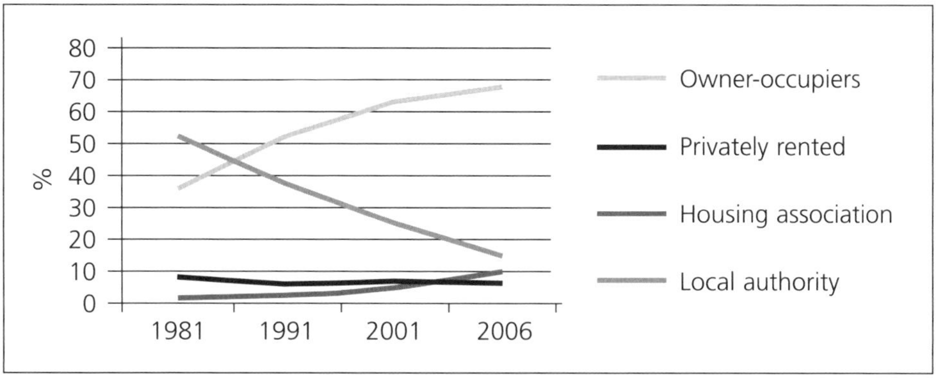

Table 1.6: Tenure as a % of all dwellings in Scotland

	1981	1992	2001	2006
Owner-occupiers	36.4	52.4	63.4	67.1
Privately rented	9.7	7.1	6.7	7.4
Housing association	1.8	2.6	5.6	10.5
Local authority	52.1	37.8	25.3	15.1

Source: Table 1.6 and Figure 1.3 adapted from Wilcox, 2008.

The 1996 Housing Act changed the responsibilities of local authorities in England and Wales significantly in relation to issues of letting of homes and dealing with homelessness and repealed the earlier provisions in the 1985 Housing Act. The implications of these acts and additional changes brought about by the Homelessness Act 2002 are considered in subsequent chapters.

The key responsibilities of local housing authorities include:

- developing and keeping up to date a strategy dealing with all the major housing issues – public and private – in their area;
- the assessment of housing needs in the area and the development of plans to meet those needs;
- where the local authority retains ownership of social housing the management of that housing stock, including the letting of dwellings, rent collection, arrears recovery and the enforcement of tenancy conditions;
- assisting housing associations and private developers to provide housing within their area: the *enabling* role;

- the provision of accommodation and other services to the homeless;
- exercising powers to tackle disrepair in private sector housing and in relation to houses in multiple occupation;
- the provision of housing advice services;
- the administration of housing benefits for both private and public sector tenants.

The responsibilities of housing authorities for housing in their area are much more extensive than simply the management of their own housing stock; indeed there is no requirement in the legislation for housing authorities to manage their own housing. As we shall see below, increasingly, local housing authorities have been transferring their housing stock to a variety of *stock transfer* organisations, or (in England) having it managed by arms length management organisations (ALMOs).

In the development of their *local housing strategies* – annually updated plans for housing in their area, required as part of their bid for resources (and examined in Chapter 4) – housing authorities are required to take a wide ranging *strategic* view of the housing needs in their area, including the provision of both rented and owner-occupied housing. This view of the local authority as having a wide ranging responsibility for housing in the area is reflected in a general desire of government to see housing authorities undertaking an enabling role – assisting other providers to achieve housing development – rather than providing new housing themselves.

The Labour government which came to power in 1997 developed a housing policy approach tied into their overarching aim of encouraging social inclusion. The green paper *Quality and Choice: a Decent Home for All*, published in 2000 set out a series of aims and objectives which laid the foundation for subsequent policy initiatives. The green paper emphasised the need for a much stronger strategic role for local housing authorities, the importance of partnership working, and the need to tackle areas of low demand. It outlined proposals to support those living in private sector tenures, improving the quality of social housing, encouraging choice in access to social housing, and the promotion of regeneration and balanced communities. The paper also emphasised the need to create a fairer system of affordable rents, improve housing benefit, and target support to those who are vulnerable, poor or in fear of crime and anti-social behaviour.

As part of this raft of policy initiatives the introduction of the *Best Value* regime generated a need for local authorities to examine critically the range and detail of their service provision. The service provision, together with service standards, must be carefully specified, and accounted for as local authorities are subject to inspections by the Audit Commission's Housing Inspectorate.

In February 2003 the government published The Sustainable Communities Plan (*Sustainable Communities: Building for the future*), which emphasised a focus on the creation of affordable housing, dealing with regional demand issues, tackling homelessness, improving local environments and the 'liveability' of local areas, and ensuring that all social housing is brought up to a decent standard by 2010 (ODPM, 2003). The implications of this key policy development are considered throughout the remainder of the book.

Since the early 1990s financial constraints have also stimulated some local authorities to engage in the *large scale voluntary transfer* of their stock to a new or existing housing association, since associations face fewer constraints on their ability to obtain finance for spending to refurbish housing stock. By March 2006 housing associations were managing over 46 per cent of all social sector dwellings, with over half of these accounted for by transfer associations.

However, in spite of these pressures, local authorities still remain significant landlords in their own right, as well as having the strategic and enabling role which the government has advocated.

5.6: Housing authorities in England

English metropolitan district councils

Following the Local Government Act of 1972, 36 metropolitan district councils were established in England, within the main urban conurbations of Merseyside, Greater Manchester, South Yorkshire, West Yorkshire, the West Midlands and Tyne and Wear. For example, within Tyne and Wear the metropolitan districts of Newcastle-upon-Tyne, Gateshead, North Tyneside, South Tyneside and Sunderland were created. These metropolitan district councils are now the responsible housing authorities in their areas.

Following the abolition in the mid 1980s of the metropolitan county councils these metropolitan district councils became all purpose, unitary, authorities, responsible for all local government activities in their area. The metropolitan district councils vary significantly both in terms of population size and the housing stock managed; the largest is Birmingham City Council with 75,783 households living in homes rented from the council at the time of the 2001 census.

English non-metropolitan district councils

Prior to April 1986 there were a total of 334 non-metropolitan district councils in England and Wales, but following a review of local government initiated in the mid 1990s a number of changes have taken place. In some cases shire county councils have been abolished and their functions transferred to new all purpose district councils, whilst in other areas the shire county council lost part of its geographical area to a new unitary authority.

Where unitary district councils have been established (particularly in big, non-metropolitan districts like Nottingham and Leicester) these have responsibility for housing. In the shire areas where the two tier system largely remains, the county councils have responsibility for key services such as education and social services, whilst district councils take on responsibility for more 'local' services, such as housing, planning, leisure services and refuse collection. However further changes have since taken place with counties such as Cornwall and Durham becoming unitary with the consequent abolition of the district councils in these areas.

London

Within London there are 32 borough councils which together with the City of London operate as unitary authorities and have responsibility for most local government matters, including housing, in their area. Each of these councils has a landlord function with the housing stock ranging from 1,887 rented homes in the City of London to 40,972 dwellings in the London Borough of Southwark (CIPFA Housing Revenue Account Statistics, 2008). The Greater London Authority and its Mayor have broad responsibility for strategic planning in the metropolis and this has led to a number of significant interventions in London housing policy, particularly to encourage more affordable housing as part of new developments.

5.7: Housing authorities in Wales

In Wales a review of local government was conducted in the mid 1990s by the Welsh Office and this review has led to the abolition of all of the previous eight county councils and the 37 Welsh district councils.

In their place a new structure of local government was introduced consisting of 24 new unitary, all purpose, councils, all of which have a responsibility for their housing. Since 1 July 1999, the Welsh Assembly Government has taken responsibility for, amongst other things, developing housing policy, social housing regulation and investment, and strategic issues.

5.8: Housing authorities in Scotland

Prior to April 1986 mainland Scotland had nine regional councils and 53 district councils. In addition there were three separate islands authorities for Western Isles, Shetland and Orkney. In Scotland the housing function had been carried out by the district councils and the islands authorities.

Following a review conducted by the Scottish Office, local government in Scotland was reorganised in April 1986 with the creation of 32 new unitary authorities and the abolition of the regional councils, though the three authorities for the Scottish islands remain.

In the new structure all of the unitary authorities including the islands councils have responsibilities for all local government services including housing. The smallest authority is Orkney with a population of 20,000 and the largest is Glasgow City Council with a population of 579,000.

The Scottish parliament was opened on 1 July 1999, directing the work of the newly created Scottish Executive, with more extensive powers and responsibilities than the Welsh Assembly. Among these is the power to pass legislation on housing issues in Scotland, although social security matters – and therefore housing benefit – are retained by the UK parliament at Westminster.

5.9: Northern Ireland

The Northern Ireland Housing Executive is the provincial housing authority, responsible for a range of strategic enabling functions, together with the development and management of its own stock of stock of 92,115 dwellings (NIHE, 2007).

Originally established by the Housing Executive Act (Northern Ireland) 1971 (since superseded by the Housing (Northern Ireland) Order 1981) the Housing Executive assumed the housing responsibilities of some 65 separate authorities and became Northern Ireland's single comprehensive housing authority.

Housing associations

Although local authorities remain the most important provider of social housing in Great Britain, the sector with the key role now in providing new social housing is the housing association sector. Under the 1985 Housing Associations Act a housing association is defined as a:

> *Society, body of trustees or company;*
>
> *a) which is established for the purpose of, or amongst whose objects or powers are included those of, providing constructing improving or managing, or facilitating or encouraging the construction of, housing accommodation and which*
>
> *b) does not trade for profit....*

Housing associations are essentially non-profit seeking organisations which exist to provide housing for people in need. They are independent bodies usually controlled by unpaid voluntary committee members (although English associations are now able to make payments to board members within limits established by the Housing Corporation). Most housing associations will have received public subsidy in the form of grants from the Housing Corporation (now the Homes and Communities Agency), Communities Scotland (now the Scottish Government), and in Northern Ireland the Department for Social Development, and are therefore subject to public regulation. In Wales registered housing associations are regulated and funded by the Welsh Assembly Government. At 31 March 2008 there were 75 associations registered with the Welsh Assembly Government, owning a total of 96,764 homes (WAG, 2008).

Due to the devolved government arrangements, the different bodies monitoring housing association activity in each of the constituent parts of the UK record and publish different statistics relating to their activity. The following sections outline the situation, making use of data published by each of the regulatory bodies.

Types of housing associations – England

There are a number of different categories of housing association which usually reflect the type of housing they provide or the particular housing need that the association wishes to meet. The majority of housing associations are general needs associations. This means that the association has been established to meet a range of needs and will provide housing for families, couples, single people and the elderly.

However, there are a number of specialist housing associations such as:

Abbeyfields

These are smaller housing associations, usually only owning a handful of properties, which specialise in providing shared housing for the elderly. The usual model is for three or four elderly people to share a house with a housekeeper being employed to offer care and support to the residents.

Almshouses

These are perhaps the earliest form of sheltered housing, with some having their roots back to the 12th century. They provide sheltered housing for the elderly and are found throughout the UK, often owning a handful of properties.

Hostels

Many housing associations provide hostel accommodation. Hostels will normally provide shared accommodation with each household having their own bedroom facilities but with cooking and bathrooms usually being shared, and with the housing association normally providing support workers, usually with specialist skills in meeting the needs of hostel residents. These needs will vary, and hostels are provided to help amongst others women fleeing domestic violence, the homeless, the mentally ill, people with physical disabilities and young people who have left the care of the local authority.

Co-operatives and co-ownerships

Co-operatives are a form of housing association in which the accommodation is collectively owned and managed by the people who live in it, although the members' only stake in the equity (value) of the properties is their £1 membership share.

Co-ownerships are a very different form of co-operative housing, which gained popularity in the late 1960s and early 1970s. When a member leaves this accommodation they are entitled to a share of some of any increase in the value of the property, depending on how long they have lived there and paid rent.

Sale/leasehold associations

A number of specialist housing associations have been set up which have concentrated on providing housing for low-cost home ownership, rather than for rent. This can take the form of shared ownership housing where residents will part buy their home on a mortgage and rent the remainder from the housing association, with the option of increasing their share (*staircasing*) to full ownership when their resources allow. Some specialist *leasehold schemes for the elderly* (now called shared ownership for the elderly) have been set up where elderly persons can buy a property at 75 per cent of its market value, the housing association retaining ownership of the remaining equity in the property. Many general needs associations now operate low-cost home ownership schemes alongside their rented provision although in some cases they have set up specialist associations to deal with this particular type of provision.

According to the Housing Corporation there were 1,879 housing associations registered in March 2008. The majority of these were registered as Industrial and Provident Act Societies.

Table 1.7: Housing associations registered with the Housing Corporation in England at March 2008

Industrial & Provident Act Societies (Charitable rules – 681/Non-charitable rules – 413)	1,094
Registered charities only	410
Registered companies only	65
Registered as both a company and a charity	310
Total	1,879

Source: *Housing Corporation Annual Report, 2008.*

The breakdown of housing associations by type of associations is shown in Table 1.8.

However, although there are 1,879 associations, the anlaysis of the sector by stock size shows that most of the housing stock is held by relatively few housing associations. In 2008 there were 43 associations holding more that 10,000 homes whilst there were 1,354 associations with less than 250 homes (see Table 1.9).

Table 1.8: Types of housing associations

Distribution of housing associations by Housing Corporation field and type

Registry type	London	South East	South West	Central	North	National
Almshouses	63	68	52	113	80	376
Abbeyfield	28	52	53	44	53	239
YMCA/YWCA	9	3	4	14	8	38
Co-operatives	138	6	4	27	68	243
Co-ownerships	6	2	–	10	7	25
Letting	127	104	62	157	156	606
Letting/Hostel	79	52	38	70	52	291
Hostels	15	5	5	12	6	43
Sale or lease	11	4	1	2	9	27
Field totals	**476**	**296**	**219**	**449**	**439**	**1,879**

Source: *Housing Corporation Annual Report, 2008.*

Table 1.9: Analysis of the housing association sector by stock size

Number of properties	Number of RSLs	Percentage of RSLs
Less then 250	1,354	72.1%
250 – 2,499	246	13.1%
2,500 – 4,999	137	7.3%
5,000 – 7,499	74	3.8%
7,500 – 9,999	24	1.3%
10,000 – 12,499	15	0.8%
12,500 – 14,999	11	0.6%
15,000 – 17,499	5	0.3%
17,500 – 19,999	3	0.2%
More then 20,000	10	0.5%

Source: *Housing Corporation Annual Report, 2008.*

At 31 March 2007 the housing associations registered with the Housing Corporation owned 2,207,300 homes (www.rsrsurvey.co.uk). However, the bulk of this housing is owned by a handful of associations. Table 1.10 shows the ten largest associations in England at March 2008.

Table 1.10: Largest housing associations in England at March 2008

Rank	*(Rank for Owned only)*	HA name	HA stock		
			Owned	Managed	Owned & managed
1	*1*	Home Group Limited	44,554	1,709	46,263
2	*3*	Sanctuary	32,853	10,705	43,558
3	*2*	Places For People	42,660	491	43,151
4	*4*	Wakefield	30,997	66	31,063
5	*7*	London & Quadrant	30,409	577	30,986
6	*6*	Anchor Trust	30,544	303	30,847
7	*5*	Midland Heart	30,621	169	30,790
8	*8*	Gentoo Sunderland Ltd	29,621	22	29,643
9	*12*	Hyde	20,950	8,048	28,998
10	*11*	Riverside	21,481	5,838	27,319

Source: www.rsrsurvey.co.uk (2008).

A feature of the English Housing sector is the development of 'Groups', where one housing group has a number of subsidiaries. Table 1.11 provides details of the largest ten housing groups.

Table 1.11: Largest housing association groups in England at March 2008

Rank	Group or HA name	HA name *(group member HAs which do not own stock are not shown in this list)*	Owned stock	
			HA total	Group total
1	Sanctuary	Sanctuary	32,853	
		Shaftesbury	7,166	
		Hereward	4,509	
		Beth Johnson	4,032	
		Charter Community	3,587	
		Rochford	1,735	
		Banbury Homes	1,555	
		Kingsmead Homes	744	
		Asra	751	56,962

Table 1.11: Largest housing association groups in England at March 2008 *continued*

Rank	Group or HA name	HA name (*group member HAs which do not own stock are not shown in this list*)	Owned stock	
			HA total	Group total
2	Guinness Trust	Guinness Trust	21,641	
		Northern Counties	18,355	
		Hermitage	4,045	
		Midsummer	2,959	
		Midsummer Homes	1,583	
		Gcs	1,139	
		Clapton Community	798	
		Guinness	603	
		Kennet	421	
		Other	181	
		Wycombe Friendship	136	51,861
3	London & Quadrant	London & Quadrant	30,409	
		Ujima	4,521	
		L & Q Beacon	4,352	
		L & Q Threshold	4,059	
		L & Q Bexley Homes	3,474	
		Tower	3,364	
		Opus	983	
		Threshold Key Homes	336	
		Lien Viet	105	51,603
4	Riverside Group	Riverside	21,481	
		English Churches	12,081	
		Carlisle	6,044	
		Berrybridge	2,826	
		Lee Valley	2,037	
		Bowlee Park	2,030	
		Community Seven	1,106	
		Riveside North	954	
		St Micheals	13	48,609
5	Places For People	Places For People	44,159	
		Bristol Churches	2,366	
		Kush	897	47,422
6	Home Group Limited	Home Group Limited	44,554	44,554

Table 1.11: Largest housing association groups in England at March 2008 *continued*

Rank	Group or HA name	HA name *(group member HAs which do not own stock are not shown in this list)*	Owned stock	
			HA total	Group total
7	Affinity Sutton	William Sutton	20,310	
		Broomleigh	13,036	
		Downland	10,790	
		Brighton	362	
		Aashyana	24	44,522
8	Circle Anglia	Circle 33	14,667	
		South Anglia	6,647	
		Russet	6,515	
		Wherry	6,033	
		Roddens	3,750	
		Mole Valley	3,516	
		Old Ford	2,598	43,726
9	Wakefield	Wakefield	30,997	30,997
10	Hyde	Hyde	20,950	
		Martlet Homes	5,200	
		Hyde Southbank	2,304	
		Minster General	1,539	
		Hillside	718	30,711

Source: www.rsrsurvey.co.uk (2008).

Types of housing associations – Scotland

A particular feature of the Scottish housing association movement is the development of co-operative and community-based housing associations. Table 1.12 gives details on the number of Scottish housing associations. Between them they own over 258,000 homes.

Table 1.12: Numbers of Scottish registered social landlords at 31 March 2008

Category	Total
General needs	185
Abbeyfield Societies	52
Small specialist	11
Co-ownership	1
TOTAL	**259**

Source: Communities Scotland on-line RSL directory, 2008.

Although Scottish housing associations own over 258,000 homes, most of the properties are owned by the largest associations. As can be seen below, 12 housing associations own almost 115,000 homes.

Table 1.13 Largest Scottish housing associations

Type of HA	No	Homes owned
Stock transfers	3	91,212
Other associations	9	23,679
Total	**12**	**114,891**

Source: Communities Scotland on-line RSL directory, 2008.

Types of housing associations – Wales

In Wales registered housing associations are regulated and funded by the Welsh Assembly Government. At 31 March 2008 there were 75 associations registered with the Welsh Assembly, owning a total of 96,764 homes (Welsh Assembly Government, *RSL – Stock Estimates for Wales*, 31 March 2008).

Table 1.14: Housing associations in Wales at 31 March 2008

General needs	33
Abbeyfields	34
Almshouses	6
Co-ownerships	2
Total	**75**

Source: Adapted from Welsh Assembly Government, *RSL – Stock Estimates for Wales*, 31 March 2008.

As with England and Scotland, the majority of housing associations in Wales own only a handful of homes, with 42 of the associations owning 250 homes or less, with only 24 associations owning more than 1,000 homes. Indeed, these 24 Welsh associations own over 88 per cent of the total stock.

Table 1.15: Distribution of Welsh housing association stock by size of association as at 31 March 2007

Size of HA (homes)	No of HAs	% of HAs
0-25	33	44
26-100	6	8
101-250	3	4
251-1,000	9	12
1,000-2,500	16	21.3
2,500 +	8	10.7
Total	**75**	**100**

Source: Adapted from Welsh Assembly Government, *RSL – Stock Estimates for Wales*, 31 March 2008.

Housing associations – Northern Ireland

At 31 March 2008, 36 housing associations in Northern Ireland are registered with the Department for Social Development. Registration gives access to Housing Association Grant, and places the association within the Department's regulatory regime. The 36 associations between them own 29,461 dwellings (Department for Social Development, 2008) with Belfast Improved Houses owning the most at 4,496 homes.

Most of the associations manage housing. However the Northern Ireland Co-ownership Housing Association (NICHA) provides opportunities through equity sharing home ownership schemes and at 31 March 2007 NICHA had 19,276 owners with 16,034 of them now owning their home in full (NI Co-ownership Housing Association, *Annual Report, 2006/7*).

Table 1.16: Housing associations in Northern Ireland at October 2007

General needs (including mixed general needs and supported)	24
Supported associations (incl. Abbeyfields)	11
Co-ownerships	1
Total	**36**

Source: Adapted from Department for Social Development data, April 2008.

The situation within the Northern Ireland housing association sector is again similar to the other countries. Of the 36 associations, only three own more than 4,000 homes.

Arms length management organisations

A local authority in England is able to set up an arms length management organisation (ALMO) as a company to manage and improve all or part of its housing stock. Unlike a stock transfer to a housing association, the ALMO is wholly owned by the local authority and operates under the terms of a management agreement set out by the authority.

Like a housing association, the ALMO is managed by a board of directors which includes tenants, local authority nominees and independent members. The local authority retains ownership of the housing and tenants remain secure tenants of the local authority.

ALMOs were primarily allowed by government as a means for local authorities to secure additional funding to achieve the Decent Homes Standard of the local authority if its tenants did not want to transfer the homes to a housing association, but at the same time securing management changes by obliging councils (after consulting tenants) to set up separate companies to which management (but not ownership) is transferred.

According to *Social Housing* (2008) there were 71 ALMOs at March 2007 managing 922,700 homes (Financial Information Company Ltd., 2008). ALMOs which deliver a 2 or 3 star Audit Commission inspection are able to access additional funding for modernising in the form of additional borrowing approvals.

The National Federation of ALMOs has published a *Key Facts* document which says:

- The first ALMOs were established in April 2002.
- The total ALMO managed stock is set to exceed one million homes by the end of 2008 – more than half of all local authority housing.
- £3.7 billion since April 2002, and a further £2.4 billion in the period 2008-2011, has been committed to improving the council housing managed by ALMOs.

(NFA, *Key Facts*, 2008).

6. The management of social housing organisations

The provision and management of social housing demands a wide range of knowledge and expertise. As shown in the previous section, most of the affordable housing stock is provided by relatively large organisations, though there are some which are exceedingly small. The task of managing them is a complex one, just as it is for any private sector organisation with a wide variety of functions. The main difference is that, since social housing organisations do not exist to make a profit, there is no simple measure of 'success', as there is for a private firm. As for all parts of the public sector, the social housing organisation cannot examine its profitability to see how well it has performed. For this reason, performance is gauged from a series of *performance indicators*, which relate to some of the key tasks undertaken by housing managers. In addition, success is measured increasingly through inspection of the quality of housing services by external bodies.

What are these tasks in housing management? First, if properties are to be built or refurbished, the key requirement is that *finance* is obtained. In general, this will be sourced from a combination of grants from the government, borrowing from the private sector, and from income generated from rents. Obtaining and managing this finance has become increasingly important for many social housing organisations. In addition, housing organisations must ensure that the income received from rents is managed wisely, to ensure that funds are available to provide an appropriate range and quality of services to the tenants on a week-to-week basis.

In those organisations where some or all of their services are decentralised, so that services are provided from a number of different locations, each manager may have control of a *budget* to pay some or all of the costs of management activities. These resources must be carefully managed to ensure that they are spent in an appropriate and timely manner. Indeed, in the light of increasing restraints on the resources available to social housing over recent years, managing the organisation's financial resources well has become a key issue.

Smaller associations undertake no new housing development and very few local authorities have sufficient resources to build new homes. However, *all* affordable housing providers will need, at some stage, to refurbish ageing properties, and most large housing associations undertake new development. This demands the ability to undertake a range of development tasks, ranging from identifying suitable sites, to managing the design of the planned development or refurbishment and arranging for the building work. Hence, the management of social housing may also require knowledge of the process of development, the roles of the key professionals, and the ways in which a high quality of development can best be achieved.

Once the properties have been built, they must be let to new occupiers, the *tenants*, and suitable arrangements must be made to collect rent and minimise arrears, to manage the letting of vacant properties, and to arrange for their repair and maintenance. These latter tasks are perhaps conventionally thought of as the key tasks of social housing managers, and they are certainly the tasks which have the most immediate and direct impact on the tenants. Increasingly, however, as explored above, some knowledge of finance and development issues is also required for effective management.

Since the managers of affordable housing have an obligation to ensure that their properties are available to households in housing need, identifying and defining *needs* is also an important task. The aim is to identify all of those needs which are unlikely to be met by the private sector, usually because the households lack the ability to pay. As identified above, local authorities have an obligation to identify housing need in their area, and to plan an annual housing strategy which addresses these needs. Chapter 2 considers the nature of the housing needs which are generally met by social housing organisations, while Chapter 4 examines the role of the *Housing Plan* in bidding for public finance.

Unlike private sector firms, the people responsible for strategic management issues in affordable housing organisations generally form an *unpaid, voluntary committee or board*. In local authorities, these are the elected members, the councillors who act as *cabinet members with responsibility for housing* or *portfolio holders for housing*. Housing associations and ALMOs have boards (sometimes paid in the housing association sector) and these boards take key decisions, with advice from the senior management team. Senior managers need, therefore, to be fully conversant with committee procedures and it is their job to 'operationalise' the decisions taken in board – to turn the policies into reality in the organisation. However, these are high level management tasks, beyond the scope of an introductory text.

As might be anticipated from the wide variation in the numbers of properties controlled by different housing organisations, the numbers of staff employed to undertake the management of the stock varies considerably. In very small associations it is likely that almost all of the work involved in running the association will be carried out on a voluntary basis by committee members. Large associations on the other hand employ significant staff numbers – often rivalling the larger local authorities.

Local authorities with their own housing stock all employ some staff to undertake housing management – although some have set up arms length management organisations which employ the staff. However, as you will discover in Chapter 4, there are huge variations in the scale and location of some of these tasks in the organisation, so some important management tasks may be undertaken by departments other than the housing department; for example, it is quite common for housing benefit payments to be administered by the Finance Department. In addition, local authorities have a much broader range of responsibilities for housing than associations, as identified earlier in this chapter. Hence, in a local authority, there will be strategic policy-makers and other staff dealing with private housing, as well as housing managers.

This book mainly sets out to explore the nature of the management roles and responsibilities carried out by affordable housing organisations, and most of the remainder of the book is directed to that objective. However, before doing so, the next chapter examines the context within which social housing operates and its place in the housing system of the UK.

References and further reading

Birchall, J. (ed.) (1992) *Housing Policy in the 1990s*, Routledge, London.

Burnett, J. (1978) *A Social History of Housing, 1815-1979*, David and Charles, Newton Abbot, Devon.

CIPFA (2008) *Housing Revenue Account Statistics*, CIPFA, London.

Department for Communities and Local Government (2007) *Homes for the future; more sustainable, more affordable,* Stationery Office, London.

Department for Communities and Local Government, *Live Tables*: www.communities.gov.uk

Department for Social Development (2008) *Northern Ireland Housing Statistics 2007-08*, DSD, Belfast.

Financial Information Company (2008) 'Special Report ALMOs', *Social Housing*, Vol 20 No.5, Financial Information Company Ltd., London.

Grant, C. (1992) *Built to Last? Reflections on British Housing Policy*, Shelter, London.

Housing Corporation (2008) *Housing Corporation Annual Report and Accounts 2008*, The Stationery Office, London.

Malpass, P. and Murie, A. (1999) *Housing Policy and Practice*, 5th ed, Macmillan, Basingstoke.

Merrett, S. (1979) *State Housing in Britain,* Routledge and Kegan Paul, London.

National Federation of ALMOs (2008) *Key Facts*, NFA, York.

Northern Ireland Housing Executive (2007) *Annual Report*, NIHE, Belfast.

Office of the Deputy Prime Minister (2000) *Quality and Choice: A Decent Home for All*, ODPM, London.

Office of the Deputy Prime Minister (2003) *Sustainable Communities: Building for the future*, ODPM, London.

Paris, C. (ed.) (2002) *Housing in Northern Ireland*, CIH, Coventry.

Pawson, H. and Fancy, C. (2003) *Maturing Assets: The evolution of stock transfer housing associations*, Policy Press, Bristol.

Perry, J. (2000) 'The End of Council Housing?' in S. Wilcox (2000) *Housing Finance Review 2000/2001*, JRF/CML/CIH, York, London and Coventry.

Power, A. (1993) *Hovels to High Rise: State Housing in Europe since 1850*, Routledge, London.

Statistics for Wales (2008) *Registered Social Landlords – Stock Estimates for Wales 31 March 2008*.

Sim, D. (ed.) (2004) *Housing and Public Policy in Post-Devolution Scotland*, CIH, Coventry.

Smith, R., Williams, P. and Stirling, T. (2001) *Housing in Wales*, CIH, Coventry.

Welsh Assembly Government (2008) *RSL – Stock Estimates for Wales, 31 March 2008,* WAG, Cardiff.

Wilcox, S. (2008) *UK Housing Review 2008/09*, CIH/BSA, Coventry and London.

Websites

www.cih.org

www.communities.gov.uk

www.dsdni.gov.uk

www.homesandcommunities.co.uk

www.housing.wales.gov.uk

www.rsrsurvey.co.uk

www.scotland.gov.uk

www.scottishhousingregulator.gov.uk

www.statistics.gov.uk/census

www.tenantservicesauthority.org

www.nihe.gov.uk

CHAPTER 2: What is the context of affordable housing?

1. Introduction

The need for shelter is a fundamental human requirement and the quality and availability of housing affects all of us. However, 'housing' is not a single entity; it is a heterogeneous item, available in many different locations, in different sizes and styles, of variable quality, and in a number of distinct tenures. This chapter considers the various ways in which households in the UK might satisfy their need for housing, through a discussion of the UK housing system and the different ways in which housing is made available to households. It explores the context in which the affordable housing sector operates, to set the scene for the issues considered throughout the subsequent chapters of this book.

The chapter begins by examining key concepts relating to the requirement for housing, such as housing *desire, need*, and *demand*. It also identifies the main tenures, which have implications for the rights and responsibilities of the dwelling's occupants. It examines influences on the demand for housing, and the ways in which this can vary over time and between tenures. It considers the problems arising from the fact that private housing markets can only respond to the desire for housing when it is accompanied by an ability to pay. The inability of households to pay has resulted in the concept of housing 'need', as distinct from housing demand, and the provision of *affordable* housing to meet housing needs. It also explores the ways in which housing need has been defined by both governments and affordable housing providers and why this concept changes over time.

In the course of this discussion the chapter examines economic and social factors which impact on the social housing system and also introduces some government policy initiatives and key legislation implemented by successive governments to 'steer' the context in which affordable housing is delivered.

2. Housing desire, demand and need

2.1: Housing desire

This can be conceived as a household's *preferences* for housing. It will include not only preferences for the size of the accommodation, its physical attributes and qualitative standards, but also preferences for tenure type and location. This means that all households, or potential households, will have particular desires in relation to their homes.

2.2: Housing need

The assessment of housing need – the process of which is considered in more detail later – involves the identification of the minimum housing standards which are required by particular households, and the measurement of whether households achieve those standards. It involves a qualitative judgement about the requirements of different households, and as a result, perceptions of housing need can change over time. Different societies may also have quite different perceptions of housing need.

The concept of housing need is a crucial element in the allocation (or letting) of social housing. In general, only those households considered to be in *housing need* will be offered a social housing dwelling, which may, or may not, meet with their desires or aspirations. This is in contrast to private sector housing provision, which is allocated largely in response to demand. The introduction of choice-based lettings by some social landlords is an attempt to recognise that households' preferences should also ideally be met. See Chapter 6 for more discussion of these approaches.

2.3: Housing demand

The term *demand* (or, more accurately, 'effective demand') is used here as an economic term to describe the situation in which housing 'consumers' have a desire for particular accommodation and have the financial resources to pay it. In this precise economic definition, therefore, 'effective demand' only exists if individuals' desires or needs coincide with an ability to pay the market price (or rent) for that accommodation. The desire for housing, or the need for it, do not, in themselves, permit the household to demand it.

3. Tenure

Within the United Kingdom at any one time, housing may be located in any one of four main tenure types. The crucial determining factor of which tenure a particular dwelling is in will be the ownership of the accommodation. The four main tenures are owner-occupation, local authority (council) housing, housing association, and private rented accommodation.

Owner-occupied dwellings are owned by the occupants, either outright or purchased with the assistance of loans – usually mortgages, for which the home will act as security for the loan. Within the United Kingdom this is the far largest tenure type with over 70 per cent of the population living in such accommodation at March 2006 (Wilcox, 2008). The other three tenures consist of accommodation which is owned by someone other than the occupier, who pays rent to the owner.

Local authority housing is the stock of dwellings owned by local councils; as the owner-occupied sector has continued to expand in recent years through the right to buy there has been a corresponding reduction in the stock of council housing. At the same time there has been increasing numbers of local authorities transferring their housing stock to existing or newly created housing associations. The reasons for these changes are considered later in the section on housing supply. Together, local authorities and housing associations make up the *social rented sector*. This sector accounts for around 18.5 per cent of the total housing stock in the United Kingdom (Wilcox, 2008).

The private rented sector consists of those dwellings owned by private individuals and companies, and let for rent usually with a view to making a profit. From a situation at the end of the First World War in which over 90 per cent of the UK housing stock was within this tenure, this sector has reduced to around 11 per cent of the total stock (Wilcox, 2008).

Owner-occupied and private rented accommodation are secured in a private market context which means that the ability to obtain properties in these tenures is dependent on the ability to pay the market price or rent. The next three sections examine the operation of these private markets, first by examining how markets operate, and then looking at demand from households and exploring the influences on the supply of housing. Within the affordable tenures, potential occupiers are prioritised on the basis of housing need, which is examined in Section 7.

4. Private housing markets

A market is any arrangement which permits the exchange of goods or services, whether for money or other consideration. In the case of housing, this refers to the arrangements by which dwellings are bought and sold, or let. Traditionally, economists have focused on the operation of markets, and the way in which markets are assumed to reach an 'equilibrium', when they achieve a balance between supply and demand. In the long term, the supply of housing should equal its demand, because price will provide the 'equilibrating mechanism' linking the two.

In very simple terms, the process by which a market reaches equilibrium is as follows:

As demand for a product increases the price will rise, because the lack of sufficient supply will result in consumers 'bidding up' the price; they will be competing for a scarce product, which always results in a higher price.

As the price increases, manufacturers (or, builders and sellers, in the case of houses) will be encouraged to produce (or sell) more of the item. As more become available, the price will stop increasing and a new equilibrium will be found where the number of articles (houses) demanded is equal to the number being supplied.

The price remains steady until levels of demand or supply alter again. If supply expands so that it exceeds demand, or if demand falls, the price will soon start to fall. There will be insufficient buyers to take up the supply. Falling prices will eventually result in a contraction in the supply, as builders put off new developments and owners delay selling their homes. Eventually, equilibrium is restored, and prices become steady again.

Whereas the theory of supply and demand and price equilibrium may be particularly accurate in describing the market for many products, such as shoes or loaves of bread, the supply of housing is rather 'inelastic' (unresponsive to price changes), in that an increase in demand with an associated increase in price cannot quickly be followed by an increase in supply. Housing supply – the 'flow' of houses into the market, those offered for sale or rent at any one time – responds only slowly to changing prices. This is because of the long lead-in times involved in the production of new houses compared to shoes or loaves of bread.

The Barker Review into Housing Supply in December 2003 reported that:

...formal estimates of supply responsiveness suggest that housing output in the UK responds relatively weakly to changes in house prices. Against a background of rising demand, this will contribute to higher house prices than otherwise might be the case. International comparisons show that the supply of housing in the UK is less price responsive than in most other major economies. Our housing supply is only half as responsive as the French housing market, a third as responsive as the US market, and only a quarter as responsive as the German market. Studies also show that supply has become less responsive over time. Before the war it was up to four times as responsive as it was through most of the post-war period and the responsiveness of housing supply has declined further in the 1990s, falling almost to zero, implying no change in housing output in response to increases in price. Increasing demand has therefore fed directly into higher house prices (Barker, 2003).

This means that the operation of housing markets is particularly complex. The complexity of factors affecting both the demand for and supply of housing, and the ways in which these differ between each tenure, are now considered in greater detail.

5. Demand

Demand arises from households either seeking to set up home for the first time or to move to a different property. The factors which influence the *overall* level of demand for accommodation will also have an influence on the levels and types of demand for accommodation within the different tenures in different ways.

The overall demand for housing is affected by a wide range of factors. These include:

5.1: Demographic factors

The demand for housing will be affected by a range of demographic (population) factors.

Size of the population

Self evidently, the size of the population will have an impact on the numbers of people requiring accommodation, and therefore on the level of demand. The United Kingdom population has undergone a fairly steady increase over the past five decades, rising from 50.25 million in 1951, to 60.6 million in 2006. However, the rate of growth has been reducing over this period, and future projections suggest that by the year 2031 the total population level will have begun to decrease (Census, 2001; *Social Trends*, 2008).

Composition of the population

Such changes in the total population will clearly have an influence on the number of people requiring accommodation, but this in itself will only be one factor affecting the number of homes required. A further influencing factor is the composition of the population, which means the number of people in different age groups, as well as the way in which it is structured – the relative size of each age-grouping.

Census data show that there has been a significant increase over the past 40 years in the proportion of the population which is over 65 years of age; and this is most marked in the group aged 75 years and over. In addition, future projections suggest that this trend is likely to continue, and that by 2021 the number of people over the age of 65 will exceed that of the population under 16 (Census, 2001; *Social Trends*, 2008).

This pattern can be expected to have implications not only for the level of demand for accommodation, but also for the demand for housing featuring designs which are appropriate to the needs of older people. As such, the changing age profile can be expected to have an impact on both the level of demand, and the types of accommodation being required.

Migration

Another demographic factor which will impact on levels of demand for accommodation is the extent of migration among the population. At a national level, the relative rates of outward migration (emigration) and inward migration (immigration) will affect the size of the population. In recent years we have seen a significant increase in the UK population with migration from abroad accounting for around half of the growth in the last ten years. The UK population stood at 60.6 million in 2006 and is expected to rise to around 71 million by 2031 before stabilising. Of this increase it is anticipated that 4.75 million will be as a result of further international inward migration if present trends continue (ONS, 2008a).

Figure 2.1: Recent UK migration

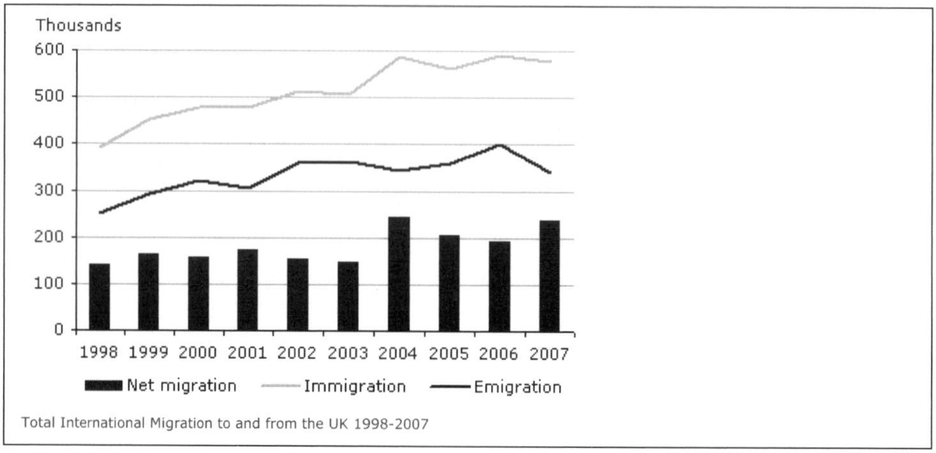

Source: www.statistics.gov.uk

Figure 2.1 shows that in 2007 there was net inward migration with around 237,000 more people migrating into the country than migrating outwards. In 2004, the gap was the highest since publication of data began in 1991. Perry (2007) suggests that rather than being part of a long-term trend, the current figures probably reflect movement amongst workers from countries joining the expanded European Union exercising their new found freedom of movement to work within other EU states. In the net inflows shown in Figure 2.1, the numbers from the 'accession states' account for 49,000 in 2004 and 64,000 in 2005.

Government statistics also show an increasing proportion of the UK population being made up of people born in other countries as shown in Figure 2.2.

Census data represented in Figure 2.2 show that one in every twelve people living in Britain is now foreign-born. In 2004, figures on all the foreign nationals living the UK showed that 'traditional' migrant groups such as people from Ireland and India are still at the top of the list, along with others from mainly better-off countries such as the USA, Germany and France. However also in the 'top 20' are much poorer countries such as Zimbabwe (no.11), Somalia (no.13) and Turkey (no.16) (Perry, 2007).

Overall levels of net inward migration will have an impact on the overall population, and therefore the level of demand for housing. In addition, cultural factors affecting

Figure 2.2: Foreign-born as a percentage of UK population

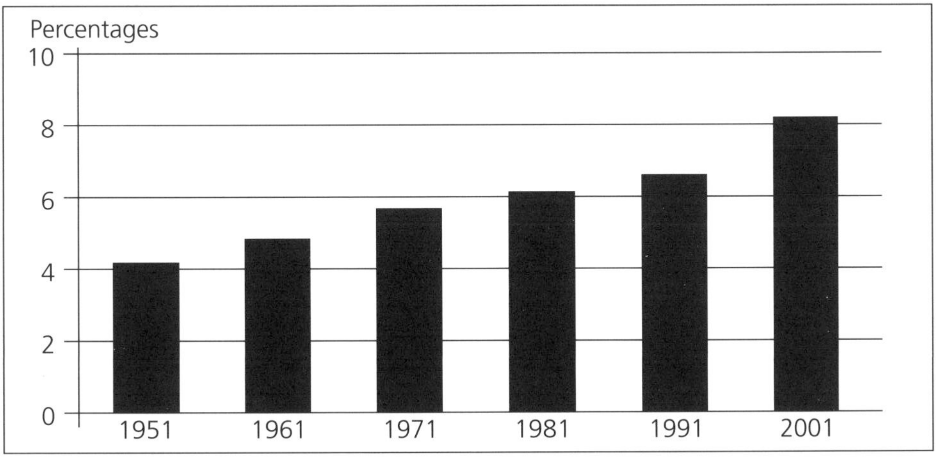

Source: www.statistics.gov.uk

the size of households, rates of household formation (considered below) and attitudes to ownership and renting amongst different ethnic groups will affect not only the level of demand for housing, but also the type and nature of dwellings required.

Levels of internal migration may also be significant. For example, during the 1980s and early 1990s rising levels of unemployment elsewhere in the country resulted in net migration of people into the South East of England with an associated impact on the levels of demand for accommodation in that region. During the late 1990s there was a net loss of population from London as people moved elsewhere in the South East and South West. Indeed, there has been a continuing urban to suburban and rural drift, resulting in population decline in many major cities (such as Glasgow and Newcastle-upon-Tyne) throughout the UK.

Levels of migration will also have a tenure specific impact. Traditionally in the UK young single people have always been the most mobile group within the population. In addition to the influence this will have on total demand for accommodation, there will be a disproportionate demand for particular tenures. The relatively long time taken to enter and exit from owner-occupation through selling and moving elsewhere, as well as the high costs of this process (so-called 'transactions' costs') will tend to discourage highly mobile groups from choosing this type of accommodation. Access to local authority and housing association dwellings have traditionally been lengthy processes due to high levels of demand and the bureaucratic rationing mechanisms adopted by many through their allocations and lettings policies as a way of dealing with that excess demand. As a result the private rented sector has tended to allow the quickest and easiest entry and exit for the highly mobile within the population, and the young single are the largest group represented among tenants of private rented dwellings.

Employment

Clearly, demand can be influenced by issues related to the labour market. The requirement to move for employment purposes is, however, only one of a range of ways in which mobility impacts on housing demand. It will also be affected by the age of individuals, with young single people traditionally being the most mobile group within the UK population. As such, the numbers of this group in the overall population will impact on the overall level of demand.

Family life cycles

Family life cycles also have an influence on the levels of demand and the type of accommodation required. As the number of children in a family increases, larger accommodation is usually required. Similarly, as the household ages, smaller accommodation or even a home suited to limited mobility may be required. Key times for households to move include leaving home for the first time, marriage, childbirth, changing employment, and retirement.

Household formation

As the children of the family grow, and begin to form new independent households there is a demand for more accommodation to house this increased number of household units. The rate at which new households form will therefore affect demand levels. The Government Statistical Office, in the 2008 edition of Social Trends, observes that:

> *Traditionally the majority of people in the UK shared living arrangements with others in the same household. However, over the past few decades changes in the age profile of the population, in society's values and attitudes, and in social legislation have led to new structures and characteristics of households and families. More people are spending time living on their own, whether before, after, or instead of marriage or cohabitation* (ONS, 2008a).

Census data show an expectation that the number of separate households in the United Kingdom will continue to increase throughout the near future. In 2007 there were 24.4 million households, an increase of almost a third since 1971 (ONS, 2008a).

As discussed above the total numbers in the population are expected to continue to increase throughout the same period. This increase, together with the increasing numbers of the population who are living in single person households, is likely to result in a significant increase in demand for accommodation, and an increased emphasis on single persons' dwellings.

Size of households

A further demographic factor which impacts on the level of demand is the size of individual households. This can also be expected to affect not only the number of dwellings required but also the size of those dwellings. Household size can also affect levels of demand resulting from households sub-dividing if existing accommodation is not sufficient to meet existing needs. For example, an older child of a family which is overcrowded in their present accommodation might be influenced to leave the family home and form a single person household earlier than would have otherwise occurred in order to ease the overcrowding situation.

Throughout the past four decades, as the number of households has steadily increased, the mean average of people within each household has steadily reduced as smaller family sizes, single person households, and divorce have become more commonplace. Government data indicates that the proportion of the population living in single person households increased from 14 per cent in 1961 to 29 per cent in 2007. At the same time the proportion of the population living in households of four or more people reduced from 34 per cent in 1961, to 21 per cent in 2007 (*Social Trends*, 2008). Clearly such demographic and social changes impact on the level of demand for accommodation with more households requiring dwellings, and with a need for smaller individual units of accommodation. However, Barker (2003) cautions that one should not assume, particularly in an era of rising incomes, that all smaller households will '*...necessarily want smaller housing*'.

From 1991 to 2016, 28 per cent of the growth in English households is predicted to come from higher household formation rates or in other words where people are less likely to be forming a household as a couple (Barker, 2003).

5.2: Income and wealth

Levels of income, and the distribution of income throughout the population have an impact on demand. The level of a household's income will affect its ability to express its housing desires through the market. For example, a young person living with relatives, who aspires to independence will need to achieve sufficient income to fund the independent accommodation they seek.

Similarly, if a household aspires to move into larger accommodation, or to a dwelling in a more desirable area, it is likely that their ability to achieve this wish will be linked to their level of income. As the level of this household's income increases, they are more likely to be able to afford their desired accommodation.

The *distribution* of income throughout the population will also be important. Increasing levels of income among greater numbers within the population, i.e. a more equal income distribution, will multiply the above effect with more households being in a position to afford their desired accommodation.

A further relevant factor is, however, the perceived permanence of the income. A temporary increase in income is unlikely to result in a household expressing a different housing preference, for instance by moving from rented into owner-occupied accommodation, as any such change would be unlikely to be sustainable in the long term. A subsequent fall in income could have serious implications for the household.

Incomes also have significance for the ability of households to choose particular tenures. There is a marked difference between the incomes of households in owner-occupation and those in council renting, for example. The *General Household Survey*, conducted in 2006 (ONS, 2008b), found that the mean average weekly income of households in owner-occupied dwellings was £737, whereas the average for council tenants was £256. Housing association tenants were seen to have similarly low incomes, with an average of £251; with private rented tenants falling in between the two extremes with an average of £596 for those in unfurnished tenancies, and £605 for those in furnished tenancies.

Figure 2.3: Average income of households within different tenures

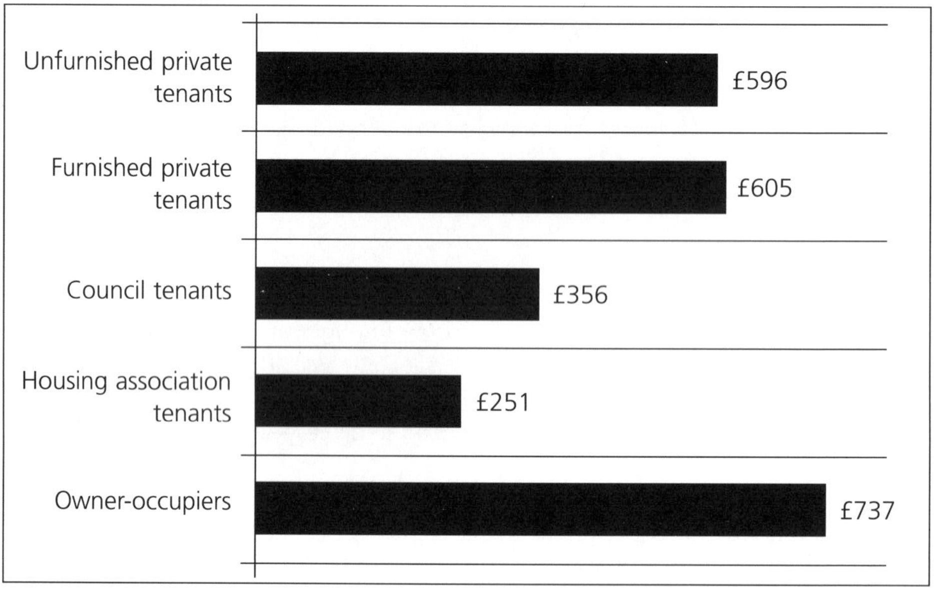

Source: Adapted from ONS data, 2008.

It can be concluded from these figures that as income increases households are more likely to move from social rented accommodation to home ownership. It can also be concluded that the first choice tenure for many of the UK population is owner-occupation. When this accommodation is not available the option of renting will be considered. In most cases it could be anticipated that renting with the 'social' landlords – local authorities and housing associations – will be preferred, due to the emphasis on affordable rents. For higher-income groups, however, for whom owner-occupation might not be an option, due, for example, to the need for job-related mobility, higher quality private rented accommodation might be a preferred option.

In general, however, rising incomes will generally lead to an increase in demand for owner-occupied housing. In the UK, although not necessarily elsewhere in Europe, the demand for rented accommodation tends to fall as incomes rise. For instance, there has been a significant change in the profile of the occupants of the UK social housing sector in the past 30 years. This trend is considered in detail later, in Section 9 of this chapter. Among households with lower-income levels, however, the effect of rising income may be a qualitative one, stimulating demand for better quality rented accommodation if the costs of home ownership are still prohibitive.

Closely related to income is the concept of social class or 'socio-economic group' which will also influence tenure choice.

Table 2.1: Proportion of UK population living in each tenure by socio-economic group (%), 2006

	Owned outright	Owned with mortgage	Rented from social sector	Rented privately	All tenures
Large employers and higher managers	14	77	2	7	100
Higher professional	20	65	1	14	100
Lower managerial and professional	14	68	6	12	100
Intermediate	17	59	13	11	100
Small employers	26	54	7	13	100
Lower supervisory and technical	14	62	13	11	100
Semi-routine	17	38	30	15	100
Never worked and long-term unemployed	12	2	73	13	100
Economically inactive	54	7	33	6	100
All socio-economic groups	31	40	20	10	100

Source: Adapted from Table 10.5 *Social Trends* 38: 2008.

The main trends which emerge from the statistics are the decreasing use of rented accommodation when moving from 'lower' to 'higher' socio-economic groups. At the same time there is a converse trend toward an increase in the proportion of owner-occupiers when moving from 'unskilled manual workers' to 'professionals'. Such statistics can support the contention that most of the population will aspire toward owner-occupation, as those in the 'higher' socio-economic groups are more likely to be in a financial position, with secure employment or continuing expectations of a sustained level of income, to take on the financial responsibilities associated with home ownership.

This also means that at the local – or regional – level, the occupational distribution can have important implications for the demand for particular tenures. The extent to which the local economy of any particular area is dependent on employers with a preponderance of workers from a particular socio-economic grouping, will influence local demand for those tenures which are traditionally available to these groups. For example, in a local area in which there is a preponderance of industries in which there is a high concentration of unskilled manual workers we would expect to see a high demand for rented accommodation, in particular social housing. In another area in which there was a high proportion of professional groups, for instance in a commuter belt, there is likely to be a higher demand for owner-occupation and a lower level of demand for rented dwellings.

Wealth and the way in which it is distributed is a key factor affecting the demand for accommodation. In the UK today most households' assets are held in the form of housing. The ownership of residential property is seen as socially desirable, a situation which has been encouraged by an intensification of the policies of successive United Kingdom governments to encourage owner-occupation as the 'natural' tenure choice.

Another conclusion which might be drawn is that some of the increase in demand for this tenure is due to those households who can afford it deciding on owner-occupation in order not to be 'left behind' by rising house prices which might exclude them from a future option to purchase their own accommodation. Households who, given other circumstances, might prefer to take advantage of the more flexible rented sectors as they experience life changes may decide to buy earlier than would have otherwise been the case, fearing that house price inflation will take the option of home ownership beyond their financial reach.

5.3: The availability of finance

Since housing tends to be a very expensive item, most buyers rely on borrowing to fund their purchase. This means that it is not only the household's income which is significant, but also how readily they are able to borrow the necessary finance. During the 1980s and 1990s the expansion in the availability of housing finance through capital market deregulation undoubtedly contributed to the explosion in demand, which generated huge price rises in many areas. A relaxation of the restrictions on lending both contributed to, and was a response to the increase in house prices which occurred during this period. From 2008 onwards the lack of availability of mortgage finance as a result of the 'credit crunch' was a major reason behind the significant slowdown in the housing sales market and the collapse in house prices. This is explored in more detail in Chapter 4.

In addition, the returns available from substitute investments may affect demand, both from owner-occupiers and from landlords. Potential purchasers of dwellings may choose to invest any additional income or wealth elsewhere, if this gives better returns than they would anticipate from the ownership of residential property. Existing private landlords might also decide under certain economic conditions that investment in other markets is more attractive and decide to move out of private landlordism. Any such decisions will reduce levels of demand for accommodation among this group. This was seen in the credit crunch which hit the UK housing market in 2008 following the collapse of the US sub-prime mortgage market. The fall in house prices and the relative difficulty in obtaining mortgages impacted significantly on the buy to let market.

5.4: Price

The price of accommodation, whether the cost of buying or the level of rents, has an impact on demand. As the effective demand for accommodation will be a function of the ability of potential occupants to pay for accommodation, it follows that when the price for particular accommodation is lower, the level of demand will be influenced by this situation and will increase. Conversely, price increases can have an influence on reducing demand.

As the price of accommodation fluctuates there will be an impact on rates at which new households form, with lower prices allowing more new households – or those 'concealed' households previously living with relatives – to be in a position where they are able to afford to pay for independent accommodation. Similarly, as prices rise fewer of these households will be able to realise their independent ambitions and will continue to live in multi-household situations. At the same time some households who were living in independent accommodation can find themselves unable to continue meeting their housing costs at times of rising prices and may be forced to enter into multi-household arrangements, moving to live with relatives or friends until such a time as they can once again afford independent accommodation.

The factors which will be considered to be the 'price' of accommodation within different tenures will vary but many of the impacts of changes in price will be the same. There are a number of elements making up the price of owner-occupied accommodation. The purchase price of the dwelling is the main element. If purchase takes place with the aid of a mortgage the interest payments due in respect of the loan, together with any capital or endowment policy payments will be part of the 'price' of the accommodation. A further element of the price will be the costs of purchase transactions (including solicitors' fees, surveys, mortgage arrangement costs and valuation) as well as insurance and maintenance costs for which the owner-occupier is responsible.

The main element of the 'price' of rented accommodation will be the rent due to the landlord. The attraction for many who choose to rent is the payment of a one-off rent to cover all of the different elements to be met by those who own their accommodation. The price of accommodation within any tenure will have an impact on demand. Expectations of future price levels are also crucial, particularly in relation to owner-occupied property. As was suggested earlier, there is a tradition, particularly in the United Kingdom, for owner-occupation to be seen as an investment in addition to a method of satisfying an individual's housing need. As a result of this convention, the impact of house price increases is for a corresponding increase in properties available for sale as prices reach a level at which owners will decide to cash in on their investment. One result of this phenomenon, as seen during the house price boom of the 1980s, is the increase in demand for more expensive properties as long-standing owners within different property value bands 'trade up' to take account of the increase in equity caused by price rises. Equally, owners who hold residential property as an investment will choose to sell once they feel that house prices have reached a plateau, or if they feel that a fall in prices is imminent, in order to maximise the profit from their investment.

The impact of expectations of future price increases is lessened in the rented sectors because of the existence of housing benefit. A tenant of a private landlord who is entitled to housing benefit will see most of the increases in rent met by increased benefit payments, so long as the increase is considered to be within reasonable limits in terms of the rent officer's assessment of the appropriate rent levels for the *Broad Market Rental Area* (this is examined further in Chapter 4). A prospective tenant will not be dissuaded from taking up a tenancy which may have a relatively high rent if they are entitled to housing benefit, and the benefit levels are such that the rent will be paid. As such, the impact of an increasing 'price' – in this case rent – for the accommodation will have less impact on demand than the fluctuating price of owner-occupied dwellings.

Similarly, those tenants of affordable landlords who receive housing benefit will find the impact of any rent increases tempered by the benefits system. Therefore, the impact of rising rents on the demand for rented accommodation has been, to date, fairly limited. However, as discussed earlier, rented accommodation, mainly in the private sector, has traditionally been used as a starting point, or stepping stone by new households setting up home for the first time and looking in the longer term to move into other types of accommodation. One likely impact of rising rents is therefore to discourage new household formation if this 'first step' is out of the reach of some who would otherwise seek to use it.

In addition to discouraging new household formation an increase in rent levels could also be expected to encourage multiple occupation with more than one household sharing accommodation, and 'concealed' households living with others due to their lack of financial ability to obtain their desired independent accommodation.

Increases in rent can also have an impact in reducing the differential cost between renting and owner-occupation (during periods when the cost of owner-occupied housing is static or reducing), and as such can be expected to encourage the decision to enter owner-occupation among some tenants who might not otherwise have chosen this step. Similarly those who see owner-occupation as a long-term aim may make the move earlier than planned if rent levels increase and the difference between the costs of the two tenures appears less prohibitive.

The price of accommodation, whilst influencing overall demand for accommodation in all tenures, as discussed earlier, can specifically affect the demand for owner-occupied housing in different ways. In relation to first-time buyers, rising prices may have two opposing effects. As prices rise, the quality of dwellings which can be afforded will reduce. In addition, fewer first-time buyers will be in a position to enter the housing market. If, however, prices are expected to continue to rise, this may stimulate additional demand in the short run, as new buyers choose to enter the market earlier in an effort to 'beat' the increases. At the same time existing owners might be stimulated, by price rises, to 'trade up', selling their existing properties to release equity which can be used to buy more desirable, and more expensive properties.

Interest charges add to the 'price' of owner-occupied housing. Any owner with a mortgage has to meet the cost of interest payments in relation to the loan. The level of interest rates at any given time will be a cost to the owner and will influence their economic decisions about continuing in their present accommodation, or whether it is possible or necessary to 'trade' up or down. Increases in interest rates may depress demand, as was seen in the house price crash in the late 1980s. During that period the government, faced with inflation in the housing market used an interest rate policy as the main tool for controlling inflationary pressures. The rise in interest rates reduced the amounts that individuals could afford to borrow – and therefore the amount they could afford to pay when moving house – with the net result that house prices fell dramatically. During the late 1990s and into the first decade of the 21st century the country saw the lowest interest rates since the 1960s, and this contributed to a boom in house prices. In 1998 the average dwelling price in the United Kingdom was £82,000 (ONS, 2000). By 2007, this had risen to £172,995 (CLG, 2008a).

From 2008 onwards house price inflation in the UK was slowing and, in most parts of the country, prices had begun to fall as a result of the credit crunch, the lack of availability of mortgage finance and the worldwide recession.

5.5: Perceived availability

The level of availability of accommodation, or the perception among households of its availability, will have an impact on levels of demand. If there is a perception that dwellings are not available those new households who might be looking to form and seek independent housing will be discouraged from doing so. Similarly, if a particular tenure is perceived as unavailable, then those demanding accommodation will be forced to transfer to alternative tenures. For example, in areas where the local authority has a lettings policy which precludes single people under a certain age from joining the waiting list, or has very little single persons' accommodation among its housing stock, young single people will have to look to other tenures, typically the private rented sector, to meet their housing need. Traditionally in the United Kingdom, the private rented sector has often provided an essential first stage for young people leaving home, including students and those saving a deposit to buy their own home. It also serves as a complement to the social rented sector to meet demand for accommodation from those people on low incomes, and those who prefer to rent rather than to buy.

Research suggests that many new households appear to choose their parents' tenure type, possibly because it is the tenure with which they are most familiar. An OPCS *Survey Into Recently Moving Households* in 1984 looked at the 'housing pathways' followed by different households – that is, the history of the different tenures and types of accommodation occupied by a sample of those who had recently moved house. The survey identified that newly forming households were likely to move directly from parental homes into owner-occupation (33 per cent of those surveyed) and furnished renting (35 per cent). A further 15 per cent moved directly into local authority rented accommodation. Whilst this balance is not equivalent to the proportions of the stock in each of the different tenures, there are limitations on access to social rented housing and owner-occupation, and therefore these tenures might be under-represented among those taking the first step to independence. The survey showed, however, that a significant proportion of the population follow their parents' tenure choice, or would choose to if finance and availability allowed. Further research in 2006 identified that newly forming households were likely to move directly from parental homes into owner-occupation (22 per cent) and furnished renting (25 per cent). A further 14 per cent moved directly into local authority rented accommodation, with 9 per cent moving into a housing association tenancy (CLG, 2008b). The change in tenure movement between the two dates – particularly the reduction in movement into owner-occupation and furnished renting – is likely to reflect the difficulties faced by newly forming households in affording private sector accommodation due to owner-occupied house price rises and the associated higher rents required by private landlords.

5.6: The impact of government policies

Government policies will clearly have an enormous influence on demand for particular tenures. For example, rent controls and increased security of tenure following the 1977 Rent Act encouraged the demand for private rented accommodation, though this was increasingly unavailable due to the impact of these restrictions on the attractiveness of rented accommodation as an investment opportunity for private landlords, and much of the demand switched to public rented housing.

Successive governments, of different political hues have promoted home ownership through a range of policies. For example, the right to buy provisions originally introduced in the 1980 Housing Act have contributed greatly to the increase in owner-occupation over the past 25 years. Since the implementation of the right to buy for tenants of local authorities and many housing associations, the levels of discount available on the sale price have been periodically increased, thus reducing the cost of purchasing for many tenants. At the same time changes in the financial regimes for both local authorities and housing associations have put pressure for rent increases, in turn lessening the differential between the cost of renting and purchasing as part of a government policy of encouraging owner-occupation as widely as possible. Recent changes in government policy in relation to right to buy, including increases in tenancy qualifying periods and reductions in discount levels in areas of high housing market pressure, have been designed to slow the transfer of housing out of the affordable housing sector.

Figure 2.4: Summary of the factors affecting demand for housing

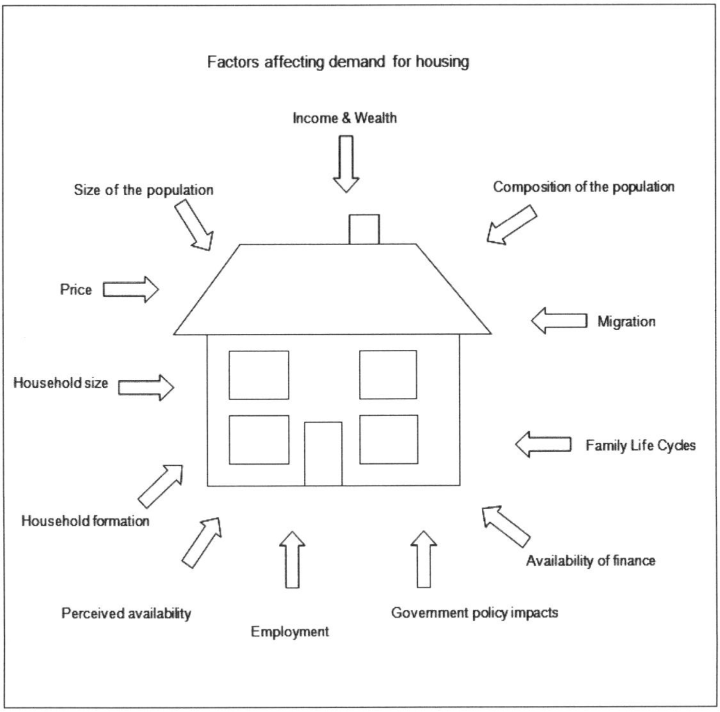

Source: Paul Grainger.

6. Housing stock and the supply of housing

The supply of housing is the quantities of accommodation made available to households either through the market system or through the social rented tenures. Hence it is the amount of property actually available to buy or rent at any given time. This is different to the stock of housing which is the total quantity of dwellings existing in a particular locality.

Since the 1980s there has been a continuing increase in the stock of housing in the owner-occupied sector. At the end of 2006, over 70 per cent of the total housing stock of the UK was within this tenure, with 18.5 per cent rented from affordable landlords and 11 per cent in the private rented sector (Wilcox, 2008). A fuller picture can be gained by looking at the age and type of dwellings available within each tenure.

6.1: Composition of the stock in each tenure

Within tenures the stock tends to have different characteristics. This can be illustrated by considering the example of the English housing stock.

Table 2.2: Age of accommodation in each tenure (England) – percentages

	Owner-occupied	Housing association	Local authority	Private rented
Pre-1919	22.16	10.24	4.88	42.23
1919-1944	19.12	8.32	16.72	14.74
1945-1964	18.13	23.15	37.44	10.85
1965-1979	21.85	26.25	34.07	14.73
Post 1980	18.74	32.04	6.89	17.47

Source: Adapted from the *English House Condition Survey 2005*, CLG, 2007b.

It is clear from Figure 2.5 that there are marked differences between tenures in the age of accommodation currently in use. Within the private rented sector over 57 per cent of properties were built prior to 1944. Of the dwellings owned by owner-occupiers 41.28 per cent are of this older stock. Local authority and housing association dwellings are of more recent construction with only 21 per cent and 18.56 per cent respectively being more than 50 years old. It can also be seen that there are some differences in the types of accommodation between tenures.

Figure 2.6 shows that within the owner-occupied sector over 82 per cent of the housing stock consists of houses, with only just under 8 per cent of dwellings being flats and 10 per cent bungalows. In contrast within the housing association sector almost 42.5 per cent of dwellings are flats, and only slightly more than 48 per cent

Figure 2.5: Age of accommodation in each tenure (England)

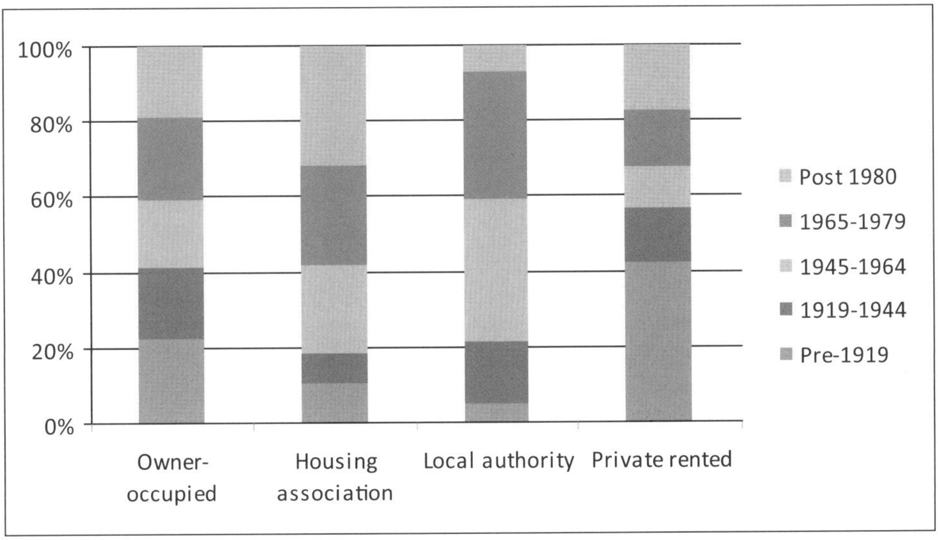

Source: Adapted from *English House Condition Survey 2005*, CLG, 2007b.

Table 2.3: Type of accommodation in each tenure (England) – percentages

	Owner-occupied	Housing association	Local authority	Private rented
Houses	**82.02**	**48.07**	**47.23**	**59.87**
Of which:				
house, small terraced	10.97	13.64	12.33	17.47
house, medium/large terraced	17.30	17.22	15.14	15.36
house, semi-detached	30.84	16.61	19.34	18.12
house, detached	22.92	0.61	0.42	8.92
Bungalows	**10.00**	**9.46**	**9.65**	**4.58**
Flats	**7.98**	**42.46**	**43.12**	**35.55**
Of which:				
flat, converted	1.88	4.29	1.94	12.53
flat, purpose built low-rise	5.66	35.97	34.44	20.79
flat, purpose built high-rise	0.44	2.20	6.74	2.23

Source: Adapted from *English House Condition Survey 2005*, CLG, 2007b.

are houses with the remaining 9.4 per cent being bungalows. Whilst we noted in Table 1.3 in Chapter 1, that the total numbers of dwellings in each tenure indicate that the housing association sector is the smallest tenure, the preponderance of flats within this sector is significant in terms of the types of developments traditionally undertaken and the ethos behind much of the voluntary housing movement in catering for other than 'traditional' general needs family housing.

Figure 2.6: Type of accommodation in each tenure (England)

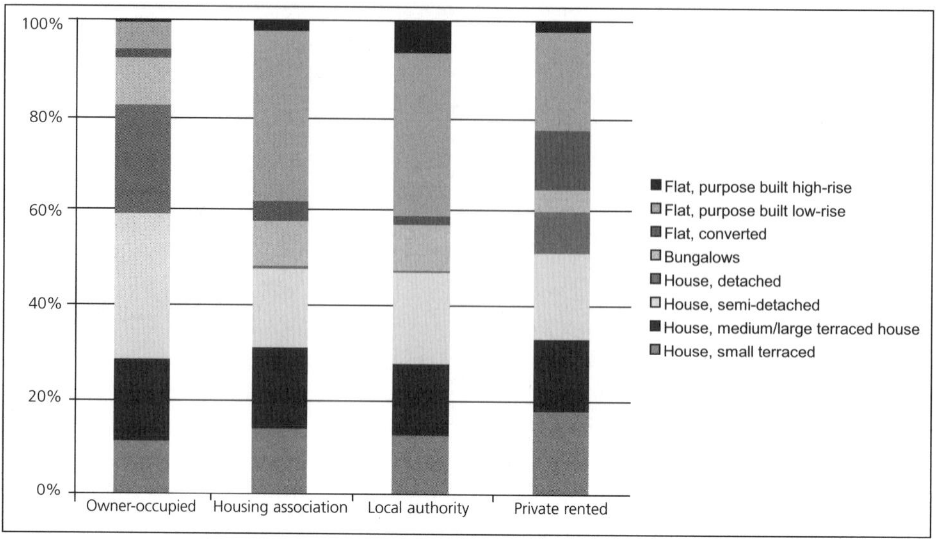

Source: Adapted from *English House Condition Survey 2005*, DCLG, 2007b.

The tables and figures also show that 47 per cent of local authority dwellings consist of houses, reflecting the large-scale local authority house building which took place following the First World War and enjoying a particular boom during the 1950s. It is worth noting that England is unusual in the low proportion of flats in its housing stock, compared with the rest of Europe. Many other European countries have one-third or more of their housing stock in the form of flats rather than houses, even in countries like Spain where home ownership is high. Within the UK, Scotland is more like the rest of Europe in having a much higher proportion of flats, across tenures, than England, Wales and Northern Ireland (Perry, 2001).

6.2: General influences on the supply of housing

It will be useful now to look at some of the factors which will have an impact on the supply of housing within all of the tenures.

The supply of housing within tenures is affected by a range of factors, which include:

(a) Patterns of household life cycles which will have an impact on the availability of housing. As the numbers of households increase, causing an expansion in demand, so there will be an associated impact in reducing the supply as available accommodation is taken up in increasing numbers.

(b) The mobility rates of existing occupiers will affect how often dwellings become available to rent or buy. Increasing supply can be expected, particularly in the private rented sector which is used by those groups such as young single households who, as seen earlier are among the most mobile in the population. Clearly, high levels of mobility will result in high levels of turnover and thus increased availability of accommodation. Conversely, family housing within the social sector, for which there are usually longer waiting times to gain access, and greater security of tenure than in the private sector, will tend to have comparatively lower levels of turnover. The net outcome will be less supply of available accommodation within existing stock in this sector when compared to private rented accommodation.

(c) Government policies in relation to taxation and planning regulations will also have an impact on the supply of housing. Tax concessions may be used to stimulate additional supply to particular tenures, whereas tax increases are likely to adversely impact on housing supply. Planning regulations may be used to influence the types, tenures and locations of new housing.

A key question examined in the Barker Review (2003) was to examine the constraints on housing supply which was preventing the output of new housing responding to price signals. The Review identified a number of factors linked to market failures and the policy environment.

These included:

- industry constraints such as the lack of competitiveness of house builders;
- capacity constraints in relation to skills and innovation as well as the lack of availability of finance to house builders;
- the impact of policy on such matters as tax, planning regulations and housing subsidies;
- the lack of availability of land caused by risk averse attitudes of the house building industry, the complex nature of sites, difficulties in land assembly, the planning system's influence on land availability, the need to improve infrastructure, the unpopularity of building development to the general public.

We will now examine ways in which the stock of each tenure can increase.

6.3: The supply of privately rented housing

The rate at which new privately rented accommodation becomes available is affected by economic investment decisions reached by existing and would-be private landlords. The return on investments in private rented accommodation – chiefly the income from renting – is a major factor determining whether new housing stock will enter the tenure. The level of returns realised by landlords will be influenced by other factors, such as government regulation through rent controls or the restriction of housing benefit levels; and the existence of tax concessions. As house prices increased the attraction of housing as a longer-term capital investment increased, and properties purchased for their long-term investment value were likely to find their way into the private rented sector until the price reached a level at which the landlord chooses to realise the capital tied up in the property. Asset values will be affected by a range of market factors, among them the security of tenure enjoyed by tenants. The deregulation of tenancies through the 1988 Housing Act was an attempt by central government to make private renting more attractive to potential landlords with decreased security of tenure enabling landlords to obtain vacant possession more easily and therefore liquefy (sell to turn into cash) their assets more quickly. Up until quite recently, the growth in capital values made possible because of rising house prices, led to a rapidly-developing buy to let market, funded by specialist mortgage products and providers.

The upturn in the numbers of privately rented dwellings from the 1989 low point followed a number of government policy initiatives which had the stated aim of stimulating growth in the tenure. Assured tenancies, which had been a small-scale and rarely used initiative within the 1980 Housing Act, were redefined and extended by the 1988 Housing Act to cover all new lettings within the 'independent rented sector', a newly defined tenure grouping including both private renting and housing associations. The new 'assured tenancy' offered less security of tenure than the previous 'secure tenancy' by extending the mandatory grounds for a landlord to obtain possession.

The supply of housing for private renting is also affected by the availability of finance. Lending to private landlords is in turn affected by the perceptions of financial institutions about likely available rental income and long-term asset value, and thus whether private renting is seen as a good investment. The availability of private finance is also of key importance to both the refurbishment of dwellings and the development of new stock by housing associations, as the reduction of grant levels from central government pushes them to rely increasingly on the money markets to raise funds.

The attractiveness to both lenders and landlords of investment alternatives impacts on the availability of finance to fund new private rented stock. If revenue and capital returns from residential property are expected to yield less than other investment opportunities, there will be less finance available to fund the purchase of housing stock for private renting purposes.

A further crucial factor is the mobility of existing tenants. Traditionally in the UK, the private rented sector has been seen as having the advantage of flexibility for tenants due to it being relatively easy to gain access quickly, subject to having the ability to pay, when compared to social rented housing or owner-occupation. As such, the more mobile sections of the community have traditionally made use of this tenure which allows swift entry and exit. High levels of tenant turnover within this sector can be attractive to potential landlords who will see only a few long-term tenants inhibiting their ability to liquefy their assets through sale of the property once the market price is appropriate.

6.4: The supply of owner-occupied housing

Since the supply of existing owner-occupied accommodation relates to the movement decisions of households, those factors which contribute to demand for this tenure will also influence supply.

Unlike in much of the rest of Europe and North America, most new building in the UK is speculative. As such, the provision of new housing within this tenure is largely based on expectations of future price changes. These expectations in turn depend on the flow of funds to housing finance markets, the current level of vacant dwellings for sale, and the time taken to sell current houses – the rate of turnover. Unlike many other markets where an increase in demand will result in a fairly swift increase in supply, housing supply is relatively inelastic (unresponsive to price changes in the short term) due to the lead-in periods necessary to construct new housing stock. Housing developers will find the conditions for construction more favourable in a situation where the building societies and banks are able or willing to lend sufficient funds to potential buyers.

Equally, in a situation where there are less properties on the market, and they are selling fairly quickly, there will be an impact in increasing prices, which will in turn encourage the development of new properties for sale.

Allied to these factors, the costs of land, construction costs, the cost of borrowing (interest rates) will all impinge on the decisions of developers, as will the availability of finance to builders, which in turn will be affected by costs and prices outlined above. It is clear then that each of the different factors influencing the cost of developing and the anticipated profits to be made from investing in new development are all closely linked and in many ways interdependent.

Developers will also take account of the profitability of other work – non-residential building work – in deciding whether to develop further housing. The inelasticity of supply in the housing market is also a product of the time lags and delays caused by factors such as planning controls, seasonal factors, and occasional shortages of labour and materials. Each of these factors will also have an influence on the rate at which new housing enters this sector.

As with other housing tenures, government policy has an impact on the supply of owner-occupied dwellings. One of the major policy initiatives in this area has been the right to buy provisions that were considered earlier in relation to the demand for accommodation. Right to buy sales contributed markedly to the increase in the number of dwellings in the owner-occupied sector since the 1980s. Some of those properties purchased by tenants will have also found their way into the private rented sector.

6.5: The supply of affordable rented housing

Unlike the other tenure types affordable rented housing, whilst it has always operated within the context of the market, is far more dependent on the context of political and administrative decisions, from central government, local government and bodies such as the Homes and Communities Agency. The new building of social rented housing in the UK has been solely dependant on government policies in relation to borrowing and capital finance. Since 1979, policies to restrict levels of borrowing by local authorities have reduced their ability to provide new housing for rent, in line with a general trend in government policy toward the privatisation and deregulation of housing provision. At the same time there has been encouragement to housing associations to take over the role of the main developers of new social rented housing, but making use of increased levels of private finance as grant levels have reduced. In addition, in any particular local area the political views of the local authority will also have an impact on the types of development and the way in which that development is carried out.

The supply of social rented housing is also affected by the use made of existing stock. The first key factor is the size of the housing stock. Clearly the more social rented housing stock there is, the more likelihood of housing within that sector becoming available to meet demand. This is not to suggest, however, that size is the only determining factor. The level of turnover within the stock is crucial. For example, an affordable landlord with a large stock in which there was no turnover is never going to be in a position to meet the housing needs of any but its existing tenants.

An example will illustrate the impact of turnover and its relationship to stock size. Assume that there are two affordable housing landlords, one with a stock of 20,000 properties and the other with 5,000 dwellings. If the smaller landlord has a turnover of 10 per cent of dwellings during a year, this would equal 500 properties becoming available for re-letting. If during the same period the larger landlord has a turnover of 2 per cent of its dwellings, this would equal 400 homes available for new letting. Leaving aside considerations of the popularity of areas with these respective turnovers, it is clear that in terms of total dwellings being supplied from within the existing housing stock for letting, turnover can have a bigger impact than total stock alone.

Related to the issue of turnover is the mobility of existing tenants. Traditionally, social rented housing has been more difficult to gain swift access to than private rented accommodation, due to the often bureaucratic processes used to administer the rationing process. This has tended to reduce the use of social rented housing among the most mobile groups in society, however a certain level of mobility will obviously occur, and will impact on the level of turnover in the housing stock. As the level of mobility among tenants increases, whether due to factors such as movement to seek employment elsewhere, or tenants choosing to leave the tenure to move into other accommodation, then there will be an increase in supply of dwellings from within the existing housing stock.

Similarly, when levels of mobility decrease, the supply of dwellings from within the existing stock falls. Since the late 1990s the relationship between housing costs and household income (the house price to earnings ratio) has been steadily increasing making owner-occupation less affordable (Palmer *et al.*, 2006). Research has also shown that the numbers of households moving out of the social rented sector to private sector housing has declined significantly over recent years, reflecting the decreasing affordability of both owner-occupied and private rented housing over that period. Indeed whilst some movement has occurred as social housing tenants leave the sector to move into private tenure homes, the main reasons for social dwellings becoming available from within the stock are through the death of a tenant, or the tenant moving in with another household or into long-term care (Perry and Capie, 2008).

Just as the supply of new dwellings affects the level of supply, so the rate at which accommodation leaves the social rented sector will have an impact. Earlier there was consideration of the impact on the supply of owner-occupied dwellings of the provisions of the 1980 legislation which gave certain social rented housing tenants the right to buy their homes. There has at the same time been a substantial reduction in the numbers of social rented dwellings.

As noted above, whilst the numbers of properties owned by both local authorities and housing associations being bought by tenants under the right to buy has fluctuated year by year there has been a steady continuing sale under this policy. At the same time the numbers of new properties being produced within the social housing sector has been consistently substantially lower than the numbers of properties leaving the sector. The net result of this disparity has been a reduction of the number of properties in the social rented sector. The impact of this reduction on the availability of social housing is not as severe as might appear at first glance. In a majority of cases right to buy purchasers remain in occupation for significant amounts of time. Wilcox (2007) has identified that ex-tenants buying their homes stay in occupation on average for a period of 15 years following the purchase. This suggests that if those buyers had remained as social tenants their dwellings would not necessarily have become available to let from within the stock. Instead the impact of the right to buy on relets is deferred, with a fairly long time lag as the 'loss' to the sector in terms of available re-lettable dwellings is not felt immediately, but – on average – 15 years after the sale.

Levels of supply will in addition be influenced by the void management policies of affordable landlords. Clearly, efficient policies will reduce void times and thus speed turnover to ensure swifter availability for renting of properties vacated. The policies of the landlord will also have a differential impact on the availability of dwellings for different groups within the population. If a landlord has a policy of allocating dwellings only to tenants above a certain age, or with certain family characteristics, then clearly those who fall outside those limits will have less access to the stock of social rented housing. Similarly, an increased willingness on the part of the landlord to transfer tenants between properties will increase the supply of accommodation appropriate to the needs of tenants and potential tenants.

6.6: Changes in housing supply between tenures

So far there has been consideration of a range of factors which might affect the rate at which housing becomes available within each of the tenures. There is, however, scope for substantial movement of properties from one tenure to another. The total number of dwellings in Great Britain has steadily increased throughout the past century. For example, in 1901 the total national housing stock stood at 6.3 million; by the end of 2005 the figure had increased to 21.7 million. During the past two decades the stock of owner-occupied dwellings, and the stock within the housing association sector has increased. The stock within the owner-occupied sector has risen from 12.17 million to 15.3 million, whilst the stock held by housing associations has increased from 0.472 million to 1.8 million during the same period. The stock of dwellings in the private rented sector remained fairly steady, changing from 2.37

Figure 2.7: Tenure change from 1985 to 2005 (nos. of dwellings in millions)

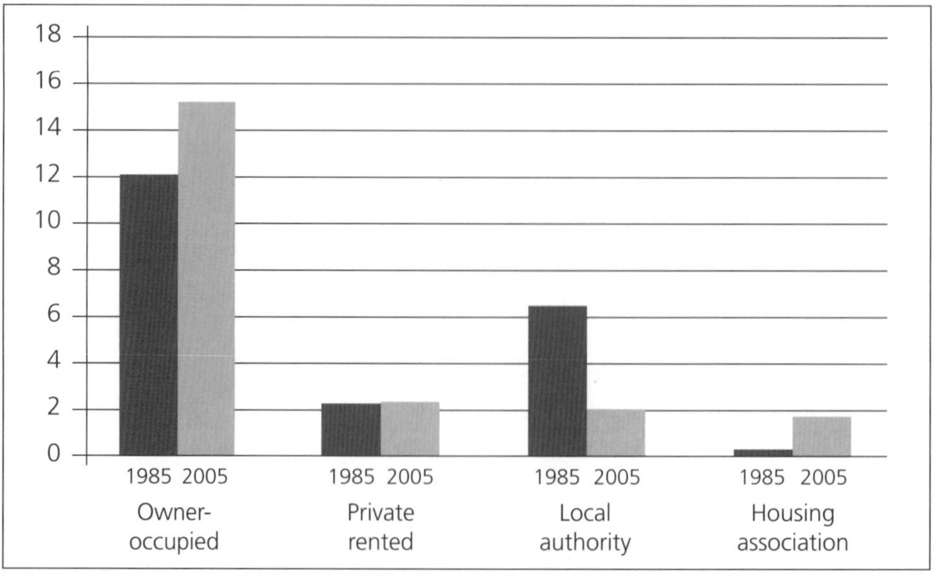

Source: CLG, 2007b.

million to 2.46 million. The only sector to have experienced substantial reductions during this period is the local authority housing stock, falling from 6.57 million to 2.16 million between 1981 and 2005 (CLG, 2007b).

7. Assessment of housing need

As discussed during the introduction to this chapter, inherent in the market system is a requirement for households to have the ability to pay for their preferred accommodation if such housing desires are to be transformed into demand. Analysis of market conditions such as price levels, and effective demand (i.e. demand which is backed up by the ability to pay) can only give part of the picture of the overall levels of housing needed, and what types of accommodation are required. It cannot give the full picture because any such consideration will not take account of those households in need who do not have the finance required to satisfy their needs. Instead, it is necessary to draw together information from a number of sources in order to arrive at a complete assessment of housing need.

Traditionally, many local authorities in the United Kingdom relied on their waiting lists as a measure of housing need. They would often base decisions for new building on the perceived shortfalls reflected through the types of accommodation, and in the locations, for which they had the greatest numbers registered on waiting lists. During the immediate post-war period, when large-scale local authority housing development was taking place – particularly in Scotland and the North of England – the numbers of applicants for whom the authority could not provide accommodation was often the major factor influencing the type of new development taking place. At the same time many local authorities had waiting lists through which lettings were solely based on date order. Many authorities had restrictions on who could join their lists with, for example, applicants having to have reached a certain age or have lived in the local area for a given period of time before becoming eligible to register on the list. Such restrictions would clearly distort any assessment of 'need' using the lists as a basis.

As the role of local authorities as developers of new social rented housing has diminished they have been subject to increasing encouragement from central government to expand and develop their role as 'strategic enablers'. Whilst the strategic planning role had already existed for local authorities for some time the emphasis on this aspect of their activity was brought into sharper focus by government proposals in the 1987 white paper, *Housing: The Government's Proposals*, which specifically stated that:

> *...the future role of local authorities will essentially be a strategic one: identifying housing needs and demand, encouraging innovative methods of provision by other bodies to meet such needs, maximising the use of private finance, and encouraging new interest in the revival of the independent rented sector.*

The crux of this role, then, is for authorities to take overall responsibility for assessing the level of housing need within their area, and for the encouragement of partnership arrangements with both the private sector and housing associations to facilitate the development of accommodation to meet that need.

It was noted earlier that the census measure of the total numbers of the population will not give a fully accurate picture of the level of demand for housing. It is, however, a useful starting point for the analysis of housing needs. The census data that were considered earlier in relation to the total population, numbers of households, and household size give a useful basis for assessment, looking at the way in which the population is structured in terms of the age profile and the way in which households are structured. Factors such as the birth rate and mortality rates can also contribute to building up a picture of likely future housing need in terms of overall stock, and also the types and sizes of dwellings which will be required.

Guidance issued by the Department for Communities and Local Government (CLG) (CLG, 2008c) recommends that local authorities consider ten elements for ensuring that housing strategies are 'fit for purpose'. One of the key elements relates to 'needs analysis' and recommends that:

- The strategy must be based on a robust, up to date, housing needs assessment, which is likely to use information from a range of sources, e.g. a needs survey, planning and health, demographic data.
- A clear picture should be presented of the housing market(s) in the area covering current and likely future supply and demand, house prices, household incomes, household projections.
- There should be an up to date summary of the condition of the housing stock in all tenures based on a recent stock condition survey.
- Information should be presented on special needs client groups (e.g. black and minority ethnic, elderly, disabled, lone teenage parents) and on homelessness.
- Performance on key areas of service performance should be shown.

Communities Scotland introduced a *Local Housing Need and Affordability Model for Scotland* in 2003 (revised and updated in 2006), which aims to provide a snapshot picture of the annual net need for affordable housing in each Scottish local authority area. The model recognises the need for local authorities to use its data in conjunction with additional local consideration to be given to stock size imbalances and stock which is unsuitable or in poor physical condition.

8. Housing quality

As has already been considered, there is a range of factors influencing the supply of dwellings to each housing tenure. A further crucial issue for consideration is the impact of such socio-economic and demographic factors on the quality and standard of the accommodation. A useful starting point in any consideration of the quality of accommodation is to look at a definition of what might be considered to be standards of 'reasonableness' or 'fitness' in relation to dwellings.

8.1: Condition surveys

Regular, five yearly, house condition surveys are carried out for England by the government and within the three devolved governments. Each of the surveys considers whether dwellings have a range of basic amenities and the physical condition of the properties.

The 2006 *English House Condition Survey* (published in 2008) found that the number of dwellings which did not meet the Decent Homes Standard (unfit, in disrepair, in need of modernisation or failing to provide sufficient thermal comfort) had fallen to 5.9 million (26.8 per cent of the total stock) from 9.4 million (46 per cent) in the ten years since the 1996 survey.

The reason for most properties failing to meet the Decent Homes Standard was a lack of thermal comfort – 4.1 million homes (50.6 per cent of all non-decent dwellings). 1.7 million were in disrepair, and 550,000 required modernisation (CLG, 2008d).

Since April 2006, the Housing Health and Safety Rating System – a comprehensive and systematic risk assessment of hazards – replaced the fitness standard as part of the decent homes criteria. In April 2008, the EHCS was integrated into the new *English Housing Survey* (EHS), therefore the last EHCS took place in 2006.

The Northern Ireland survey in 2004 found that 25,630 dwellings, 3.8 per cent of the total housing stock, lacked basic amenities. The condition of the dwelling stock was not uniform, with 6.8 per cent of rural dwellings failing to meet basic standards compared with 2.5 per cent of urban dwellings. The main causes for properties being defined as unfit were unsatisfactory facilities for the preparation of food (17,730), and disrepair (19,840). The survey concluded a clear relationship between age and the Decent Homes Standard. One half of those dwellings built before 1919 were non-decent, and this proportion reduced steadily until it was minimal for those properties built since 1980. Elderly heads of household were more likely to live in non-decent homes – 46 per cent compared to the overall average of 30 per cent for all households (NIHE, 2008).

The *Welsh House Condition Survey* of 2004 (WAG, 2008) identified 57,700 dwellings failing to meet the fitness standard, representing 4.8 per cent of the total housing stock at that time. Of those dwellings built before 1850, 11.8 per cent were unfit, a level which reduces steadily with newer properties with only 2.4 per cent of those properties built since 1965 failing to meet the standard.

The *Scottish House Condition Survey* of 2006 identified that less than 1 per cent of the housing stock fell *below the tolerable standard*, due to reasons such as dwellings being structurally unstable; damp or poorly ventilated; lacking a wholesome water supply, WC or bath/shower facilities, effective drainage and facilities for cooking food.

8.2: Who lives in poor housing?

The proportion of the housing stock which is unfit reduces as consideration turns to properties of more recent construction. There are, however, a number of factors in addition to age which impact on the standard of dwellings. The *English House Condition Survey* gives information on the household make up of those households in the worst dwellings. Consideration of these data provides some useful insights.

Almost 6 million households live in non-decent homes, 4.8 million of these in the private sector and nearly 1.2 million in social housing tenancies. Older households are more likely to live in non-decent homes in the private sector, with 34 per cent of those households including someone over 75 years of age, 38 per cent of single persons over the age of 65, and 44 per cent of households who have been resident for 30 years or more living in non-decent private sector housing.

In the private sector some types of households are more likely than average to live in non-decent homes: 41 per cent of the poorest fifth of private sector households are living in non-decent homes, as are 43 per cent of those below retirement age who are either economically inactive or unemployed and some 40 per cent of ethnic minorities. In contrast, there is relatively little difference between the quality of housing occupied by different groups within the affordable rented sector.

Ethnic minority households (28 per cent) are nearly three times more likely to live in poor neighbourhoods than white households (10 per cent). Poor neighbourhoods have relatively high concentrations of pre-retirement households on low income, those who are unemployed or economically inactive, lone parents, and other people living alone or sharing.

Residents of poor neighbourhoods are much more likely than those living elsewhere to view their neighbourhood as having a wide range of problems linked to the environment and its upkeep and to criminal and anti-social behaviour. The most common problems indicated by residents of predominantly local authority-built poor neighbourhoods are the amount of litter and rubbish around (62 per cent of all households in these neighbourhoods), fear of being burgled (51 per cent), vandalism and hooliganism, troublesome teenagers/children, and the general level of crime (all 45 per cent). For households in private sector, poor neighbourhoods (who are most likely to live in city and other urban centres) the most common problems are the amount of litter and rubbish (55 per cent), street parking (55 per cent), fear of burglary (45 per cent) and heavy road traffic (40 per cent).

Survey data would also suggest that age and income levels are key factors as to whether owner-occupiers are likely to carry out repair and maintenance work on their homes. As income increases, the likelihood of people spending more money on repairs to their property increases. Data from the survey suggest that households in the lowest income bands were most likely to live in the worst dwellings. This would suggest that those with the lowest income are able to only afford the worst property and are less able to afford repairs.

As owner-occupiers age, the likelihood of spending money on repairs would appear to decrease. A greater proportion of both the elderly and the younger age groups were found to live in the worst dwellings. As with income, this suggests that the dwellings these groups inhabit were in poorer condition to begin with and that repairs are less likely to have been carried out (ODPM, 2003).

There is also a link between age and income. The younger the occupier is, the more opportunity there is to earn money which might be spent on improvements in the house. In the same way that the above data shows the link between the income and the dwelling condition of owner-occupiers, there will also be a link between the availability of finance to landlords and stock condition. If finance is available to landlords, both private and public sector, there are more options available to them in maintaining their dwellings. In relation to local authority landlords there is a crucial impact of government financial controls in determining the amount of resources available to repair and maintain the stock. An associated factor will also be the spending decisions made by local politicians in how to ration and allocate the central government determined total sum.

A further influence on private landlords' decisions to spend on maintenance will be the rate of return on rented accommodation. At the present time there is a relatively poor rate of return for private landlords, and therefore a lack of incentive to invest in improving the condition of housing stock among this group.

As the owner-occupied sector has increased, an increasing proportion of home owners will be relatively poorer. Some commentators have noted that the government's push to increase the owner-occupied sector has taken numbers beyond limits which are sustainable by the market. In the worst cases the result might be repossession for those encouraged to take on financial responsibilities they cannot afford to meet. For others the impact will be a lack of ability to meet the costs of repairs and maintenance.

8.3: Improving housing quality

England

The *English House Condition Survey* (which was carried out every five years until 2006; after which it was incorporated into the *English Housing Survey*) last reported in 2008, based on a survey completed in 2006. The survey showed that 27.5 per cent of the English housing stock was classified as failing to meet the Decent Homes Standard. This represented a total of 5.9 million homes. This was an improvement on the situation in 1996, when 9 million homes (44.7 per cent of the total housing stock) were found to be 'non-decent'. The 2006 survey also identified that levels of disrepair had reduced since 1996 across all tenures, with particular improvements for private rented local authority and housing association tenants, as we can see from Figure 2.8 below.

Figure 2.8: House condition by tenure 1996-2006 in England (percentages of stock)

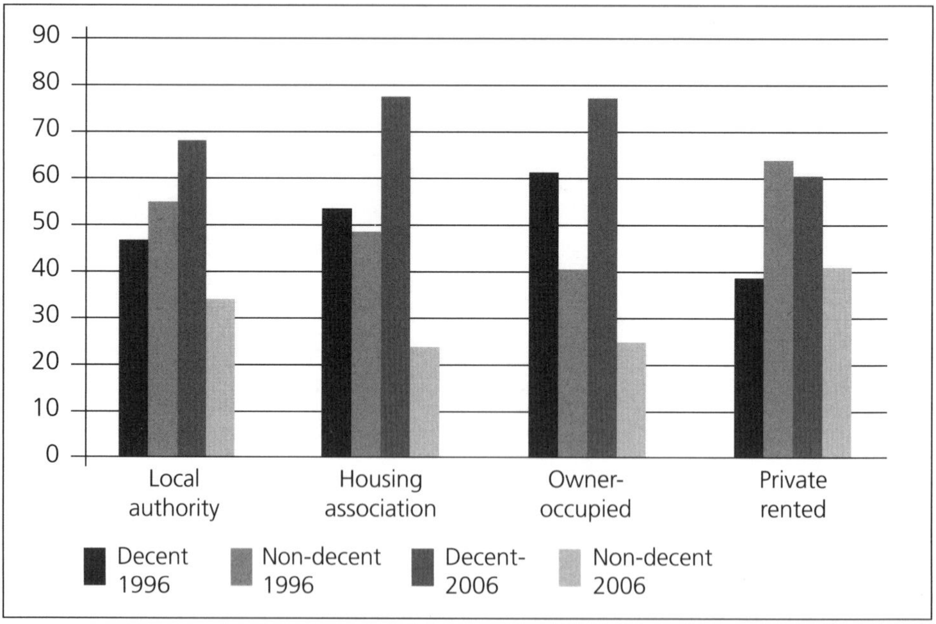

Source: Apapted from CLG, 2008d.

The government introduced the Decent Homes Standard for social housing landlords in England in July 2000, requiring that:

> *All social housing meets standards of decency by 2010, by reducing the number of households living in social housing that does not meet standards...with most of the improvements taking place in the most deprived local authority areas*
> (ODPM website, *A Decent Home: the revised guidance*, February 2002).

The initial fitness standard was revised in April 2006, with the introduction of the Housing Health and Safety Rating System (HHSRS), to allow for a more comprehensive risk assessment of the condition in each home.

The **Decent Homes Standard** states that all housing must:

- be above the statutory minimum standard (i.e. the HHSRS standards);
- be in a reasonable state of repair;
- provide reasonably modern facilities and services;
- provide a reasonable degree of thermal comfort.

English Decent Homes Standard

(a) Meeting the statutory minimum standard

In England, this is the Housing Health and Safety Rating System. The purpose of the HHSRS assessment is not to set a standard but to generate objective information in order to determine and inform enforcement decisions.

There are 29 categories of hazard, each of which is separately rated, based on the risk to the potential occupant who is most vulnerable to that hazard. The individual hazard scores are grouped into 10 bands where the highest bands (A-C representing scores of 1,000 or more) are considered to pose Category 1 hazards. Local authorities have a duty to act where Category 1 hazards are present.

Local authorities may take into account the vulnerability of the actual occupant in determining the best course of action.

For the purposes of the Decent Homes Standard, homes posing a Category 1 hazard are non-decent on its criterion that a home must meet the statutory minimum requirements.

(b) Meeting the reasonable repair test

A property is in reasonable state of repair unless:

- one or more key building components are old **and** because of this need replacing. Key components are:
  External walls(80 years+)
  Roof (50 years+)
  Windows and doors (40 years+)
  Chimneys (50 years+)
  Central heating boilers (15 years+)
  Gas Fires (30 years+)
  Storage heaters (30 years+)
  Electric (30 years+).

- Or, two or more other building components are old and because of their condition need replacing or major repair:
  Kitchens (30 years+)
  Bathrooms (40 years+)
  Radiators (40 years+).

(c) Meeting the reasonably modern facilities and services test
If three or more of the following are lacking then the home is not decent:

- Kitchen 20 years old or less
- Kitchen providing adequate space and layout for food storage and food preparation
- Bathroom 30 years old or less
- Appropriately located bathroom and WC
- Adequate noise insulation
- Adequate size and layout of common entrances for blocks of flats.

(d) Meeting the thermal comfort test
A dwelling must have both:

- Efficient heating (programmable central heating systems)
- Effective insulation (cavity wall insulation where possible plus 50mm loft insulation for gas/oil heating and 200mm for electric systems).

Figure 2.9: Number of non-decent local authority homes England 2000-01 to 2007-08

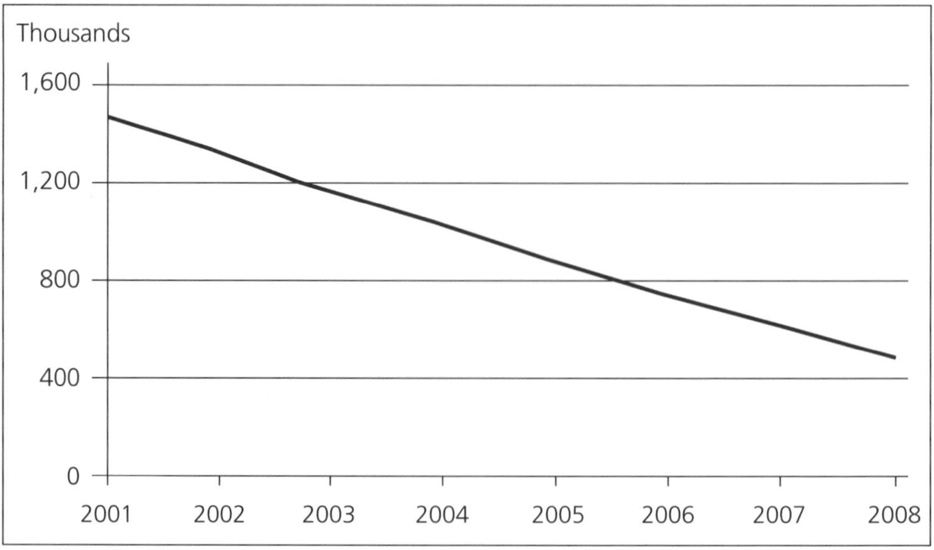

Source: CLG, 2009.

In its housing statistical report published in 2009 the government reported that the number of non-decent local authority dwellings in England at 1 April 2008 was 489,000 (compared to 617,000 in 2007). This figure represented 27 per cent of local authority homes.

Northern Ireland

The Northern Ireland Assembly has adopted a parallel approach in which the Decent Homes Standard, taking account of fitness, state of repair, facilities and services, and thermal comfort are considered. In 2008, the Northern Ireland Housing Executive had measured whether dwellings met the Housing Health and Safety Rating System as part of the 2006 *House Condition Survey* but the Assembly had yet to formally adopt it as a requirement to be met as part of the standard (NIHE, 2008). Data compiled from the survey into the condition of Northern Ireland's housing shows a steady improvement over the past 30 years, as can be seen in Figure 2.10.

Figure 2.10: NI house conditions 1979 to 2004 (thousands of dwellings)

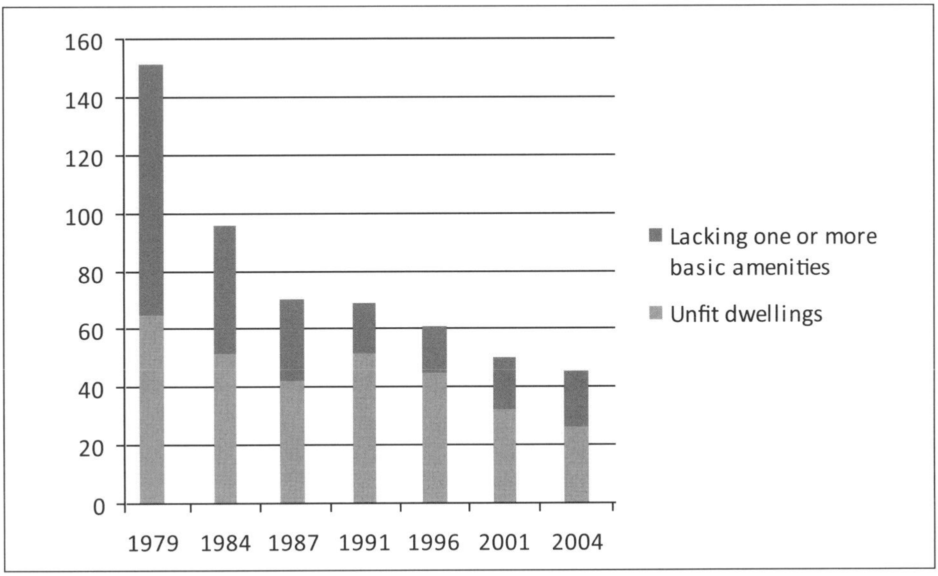

Source: Adapted from NI Department for Social Development, Housing Statistics 2005-06.

Wales

A similar standard applies in Wales, set by the Welsh Assembly Government. The Welsh Housing Quality Standard (WHQS) aims to provide a common target standard for the physical condition of all housing in Wales. The Welsh Assembly Government expects all affordable landlords in Wales to adopt the standard and to devise realistic programmes for bringing all of their properties up to it by 2012. Data from the survey into the condition of Welsh housing shows improvement over the past two decades.

Figure 2.11: Welsh House Conditions 1986-2004 (thousands of dwellings)

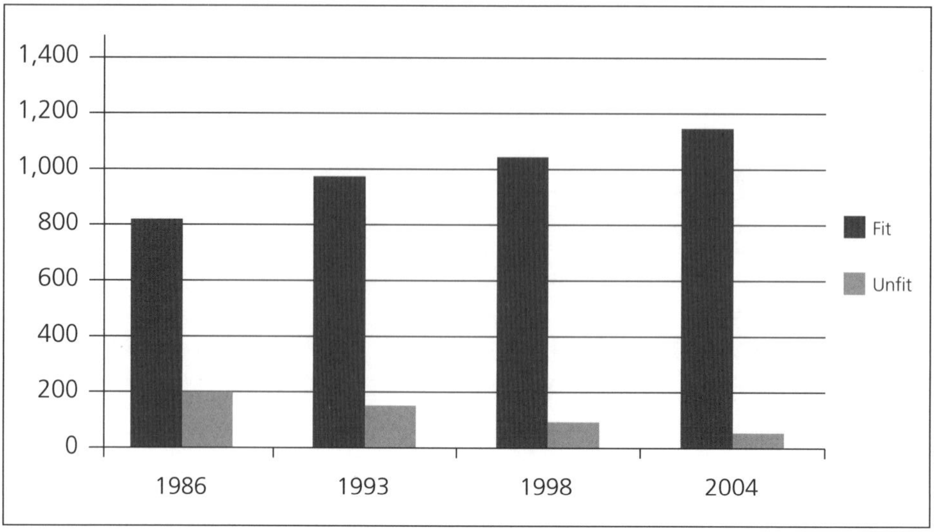

Source: Adapted from *Living in Wales 2004* – Report on Unfitness and Repairs, 2005.

Welsh Housing Quality Standard

Better Homes for People in Wales (2001) stated the National Assembly for Wales's vision that '*all households in Wales...shall have the opportunity to live in good quality homes that are:*

- *In a good state of repair*
- *Safe and secure*
- *Adequately heated, fuel efficient and well insulated*
- *Contain up-to-date kitchens and bathrooms*
- *Well managed (for rented housing)*
- *Located in attractive and safe environments*
- *As far as possible suit the specific requirements of the household (e.g. specific disabilities)*'.

Scotland

Figure 2.12, below, demonstrates improvements in the numbers of Scottish dwellings failing to meet the tolerable standard, reflected in a comparison of data from the 1996, 2002 and 2004-05 *Scottish House Condition Surveys*.

The proportion of unfit housing, and particularly the level of unfit housing within the social rented sector showed some improvement in the periods between the surveys.

The Scottish Executive announced in February 2004 the details of its Housing Quality Standard. To meet the standard, homes have to be free from serious disrepair, energy

Figure 2.12: Scottish dwellings below tolerable standard 1996, 2002 & 2004-05 (thousands of dwellings)

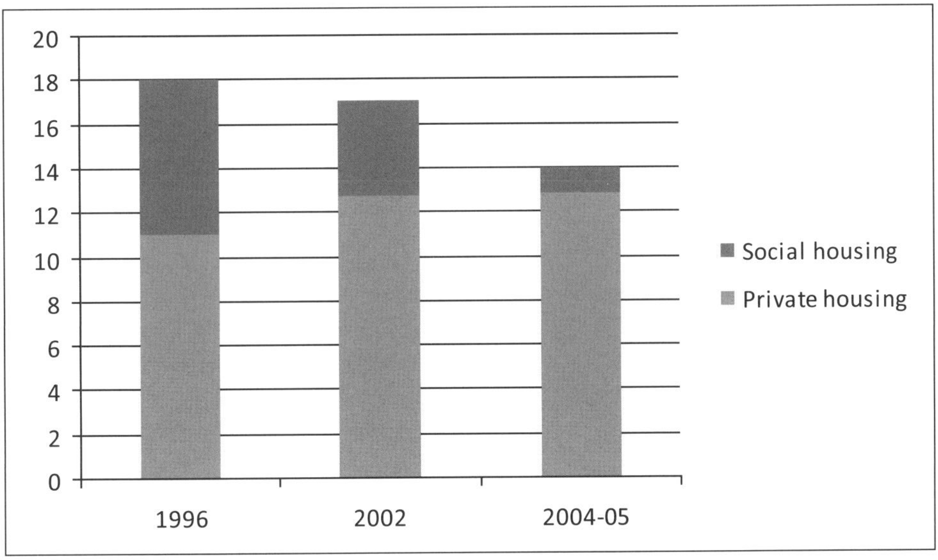

Source: Adapted from *Scottish House Condition Surveys* 1996, 2002 and 2004-05.

efficient and safe and secure. Landlords have been given until 2015 to achieve this target with each required to have a delivery plan setting out how they intend to achieve the target.

Scottish Housing Quality Standard

- compliant with the tolerable standard;
- free from serious disrepair (this applies to all elements of the building);
- energy efficient (effective insulation, insulated hot water systems, energy efficient full central heating);
- provided with modern facilities and services (bathrooms with a WC, bath/shower and hand basins in 'good and usable' condition, kitchen fittings in good condition with adequate storage);
- healthy, safe and secure (lead free internal pipes, mechanical ventilation where appropriate, external noise insulation, smoke detectors, safe electrical and gas installations, internal common areas in a good and safe condition, secure front and rear doors and entry systems operative).

Figure 2.13 shows the numbers of dwellings meeting the Scottish Housing Quality Standard (SHQS). Within the social housing sector there has been a steady increase in the numbers passing the SHQS, and a reduction in the numbers of dwellings failing the standard. This suggests that affordable landlords are taking steps to meet the government's target. The increase in the numbers meeting the SHQS in the private sector is not matched by a significant decrease in the numbers failing to meet standard in that sector. This would appear to suggest that whilst newly constructed private sector dwellings are meeting the standard, older private sector housing is improving at a slower rate than that in the social housing sector.

Figure 2.13: Passing and failing the Scottish Housing Quality Standard by tenure (thousands of dwellings)

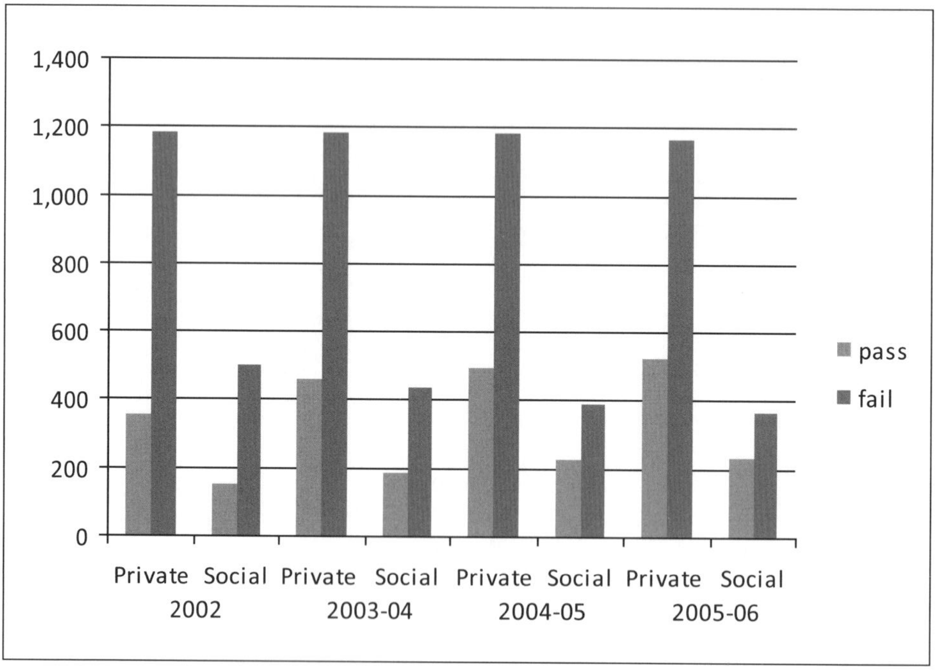

Source: Data adapted from the *Scottish House Condition Survey* 2005-06.

The requirement to meet the varying housing standards operating in the different countries of the UK is a factor which impinges on the financial planning of all affordable landlords. The implications of the issues arising are considered in the next chapter. At the present time there are no plans for the standard to be applied in the private sector.

9. Access to the affordable housing sector

As we have seen earlier in this chapter, the nature and extent of the affordable housing sector has changed over time, particularly since the step change in government policies following the 1979 election, resulting in a reduction of the local authority sector and a decline in the proportion of the population living within affordable housing. We noted that the main trends in government policy during this period have been a reduction in the landlord role of local authorities – driven by the introduction of the right to buy and restrictions on the spending capabilities of local authorities. At the same time, whilst housing associations took the main role in the provision of new social housing, this new development has not been at a rate allowing replacement of the number of dwellings leaving the sector.

Figure 2.14: Changing tenure balance 1971-2006 (UK)

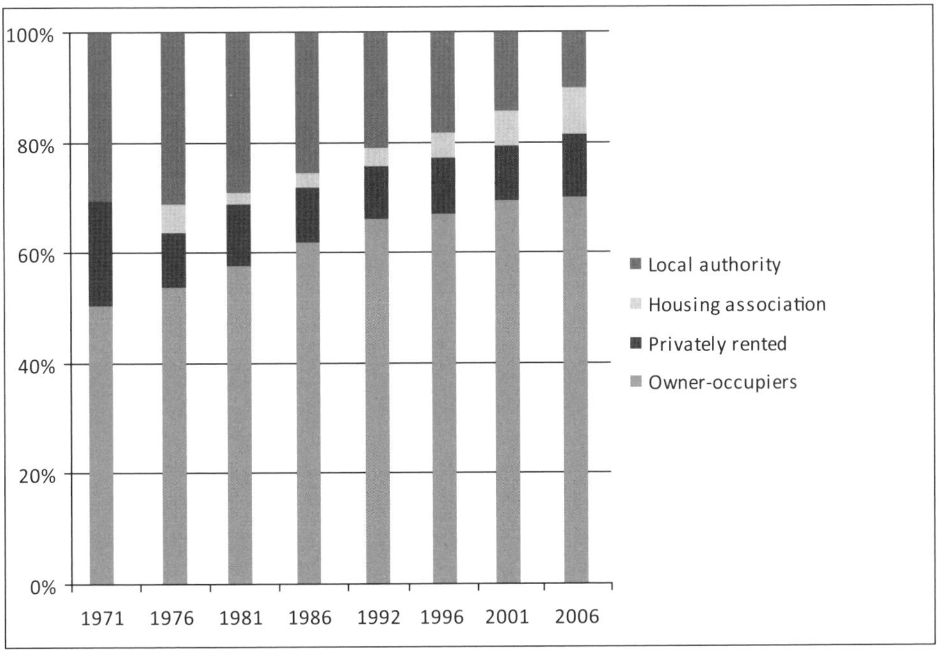

Source: Adapted from Wilcox, 2008.

Figure 2.14 shows the steady increase in the proportion of the housing stock held by owner-occupiers whilst the stock of local authority housing has steadily reduced. At the same time, housing associations have gained an increasing percentage of the nation's dwellings, but not at a sufficiently high level to replace the lost council stock. Between the introduction of the right to buy in 1980 and 2006, 2,399,407 social housing dwellings, most of them owned by local authorities were bought by sitting tenants (Wilcox, 2008). This represents a mean average figure of 89,977 for each of the 26 years in that period. Although rising, the number of new social housing dwellings is still far below that required. There were 42,000 new units of affordable housing produced in 2006–07, compared with an estimated 48,000 required to keep up with demographic change (Palmer *et al.*, 2007).

Levels of demand for social housing will often be affected by the availability of housing in the other tenures, particularly access to owner-occupation. Affordability, notably the perceived lack of affordable housing, is often seen as one of the key problems relating to housing in this country. In the five years up to 2007 annual mortgage costs for first-time buyers have risen sharply and reached a historically very high level compared to earnings (Palmer *et al*, 2007). It had been noted that housing costs comprise one quarter of net household income for households in the poorest fifth of the population, compared to 15 per cent on average and 10 per cent for the richest fifth; levels comparable with a period in the early 1990s when a sudden fall in house prices resulted in high levels of negative equity and an affordability crisis for new and recent first-time buyers.

9.1: Affordable housing tenants

During the first two decades of the right to buy policy the most desirable council housing was bought by the most affluent tenants in the middle stages of the family life cycle. The youngest and oldest tenants were the least likely to buy, resulting in fewer remaining tenants in the 40 to 60 age range, together with an increased proportion of the young and older populations, and those who were either not economically active or working but in receipt of lower incomes (Jones and Murie, 1998).

We have already seen (Table 2.1) that those living in social housing tend to be predominately within particular socio-economic groups, with 73 per cent of all of those people in the population who have never worked or who are long-term unemployed renting within the social housing sector. A comparison of the employment status of social housing tenants over the past three decades gives an indication of the changing nature of the tenant profile during this period.

Table 2.4: Employment status of heads of household in social housing in England

(percentages)	1977-78	1981	1984	1988	1991	1995-96	2000-01	2005-06
Full-time employment	52.3	43.0	32.0	25.8	25.2	22.2	23.2	21.0
Part-time employment	3.6	5.0	4.0	5.7	5.0	6.2	8.4	9.0
Unemployed	5.8	8.0	13.0	11.8	11.1	11.9	6.1	6.0
Retired	21.1	29.0	27.0	38.5	40.4	37.7	36.3	34.0
Other: economically inactive	17.2	15.0	24.0	18.2	18.3	22.0	26.0	30.0
Total	100	100	100	100	100	100	100	100

Sources: Adapted from Holmans, 2005, and Wilcox, 2007.

If we present the data from Table 2.4 as a stacked bar chart it clarifies some trends for us.

From Figure 2.15 it can be seen that since the late 1970s the proportion of social housing tenants in employment has reduced, whilst the proportion of economically inactive has increased. Amongst this group the numbers of retired tenants have increased. A reduction in the numbers registered as unemployed after the mid-1990s

Figure 2.15: Employment status of heads of household in social housing in England

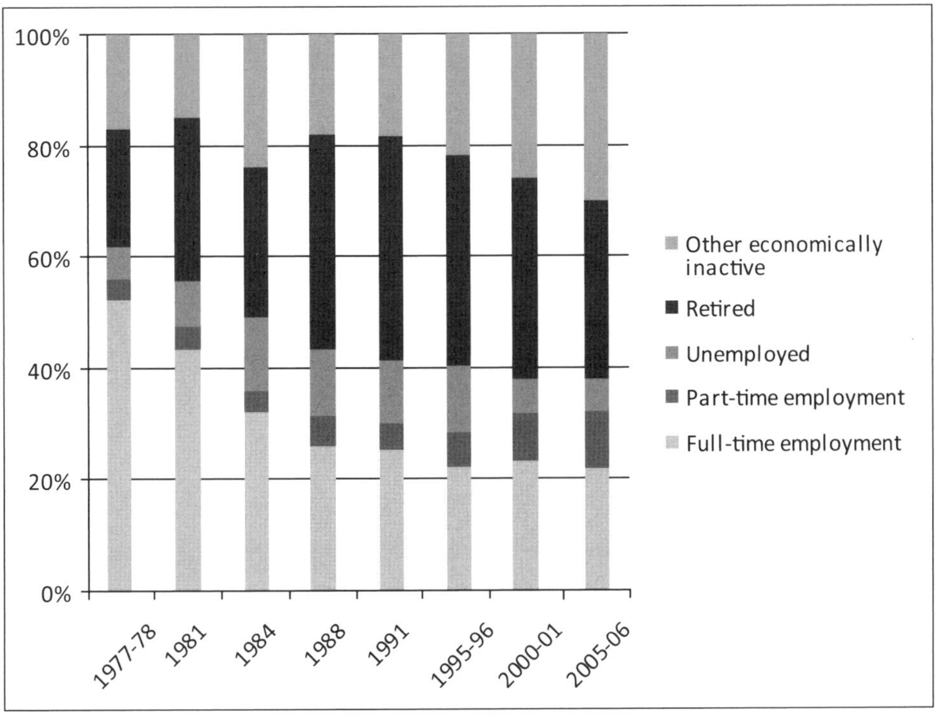

Sources: Adapted from Holmans, 2005, and Wilcox, 2007.

in part reflects reducing levels of unemployment in the economy at large, but also a tendency for many economically inactive people to be transferred from being counted as long-term unemployed and onto sickness and invalidity benefits, and therefore to have their status reclassified. A number of explanations have been given for the changing profile of social housing tenants during the past three decades. As the stock of social housing reduced after 1980 it was largely the case that the sitting tenants exercising the right to buy were predominately in the 40 to 60 age range, with families, likely to be employed (and therefore able to get a mortgage) and more likely to be living in, and keen to buy, attractive family housing of traditional design and construction (typically brick built semi-detached houses) and situated in popular areas.

The impact of this trend on the remaining tenant profile was that an increasing proportion of the tenants were either young or elderly, and less likely to be economically active. The housing stock which remained unsold was more likely to be of non-traditional design and construction (flats and maisonettes, built using 'system-building' techniques) and in areas that had been traditionally less popular and more difficult for the landlords to let. At the same time, local authorities were required to abide by the terms of the Housing (Homeless Persons) Act 1977, which gave responsibilities for housing the homeless. This act, amended and updated in 1985, 1996 and 2002 has continued to place responsibility on local authorities for securing permanent or temporary housing solutions for homeless people ever since.

The proportion of new lettings being given to the homeless increased as the total stock diminished, and housing associations – many of whom were originally established to assist the poor, as we noted in Chapter 1, focused their stock on providing affordable housing to the needy. A partial outcome of this confluence of policy and practice decisions was the increasing residualisation of social housing as the poorest in society tended to be concentrated in the poorest accommodation in the poorest areas. This tendency has led to a number of impacts for affordable landlords in the approaching the way they manage their housing stock.

It would, however, be too simplistic to suggest that all social housing has been residualised in this way. In order to gain a clear picture of the sector today it is useful to examine the demographic characteristics of those living in social housing in more detail. Research conducted by the Housing Corporation's Centre for Research and Market Intelligence (Perry and Capie, 2008) has identified a number of attributes of the remaining population of the affordable housing sector, including social rented housing and those accessing owner-occupation via low-cost home ownership. Tenants of affordable landlords tend to be concentrated at the extremes of the age range, with those between the ages 45-75 representing a relatively small group compared to the other ages.

Amongst the social tenant group there are more single parents and single person households than in the other tenures. Incomes amongst social housing tenants tend to be significantly lower than in other tenures, with less than half of working age tenants being economically active. The chances of households in social housing to contain a member with employment have continued to reduce. As a result, average incomes amongst those in social housing continue to be lower than those in other tenures, and social housing tenants are more likely than those in other tenures to have an illness or disability.

In addition, black and minority ethnic households are more likely to live in social housing, with some groups (Bangladeshi, black and mixed ethnic households) more likely than others (Indian and Chinese) to occupy the tenure.

Perry and Capie identified four key 'types' of social housing tenant, categorised as 'young urbanites', 'working families', 'non-working poor' and 'older settled households'.

Young urbanites tend to be under the age of 35, less than half have children, and tend to live in flats or maisonettes with one or two bedrooms. Most of this group live in London, the south and east of England.

Working families tend to be more likely to be working than the other groups. Most are between the ages of 25-45, married with children and living in (mainly semi-detached) houses. This group tend to be mobile. Over a third had moved within the last year and the majority had moved within the last five years. Most live in London or southern England and tend to be in professional or 'white collar' occupations.

> *Where they live, and their typically large household sizes, suggest that these residents may be not be able to afford sufficiently big accommodation in the private sector despite having incomes that are above average for the social housing sector* (Perry and Capie, 2008, p6).

The main characteristics of the 'non-working' poor are that they tend to be of working age, despite not being in employment. They tend to be more concentrated in the north of England than the group identified as 'working families', are less likely to be married, more likely to have lower incomes and less likely to have studied beyond the age of 16. They are also less mobile than the other groups, less likely to have moved within the last three years, and more likely to have moved to their current accommodation from another social housing dwelling.

The remaining group – 'older settled households' are mostly retired or not in work, and aged over 55, with most over the age of 65. Almost none of these households have children and just over half are single person households, most being divorced, separated or widowed. Incomes tend to be low to moderate and the group are less mobile than the other groups; most have been resident in their current homes for over ten years.

The first two groups 'young urbanites' and 'working families' are considered to be more likely to seek other housing, potentially in other tenures if and when available as an option. The remaining two groups are considered more likely to remain in social housing as a long-term housing solution.

9.2: Those moving into the affordable housing sector

In 2004 (the example year for the study), 71,000 households entered the affordable sector from private rented housing, 32,000 from owner-occupation and 91,000 as newly forming households (Perry and Capie, 2008). Most of the people moving into social housing tenancies and low-cost home ownership were under the age of 45. The reasons for accessing the sector tended to be varied between the identified groups. The groups most likely to be in employment tended to have come from the private sector and may see social housing as a short-term measure at a time of declining levels of affordability in other tenures, particularly owner-occupation. The older settled households had either been tenants for a long period or had moved into social housing as they developed a need for specialist or supported housing. There was an equal split between those living in two and three bedroom homes (likely to have been long-term tenants with families who had grown and moved away), and those in bungalows.

9.3: Those leaving the affordable housing sector

Those leaving the sector are more likely to be within the 25-45 age group and to be in employment. Over 70 per cent of those leaving the sector were found to have jobs. During 2004, 50,000 households moved from social housing into private rented housing, 22,000 to take up owner-occupation, and an additional 60,000 bought as sitting tenants (generally via the right to buy). Once again the tendency for the economically active in the middle stages of the family life cycle to leave the sector is likely to further contribute to the concentration of higher proportions of tenants being in the outlying younger and older age groups and more likely to be on low incomes.

The past three decades have seen a significant change in the characteristics of the tenants of social housing. During the 1980s and 1990s, social housing has increasingly housed poorer and poorer people, as working households left the sector, often through the right to buy, and affordable landlords sought to focus a diminishing resource on assisting those in the greatest need. The result has been an increase in unemployed, sick and disabled households, with a relatively high proportion of single parents, the young and older people living in social housing.

10. Summary

From this chapter we have seen that there is a range of contextual factors which impact on the housing system and the types and quality of housing available within different tenures. We have also noted that many economic and social factors have an impact on access to housing and the type of housing available. It can also be seen that government policy initiatives are used to steer and encourage changes in the housing system, through a range of measures from setting standards for decent homes to encouraging the privatisation of public sector housing. Often the government will use legislation to change the legal rights of tenants (such as the introduction of the right to buy) or to alter the role of local government, or the housing associations.

The key themes arising are used as the basis for discussion of key areas of the provision and management of affordable housing through the remaining chapters of the book.

References and further reading

Barker, K. (2003) *Review of Housing Supply: Securing our Future Housing Needs: Interim Report – Analysis,* ODPM, London.

Communities Scotland (2003) *Scottish House Condition Survey 2002*, Scottish Executive/Communities Scotland, Edinburgh.

Communities Scotland (2006) *Local Housing Need and Affordability Model for Scotland Update*, Communities Scotland, Edinburgh.

Department for Communities and Local Government (2007a) *Housing Market Report: March 2007*, CLG, London.

Department for Communities and Local Government (2007b) *English House Condition Survey 2005*, CLG, London.

Department for Communities and Local Government (2008a) *Median house prices by district, table 582, based on the sale price of property taken from the Land Registry's sold price data: Q2/2007*, CLG, London.

Department for Communities and Local Government (2008b) *Survey of English Housing*, CLG, London.

Department for Communities and Local Government (2008c) *Housing Strategies: fit for purpose*, CLG, London.

Department for Communities and Local Government (2008d) *English House Condition Survey 2006: Decent Homes and Decent Places*, CLG, London.

Department for Communities and Local Government (2009) *Local Authority Housing Statistics, England 2007/08*, CLG, London.

Holmans, A.E. (2005) *Historical Statistics of Housing in Britain*, Cambridge Centre for Housing and Planning Research, Cambridge.

Jones, C. and Murie, A. (1998) *Reviewing the Right to Buy*, JRF, York.

Kemp, P. (2004) *Private Renting in Transition*, CIH, Coventry.

National Assembly for Wales (2001) *Better Homes for People in Wales*, Welsh Assembly, Cardiff.

Nationwide (2008) *House Prices: April 2008*, Nationwide (available at: http://www.nationwide.co.uk/hpi/historical/Q1_2008.pdf), Northampton.

Northern Ireland Housing Executive (2003) *Northern Ireland House Condition Survey 2001*, NIHE, Belfast.

Northern Ireland Housing Executive (2008) *2004 Interim House Condition Survey: Statistical Annex*, NIHE, Belfast.

Northern Ireland Housing Executive (2008) *Northern Ireland House Condition Survey 2006*, NIHE, Belfast.

Office for National Statistics (2000) *Social Trends 30*, HMSO, London.

Office for National Statistics (2003) *Social Trends 33*, HMSO, London.

Office for National Statistics (2008a) *Social Trends 38*, HMSO, London.

Office for National Statistics (2008b) *General Household Survey 2006,* HMSO, London.

Palmer, G., Kenway, P. and Wilcox, S. (2006) *Housing and Neighbourhoods Monitor*, JRF/NPI, York.

Palmer, G., MacInnes, T. and Kenway, G. (2007) *Monitoring Poverty and Social Exclusion 2007*, JRF/New Policy Institute, York.

Perry, J. (2001) 'International Comparisons', in S. Wilcox, *Housing Finance Review 2001/2*, CIH/Council of Mortgage Lenders, Coventry and London.

Perry, J. (2007) *Community Cohesion and Housing*, CIH, Coventry.

Perry, J. and Capie, R. (2008) *Who Lives in Affordable Housing*, CIH/Housing Corporation, Coventry.

Scottish Government (various dates) *Scottish House Condition Survey: Key Findings*, Scottish Executive, Edinburgh.

Shelter (2002) *Time for a Change: Reforming the Right to Buy*, Shelter, London.

Welsh Assembly Government (2008) *Living in Wales: Welsh House Condition Survey, 2004,* Statistical Directorate, Cardiff.

Wilcox, S. (2007) *UK Housing Review 2007/08*, CIH/BSA, Coventry and London.

Wilcox, S. (2008) *UK Housing Review 2008/09*, CIH/BSA, Coventry and London.

CHAPTER 3: Who runs affordable housing?

1. Introduction

During the last 20 years the way in which housing services are organised and the polices which housing organisations pursue have changed significantly. Much of these changes have been led by changes in government policy designed to address some of the real weaknesses in the management of affordable housing which came to be highlighted in the 1980s. Some of the changes were driven by economic policy and some by political dogma.

2. Local authority housing services

Chapter 1 described in detail the development of local authorities as landlords since the First World War. As local authorities became landlords of significant numbers of homes very few of them had a co-ordinated approach to the management of their housing services. This was because the housing management function was relatively new and involved a number of local government disciplines and perhaps it was not surprising that the task of providing and managing social housing fell to a number of different departments. In the inter-war years it was still relatively rare to find a local authority housing department which carried out most of the key housing management functions itself. However, as the numbers of properties owned by local authorities increased then the need for a more co-ordinated approach to housing management led to more and more functions being brought together into a separate housing department. Of course, practice varied from local authority to local authority and even in the 1950s and 1960s it was still common to find a number of different departments undertaking housing responsibilities.

This fragmentation of service delivery was a cause for concern in the housing profession and in 1969 the Cullingworth Report (*Council housing; purposes, procedures and priorities*) advocated the establishment of a separate housing department responsible for all housing functions of the local authority. This was echoed in 1972 by the Institute of Housing in their report, *The Comprehensive Housing Service: Organisation and Functions* and this influenced the way in which housing services were organised in the new local authorities which were established in the major review of local government of 1974.

However, even in the 1980s a significant number of local authorities had still not set up a housing department with responsibility for the key housing management functions. The Audit Commission in 1986 wrote of local authorities:

> *...some have all of the housing functions under the direct control of a chief housing officer; others operate with the financial aspect outside the housing department under the treasurer; yet others have no separate housing organisation at all, typically with the treasurer in control of the management of all council housing* (Audit Commission, 1986).

In their report, the Audit Commission had indicated that 12 small housing authorities had no separate housing department, whilst 108 authorities had the treasurer responsible for rent collection, rent accounting, arrears recovery and housing benefit. The Audit Commission strongly advocated the creation of a single housing department and after the 1986 report local authorities increasingly recognised the benefits to be obtained from having one department co-ordinating all housing activities.

In 1993, the Centre for Housing Policy at the University of York still found that a truly comprehensive housing department was the exception rather than the norm. The research showed that only 29 per cent of local authorities had a separate housing department which carried out all housing management functions. On average 30 per cent of housing management work was still carried out by departments other than housing. The local authorities which were most likely to have a housing department carrying out most functions were those with the most properties. Indeed 85 per cent of local authorities with 30,000 properties carried out more than 70 per cent of housing management functions in the housing department alone compared to only 40 per cent of authorities with less than 5,000 units.

The Audit Commission in their 1986 report suggested that the department most likely to be involved in housing management activities outside of the housing department was the Borough Treasurer. Although the 1993 research reported that over 20 different types of local authority departments were involved with housing management, it was clear that the Treasurer's department was most likely to be undertaking some aspect of housing management work, whether rent collection, rent arrears recovery, or managing housing benefit.

3. The organisation of housing association services

Most housing associations are small compared to local authorities; a medium-sized housing association will own between 1,000 and 5,000 homes, which of course would be considered small by local authority standards. There are significantly more housing associations than local authorities and within the housing association sector there is greater diversity in terms of the number of homes that associations manage ranging from almshouses with perhaps three homes to large national housing associations managing over 60,000 homes. Many housing associations, unlike local authorities, are not based in one geographical location and may well operate in a number of local authority areas or even nationally, such as the Anchor Trust.

In contrast to local authorities, some housing associations will specialise in meeting the housing needs of a particular client group rather than aiming to meet general needs, which is the remit for a local authority. For example, Habinteg is a national housing association which concentrates on meeting the needs of people with disabilities. In recent years a number of black and minority ethnic (BME) associations (such as Asra and Presentation) have been established to meet the housing needs of BME communities.

Given these significant organisational differences between housing associations and local authorities it is not surprising that housing associations often deliver their housing service in a different way to local authorities. Perhaps the most significant difference is that housing associations are more likely to directly control all of their housing management services. This was confirmed by the 1993 York research which showed that housing functions were unlikely to be outside the direct administrative control of housing associations, with over 90 per cent of associations directly controlling rent collection and arrears recovery, void control, repairs and lettings. Some associations will of course have to contract out some of their work to outside agencies, whilst remaining in control of the work as the client. This may be because they do not have the staff or expertise within the association to carry out these functions.

For example, the 1993 research showed that 47 per cent of associations employed an outside agency to administer at least one of their key functions, such as training, IT services and the management of supported housing being the most likely to be contracted out to another body. The 1993 research suggested that this difference between local authority and housing associations reflects the different context in which they work:

> *...housing departments exist within a relatively large bureaucracy with a great many functions, in which tasks outside the immediate expertise of the department may well be handled by specialists in another department. Housing associations are 'housing only' organisations and may therefore be obliged to seek outside help with areas outside their main functions* (York, 1993).

4. The changing face of social housing

Today, affordable housing is now delivered in number of different ways, through local authority housing departments, housing associations and arms length management organisations managing local authority homes.

In the local authority sector there are local authority housing departments, arms length management organisations, Tenant Management Organisations and 'Supporting People' administering bodies. Private sector developers can now access the Social Housing Grant and a number of private sector housing managers are working in the sector. The Audit Commission in England carries out inspections, the Homes and Communities Agency is delivering the regeneration agenda previously shared by the Housing Corporation and English Partnerships, the Welsh Assembly Government has its own arrangements as does the Scottish Government. The Tenant Services Authority regulates housing associations and private sector leasing providers in England. Local authorities and ALMOs will come under TSA regulation in 2010. (The Welsh Assembly Government and Scottish Housing Regulator have similar remits in their respective countries.) These have been rapid changes in the housing sector and in this section we will trace the roots of these developments.

4.1: 1986: managing the crisis in council housing

In 1981 there were 6.78 million social housing dwellings in the UK. Of these, 6.3 million (or 93 per cent) were owned by local authorities. By 2006 the picture had changed significantly with the total UK affordable housing stock having fallen to 4.89 million of which only 1.8 million were directly managed by local authorities (37 per cent), with the 2.19 million managed by housing associations (45 per cent) and 0.9 million by ALMOs (18 per cent) (National Federation of ALMOs, 2006). This is a massive change in numbers and management arrangements.

Although it is difficult to pinpoint the beginnings of a policy shift which has so significantly changed the way in which the sector delivers housing, a good starting point would be 1986. In that year the Audit Commission published what is perhaps one of the most important reports on housing in the last 50 years. It was written at a time when there was an increasing recognition both within and outside the profession, that housing management, particularly within local authorities, was in a crisis. Problems of rent arrears, difficult to let estates, crime and vandalism were all in the news.

This culminated in the Audit Commission publishing its damning report, '*Managing the Crisis in Council Housing*'. The report said in its opening paragraphs:

> *'Crisis' is a heavily overworked word. Yet it is difficult to find a more appropriate way to describe the state of much of the stock of...council owned dwellings in England and Wales...A combination of short sighted national housing policies since the 1960s and shortcomings in local administration has produced a major management challenge in many urban areas* (Audit Commission, 1986).

The crisis which the Audit Commission identified included problems such as:

- Defective dwellings
- Deteriorating stock
- Shortages of housing for rent
- Increases in homelessness

- Low rents
- Weak management control.

The response to the report was far reaching. The Conservative government had already introduced the right to buy in 1980 allowing council tenants to purchase their homes at a significant discount. This policy had been driven by a political desire to extend what were seen as the benefits of home ownership to households living in council accommodation who could afford to buy. It was also driven by a desire to begin to break down some of the mono-tenure estates across the country by introducing multi-tenure into these areas.

The 1986 report prompted the government to go further. In its white paper *Housing: the Government's proposals*, the government set down four key objectives for housing policy in England and Wales:

- to reverse the decline in rented housing and improve its quality;
- to give council tenants the right to transfer to other landlords if they chose to do so;
- to target money on the most acute problems;
- to continue to encourage the growth of home ownership.

4.2: 1988 Housing Act and the growth of housing associations

The resulting 1988 Housing Act set the framework in which these objectives were to be achieved. In the private sector, rent controls which had previously existed under the fair rent regime were replaced with a new regime of assured and assured shorthold tenancies for almost all new lettings, which gave greater powers to landlords and relaxed the previous rent constraints as set out in the fair rent regime.

In order to encourage new house building by housing associations to meet the increasing housing needs of the population the government also introduced assured tenancies into the housing association sector and enabled housing associations to develop mixed finance schemes, with Housing Association Grant allied to private borrowing. By introducing private finance into new development the Housing Association Grant could be spread over more developments and more homes created. This, however, had to be at the expense of higher rents to service the mortgage loans and to meet the association's repairs and management costs, hence the need to introduce assured tenancies, free from rent control into the sector.

The act also gave further encouragement to the voluntary transfer of housing stock by local authorities to housing associations. Local authorities contemplating this option (which was largely driven by a desire to enable homes to be modernised by housing associations which were free of borrowing restrictions imposed on local government) had to demonstrate that the proposals had the support of tenants.

It was the 1988 Act that led to the significant development of large scale voluntary transfers (LSVT), which by 2008 meant that more affordable housing is owned by housing associations than by local authorities.

4.3: Housing Action Trusts

In a number of specific geographical areas the government decided that more targeted intervention was required and enabled the establishment of Housing Action Trusts to regenerate some of the most deprived local authority estates in England. HATs were non-departmental public bodies, each managed by a board appointed by the government, with boards including residents, elected as representatives of the estates, and members of the local authority. They were set up to repair and improve their housing; to manage their housing effectively; to encourage diversity of tenure; and to improve the social, environmental and living conditions of their areas. Trusts were set up in six areas as set out in Table 3.1. On closure, tenants were consulted on who should take over; in some cases the Trusts were transferred to housing associations or back to the local authority.

Table 3.1: Housing Action Trusts

Housing Action Trust	Closure date
North Hull	March 1999
Waltham Forest (East London)	April 2002
Tower Hamlets (East London)	June 2004
Castle Vale (Birmingham)	March 2005
Liverpool	September 2005
Stonebridge (Brent, London)	August 2007

The 1988 Housing Act therefore sowed the seeds of the housing sector we see today with the decline of council housing, the growth in housing associations (and in particular LSVTs), and the introduction of private finance to deal with both improving homes and delivering new homes for rent and sale.

4.4: 1997 onwards: the impact of the new Labour government

The years from 1988 to the election of a Labour government in 1997 were marked by a continuing trend to stock transfer and continuing right to buy sales as shown by Table 3.2.

This shows that in the late 1980s the right to buy remained very popular with a big increase in sales at time of the 1988 Housing Act, which further increased discounts for purchasers. The success of the right to buy policy is shown in Table 3.3 with the

Table 3.2: Right to buy sales in Great Britain 1980-99

	Local authorities	+ New towns	+ Housing associations	= Total
Total sales 1980-85	607,318	15,023	21,282	**643,623**
1986	89,251	1,656	4,949	**95,856**
1987	103,309	2,277	5,462	**111,048**
1988	160,569	3,275	10,221	**174,065**
1989	181,370	4,608	9,972	**195,950**
1990	126,215	2,522	7,014	**135,751**
1991	73,548	1,501	4,610	**79,659**
1992	63,986	1,182	3,456	**68,624**
1993	60,256	1,192	3,187	**64,635**
1994	65,177	1,417	3,541	**70,135**
1995	49,343	1,309	2,815	**53,558**
1996	44,860	249	4,168	**49,277**
1997	57,996	0	6,380	**64,376**
1998	55,914	0	5,904	**61,818**
1999	67,483	0	8,672	**76,155**

Source: Wilcox, 2008.

numbers of homes in local authority ownership in England falling by 1.25 million (from 4.43 million to 3.178 million) as a result of both the right to buy and stock transfer. This is mirrored by an increase in stock owned by housing associations of 670,000 through some new building but mainly as a result of large scale voluntary transfer.

Figure 3.1 shows the numbers of stock transfers and dwellings transferred in England up to March 2001. As can be seen, around 450,000 homes were transferred in the 12 years prior to 2000 to housing associations but 700,000 homes had been sold under the right to buy.

4.5: New Labour: new housing policy

When the Labour government was elected in 1997 it was committed to following strict fiscal guidelines and initially did not have a significant housing agenda, although it did seek to stem the decline in investment by allowing the 'reinvestment' of the unspent proceeds from earlier council house sales.

Table 3.3: Tenure in England 1986-99 (thousands)

	England Owner-occupiers	+ Privately rented	+ Housing associations	+ Local authority	= All dwellings
1986	12,015	1,953	475	4,439	**18,882**
1991	13,237	1,927	608	3,899	**19,671**
1992	13,333	2,012	646	3,844	**19,836**
1993	13,434	2,079	714	3,760	**19,987**
1994	13,553	2,141	779	3,666	**20,139**
1995	13,700	2,184	857	3,565	**20,305**
1996	13,865	2,191	942	3,470	**20,468**
1997	14,040	2,196	985	3,401	**20,622**
1998	14,237	2,192	1,040	3,309	**20,778**
1999	14,443	2,171	1,146	3,178	**20,927**

Source: Wilcox, 2008.

Figure 3.1: Stock transfers in England

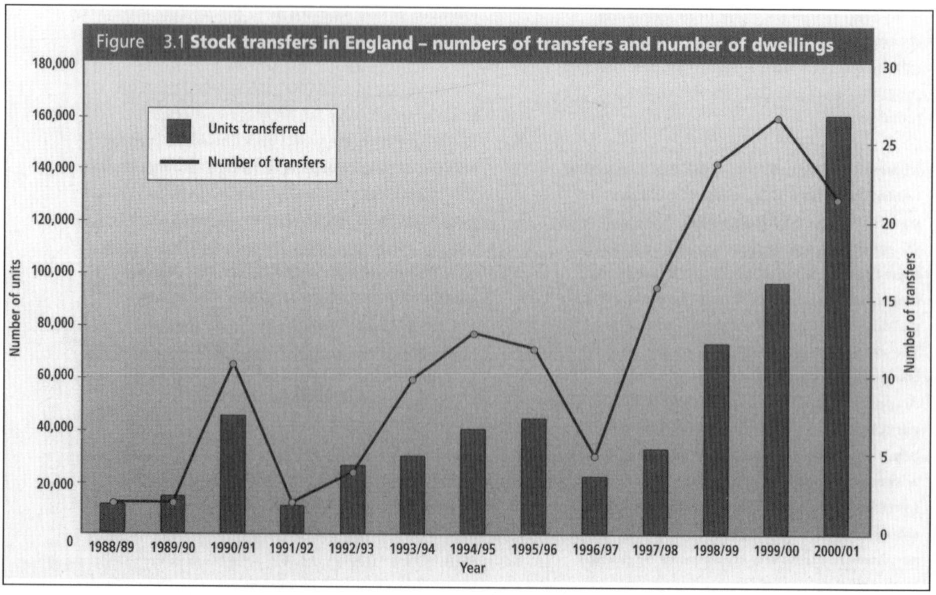

Source: *Housing Finance review 2000/2001*.

However, early in 2000 the new government began to set the scene for a dramatic shift in policy from which we can now trace the development of ALMOs, the move to development partnering and the continuing popularity for local authorities of voluntary transfers.

In April 2000 it published a green paper (*Quality and Choice: a Decent Home for all*, DETR, 2000), which set out an approach to housing policy that sought to continue to drive up the quality of affordable housing and at the same time introduce more choice into the sector as a way of dealing with social exclusion.

The green paper recognised that there had been significant improvements in affordable housing:

> *Yet despite the improvements that have been achieved in the last 150 years, a sizeable minority of people face severe problems with housing:*
>
> - *Too many live in poor-quality housing or find that their landlord, private or public, does not provide a proper service. It would cost about £19 billion just to bring the worst council housing up to a decent modern standard.*
> - *Many live on estates which have been left to deteriorate for too long, and which contribute to ill health, crime and poverty.*
> - *Many families and individuals, including elderly and vulnerable people, live in housing that is not energy efficient and in which it is difficult to keep warm.*
> - *Most public-sector tenants have been denied choice, offered housing on a take-it or leave-it basis and charged rents that are not comparable for comparable homes.*
> - *The most disadvantaged have often been concentrated in the poorest housing.*
> - *Some homeowners, including many retired people, cannot afford to maintain their own homes.*
> - *Others who have bought cannot afford mortgage payments, for example after losing a job.*
> - *Some people are homeless, or even sleeping rough.*

The green paper made a number of proposals:

- Promoting a stronger role for local authorities in housing and in particular to encourage all authorities to take a strategic view of needs across all housing.
- Proposals to support sustainable home ownership including helping key workers and other people on modest incomes to buy their own homes.
- New approaches to improve the quality of social housing and housing management aiming for a step change in the quality of the stock and the performance of social landlords.
- Encouraging the creation of new arms length management organisations to manage local authority owned housing, with the best performing authorities

which established such companies given extra scope to borrow where there is a proven record of efficient management and investment and a clear business plan for the stock.

- Improvements to the delivery of affordable housing, so that it is provided where it is needed and in a form that is sustainable.
- Reforms to lettings policies to give tenants in affordable housing real choice over the homes they live in allowing flexibility for local lettings policies to deal with particular problem estates and other local priorities.
- Options for restructuring rents in the social housing sector to put rents on a fairer, affordable basis.

This green paper set the scene for housing policy for the period from 2000 onwards. In particular, it introduced the Decent Homes Standard and the need to ensure that all affordable housing in England and Wales met the standard by 2010. Arguably, this requirement has had the biggest impact on the way in which affordable housing is managed and who does it over the last 50 years.

4.6: Decent Homes Standard and its organisational impact

The condition of local authority housing in 2000 meant that for many local authorities achieving the Decent Homes Standard would be difficult given the backlog of improvement work required and the capital funding restrictions imposed by central government. This meant that every local authority had to consider how best to achieve the Decent Homes Standard and essentially they had four options:

- Could they achieve the standard using existing resources through the housing investment programme?
- Or if not, should they consider other options such as:
  Private finance initiative
  Stock transfer
  Arms length management organisations.

In practice, some councils were able to demonstrate that they were able to finance the necessary improvements within their existing resources, but the majority had to consider the other three options. Although the private finance initiative has been used to modernise some council stock it has proved to be a complex and expensive way of improving housing and at best PFI has had only a marginal impact on housing policy since 2000.

By far the most popular options adopted in response to the Decent Homes Standard challenge were voluntary transfers of housing stock to a housing association or the establishment of an arms length management organisation. We have already looked at the growth of stock transfer housing associations, which originally were an initiative given full support in the 1988 Housing Act. We now turn to ALMOs.

4.7: The development of arms length management organisations

The government had encouraged councils in the green paper to separate out their strategic and management roles as a way of tackling the backlog of renovation and modernisation work over a faster timescale and of improving services to tenants through new:

> *...management organisations, more focused on and better able to respond to the needs and aspirations of tenants.*

As an incentive to establish arms length management organisations the government decided that local authorities pursuing this option could secure additional capital funding if the new arms length body had received an 'excellent' (3 stars), or later this was reduced to a 'good' (2 stars) rating from the Audit Commission's Housing Inspectorate. To access this additional funding an authority must:

- have established an arms length management organisation to manage its housing stock and associated investment;
- have demonstrated a high level of performance as measured against the Best Value national housing indicators and achieved at least a 2 star rating from the Audit Commission following a housing inspection;
- have demonstrated sound financial planning, management and long-term financial viability through a high quality business plan; and
- have provided a clear plan showing how it proposes to move to a structure of rents and a lettings scheme that is in line with government guidance on rent restructuring and choice-based lettings.

This led to the creation of substantial interest from local authorities in ALMOs as a way of obtaining funding to modernise homes to the Decent Homes Standard whilst at the same time retaining ownership.

An ALMO is a legal entity which is independent of the local authority and is usually established as a not-for-profit company limited by guarantee. It has its own board consisting (like stock transfer associations) of tenants, local authority councillors and independent members. It manages the sponsoring council's stock under a management agreement which should be at arms length from the council so that the ALMO is able to make decisions on the management of the stock independently of the council.

ALMO tenants remain council tenants and retain the right to buy, but the management service is provided by the ALMO itself rather than the council. This initiative only applied to England and was not taken up by the Scottish Government or the Welsh Assembly Government.

As access to funding is linked to achieving a 2 or 3 star result at inspection it is perhaps not surprising that ALMOs have tended to do well at inspection (or at a quick re-inspection following a poor result).

Table 3.4: Audit Commission inspection results for ALMOs at March 2007

3 star excellent	9
3 star promising	5
2 star excellent	6
2 star promising	28
2 star uncertain	4
1 star	7
To be inspected	12
TOTAL	**71**

Source: Adapted from *Social Housing*, 2008.

As can be seen by comparing Tables 3.4 and 3.5, ALMOs have fared significantly better in inspections than their housing association counterparts:

Table 3.5: Housing association inspection results to December 2006

3 star excellent	1
3 star promising	0
2 star excellent	7
2 star promising	27
2 star uncertain	3
1 star	70
0 stars	13
TOTAL	**121**

Source: Extracted from Audit Commission Inspection reports.

Social Housing also reported that 66 per cent of ALMOs improved their grades on re-inspection, whilst 31 per cent remained the same. Only 1 ALMO had a worse score on re-inspection. This is important, since an organisation which obtains an uncertain prospects score is subject to re-inspection, and if a 2 or 3 star ALMO falls to a 1 star on re-inspection it will have its additional funding suspended pending a re-inspection.

ALMOs have grown rapidly as a means of delivering much needed investment into council housing stock. Indeed, in May 2008, *Social Housing* journal reported that here were over 71 ALMOs, employing over 21,000 staff and managing almost 900,000 units. This is an important development since the 2000 green paper and means that ALMOs are now a significant organisational vehicle in the management of affordable housing. Of these ALMOs the largest to date has been Sheffield Homes with a stock of 42,650 units and the smallest, Carrick Homes, managing 3,710 homes.

In 2007, the financial benefits to ALMOs were extended when the Housing Corporation opened up the Social Housing Grant regime to high performing ALMOs and three ALMOs (Brent Housing Partnership, Derby Homes and Sheffield Homes) with 3 stars and promising prospects were awarded SHG allocations to develop new housing in the first round of the National Affordable Housing Programme 2008-11.

Interestingly, the ALMO model has proved to be a peculiarly English model with the Welsh Assembly Government restricting options to achieve the Welsh Housing Quality Standard to local authorities themselves or via stock transfer (preferably to a Community Mutual Model). In Scotland, transfer has been the only other option and apart from the massive transfer to Glasgow Housing Association, transfer has not taken off significantly in Scotland.

4.8: The Sustainable Communities Plan and its impact on housing organisations.

Sustainable Communities: Building for the Future was published in early 2003. It had a number of elements designed to ensure the creation of sustainable communities in the 21st century. The plan said that a key objective of government housing policy was providing homes where people want to live. This simple statement hid what is a hugely complex issue.

In large parts of the south east of England there was a gross shortage of housing in all tenures, leading to house price inflation, high market rents and a shortage of affordable rented homes leading to long waiting lists and thousands in temporary accommodation. In spite of this problem, house building in both the private and affordable housing sectors had been in decline for decades. Local authority house building effectively stopped in the 1970s and the level of investment by housing associations had not kept pace with the level of need.

Table 3.6: Housing completions in the UK

	1970	1980	2007
Local authorities/new towns/government departments	179,373	88,590	373
Housing associations	8,511	21,422	26,355
Private sector	174,342	131,974	195,875
Total	**362,226**	**241,986**	**222,603**

Source: Wilcox 2008.

In the private sector too, house building had failed to keep pace with the demand for home ownership. As the Communities Plan said:

> *Successive governments have failed to tackle the issues and the gap between the need for new housing and what is being provided is widening* (ODPM, 2003).

The plan highlighted that the most significant areas of housing pressure were in London and the south east and the government's strategy to increase supply here had a number of elements:

i) Enabling private developers to build more homes of the right type in the right place

A key action here was to improve the planning framework to make it easier and quicker for new development to proceed. The government also decided that the additional new housing should be located in four growth areas:

- Thames Gateway, *which covers the north and south banks of the Thames into north Kent as far as the Isle of Sheppey and south Essex as far as Southend.*
- Milton Keynes/South Midlands, *to the north of London*
- Ashford, in Kent, *to the south east of London*
- London-Stansted-Cambridge corridor, *which extends broadly to the north east of London up the M11. In February 2004 Peterborough was added to this growth area.*

ii) Funding the provision of more affordable housing for the homeless and key workers

The funding made available to the Housing Corporation was increased to boost the supply of new housing in the south east of England over this three year period. English Partnerships (which was responsible for the government's landholdings in England) was given additional funding to assemble sites for housing development, to work alongside the Housing Corporation.

iii) Making better use of the existing housing stock

One of the paradoxes is that in a time of massive housing shortage there are large numbers of empty homes available in the public and private sector. Often there are good reasons for the properties being empty, such as the need for major repairs or modernisation, but in other cases it is difficult to see why the homes are not put back into the market. The government in its Communities Plan indicated that it wanted to bring more of these long-term empty properties back into use through proposals such as:

- allowing local authorities to lease (compulsorily) long-term empty homes;
- charging the owners of empty homes up to 90 per cent of the council tax;
- encouraging affordable housing tenants to relocate from high demand areas to lower demand areas;
- supporting choice-based lettings schemes;
- funding and supporting care and repair partnerships which can ensure that older properties can be adapted for the use of older tenants.

iv) Other reforms to improve delivery

The changes announced in the Communities Plan (in particular the expansion in the provision of housing across all tenures) was also accompanied by some radical changes to the way in which housing was delivered. This included the creation of regional assemblies with housing responsibilities (to be abolished in 2010) and regional housing boards, intended to ensure that housing strategies, and the allocation of finance, best reflected the needs of the particular region.

4.9: Housing Market Renewal Pathfinders

In some parts of the north of England and in the midlands the housing problem is the reverse of that in the south east, with an excess supply of housing, low average house prices, a glut of rented homes leading to empty estates and vandalism. This low demand is not a new problem and the first signs were noted in the north east in the early 1990s but it has accelerated ever since. The reasons for low demand are complex but are linked crucially to economic conditions and the availability of jobs. Over the last 50 years, the large manufacturing base, often concentrated in the urban areas of the north and midlands of England, central Scotland, south Wales and parts of Northern Ireland, has all but collapsed. With this, there has been a reduction in jobs, increased unemployment and a migration of people, often from conurbations to the more attractive suburbs and rural areas, where the economy is more buoyant. The outcome has been an excess of housing supply in some areas.

The Communities Plan set out the government's strategy to deal with the dilemma of how to bring back life to those areas where there is low demand for housing. In some cases there is wholesale abandonment of homes and a need to re-build sustainable communities where people want to live.

The government's approach to these serious problems has been to create nine Market Renewal Pathfinder Areas. These areas covered almost 50 per cent of the homes which have been affected by low demand and abandonment and where 20 per cent of all of the English non-decent homes stock is situated.

Pathfinders are partnerships between the local authorities, housing associations, the Housing Corporation, English Partnerships, Regional Development Agencies and other key stakeholders in the relevant area and they were tasked with producing strategic plans for the revitalisation of the total housing market in these area on a permanent basis. Plans for each Pathfinder area do of course differ but they include actions such as:

- demolition
- refurbishment
- building new homes of a kind that people want
- the development of sustainable communities

- wider use of compulsory purchase orders of land and property
- use of 'gap funding' to subsidise developments where the costs of development exceed estimates of sale values
- community safety
- encouraging economic development through regional development agencies and business links.

Figure 3.2: Market Renewal Pathfinders

Bridging Newcastle Gateshead – Newcastle and Gateshead
Gateway Hull and East Riding – Hull and East Riding of Yorkshire
Transform South Yorkshire – Sheffield, Barnsley, Rotherham and Doncaster
Urban Living – Birmingham and Sandwell
Renew North Staffordshire – Stoke, Newcastle-under-Lyme and Staffordshire Moorlands
Manchester Salford – Manchester and Salford
Newheartlands – Liverpool, Sefton and Wirral
Partners in Action – Oldham and Rochdale
Elevate East Lancashire – Blackburn with Darwen, Hyndburn, Burnley, Pendle and Rossendale

The Pathfinders were funded out of the government's Housing Market Renewal Fund to £500 million and this was increased in 2005 to £1.2 billion for the period up to March 2008. In addition, the government announced funding of £65 million to three new areas:

West Yorkshire
Tees Valley Living
West Cumbria/Furness.

This approach to low demand and neighbourhood regeneration is not entirely new. Previous initiatives have included Housing Action Areas and General Improvement Areas (to improve private sector housing), Estates Action and Estates Renewal Challenge Fund (to tackle poor quality council housing), City Challenge, and Single Regeneration Budgets. However, what was new about the 2003 Plan was the priority and emphasis attached to tackling the problem of low demand and abandonment.

4.10: The organisational impact of the Sustainable Communities Plan

The Plan had a twin track commitment of delivering new homes and ensuring that existing homes were brought up to the Decent Homes Standard. In order to achieve the latter the government said that every local housing authority in England had to carry out an options appraisal by 2005 to determine how it might achieve the Decent

Homes Standard. As we have seen, the major impact of this has been the development of ALMOs and the continuing popularity of stock transfer.

In relation to the delivery of new homes the Sustainable Communities Plan had an organisational impact that was less well foreseen. In response to the government's renewed emphasis on delivery of housing units and achieving value for money, the Housing Corporation in England began to look at how best it might deliver more housing through its Social Housing Grant programme.

It decided that in order to deliver more units for the same grant it would begin to concentrate its development activities on a limited number of developing associations, knows an Development Partners. In 2004-06 the number of Development Partners who could access Social Housing Grant was restricted to 71.

One impact of this development was that a number of housing associations decided to merge to form larger entities with more resources and better able to meet the development challenges thrown down by government. Others took the same route because of the increasing emphasis on value for money and efficiency and a recognition that for some, merging with another organisation or developing a group structure, would be beneficial.

Group structures are where two or more housing associations came together in a legal partnership, retaining their separate legal identities but sharing corporate services (Finance, Human Resouces, IT, Development etc.) from a parent association. The period from 2004 has seen a rapid expansion in group structures and mergers in the housing association sector driven by this development agenda and a continuing concentration of development resources in a small number of large, developing associations. Again this seems to be a peculiarly English trend with no such pattern being found in Scotland and Wales.

5. Social exclusion and neighbourhood management

The new Labour government of 1997 not only introduced a new dynamic into housing in relation to decent homes, they also had a strong commitment to tackling social exclusion. The government said that social exclusion was about more than income poverty. It is a short-hand term for what can happen when people or areas have a combination of linked problems, such as unemployment, discrimination, poor skills, low incomes, poor housing, high crime and family breakdown. These problems are mutually reinforcing.

The Cabinet Office said:

> *Social exclusion is an extreme consequence of what happens when people don't get a fair deal throughout their lives, often because of disadvantage they face at*

birth, and this disadvantage can be transmitted from one generation to the next (Cabinet Office, undated).

In order to deal with social exclusion the government established a Social Exclusion Unit in 1997 to reflect its determination to take a cross-government approach to improving the life chances of the most disadvantaged in our society. The SEU produced over 40 reports, and many of these have led to significant changes. For example:

- The report on rough sleeping led to the creation of the Rough Sleepers Unit. The Rough Sleepers initiative led to a 70 per cent reduction in the number of people sleeping rough.
- The national strategy for neighbourhood renewal led to the creation of the Neighbourhood Renewal Unit to pilot initiatives, often on housing estates, to narrow the gap between deprived neighbourhoods and the rest of the country.
- The report *A Sure Start to Later Life: Ending Inequalities for Older People* set out 30 cross-government actions to tackle exclusion and isolation. A key action was the reforming of services tailored around the older person which addressed material well-being, physical and mental health, housing issues, neighbourhood exclusion, and ageism. The Department for Work and Pensions (DWP) piloted a series of 'one-stop shops' to test of how joined-up tailored services can tackle current, and prevent future, exclusion amongst older people.

5.1: Neighbourhood Renewal Unit

The NRU runs a number of the government's cross-sector regeneration programmes, including the:

- **New Deal for Communities** programme, which are partnerships tackling the five key themes:
  poor job prospects
  high levels of crime
  educational under-achievement
  poor health
  problems with housing and the physical environment.
- **Neighbourhood management**: working with local agencies to improve and link their services at a local neighbourhood level, often on social housing estates.
- **Neighbourhood wardens**: providing a highly visible, uniformed, semi-official presence in residential and public areas, town centres and high-crime areas.

5.2: Neighbourhood management

Of these initiatives one which has had most impact on social housing has been neighbourhood management which has often been focused on social housing estates. The Neighbourhood Management Pathfinder programme is a process not a project. It involves communities working with local agencies to improve services at neighbourhood level. The programme has been designed to bring together key stakeholders (housing, health, education, social services, police etc.) in an area to seek to tackle quality of life ('liveability') issues in communities through:

- improving the management of the local environment;
- increasing community safety;
- improving housing stock;
- working with young people; and
- encouraging employment opportunities.

Many Neighbourhood Management Pathfinders have also established neighbourhood warden schemes as a way of addressing many of these issues.

The neighbourhood management process is based on the work of the Priority Estates Project in the early 1980s and is now seen by many as one of the best ways to deliver effective neighbourhood renewal.

6. Housing inspection

6.1: The development of housing inspection in England

In 1997 the government indicated that it intended to replace the previous regime of Compulsory Competitive Tendering of housing services with a Best Value regime. Under CCT, key services were contracted on the basis of a competitive tender and this regime was applied to housing in 1996, although in practice there was little external competition for housing services.

Under the new Best Value regime local authorities were required to demonstrate through comprehensive service reviews that they had examined other options for the delivery of services, other than an in-house one. In particular, Best Value involved local housing authorities (and later housing associations) reviewing services using the four 'Cs':

- **Challenge**: the process of testing why and how services should be provided.
- **Compare**: the process of comparing the service provided by the organisation with other organisations.
- **Consult**: the process of consulting with tenants and other stakeholders on their views of the service being provided.
- **Compete**: the process of examining the prospects for placing the service out to competition to deliver improved services.

This new regime meant that authorities no longer had to place their housing service out to competitive tender but instead could subject the service to a series of Best

Value reviews. Some councils undertook such a review of the whole service, but in most cases reviews were conducted on parts of the service (such as repairs, lettings or sheltered housing services).

In exchange for removing the CCT requirements, the government decided to ensure that Best Value reviews were rigorous by subjecting them to independent inspection by the Audit Commission, whose remit was therefore extended through the creation of a specialist Housing Inspectorate (which commenced inspections in April 2001).

This Inspectorate's initial role was to test the rigour with which councils had carried out Best Value reviews and then to comment on how good the service was and whether it was likely to improve.

The Audit Commission is an independent body, responsible to parliament, which exists to ensure that public money in England is spent economically, efficiently and effectively in local government, housing, health, criminal justice, and the fire and rescue service. It is made up of a number of Commissioners appointed by the Secretary of State for Communities and Local Government. The Audit Commission appoints independent auditors to local government, health and criminal justice organisations, and regulates the work they do.

In addition to its audit work the Audit Commission also inspects key public services and reports back to the public on the results. These inspections assess the quality and cost-effectiveness of services and in cases of serious underperformance by a local authority the Commission has the power to recommend that the Secretary of State use his or her discretion under section 15 of the Local Government Act 1999 to give direction to an authority.

Whilst the Housing Corporation had long regulated the work of housing associations it was only in 2001, that it too, formally set up an inspection programme similar to that operated by the newly established Audit Commission's Housing Inspectorate for local authorities. The Housing Corporation inspection regime was designed to answer two key questions:

- How good was the service?
- How good was the association at continuous improvement?

The improvement question was slightly different to that for local authorities being inspected under the Best Value arrangements. The inspection process was piloted in 2001-02 and commenced formally in April 2002. However, the existence of two similar inspection regimes run by different organisations operating a slightly different methodology was seen by many as wasteful and in September 2002 the Deputy Prime Minister decided to combine inspection activities for all social housing landlords into one organisation. As a consequence, in April 2003 the responsibility for the inspection of housing associations transferred from the Housing Corporation to the Audit Commission's Housing Inspectorate.

Initially, the Audit Commission's Housing Inspectorate assessed the effectiveness of Best Value reviews in its inspections, but after 2003 it introduced a new model of inspection based on Key Lines of Enquiry. These Key Lines of Enquiry (KLOEs) set out questions and statements around services which provided more consistent criteria for assessing and measuring the effectiveness and efficiency of housing services. These KLOEs were designed to provide inspectors, inspected bodies and others with a framework through which to view and assess services. Descriptors of excellent and fair services were drawn up to help organisations to understand how the quality of services is judged against the KLOEs. The list of KLOEs (as at December 2008) were:

Landlord services

Stock investment and asset management
Tenancy and estate management
Housing income management
Resident involvement
Allocations and lettings (as appropriate)

Local authority strategic housing role

Strategic approach to housing
Homelessness and housing advice
Private sector housing
Supporting people
Allocations and lettings (as appropriate)

Specialist functions

Supported housing
Management of leasehold and shared ownership housing
Management of right to buy and right to acquire schemes
Housing regeneration and neighbourhood renewal

Cross-cutting areas

Access and customer care
Diversity
Value for money

What are the prospects for improvement?

At the end of each housing inspection, the Audit Commission inspectors make two judgements:

1. How good are the inspected services? – rated from 3 stars (excellent) to 0 stars (poor).
2. What are the prospects for improvement? – rated on a scale that runs from 'excellent' to 'promising' to 'uncertain' to 'poor'.

Figure 3.3: Housing inspectorate verdict on London Borough of Camden Supporting People service, March 2008

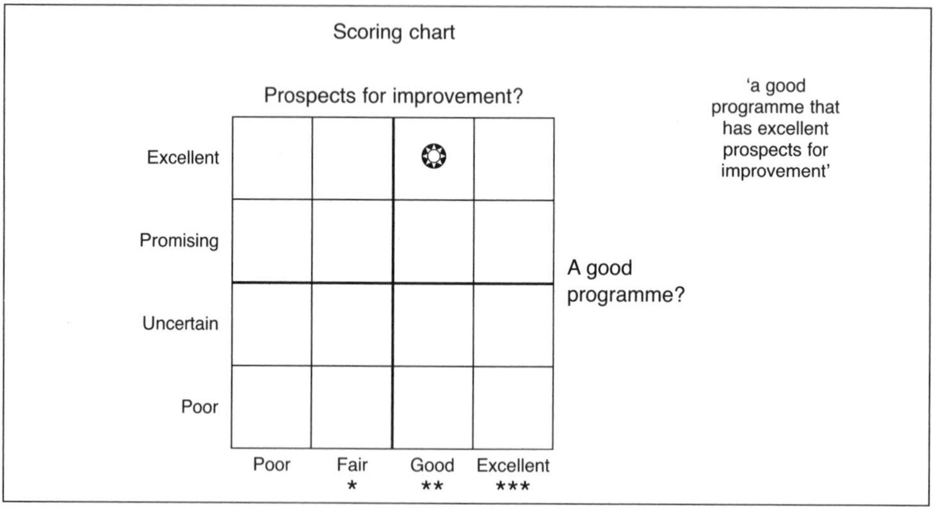

Source: Audit Commission inspection report, 2008.

Figure 3.4: Audit Commission verdict on Homes in Sedgemoor service, November 2007

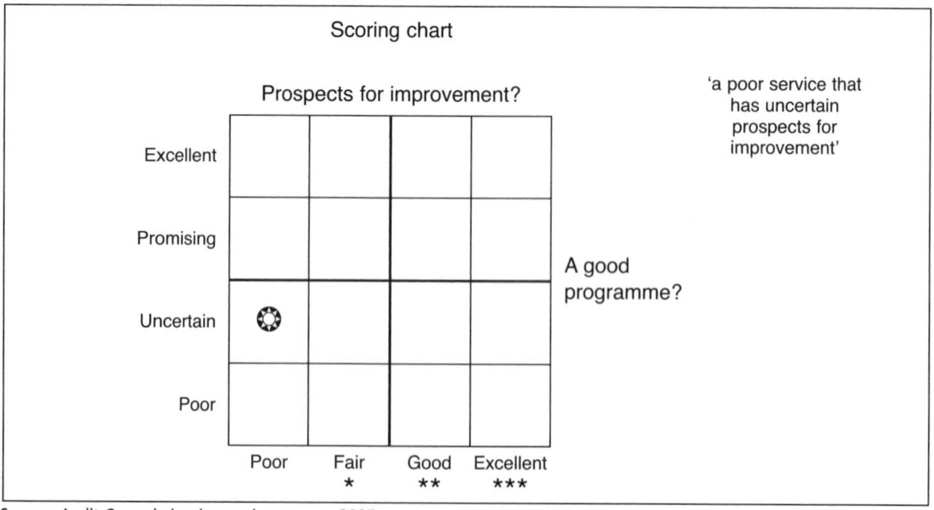

Source: Audit Commission inspection report, 2007.

The inspectors' report sets out the evidence that led to these judgements, and makes recommendations to help the inspected organisation authority achieve improvements. Set out in Figure 3.3 below is the graphical description of the Audit Commission's report into the London Borough of Camden's Supporting People service in 2008.

As can be seen from Figure 3.3, London Borough of Camden received a 2 star rating which says that the Supporting People programme in Camden is good and a service which has excellent prospects for improvement.

This can be contrasted with the 2007 scoring for Homes in Sedgemoor, which is the ALMO for Sedgemoor Borough Council. This inspection carried out in 2007 said that the service was poor (0 star) and had uncertain prospects for improvement as can be seen in Figure 3.4.

6.2: Housing inspection in Scotland

In Scotland, Communities Scotland had the obligation under the 2001 Housing (Scotland) Act to implement a single regulatory framework for all affordable landlords and homelessness functions in Scotland, and in 2004 it introduced an inspection regime, similar to that operated by the Audit Commission's Housing Inspectorate. Its first report into East Lothian Council's housing and homelessness services was published in January 2004.

Communities Scotland was abolished on 1 April 2008. On that date, most of its non-regulatory functions were transferred to the Scottish Government's Housing and Regeneration directorate. The work of Communities Scotland's Regulation and Inspection division was transferred to the new Scottish Housing Regulator.

The Scottish Housing Regulator (SHR) regulates registered social landlords and the landlord and homelessness services of local authorities. Its purpose is to:

- protect the interests of current and future tenants and other service users;
- ensure the continuing provision of good quality affordable housing, in terms of decent homes, good services, value for money, and financial viability; and
- maintain the confidence of funders.

It continues to inspect registered social landlords and the landlord and homelessness services of local authorities under powers set out in the 2001 Housing (Scotland) Act. Its purpose is to provide an independent external assessment of the effectiveness of housing service delivery and make recommendations to help landlords improve.

In each inspection, the Scottish Housing Regulator makes a judgement on:

- how good the organisation, services or areas inspected are; and
- how well the organisation, the services or areas are being managed for improvement.

Like its English counterpart each organisation inspected is then graded, but the system used is different. The Scottish Housing Regulator uses four grades to assess performance which combine judgements on the two inspection questions.

Figure 3.6 sets out the assessment for Knowes Housing Association in relation to their January 2008 inspection.

Figure 3.5: Inspection gradings used by Scottish Housing Regulator

Grade illustrations
Grade A (excellent) will apply to a service, organisation or part of an organisation characterised by major strengths, that delivers well above minimum requirements, is highly cost-effective and has a record of continuous improvement. It may be fully contributing to the achievement of wider strategic outcomes for communities. We may still find weaknesses, but there will be very few areas for improvement and few, if any, barriers to improvement. In service inspections we will find that these weaknesses do not affect the service user or hinder the ability to improve services.
Grade B (good) will apply to a service, organisation, or part of an organisation with many strengths, which delivers above minimum requirements, is cost-effective, and focuses on continuous improvement. It may be making contributions to wider strategic outcomes for communities. The strengths will outweigh the weaknesses. And the capacity to make improvements is likely to strongly outweigh any barriers to improvement. In service inspections we will find that any weaknesses are not enough, either singly or collectively, to detract from services or hinder the ability to improve services.
Grade C (fair) will apply to a service, organisation, or part of an organisation with some strengths but also some weaknesses, that meets only minimum requirements in key areas. It is not particularly cost-effective or focused on improvement. It may be contributing to a limited extent to wider strategic outcomes for communities. Strengths and weaknesses will be finely balanced. And the capacity for, and barriers to, improvement are also likely to be finely balanced. In service inspections we will find some important weaknesses, which, either individually or collectively, noticeably detract from the service or hinder the ability to improve. A grade C is likely to suggest the need for structured or timely action to put things right. However, in the inspection of a new or restructured organisation, the award of a grade C may reflect its newness and the particular point it has reached in its early development – it may show a relatively good level of achievement in a short space of time.
Grade D (poor) will apply to a service, organisation, or part of an organisation with major weaknesses, which does not deliver minimum requirements, may not be cost-effective, and is not focused on improvement. It may be making little or no contribution to wider outcomes for communities. The weaknesses will outweigh the strengths. The barriers to improvement are likely to strongly outweigh the capacity to improve. In service inspections, whatever the strengths, we find that the weaknesses very significantly undermine the service or the management of the service. A grade D suggests the need for immediate remedial action.

Source: Scottish Housing Regulator, *Guide to Inspection*, April 2008.

Figure 3.6: Inspection result for Knowes Housing Association January 2008

> ## 2. Inspection grade and overview
>
> In this section we set out our overall assessment of Knowes' performance. We detail the inspection grade and we summarise our inspection findings.
>
> **Grade**
>
> 2.1 The inspection of Knowes Housing Association took place between 14 and 25 January 2008.
>
> Knowes Housing Association has achieved a **B** grade overall. This is a **good** performance.

Source: Scottish Housing Regulator, *Knowes Housing Association Inspection Report*, April 2008.

6.3: Housing inspection in Wales

In Wales, inspections are now carried out by the Wales Audit Office using a programme jointly agreed between the Welsh Assembly Government and the Wales Audit Office. The Wales Audit Office was created on 1 April 2005 following the 2004 Public Audit (Wales) Act. That act brought together the former offices of the Audit Commission in Wales (ACiW) and the National Audit Office (NAO) in Wales into one body headed by the Auditor General for Wales (AGW).

Previously, the role of the NAO in Wales was to audit, on behalf of the AGW, the National Assembly and its sponsored and related public bodies. The ACiW was responsible for auditing and inspecting local Welsh public services. Both bodies also carried out value-for-money studies and reported on their findings. Wales now has a single audit and inspection body, responsible annually for the audit of over £19 billion of public expenditure at all levels of administration.

Inspections of housing associations in Wales are carried out under section 96c of the 1988 Government of Wales Act. The inspections assess how associations are meeting the expectations of the Welsh Assembly Government, as set out in its Regulatory Code for Housing Associations in Wales, March 2006.

The focus of inspections is on the quality of landlord services provided to residents. Inspectors seek to answer two key questions:

- Does the association deliver good quality services?
- Does the association secure continuous improvement in services?

The first question is applied to individual service areas, and the second is applied to the association as a whole in relation to inspected services. The judgements to be reached on each question are:

Does the association deliver good quality services?
Judgements:
- Excellent
- Good
- Satisfactory
- Scope for considerable improvement
- Fails to comply with the regulatory code.

Does the association secure continuous improvement in services?
Judgements:
- Demonstrates strong corporate and strategic capabilities
- Is raising standards in service delivery
- Shows weaknesses in processes and performance
- Fails to demonstrate capability.

Set out below is a summary ofthe December 2007 inspection judgment on Seren Group.

Figure 3.7: Inspection result for Seren Group

The Group was providing 'excellent' services in two areas, 'good' services in three areas and 'satisfactory' services in three areas.

The Group was 'raising standards in service delivery'.

Unlike the position in England and Scotland, local authority housing in Wales is not subject to the same inspection regime as the housing association sector.

7. The changing face of housing regulation in England

In 2006 Professor Martin Cave, Director of the Centre for Management under Regulation at Warwick University was appointed by the Secretary of State for Communities and Local Government to undertake an independent review of social housing regulation in England. The review was asked to look at how the regulatory system for social housing could be reformed to better support tenants and drive up standards of housing provision, reduce burdens on social housing providers and to reflect current and future government priorities.

The Review, *Every Tenant Matters: a review of Social Housing regulation* argued that the current system of social housing regulation in England had a number of drawbacks, such as an inadequate concern for tenant interests, over-regulation of some providers, the unacknowledged implementation of policy through regulation, poor efficiency incentives, and a failure to fully use available capacity to expand the provision of new affordable housing.

But the Review concluded that regulation of social housing is necessary because the use of sub-market rents limits tenant choice and gives limited incentives to landlords to provide good management.

The Review therefore proposed a new system based on the following objectives:

- to ensure continued provision of high quality social housing;
- to empower and protect tenants; and
- to expand the availability of choice of providers at all levels in the provision of social housing.

These objectives should be achieved, the report argued, with a minimum degree of intervention and crucially that the same approach should be adopted where possible across all providers of social housing. This contrasted with the current system where the Housing Corporation regulated housing associations but did not regulate local authority housing providers.

The Review argued that it would be beneficial therefore to have a single regulator and a single system of regulation for all social housing providers (both owners and managers), such as housing associations, local authorities, ALMOs and private sector. This would allow a clearer comparison of services and standards of provision across what Cave called the '*social housing domain*'. It recommended that the new single regulator should control inspection of social landlords, though it would be able to contract for inspections (for example, through the Audit Commission) rather than undertaking them directly.

The Review argued for a new social housing regulator, statutorily independent (with a board of directors appointed by government), with the objectives set out in statute and powers to collect information and to take action to enforce decisions. It also said that the costs of running the regulator should be paid for by those it regulates.

The Review concluded that the best system of regulation would be to have regulatory powers backing up a system that encouraged improvement by, for example, tenant satisfaction monitoring, provider benchmarking and other co-operative mechanisms. The government would have a statutory power to make strategic directions to the regulator in two key areas: an overall strategy for rent setting and the standards that should apply to the 'core housing function'. The regulator would follow these directions to set detailed regulatory requirements and would maintain a clear statement of obligations placed on providers.

The Review said that the core functions of social landlords, including management and maintenance and a role in anti-social behaviour issues, should be subject to regulation by the regulator. The scope of the core function would initially be set by government in statute, although details and implementation would be for the regulator.

The Review recommended that all providers should have a new statutory duty to engage constructively with local authorities in respect of their place-shaping functions, e.g. by local partnerships and agreements. The Review recommended that where information provided shows good performance and there are no contra-indications, the regulator should not intervene. However, if there was cause for concern, the regulator would investigate and where necessary apply its intervention and enforcement powers.

The regulator's statutory intervention powers would be wider than those held by the Housing Corporation. They would include new intermediate powers such as enforcement notices and penalties. Continued failure to improve could lead to administrative penalties, restrictions on rent increases, appointing new board members, or, in extremis, a formal inquiry leading to a forced change of management or ownership, or winding up the organisation. Forced changes would be competitive and tenants would be engaged. Certain interventions may be inappropriate for some providers, i.e. in the cases of a local authority or a for-profit organisation appointing new board members.

The Review also advocated a greater diversity of providers. Housing associations and unregistered bodies (including for-profit organisations and local authorities that have set up special purpose vehicles/ALMOs) would, as at present, be able to develop using Social Housing Grant, but in addition there could be a range of arrangements for management. For example, a housing association could contract with an ALMO to undertake management and an organisation could register as a manager, independently of being an owner or a developer. This would be formalised under regulation and enable regulatory action where appropriate against a registered manager. The key other difference was that a for-profit body could register with the regulator and receive grant with control being achieved by regulation rather than through contractual arrangements.

7.1: The 2008 Housing and Regeneration Act

The government largely accepted the findings of the Cave Review and decided to disband the Housing Corporation and English Partnerships in December 2008 and create two new bodies.

The Homes and Communities Agency was formed through the effective merger of English Partnerships and the investment division of the Housing Corporation. The HCA became the single regeneration agency for England with a brief to increase the supply and quality of housing in England, the regeneration of communities and the development of sustainable communities.

On the regulation side there was a strong campaign by the Audit Commission to become the new regulator but in the end the government decided to create the Office for Tenants and Social Landlords which would operate under the name of the Tenant Services Authority. This new regulator was given the task of improving the regulation of affordable housing through the creation of a register of 'registered providers of housing' which could be both not-for-profit and profit-making providers. Initially the register would be restricted to housing associations and profit-making providers with local authorities and ALMOs unable to register. However, the government gave a commitment that by April 2010 the new system of regulation would apply across the entire affordable housing domain with local authorities and ALMOs required to register.

The TSA was also required to set out standards in relation to housing management services, financial management and governance. These standards, to be introduced by 2010, would be mandatory for all registered providers and a breach of the standards would trigger enforcement action.

In line with the Cave recommendations, the act significantly extended the powers of the regulator to intervene and under the act the Tenant Services Authority has a range of powers it can use to enforce standards. These include:

- **Enforcement notices**: where a provider can be required to take action specified by the TSA.
- **Penalties**: where the registered provider can be fined for failing to take action to improve standards.
- **Compensation**: where the TSA can require registered providers to pay compensation to tenants for a failure of service.
- **Manager appointments**: where the TSA can appoint a manager to run the affairs of a registered provider.
- **Management tenders**: where the TSA instructs the registered provider to outsource the management of its housing to another provider.
- **Inquiry**: where in suspected serious cases of mismanagement the TSA sets up an independent inquiry to investigate the affairs of a registered provider.
- **Extraordinary audit**: where an auditor is appointed to examine the books of a registered provider where mismanagement is suspected.
- **Management transfer**: where, following an inquiry or audit where mismanagement is found the TSA can instruct that the management of services be transferred to another organisation.

- **Transfer of land**: where the TSA can force a provider to transfer its land and housing to another organisation.
- **Amalgamations**: where the TSA can force a registered provider which is an Industrial and Provident Society to amalgamate with another provider with the same legal status.
- **Removal of officers and staff**: where the TSA can suspend and then remove board members (officers) or staff following an inquiry.
- **Appointment of officers**: where the TSA can appoint officers (board members) to an Association.
- **Funding restrictions**: in certain cases the TSA can also instruct the Homes and Communities Agency to stop funding associations which are subject to more serious enforcement action.

8. The impact of tenant involvement on the delivery of housing services

The extent to which tenants are involved in the management of housing services varies from landlord to landlord, from a situation where tenant involvement is at the legal minimum, through to housing co-operatives where tenants fully control and manage all aspects of their housing stock.

8.1: Statutory requirements

The legislation relating to the involvement of tenants in housing management is fairly weak, as under the Housing Act 1985, local authorities and housing associations are only required to consult their secure tenants on a limited range of housing management matters. Section 105 of the 1985 Housing Act requires landlords of secure tenants in England and Wales to consult them on changes to certain housing management practices or policies (with the significant exception of changes to rents and service charges).

Consultation is not defined in the legislation but will involve the landlord seeking the views of tenants affected by the change and the landlord considering the views of tenants before making any final decision on a matter subject to consultation. In addition, landlords of secure tenants have to publish details of their consultation arrangements and make these available to tenants on request.

For housing association assured tenants there is no statutory requirement for consultation. However, the Housing Corporation's Regulatory Code requires:

> *Housing associations must seek and be responsive to residents' views and priorities: reflecting these interests in their business strategy; giving residents and other stakeholders opportunities to comment on their performance, enabling residents to play their part in decision-making, providing opportunities for residents to explore, and play their part, in how services are managed and provided.*

The association is effectively accountable to all its stakeholders. Current information about the association's activities is widely available to residents and other interested parties. Residents, housing applicants and others have ready access to an effective complaints and compensation policy, administered effectively. Independent Housing Ombudsman recommendations are implemented.

Residents have the opportunity both to influence the association's activities and to become involved. The association considers a range of methods and opportunities to consult and obtain feedback from residents. It seeks to make an agreement, developed in partnership with residents, setting out how they will be involved, consulted and informed and how this will be resourced, measured, monitored and reviewed. Where they so wish, residents are supported, enabling them to obtain the knowledge and skills to play an effective part in investment in, and management of, their homes and neighbourhoods. They are encouraged and supported to explore such options.

8.2: The ladder of involvement

Although the legislation only requires housing organisations to consult tenants, tenants may be involved in the management of the housing at a variety of different levels. Indeed this involvement can work at a number of different levels ranging from:

- Information giving
- Tenant consultation
- Tenant participation
- Tenant control.

(a) Information giving

Working with tenants at this level involves providing tenants with more information about the housing service, the standards they can expect and the levels of services to be provided. This information might be given in the form of newsletters, leaflets and other publications, or it might be in the form of resident meetings or one-to-one communication.

(b) Tenant consultation

This involves housing officers actively seeking the views of tenants on housing issues. Tenants might be consulted for example about a change to allocations policy or rent setting policy. Consultation involves a commitment to ask tenants what they think, but involves no commitment to fully take account of their views. But it does enable tenants, usually through surveys, meetings or face-to-face communication to influence the housing service which is provided.

(c) Tenant participation

With tenant participation tenants are actively involved in the decision-making process. They may not have the ability to decide every issue but they will have a real voice in decision-making. For example, a form of participation might include tenant representatives sitting on an area housing committee with a vote and a true voice in the proceedings, or it might be seen in an estate committee, where residents have control over a small improvements budget. Where tenant participation occurs tenants have a real influence over the decision-making process.

(d) Tenant control

This involves tenants controlling most or all aspects of their housing service. There are a number of models of tenant control which can be seen in Britain today. In Estate Management Boards, residents control most aspects of the housing service on their estate and usually employ staff directly. In housing co-operatives tenants are shareholding members of their co-operative housing association and are fully responsible for the housing service which the co-operative, as landlord, provides. In some cases co-operative members may undertake the housing management work themselves or they may employ staff directly or indirectly, through a secondary housing co-operative to provide the housing service.

Tenant involvement is now a feature of most housing organisations although the extent of that involvement does vary. However, involving tenants in the management of the housing services is a relatively recent phenomenon and as late as 1977 the green paper on housing policy proposed a new Tenants' Charter which would encourage tenant participation in housing. The ideas as set out in the 1977 green paper were eventually incorporated into the 1980 Housing Act in the Tenants' Charter, but the extent of tenant involvement was limited to a requirement for consultation rather than participation or control.

Under the 1988 Housing Act (1988 Housing (Scotland) Act) council tenants were given the right under the Tenants' Choice legislation to transfer their homes to a new landlord. At the time this legislation was passed there was an expectation from government that large numbers of dissatisfied council tenants would vote to transfer to a new landlord. However, in practice very few such transfers took place, but one of the interesting effects of the 1988 Act was to force many local authorities to consider more seriously ways of improving their communication with tenants and involving them more actively in the management of their homes.

8.3: Estate Management Boards and Tenant Management Organisations

Whilst many tenants are happy simply to receive information from the landlord and to be consulted by the landlord on changes to housing management policy and practice there have been a number of models established through which tenants can exercise much greater control over their housing.

Where Estate Management Boards or Tenant Management Organisations are established, tenants control the housing management and maintenance of their estate by involvement in an EMB or TMO which is a legally constituted organisation which undertakes the management of an estate from a local authority under the terms of a management agreement. Through this model residents control the management of their estate through the board with much of the day-to-day management being undertaken by paid staff.

8.4: Housing co-operatives

One of the more advanced forms of tenant participation and control is through the establishment of housing co-operatives. A housing co-operative is where a group of tenants come together to form a legal entity which manages and in some cases owns the houses in which the tenants live. There are a number of different forms of housing co-operative including:

• *Par value co-operatives*
This is a co-operative in which the shareholding members, who are normally tenants or prospective tenants, each hold a one pound financial stake in the co-operative. The homes, which they live, are owned collectively by the co-operative of which they are shareholding members. As the co-operative is the landlord, all housing management functions are undertaken by the co-operative and in many cases housing management tasks are delegated to individual co-operative members, such as collecting the rents and arranging repairs. However, as this poses an additional burden on tenant members, many housing co-operatives have decided to employ paid staff themselves to carry out the day-to-day housing management work under the direction of co-operative members, or have employed another housing association or secondary housing co-operative to provide such services under the terms of a management agreement.

• *Tenant management co-operatives*
A tenant management co-operative is normally constituted in much the same way as a par value co-operative with the difference that the co-operative only manages and does not own the homes of the tenants. For example, the Langridge Crescent tenant management co-operative in Middlesbrough was initially established when the local authority agreed to transfer the management of a small estate to the tenant management co-operative. Under the terms of the management agreement between the local authority and the co-operative, the co-operative undertakes certain housing management and maintenance functions on behalf of the local authority and receives a fee from the authority for undertaking this work.

Although most tenant management co-operatives have been established on local authority estates there are a number of examples where housing associations have transferred the management of some of their estates to tenant management co-operatives under the terms of a management agreement.

8.5: What tenants want

In 2006 the NHF set up an independent Commission chaired by Ed Mayo of the National Consumer Council to look at tenant involvement. The report (*What Tenants Want*) challenged housing associations to:

- be more responsive to the aspirations of their tenants and other customers;
- be more accountable for their performance in terms of what matters to tenants, other customers and local communities;
- do more to open up opportunities for communities to have a greater say over the local service provision and the shape of their neighbourhood.

It said that tenants wanted their associations to do four things:

1. Get the basics right and go the extra mile
2. Give tenants a choice
3. Make involvement personal
4. Be accountable.

On the issue of getting the basics right it was clear that most tenants felt that it was essential that the basic service was right before landlords attempted more innovative service approaches. However, once the basics were rights, landlords who went the 'extra mile' were seen as the ideal by tenants consulted by the Commission. And this meant offering more choice to tenants and listening to their needs. This, however, was not the norm, with many tenants seeing their housing associations as paternalistic or even patronising, in their approach to tenants. Interestingly, tenants were far clearer about their responsibilities than about their rights and very few tenants knew how their housing association compared to others.

In relation to choice, the report found that more than nine out of every ten tenants say that they would like to have more choice in the service that their landlord provides. Tenants have lots of ideas on the choices they would like, from appointment times and picking contractors through to choice-based kitchens. Tenants recognise the resource limitations faced by their landlords and in the research they stressed that customers should not pay extra for what should be the core service, but some would like the choice to pay more for additional services.

Some tenants are interested in becoming involved, but the report indicated that many tenants are apathetic about this as they do not feel involvement can really make a difference. Only a minority of tenants are keen to be actively involved in decision-making, but many more wanted to be involved when there is a key decision to be taken that will affect them directly. The report also said that tenants wanted opportunities to be involved that are convenient to them and give them a personal as well as a collective say.

On the issue of accountability, tenants said that they knew how to complain to their housing association, although few who did so were satisfied with the outcome. Few tenants knew how to complain to an external body about their housing association, or, knew what to do if their complaint to their landlord was not addressed. Tenants believe that it is important to have tenants on the management boards of housing associations as they are seen to bring tenants' perspectives to the discussions of the board.

9. The efficiency agenda and its impact on housing

In August 2003 the Prime Minister and Chancellor of the Exchequer asked Sir Peter Gershon to undertake a review of public sector efficiency. It focused on the government's key objective to release resources to fund front line services by improving the efficiency of service delivery.

He published his independent Review of Public Sector Efficiency in 2004 and this marked a major step forward in embedding value for money into the planning and delivery of public services. The report concluded that there was scope for savings across the public sector of £21.5 billion annually, of which £6.5 billion could be found within local government. As a result of the report, the government introduced rigorous efficiency targets into the public sector:

- Efficiency targets increased to 2.5 per cent a year from 2005 to 2008 as Gershon estimated that £15 billion a year can be saved in the public sector.
- Savings are expected in staff costs especially from the extension of information technology.
- The major area of savings in social housing is with procurement of repairs and maintenance services.
- Local authorities need to review their current practices and convince the housing inspectorate that they are moving towards achieving greater value for money.

The report emphasised the need to ensure that efficiency gains were not delivered at the expense of quality of service delivery. Simplistic cuts in services do not count as efficiency gains. Efficiencies are achieved through reforms that:

- Maintain the same level of service provision while reducing the resources needed or deploying fewer staff.
- Result in additional outputs, such as enhanced quality or quantity of service, for the same resources. Or:
- Remodel service provision to produce better outcomes.

The efficiency gains identified by the Efficiency Review with regard to social housing all related to different areas of procurement in the following 'work streams':

- New supply

- Capital works
- Housing management and maintenance services
- Procurement of commodity goods.

The impact of the efficiency agenda has been seen in housing in a number of ways. In response to the need to access Social Housing Grant there has been an increase in the number of housing association mergers and group structures. Alongside this, housing associations have come together in development consortia under a lead Development Partner. The lead Development Partner is able to access development funding from the Housing Corporation and the associations in the development consortia are able to deliver efficiencies through improved procurement.

On the repairs and maintenance side, Gershon identified that there would be significant savings to be made through improved procurement. This has led to the development of procurement consortia within housing (such as Procurement for Housing) which act as procurement clubs, able to secure better prices from suppliers as a result of the increased purchasing power achieved through having a number of housing organisations coming together to purchase goods.

The housing association sector achieved the efficiency savings targets set by government for it and in 2008 the Housing Corporation dropped the requirement to produce an Annual Efficiency Statement, although efficiency is still assessed in inspection under the value for money KLOE.

10. Homes for the Future; more affordable, more sustainable

In July 2007 the government published a green paper (*Homes for the Future: more affordable, more sustainable*). This aimed to set out a strategic housing direction for the next generation. The government said that here had been a significant improvement in housing since it had been elected in 1997, but that there were new challenges to be faced:

- Demand for homes to buy or rent is growing faster than supply.
- It is increasingly difficult for young people to get a step on the housing ladder.
- The challenges of climate change mean there is a need to provide greener, better-designed housing for the future.

The green paper set out proposals to provide:

- More homes to meet growing demand.
- Well-designed and greener homes, linked to good schools, transport and healthcare.
- More affordable homes to buy or rent.

In relation to providing more homes, the government indicated that it needed to deliver 2 million new homes by 2016 and 3 million by 2020. In respect of better-designed homes the government said it wanted new homes to be:

> *...better homes, built to high standard, both in terms of design and environmental impact and homes that are part of mixed communities with good facilities...We need a revolution in the way we build, design and power our homes. A quarter of the UK's current carbon emissions (around 150 million tonnes of carbon dioxide each year) arise from how we heat, light and run our homes. We want to increase protection of the environment by cutting carbon emissions and we want all new homes to be zero carbon from 2016. We will strengthen building regulations by 25% in 2010 and by 44% in 2013 to set the standards we need to help achieve this. We will also set new minimum standards for water use in new homes cutting average water use by almost 20%.*

The green paper indicated that it wanted well-designed and quality homes and set out proposals to encourage innovation through a national competition to produce new settlements called eco-towns.

10.1: Making housing more affordable

The green paper noted that house prices had doubled in real terms in the last decade. In response the government proposed a major expansion in housing supply with:

- an £8 billion programme for affordable housing in 2008-11;
- at least 70,000 more affordable homes a year by 2010-11;
- at least 45,000 new social homes a year by 2010-11;
- over 25,000 shared ownership and shared equity homes a year;
- thousands more shared ownership homes provided through local housing companies;
- more affordable housing in rural areas.

The green paper proposal for the establishment of local housing companies were designed to be vehicles involving a local authority, a private developer and the Homes and Communities Agency to deliver shared ownership homes and homes for first-time buyers built on local council land. The government believed these new organisations had the potential to deliver tens of thousands of shared ownership homes over the next five years. In the private sector, the government said that it considered that the private sector could play a much greater role in offering shared equity mortgages or shared ownership homes.

11. Conclusion

This chapter has described the changing face of social housing from a situation in the early 1980s where local authorities were the main providers of social housing. In the 2000s the situation is now significantly different with the social housing sector being dominated by housing associations and stock transfer associations. A new form of local authority housing management through arms length management organisations has proved very popular and alongside this there have been Housing Market Renewal Pathfinders, Tenant Management Organisations and Neighbourhood Management initiatives.

The Audit Commission and its counterparts in other parts of Great Britain have changed the face of the sector through its inspection activities and the regulation of affordable housing is changing through the creation of a single affordable housing regulator in England (the Tenant Services Authority) and the continuous evolution of regulation and inspection models in the devolved governments of Scotland and Wales.

References and further reading

Audit Commission (1986) *Managing the Crisis in Council Housing*, HMSO, London.

Audit Commission (2007) *Inspection of Sedgemoor Homes*, The Stationery Office, London.

Audit Commission (2008) *Inspection of LB Camden Supporting People Service*, The Stationery Office, London.

Cabinet Office (undated): http://cabinetoffice.gov.uk/social_exclusion_task_force/context.aspx

Cave, M. (2007) *Every tenant matters: a review of social housing regulation*, CLG, London.

Central Housing Advisory Committee (1969) *Council housing: Purposes, procedures and priorities*, HMSO, London.

Centre for Housing Policy, University of York (1993) *Managing Social Housing*, HMSO, London.

Centre for Housing Research, University of Glasgow (1989) *The Nature and Effectiveness of Housing Management in England*, University of Glasgow, Glasgow.

Department for Communities and Local Government (2007) *Independence and Opportunity: Our Strategy for Supporting People*, CLG, London.

Department of the Environment, Transport and the Regions (2000) *Quality and Choice: a Decent Home for all*, DETR, London.

Gershon, P. (2004) *Releasing Resources to the front line*, The Stationery Office/HM Treasury, London.

Institute of Housing (1972) *The Comprehensive Service: Organisation and functions*, IOH, London.

National Federation of ALMOS (2006): www.almos.org.uk

National Housing Federation (2006) *What Tenants Want*, NHF, London.

Office of the Deputy Prime Minister (2003) *Sustainable Communities: Building for the Future*, ODPM, London.

Scottish Housing Regulator (2008) *Guide to Inspection*, Scottish Housing Regulator, Edinburgh.

Scottish Housing Regulator (2008) *Knowes Housing Association Inspection Report April 2008*, Scottish Housing Regulator, Edinburgh.

Social Exclusion Unit (2000) *The National Strategy for Neighbourhood Renewal: A framework for consultation*, SEU/HMSO, London.

Social Exclusion Unit (2006) *A Sure Start to Later Life: Ending Inequalities for Older People*, ODPM, London.

Social Housing Journal (2008) London.

Wilcox, S. (2008) *UK Housing Review 2008/09*, CIH/BSA, Coventry.

CHAPTER 4:
How is affordable housing funded?

1. Introduction

This chapter provides an overview of the main features of finance for affordable housing in the UK, and highlights the key reasons for, and implications of, a number of recent policy changes.

It begins by considering the reasons why finance is so important for the provision of housing, and some recent influences on the cost and availability of borrowed funds. The significance of finance for housing has ensured that housing finance is an important public policy issue, so it explores the nature of public finance for affordable housing. It examines recent changes which have occurred as a result of public policies in relation to the roles of the main providers of affordable: housing, local authorities and housing associations. It then explores the specific arrangements for the funding of development and rehabilitation of affordable housing – called *capital spending* – as well as finance for spending on management and repairs and maintenance, called *revenue spending*. It also briefly examines the importance of budgets and financial controls in managing financial resources and achieving financial objectives. Finally, it explores the provision of personal, financial subsidy to tenants – the housing benefit system – as well as the help available to owners.

Readers requiring a more detailed guide to aspects of housing finance should consult *Housing Finance* (Garnett and Perry, 2005).

1.1: The need for, and nature of, finance for housing

The broad term 'housing finance' includes all sources of funding for housing, whether public or private. Housing is a commodity much like any other, in that it can be produced, bought and sold, whether by private developers, affordable housing providers, landlords or individual owners. So, why is finance such an important issue in housing markets?

Housing is a very expensive item to produce and, for most households, it is by far the most expensive item in their household budget. The high cost of housing means that those who wish to buy property – including local authorities, housing associations and private landlords as well as private households – invariably have to find external sources of finance to help them, usually borrowing funds from financial institutions, such as building societies and commercial (high street) banks. Of course, these loans must eventually be repaid, whether by monthly repayments towards both capital and interest (most usual for private household's mortgages), or by regular interest payments and a later lump sum repayment of the original capital sum (usual for local authorities).

As indictated in Chapter 1, the government first became committed to the provision of finance for house building after the end of the First World War, when it provided capital subsidies toward the cost of building council homes to tackle chronic housing shortages in the UK. Much later, councils were urged to introduce rent subsidy schemes, in the form of rent-rebates. Public finance was now to be used not simply to provide new, lower-cost homes, via *capital* subsidies, but also directly to reduce weekly housing costs for households, via *revenue* subsidies. The current provision of public finance for housing still has these two distinct elements:

a) Capital finance

This pays for, or provides subsidy towards, the building (and rehabilitation) of homes. Thus, it helps to create or improve housing assets, increasing the stock of housing – the total quantity available – as well as its quality. Local authority capital investment, mainly in improving council housing, is undertaken largely by borrowing. Except for certain limited purposes, councils do not receive capital subsidy from government. Housing associations, though, may receive capital subsidy in the form of Housing Association Grant (in Scotland) and Social Housing Grant (in England, Wales and Northern Ireland). In addition, like local authorities, they also borrow money for capital investment.

Until the recent problems in the financial system and the economic downturn from late 2008 (see Section 1.4 below), the government emphasised three main 'fiscal rules' for managing public finances (see Figure 4.1), which to some extent reflected European Union requirements such as those set out in the Maastricht Treaty.

Figure 4.1: The fiscal rules

1. The 'golden rule', which says that in the long term, the government will borrow only to invest, not for current (revenue) spending.

2. Public debt must be at a sustainable levels, originally regarded as below 40 per cent of national income.

3. Only bodies owned and controlled by the private sector are exempt from these rules.

However, as a result of the need for the government to provide very large sums of money to the banking system during 2008, as well as the economic recession (which reduces tax income) from late 2008, public debt will increase to well over 40 per cent during the next few years. From 36.3 per cent of Gross Domestic Product (a measure of national income) in 2008, public debt is predicted to increase to 52.9 per cent by 2010-11, thus breaching fiscal rule 2 (*Guardian*, 25 Nov 2008).

Fiscal rule 3 indicates that housing association borrowing – unlike that by local authorities – does not count as public borrowing under the chancellor's rules, because housing associations are private rather than public sector bodies.

Capital subsidies can also assist some households to purchase properties (for example, the right to buy discounts), but, in general, this does not result in any additional stock being created.

b) Revenue finance

Revenue spending by housing organisations broadly consists of three elements of cost for:

- managing properties;
- repairs and maintenance;
- financing borrowing (paying interest and repaying the original loan).

Government revenue subsidy may assist towards these annual, operational costs of housing organisations, so that rents are lower (for example, Housing Revenue Account Subsidy received by some LAs, which takes account of all three elements of revenue costs). For households, revenue subsidy may also take the form of personal subsidy towards the costs of purchasing housing *services* – either mortgage repayment costs or rents (such as housing benefit). Hence, these revenue subsidies do not create any new or improved housing assets, but instead focus on subsidising the housing costs of (mainly) low-income households.

1.2: The importance of interest rates

Since most housing in the UK is acquired or built using borrowed finance, it is not simply the capital (purchase) cost which matters to buyers. Interest is charged on the borrowed monies, so a rise in interest rates will increase the total sum that has to be repaid to the lender. For private households, for example, their monthly mortgage costs will rise. So, because it has such a significant impact on overall costs, the interest rate will have a large influence on the demand for housing to buy.

Interest rates have been used by UK governments since the 1970s as a key weapon in the fight against high inflation (defined as a persistent rise in the general price level). If inflation is rising, an increase in interest rates deters borrowing, which reduces the amount of money available to spend. Less money to spend means less demand, and so less upward pressure on prices. In the UK, a substantial part of consumer spending is undertaken with borrowed money, most importantly in housing markets for home purchase and for home refurbishment, but also for goods such as cars and major household items. Hence, increasing interest rates and so raising the cost of borrowing should reduce demand and limit the upward pressure on prices. Reduced consumer spending should also force firms to remain more competitive and keep prices down, if they are to continue to sell their goods.

At one time, interest rates were entirely under the control of the Chancellor of the Exchequer and UK Treasury (via the Bank of England), but, by the 1990s, there were growing concerns that political pressures had resulted in interest rate changes that were not necessarily in the best interests of the economy. Hence, control over these was passed to an independent *Monetary Policy Committee* of the Bank of England, whose members meet monthly to take decisions on interest rate changes, based solely on economic data (such as output and inflation).

Due to high rates of inflation, interest rates were very high in the late 1980s and early 1990s (see Table 4.1, 'average mortgage rate'), which increased monthly repayments and caused large increases in mortgage defaults and repossession proceedings by lenders (see Table 4.1, 'mortgage repossessions'). In more recent years (late 1990s to mid 2008) inflation, and hence, interest rates have been kept at relatively low levels, which contributed to rapidly rising housing demand, and hence, rising house prices, because (despite rising prices), mortgage repayments remained much more affordable.

A sharp increase in the rate of inflation (to 5 per cent) by September 2008, partly due to rapidly rising oil and hence fuel prices, hearalded an economic downturn and a predicted severe economic recession from 2009. In an attempt to reduce the severity of this recession, the bank rate (the interest rate charged by the Bank of England) was reduced significantly, from 4.5 per cent to 3 per cent in November 2008, then reduced again to 2 per cent in December 2008 and to half of a per cent

Table 4.1: Private housing markets

	1990	2006 (Q)	2007 (Q)	Change 2006-07
Average house price	£63k	£207k	£227k	+ 9.6%
Mortgage completions (UK)	783k	301k	226k	– 24.9%
of which first-time buyers	409k	104k	81k	– 21.9%
of which first-time buyers (% of total)	52%	35%	27%	– 8% pts
Average mortgage rate (UK) (%)	14.34%	5.41%	5.88%	+ 0.48% pts
Over six months in arrears (UK)	159k	52k	57k	+ 8.6%
Mortgage repossessions (UK)	44k	12k	14k	+ 15.4%

Source: CLG, May 2008.

in March 2009. This is the lowest rate since the cenral bank was founded in 1694. However, mortgage rates generally failed to follow suit, and the LIBOR (the *London Inter Bank Offer Rate*, the interest rate which banks charge each other) has remained at much higher levels. House prices have been falling in some areas during 2008, as demand for purchases has dropped off (due to reduced mortgage availability as well as fear of unemployment). The availability of mortgages is examined next.

1.3: The availability of borrowed finance

Over more than two decades, households in the UK became used to borrowed finance for housing purchase being readily available. This was not always the case, as, until 1986, almost all mortage lending was undertaken by building societies. These 'mutual', not-for-profit organisations existed solely to provide lending to their members (rather like the much smaller-scale 'credit unions' with which readers may be familiar). Their members saved with the association so that they could later be entitled to borrow funds from the accumulated savings. This arrangement effectively limited the availability of funds for house purchase, which helped to constrain private housing demand – and house prices – during the post-war years. If demand for housing was increasing, this increased the demand for borrowing, but the building societies would quickly run out of saved funds and have to ration lending. They did this mainly by creating waiting lists, which forced households to delay purchasing and so this reduced housing demand again.

When the UK government 'deregulated' UK capital markets from 1986, commercial (high street) banks were permitted, for the first time, to lend funds for house purchase along with building societies. Unlike building societies, these banks are generally for-profit organisations, owned by large numbers of shareholders (who expect a share of the banks' profits in the form of dividends). Following deregulation, the banks were able to significantly expand the availability of funds for house purchase, and, as these banks competed for custom, a much greater variety and number of mortgage deals were made available – including, until 2008, loans in excess of the property's value, commonly 105 per cent or more. Many building societies 'demutualised' and became banks themselves, as this gave them much wider freedoms to lend and borrow; examples included Halifax, Abbey National, Bradford and Bingley and Northern Rock. The improved availability of finance unquestionably contributed to the expansion of owner-occupation in the UK from the 1980s to 2007. More recently, however, the availability of funds to borrow has been curtailed by the so-called 'credit crunch', which is explored next.

1.4: The 'credit crunch' from 2007

With the growing 'globalisation' of capital markets over recent decades – meaning that funds are traded throughout the world between banks and companies – many banks became dependent on borrowed funds from abroad. However, it emerged in 2007 that a number of US banks had loaned large sums to higher-risk borrowers (referred to by the media as *Ninjas* – no income, no jobs or assets), in so-called 'sub-prime markets'. They suddenly found that they had rising numbers of defaults on these loans: borrowers were unable to make their repayments. This led to a reduction in the funds available to lend and borrow in global capital markets, which became widely known as the 'credit crunch'; credit (borrowed funds) was no longer so readily available. Many British banks, in turn, found they were unable to renew their US and UK borrowing, so they found themselves short of funds for UK mortgage markets. In the first high profile case, the Northern Rock bank had to be rescued from potential bankruptcy by the UK government in 2007, and was later, in 2008, taken into public ownership ('nationalised').

Unfortunately, the credit crunch continued to worsen as the banks lost further confidence in lending to each other, and by the late summer of 2008, two of the main US mortgage companies – Fannie Mae and Freddie Mac – had to be taken over by the US government. The spectacular collapse of a US investment bank, Lehmans, followed, and here in the UK, the value of bank shares fell significantly on the stock exchange. HBOS (Halifax Bank of Scotland) agreed to be taken over in September 2008 by Lloyds TSB, to protect it from further speculation, and, although this created a new banking giant with about 25 per cent of the UK mortgage and savings market, the UK government rejected competition concerns and agreed to the takeover. In addition, the UK government had to establish a multi-billion pound 'rescue' fund, to make substantial additional funds available to the banks so that they could sustain some level of lending. The government also took some banks into partial public ownership as a means to inject new capital.

By late 2008, the impact of the credit crunch was being felt across the whole UK housing market, as many lenders had significantly reduced the availability of mortgage funds. Large deposits were being required and smaller mortgages being offered (as a percentage of the property's value), with only perceived low-risk borrowers being considered. Indeed, one bank, Bradford and Bingley, withdrew from new mortgage lending altogether. In addition, even though the 'bank rate' (the interest rate charged by the Bank of England, as determined by the Monetary Policy Committee – see Section 1.2 above) was reduced, banks were still charging higher sums for mortgage lending, in an effort to curb demand and ration their limited funds. This, in turn, resulted in reduced housing transactions – many fewer properties were being bought and sold – which contributed to falling property prices in many areas of the UK during most of 2008 and into 2009. (see Figure 4.2 which provides a 'snapshot' of the credit crunch effect.)

The growing economic recession towards the end of 2008 resulted in rising UK mortgage arrears and hence growing repossessions by mortgage lenders, despite government exhortations for lenders to delay repossession actions until arrears extended to at least three months. It was predicted that repossessions would reach 75,000 during 2009 (*Guardian,* 4 December 2008). As a result, in his Pre-Budget

Figure 4.2: Halifax House Price Index, November 2008: key facts

The monthly fall in house prices was 2.6%.

House prices in November were 14.9% lower on an annual basis. The UK average price had returned to the level of July 2005 (£163,445).

The house price to earnings ratio – a key affordability measure – declined significantly. The house price to average earnings ratio fell from a peak of 5.84 in July 2007 to an estimated 4.56 in November 2008. The ratio was at its lowest level for more than five years (July 2003: 4.54). The long-term average is 4.0.

The UK average house price was 124% higher than ten years ago. The current average price was more than £90,000 higher than in November 1998 (£73,129).

Housing market activity showed signs of stabilising albeit at a low level. The number of mortgages approved to finance house purchase was broadly unchanged for the fourth successive month in October at a seasonally adjusted 32,000. The recent flattening off in approvals suggests that housing market activity may be stabilising.

Source: Halifax House Price Index, November 2008.

Report in November 2008, the chancellor announced a mortgage rescue scheme to help up to 6,000 home owners facing repossession, to be 'fast-tracked' into operation by 60 councils from December 2008. Then, following the Queen's Speech at the state opening of parliament on 4 December 2008, the chancellor announced a further new 'deal' with eight key lenders, covering 70 per cent of the mortgage market. This pemits households who suffer redundancy or a 'significant fall in income', to apply to defer interest repayments for up to two years. The government has agreed to 'underwrite' (i.e. guarantee) this debt, should the borrower subsequently fail to repay the deferred interest. This applies to mortgage debts of up to £400,000 and those with savings of less than £16,000. For affordable housing providers such as housing associations, this 'credit crunch' has, in a number of cases, made it more difficult for them to secure new borrowing for housing development. It is also more difficult to find good 're-financing' deals (i.e. find lower rates of interest for their borrowed funds) – which is examined later in Section 2.3. In addition, it became more difficult to sell new low-cost and shared ownership properties, as potential buyers were unable to secure mortgages.

Meanwhile, many private developers were also finding that they could not easily sell recently competed properties, which meant that they delayed new house building starts. This is threatening the achievement of government targets for new private house building over the next few years. In an effort also to prevent escalating house-price falls (caused by falling demand), in mid 2008, the government made available at least £200 million in Social Housing Grant subsidy to housing associations, to help them to purchase some of this new, unsold stock from builders. This is explored in more detail later in Section 2.3.

1.5: Public subsidy for housing

During the 1990s, there was a fairly steady decline in public expenditure on housing in real terms (i.e. after allowing for inflation), which contributed to the continued decline in capital investment by local authorities during this period. As UK governments throughout the 1980s and 1990s were keen to change the key role of councils in relation to housing, from being key 'providers' to becoming primarily 'enablers' (facilitating other providers), there were various policy developments. Firstly, government policy focused on shifting council-owned homes into owner-occupation via the right to buy; then, later, the focus moved to transferring them to other rented tenures, particularly to housing associations, via large scale voluntary transfer (LSVT). More recently, policies focused on encouraging councils to set up separate companies to manage their stock, via arms length management organisations (ALMOs), or to bring in private finance and management via the private finance initiative (PFI). All of these objectives have been pursued via financial incentives, explored next, in 'changing roles'.

From the early 2000s, a renewed government commitment to affordable housing subsidy saw public capital expenditure increase from £5.4 billions in 2002-03 to £12.5 billions by 2006-07 (estimated outturn, Wilcox, 2007). This permitted, for example, a significant expansion in the Housing Corporation's net capital spending via English housing associations, from £916 millions in 2002-03 to £1,918 millions by 2007-08 (Wilcox, 2008), and has also permitted some councils to resume house building for the first time in decades. These public capital spending trends are illustrated by Figure 4.3, below.

Changing roles in affordable housing: the recent context

(i) Right to buy

The *right to buy* policy played the first, key role in reducing council housing stock, though it was intended also to satisfy the desire by lower-income households in council tenure to become owner-occupiers. It was introduced in the 1980 Housing Act and 1980 Housing (Scotland) Act, offering substantial discounts on the market value of the property for existing council tenants. Over time, the discounts were increased (to a maximum of 70 per cent for flats) to encourage further purchases. Northern Ireland has a more recent version of right to buy, called *Homes for Sale*.

The impact on council housing has been significant, with almost 2.4 million homes sold between 1980 and 2006 (Wilcox, 2007): around 1.79 million of these in England, 473,000 in Scotland and 136,523 in Wales. However, this policy has affected not just the quantities of council properties available for new tenants, but

Figure 4.3: Housing capital investment 1980-2007

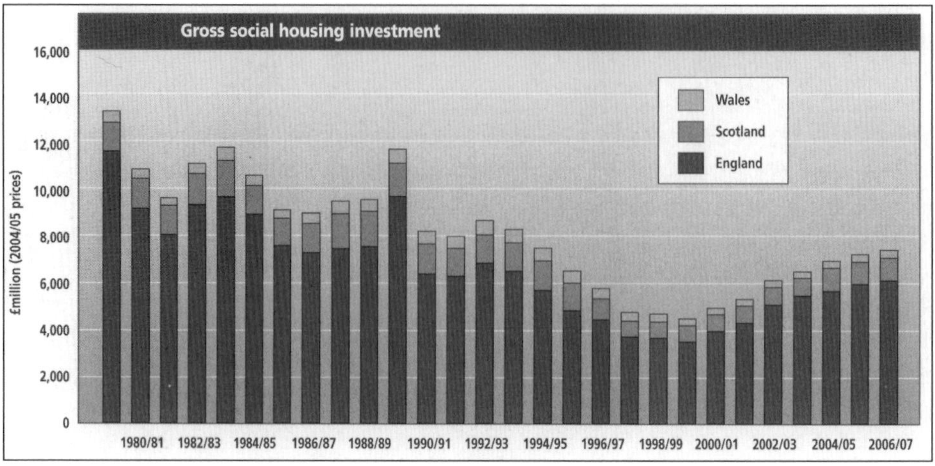

Source: Wilcox, 2007, p64.

also the qualities, since, in general, it is the best properties (predominantly houses), in the best localities, which have sold.

In addition, some of these properties have become private rented lets, which may be used to house tenants with a variety of challenging behaviours. These problems are more difficult address than would be the case if the tenants were in council-owned properies (see Chapter 6). For example, research by Jones (2002) in London suggested that up to 40 per cent of right to buy purchases were being let out (in the private rented sector), with up to a third (in the London borough of Lambeth) owned by property companies. Concern was also expressed that there were abuses in regeneration areas, with tenants hoping to gain from subsequent compulsory purchase by the local authority.

As a result of these problems and perceived abuses, the Scottish Government permitted several local authorities facing acute shortages of affordable housing to apply for exemption from the right to buy. The Whitehall government also introduced new constraints in some English local authority areas with acute housing shortages (mainly London and the south east) during 2003. New legislation reduced the maximum discount (from £38,000 to £16,000), extended the initial qualification period from two to five years, required tenants to repay the discount if they moved within five (instead of three) years, and allowed local authorities to refuse right to buy sales where demolition was expected. There is also now a five year ban on letting, and applications steered by private companies are illegal (Ambrosi, 2003). Partly because of these greater restrictions on eligibility and discounts, there has recently been a sharp decline in right to buy sales. Unquestionably, the rapid increase in house prices in the UK from the late 90s to the mid 2000s has also been a major contributor to this decline, because, as the market value of council houses has been increasing, purchase (even with the discount) has become much less affordable (CIH/HC, April 2008).

(ii) Large scale voluntary transfers

Severe restrictions on the availability of capital funds due to government controls, particularly in England during the 1990s, had the effect of forcing many local authorities to pursue alternative actions which would permit them to access sources of funding. Large scale voluntary transfer (LSVT) was used to transfer a council's housing stock to a housing association, which is then not affected by public sector borrowing constraints (see Section 1.1 above). Although the first large-scale stock transfer in England was actually a local authority initiative (Chiltern), other councils were soon encouraged to follow suit to escape restrictions on spending.

By March 2008, some 160 English councils had (with the consent of their tenants) transferred *all* their housing stock to housing associations (Wilcox, 2008). Usually, these were newly created associations, funded through private borrowing. This process involved the transfer of some 970,256 dwellings from council to housing association ownership, at a transfer price of £6,324.6 million (Wilcox, 2008). The average price per dwelling paid by the transfer organisation was a tiny £6,588 (because the prices are discounted by the need to carry out expensive modernisation of the properties and charge an affordable rent), but these transfers have nevertheless produced 'usable' receipts (see Section 2.2 on local authority capital finance) of £1,391 million for the councils concerned. However, the transferred stock is valued as the *present value* of a 30-year income stream from rents (less the costs of repairs and management), so future income streams must be discounted to give this present value. It has been argued by some councils that the government's choice of interest rate (used to discount the future income streams) was much too high, which resulted in lower valuations. LSVT has also contributed to the transformation of the composition of the HA sector in England, which has become increasingly one of large organisations.

As LSVT rents were increased (in comparison to the previous LA rents) to pay for their new, private borrowing, housing benefit costs to the Treasury rose. As a result, the government quickly introduced a 20 per cent 'levy' on those LSVT receipts that remained after all housing debt had been cleared. By March 2008, this levy had raised £331 million from English LSVTs for the UK Treasury (Wilcox, 2008). Like other English social landlords, transfer associations were also subject, from 2002, to a common government policy on rents ('rent restructuring'), which is explored in Section 3.

In contrast to the relative success of LSVT in England, Scotland was slower to take up large-scale transfers, with Berwickshire being the first, followed later by the

Scottish Borders and Dumfries and Galloway (in 2003), with Glasgow City (the largest LSVT to date) also adding around 90,000 dwellings to the transfer total during 2003. This latter transfer was facilitated by significant public subsidy, as the transfer value was insufficient to repay the outstanding housing debt, referred to as 'overhanging' debt; some £900 million was paid from the Treasury at Whitehall to cover these outstanding debt repayments. The Scottish Government also made available a £700 million subsidy in the form of HAG, to fund subsequent renovations to the properties, as well as a £100 million 'contingency fund'. In addition, private finance (from the Bank of Scotland, the Royal Bank of Scotland, Abbey National and Nationwide) was secured to provide £850 million in loans. (Evans, 2002). In order to break up its effective monopoly over social housing in Glasgow, the new Glasgow Housing Association was required subsequently to transfer its stock to other smaller organisations. However, these 'secondary transfers' faced continuing problems, and further transfers stalled due to disputes over stock valuations as well as problems with the transfer organisations securing firm commitments from banks for new borrowing. Only by late 2008 were a few of these transfers finally proceeding.

Nevertheless, a large number of smaller-scale stock transfers have taken place in Scotland over many years, often to community-based housing associations (unique to Scotland, these are managed by a locally-based committee). These were usually transfers from former Scottish Special Housing Association (SSHA) stock by Scottish Homes, supported by Housing Associaton Grant (HAG) funding. The SSHA was a public body, established in post-war Scotland to build social housing in parallel with councils. When Scottish Homes was set up to fund and regulate housing associations in Scotland (taking over from the Housing Corporation in Scotland), it incorporated the SSHA, but was required to lose its landlord role and divest itself of SSHA stock. Scottish Homes was subsequently reformed to become Communities Scotland, which was later abolished in April 2008, and its funding duties passed to the Housing and Regeneration Directorate of the Scottish Government, whilst regulation went to the new Scottish Housing Regulator.

In Wales too, LSVTs were also initially unpopular, but these have become more common in recent years. By 2008, almost a third of Welsh councils had transferred their stock (*Inside Housing*, 11 April 2008, p5).

Table 4.2 gives some indication of the overall scale of LSVT and right to buy combined, with 3.1 million homes transferred from English council ownership into either the private sector or HA ownership by March 2007.

As LSVT organisations are all housing associations, their current capital financing arrangements are as described under Section 2.3, below.

Table 4.2: Sales of local authority council houses in England

	2005-06	2006-07	Total April 1979 to March 2007
Private sales (inc. RTB)	29k	17k	2.0m
Large-scale transfers	47k	79k	1.0m
Total dwellings sold	75k	96k	3.1m

Source: CLG, May 2008.

(iii) Arms length management organisations (ALMOs)

Since 2001, English councils have also been able to bid to the government to set up ALMOs (arms length management organisations). An ALMO involves the setting up of a new, separate ('arms length') organisation to manage the council's stock, and the board of the new company will usually include councillors, tenants and independent members. These have proved popular, partly because the council retains ownership of the stock and tenants remain as council tenants, but also because the government made available to these councils significant additional revenue allowances to finance extra capital borrowing. However, access to these new resources was subject to evidence of good performance, so the new organisation had to achieve a minimum 2 star inspection rating (by the Housing Inspectorate of the Audit Commission) to secure the additional funds.

By March 2008, a total of 69 ALMOs were operating, and a total of £3.7 billion of extra funding had been allocated to help them to achieve the Decent Homes Standard (which many have already done). During 2008, the number of homes managed by ALMOs in England (over 1 million) for the first time overtook the numbers retained by councils and managed directly by them.

ALMOs are keen to continue to develop their roles post-Decent Homes Standard (DHS) and, crucially, to continue successfully once their additional DHS funding has ended. So, in April 2005, the National Federation of ALMOs, the CIH and HouseMark together produced a report on options to support possible future directions (CIH, 2005). As the report states, '*...all of the options...depend on breaking the link with the local finance system for council housing (the HRA) and the national system (the HRA susbsidy system)*' (p3). This CIH research clearly influenced government thinking on the issue, and resulted in a pilot study being undertaken from 2006 on the feasibility of ALMOs opting out of the LA subsidy system (CLG, 2008a). Details of the HRA and HRA subsidy, along with this influential research, are explored further in Section 3.2 below.

In the meantime, the government indicated that some ALMOs could bid for the capital subsidy mainly available only to HAs – Social Housing Grant (SHG) through the National Affordable Housing Programme (NAHP); this is described in further detail under Section 2.3, as well as in Chapter 5. Three ALMOs had, by April 2008, successfully bid for, and been allocated, SHG from the 2008-11 National Affordable Housing Programme to help fund new development. A further five had applied for 'pre-qualification status' (to apply for SHG) and more were expected to follow, since the requirement for eligibility was reduced from 3 to 2 stars (*Inside Housing*, 25 April 2008). However, it is generally accepted that reforms to the Housing Revenue Account Subsidy system will be necessary if the future of ALMOs is to be secured (see above) and this is explored further in Section 3.2.

(iv) The private finance initiative

Although this approach has been used extensively in the UK to provide new hospitals, schools, roads and even prisons for many years, its use for social housing is a relatively recent development. The first housing PFI was set up in 1999 in North East Derbyshire, and in 2003, the government simplified the rules to encourage further take up (*Inside Housing*, 11 April 2008, pp16-17). However, by mid 2008, only 21 housing PFI schemes had been approved.

PFI involves a private company being appointed to fund and build new housing, and/or take over ownership of exisiting housing to undertake extensive refurbishment. This means that the capital funds are being provided privately, avoiding the need for the public sector to borrow. The public body – usually a council – will then lease (rent) the assets from the company for an annual fee. Essentially, then, PFI is a device to turn what would otherwise be a capital cost for the public sector into a revenue one. Usually, the public body will subsequently provide and manage the service provision (e.g. housing management, teaching, medical staff) whilst the private company manages and repairs the buildings.

It is not yet apparent whether this alternative approach delivers value for money for housing. A review of PFI for council housing undertaken by the CLG in 2008 found that '*...non-HRA PFI costs were generally significantly higher than SHG costs*', suggesting that it is cheaper for the public sector to support housing association developments than to use PFI. However, this review is ongoing, and readers should endeavour to monitor future reviews via the CLG website: www.communities.gov.uk

(v) Conclusion

It is clear that these various policies have had a significant impact not only on council housing provision, but also the housing association sector. Right to buy has considerably reduced the numbers and qualities of council homes, and this has not been balanced by an equivalent growth in new housing association stock. Nevertheless, LSVT has resulted in the creation of many, new, much larger HAs, and private finance has become much more significant in the provision of affordable housing. The perceived success of ALMOs in delivering improved management and achieving significant home improvements for their council tenants has generated calls for steps to be taken to ensure their continuation, to which the government has responded by considering whether they might permit some councils to opt out of the council housing subsidy system – the Housing Revenue Account Subsidy. The operation and effects of current public sector subsidies for affordable housing is explored in the next two sections.

2. Capital finance for affordable housing

2.1: Introduction

Most capital spending by local authorities and housing associations has to be funded from borrowing, as revenue incomes are unlikely to provide the 'lump sums' needed for major capital works. Also, because borrowing is repaid over a lengthy time period this also has the advantage that the costs of the assets – which will last for a long time and be enjoyed by future as well as present generations – are shared more fairly between the people who will benefit from them over time.

As examined in Section 1 (above), for many years, most public subsidy for new house building was focused on housing associations, whilst local authorities were largely starved of funds even to maintain their properties adequately. Local authorities had responsibility for assessing their housing markets and identifying housing needs, but these were largely to be addressed by housing associations. More recently, however, the government has adopted a more holistic and inclusive approach, with efforts focused on better integrating the efforts of both types of organisation. The ways in which this is being encouraged will become apparent in the next section which examines capital finance issues.

2.2: Capital finance for local authorities

a) The context

As a result of efforts by the central government to control, and reduce, council spending during the 1980s and 1990s, various mechanisms were put in place to limit capital spending, including the requirement (in the 1989 Act) that councils obtain prior 'permission' from central government to borrow funds for capital projects. Permissions were given through a bidding process, which partly ensured that councils which actively pursued preferred government policies could be rewarded. Councils were allocated an 'annual capital guideline', which set out how much they could spend on capital items, and identified where it would come from – whether from borrowing (for which they needed a 'credit approval' from the government), from capital receipts (such as from right to buy sales), or from revenue sources (mainly rents). Overall, the intention was to limit drastically the ability of councils to invest in new housing or their existing stock. These detailed controls were dropped in the Local Government Act 2003 in favour of a system where the government decides the level of borrowing it will support ('supported borrowing') and leaves councils to decide for themselves how much borrowing they can afford – although within a set of rules (called 'prudential borrowing'). This is explored in detail below.

Capital spending – which must by law be kept separate from revenue spending – is recorded in the capital account. However, repayments of the loans are made from revenue accounts (mostly from rent income). In Scotland only, a council's capital account is divided into Blocks A and B. Block A is for expenditure on council housing and is also known as the 'HRA' element of capital expenditure. This is because any borrowing for council stock (in the capital account) will appear as annual debt repayments in the housing revenue account (HRA). Block B is for expenditure on other stock, such as private sector renovation grants or mortgages for right to buy purchasers. This is also known as the 'non-HRA' element. A small amount of virement (transfer) may be permitted between the two blocks of capital expenditure.

The local authority finance director (or equivalent) is responsible for all borrowing by a local authority. It is the task of the finance department to ensure that the authority obtains its funding at a fair price (rate of interest) and at timely intervals – that is, it should not unnecessarily be taking out loans which are not immediately needed. It must also ensure that all rules affecting the operation of accounts are complied with.

The borrowed money is placed in the local authority's *loans fund*. Local authorities have a major advantage over housing associations, in that they represent a much more secure 'home' for investments, as local authorities cannot go bankrupt. Local authorities are, therefore, viewed as very low risk by lenders and are generally able to obtain much more favourable rates of interest.

Local authorities have two main sources for borrowing:

i) The Public Works Loan Board

Finance for this fund is borrowed by the central government, so it should be a cheaper source than the local authorities' other external borrowing, as central government is even more of a 'safe bet'. Each authority receives a quota allocation from the Board, based on its capital programme and existing debts. The Board will also provide short-term emergency funding – i.e. it acts as *lender of last resort* for local authorities – should an authority find itself temporarily short of funds.

ii) Capital markets

Local authorities can issue their own financial instruments, such as bonds, which are sold on the capital market (through the Stock Exchange). These bonds are a form of long-term borrowing, bought mainly by large financial institutions such as pension funds and life insurance companies, which need to ensure that a proportion of their resources is kept in very secure, low-risk investments. Hence, LA bonds compete for buyers with central government and large private sector firms' borrowing which they do via issuing securities. The original purchaser can sell the bond to someone else (who then receives the annual LA interest payments), so the bonds are *tradeable* on the capital market. This also enhances their attractiveness to lenders.

The system under which councils obtain these funds for capital expenditure has undergone substantial revision since the late 1990s, by a Labour government keen to reform local authority finances. According to the CLG (2006a, p5), the objectives of the reforms were to:

- enable all local authorities to effectively and efficiently manage their businesses as landlords and better fulfil their role as strategic bodies;
- encourage sound investment decisions and good overall performance, making maximum use of the resources provided;
- ensure all available housing resources are distributed fairly in the light of the above.

The key features of this current capital financial framework are explored next.

b) Key features of the current capital financial framework for local authorities

The housing strategy

Each local authority (and the NIHE in Northern Ireland) must produce a housing strategy – called the *Housing Strategy and Housing Investment Programme (HIP)* in England, the *Housing Strategy and Operational Programme (HSOP)* in Wales, the *Strategic Housing Investment Plan (SHIP)* in Scotland, and the *Annual Housing Strategy (AHS)* in Northern Ireland. This sets out the local authority's (or, in NI, the NIHE's) assessment of housing need in its area, and the priorities for addressing these housing needs, and is updated as necessary. It covers all tenures, so authorities are expected to consult with all relevant stakeholders (e.g. tenants and housing associations) in developing the strategy. In England, local authoritiess must also take account of the regional housing strategy – see below. This strategy provides the context within which the HRA business plan is developed.

HRA business plans

Having developed the strategy, local authorities must produce HRA (council housing) business plans, to show how they intend to manage and enhance their housing assets over the longer term (up to 30 years). This is similar to the business planning process which housing authorities have had to undertake since the need to borrow private finance was introduced by the 1988 Housing Act and Housing (Scotland) Act.

According to the CLG (2006a, p5):

> *...business planning is the key to understanding what the best options are in delivering high quality, cost effective services. In particular, it enables them to*

assess whether they are in a position to meet the decent homes target within availale resources, and, if not, to look at how they might do so.

Hence, as part of their business plans, local authorities had to undertake 'option appraisals', to consider different options for securing sufficient resources to refurbish their stock, including stock transfer, or (in England) arms length management organisations (ALMOs), or securing resources under the private finance initiative (PFI).

The strategies and plans are assessed by the CLG, DSD in Northern Ireland, Scottish Government or Welsh Assembly Government (as appropriate), so that the allocation of total expenditure between the English regions, Scottish and Welsh local authorities and to the NIHE can be determined.

Allocating capital resources

Each part of the UK has a slightly different system for allocating capital resources to local authorities, and key differences are highlighted as appropriate. The allocation of capital borrowing remains focused solely on local authorities in Wales and Scotland, and on one body, the Northern Ireland Housing Executive, in Northern Ireland. In England, however, a new regional focus was introduced from 2004, when *regional housing boards* in England were given a strategic responsibility for capital spending in their areas. This is explored next.

The regional housing pot in England

The regional housing boards comprise representatives of:

- The government office for the English region, which represents departments of the UK central government, so comprises civil servants.
- The Homes and Communities Agency (formerly the Housing Corporation, English Partnerships and parts of CLG).
- Regional development agencies, which promote economic development and contribute to sustainable development; appointed by and responsible to the central government.
- Regional assemblies, which scrutinise the work of the regional development agencies, and they contain government appointees. All regions were to be given the opportunity, through a referendum, to opt for directly elected assemblies, but after the failure to achieve a 'yes' vote in the North East of England, this was abandoned. There are now proposals to abolish the assemblies by 2010, so readers should explore the current situation via the CLG website.
- Regional housing forums, which contain representatives from all organisations with an interest in housing – e.g. tenants' groups, Council of Mortgage Lenders (CML), House Builders Federation.

These regional housing boards produce an annual regional housing strategy, which takes account of the regional economic strategy (produced by the regional development agencies) and the regional planning guidance (drawn up by the regional assembly). The strategy is approved by the CLG, and it is argued that this approach can better reflect regional needs and priorities than a centralised system. Hence, in England, all local authority housing strategies have to be developed in the context of the regional strategy.

The CLG decides the value of each *regional housing pot* (RHP), which combines the funding available for both LAs and HAs, and is focused on each region. The amount of each regional housing board's RHP is derived from the housing needs formula (HNF), detailed in Figure 4.4. There are four components, which together contribute to determining the regional allocation. The relative weighting of each component may vary annually depending on current government priorities and the outcomes of spending reviews.

Figure 4.4: The housing needs formula

1. Affordable housing provision
This is assessed from:
- homelessness data (35%);
- overcrowding and concealed households (40%); and
- affordability of market housing (25%).

2. Affordable housing in growth areas
This element reflects the government's Sustainable Communities Plan to prioritise four identified growth areas in England:
- the Thames Gateway;
- London, Stansted, Cambridge and Peterborough;
- Milton Keynes and the south Midlands; and
- Ashford (Kent).

3. Decent homes
Determined from three indicators of stock condition in the LA area:
- The local authority stock condition indicator (LASCI);
- Housing association repairs and re-improvement (HARR) indicator; and
- The private sector stock condition indicator (PSSCI).

4. Regeneration
This is for local authorities with high levels of deprivation, based on the Index of Multiple Deprivation.

Source: CLG, 2006b, p3.

Supported Capital Expenditure (SCE) in England

The SCE is the amount of borrowing which the government thinks is necessary for the local authority to undertake, and that the government is prepared to recognise (i.e.

'support') through the revenue subsidy system (HRA subsidy in the case of council housing, which is explored in Section 3.2). This has replaced the previous system of 'annual capital guidelines', which were, in effect, borrowing permissions from central government, and this has been necessary due to the new 'prudential borrowing' rules (see below).

The SCE is split into two elements:

SCE (revenue) – which determines the support offered towards borrowing through the HRA subsidy system – see Section 3.2 – and

SCE (capital grant) – which determines what were previously known as specified capital grants, paid for specific activites such as adaptations for disabled people.

Once the regional housing pot is determined, based on the regional housing strategy, the distribution of SCEs for local authorities in England is determined by the relevant regional housing board. Note that this also influences the allocation of the National Affordable Housing Programme (NAHP) for housing associations (see Section 2.3, below), via the Homes and Communities Agency.

Prudential borrowing

After many years of local authority borrowing being tightly controlled by central government, 'prudential borrowing' has shifted responsibility for borrowing decisions back to the councils in England and Wales. Local authority borrowing is now undertaken in accordance with a professional code, drawn up by the Chartered Institute of Public Finance and Accountancy (CIPFA). This code gives a set of 'prudential indicators', which includes:

- past borrowing levels
- usable capital receipts
- borrowing support available from the government (SCEs) and
- revenue sources of finance.

According to CLG (2006a, p11): '*the prudential system will enable authorities to operate more flexibly to meet investment needs, but it will also require them to take responsibility for their decisions...although (the proposals) will not, by themselves, provide authorities with additional resources*'. The level of support available from the government – the SCEs – remain a key borrowing constraint, because any attempt to pay for extra borrowing beyond this via higher rents will simply result in reduced HRA subsidy (see below). In addition, local authorities cannot borrow against the value of their assets or their projected future rental streams (unlike housing associations). Hence, tight borrowing constraints, in reality, remain overall.

Value for money and performance criteria

The previous requirement for local authorities to engage in Compulsory Competitive Tendering (CCT) for local authority services – the requirement to invite competitive bids to run council services from the private sector – was replaced by the Best Value regime from 2000, often referred to as 'value for money'. This involved the need to demonstrate continuous service improvements against performance indicators, usually benchmarked against similar local authorities. In some instances, however, it also required 'market testing', to check whether the service could be provided more cheaply by another organisation.

In England and Wales, Best Value performance indicators were replaced (from April 2008) by new National Indicators, which include a bi-annual measurement of tenant satisfaction, via the STATUS survey (see Chapter 6). Housing inspectors from the Audit Commisssion examine the service and rate provision by 'star' categories (0 to 3 stars), with an indication of the likelihood of continuing improvement. So, the best achievement from an inspection is 3 stars and excellent prospects for improvement; the worst, no stars and poor prospects for improvement.

A system to pool RTB receipts nationally for redistribution (England and Wales)

Before 2007, councils could retain only 25 per cent of their right to buy capital receipts to spend on further capital projects (called 'usable' receipts), with 75 per cent 'set aside' largely to repay their past debts. A number of previously low-debt English councils had managed to repay all debts through this requirement, and they were then required to pay the set-aside sum into the council's General Fund (the revenue account for all, non-council housing spending). This 75 per cent 'set aside' is now collected by central government, for redistribution (to both local authorities and housing associations) through their subsidy systems. So, receipts from 'rich' local authorities (which sell large numbers of council houses) can be used by central government to subsidise other councils and housing associations (via SHG). Non-RTB receipts – i.e. those under the local authority's direct control, such as receipts from the sale of land – are not affected by pooling if recycled into regeneration or housing projects. This is intended to encourage a more active management of an authority's assets, thus generating addional resources to meet the need for affordable housing (CLG, 2006a, p7). However, this does not apply in Scotland or Northern Ireland.

2.3: Capital finance for housing associations

a) The context

In contrast to the 1980s, when up to 90 per cent of housing associations' development costs could be subsidised by publicly-provided Housing Association Grant (HAG), nowadays, in England and Wales especially, most of the finance needed for capital works is borrowed from private sector sources.

There are two main sources of finance:

i) Loans from banks (the 'money market')

These loans are negotiated with major commercial banks, and usually borrowed for short to medium terms. The security for the loans is provided by the organisation's assets – its housing stock – and its projected rental income. This is quite unlike local authorities, which cannot borrow against the value of assets or projected income flows; instead, local authorities are able to borrow simply because they are local authorities and, as part of government, cannot go bankrupt. Housing associations may later re-negotiate their loans, or re-finance with another lender, in an effort to obtain a better deal. This is explored further in Section 4.5.

ii) Loans from the capital market

Rather like local authorities, the larger housing associations may be able to issue bonds for sale on the stock market. This provides much longer-term finance, but, due to the hugely expensive process of issuing bonds, it is only available for raising substantial sums of money and so is only usually available to the largest organisations.

In England only, The Housing Finance Corporation (THFC) was created following the 1988 Housing Act to provide support to smaller associations which might find it difficult to access private finance. This organistion can 'pool' the borrowing requirements of a number of associations to try to secure a better deal from the banks. In addition, it can draw together the requirements of a number of associations to enable a bond issue to take place. Bazlinton (2008) reports that, by 2007, THFC had raised more than £1.6 billion for smaller associations, much of it through bonds issues.

b) Capital subsidy

Varying proportions of scheme costs may be funded by capial subsidy from the public funding bodies in each country of the UK, and each has its own system for determining which associations get what. In England, Wales and Northern Ireland, the subsidy is called the Social Housing Grant (SHG); in Scotland, it is the Housing Association Grant (HAG). Under the current capital subsidy systems, the amount of capital grant is determined at the outset, so that it is up to the housing association to ensure that costs are constrained within these limits. Rents are generally determined at the level needed to cover all annual (revenue) costs, but, in England and Wales, this must be within the constraints of the formula rents required under the rent restructuring policy (see Section 3).

The institutional arrangements for providing public subsidy to housing associations in the UK have seen considerable reorganisation in England and Scotland recent years. The main bodies – and recent changes – are:

- In England, the Housing Corporation, the main public body providing capital subsidy for housing associations in England from the 1970s until December

2008, was merged with English Partnerships, together with parts of CLG, to form the Homes and Communities Agency. The regulatory elements joined the new regulatory body, the Tenants Services Authority.

- In Scotland, when the devolved Scottish Government was created, Communities Scotland (directly administered by the Scottish Government) was formed from Scottish Homes, which was an agency similar to the Housing Corporation with its own board. Communities Scotland was subsequently abolished (from April 2008), and its non-regulatory functions switched to the Housing and Regeneration Directorate, with regulatory functions going to the Scottish Housing Regulator.

- In Wales, Tai Cymru (the Housing Corporation equivalent) was absorbed into the Welsh government before devolution took place, so that both housing association funding and regulation are the direct responsibility of the Welsh Assembly Government.

- Funding and regulation of housing associations in Northern Ireland is shared between the Department for Social Development (DSD) and the Northern Ireland Housing Executive (NIHE).

As the key features in the capital subsidy systems of these national organisations all differ in some key respects, each organisation's approach is explored separately next.

(i) The National Affordable Housing Programme (NAHP) in England

The Housing Corporation's (HC) traditional approach to subsidising housing association development had encouraged most associations to bid, even for very small projects, for a share of their annual 'Approved Development Programme' (ADP) – the value of which was determined by the CLG. This approach had successfully supported a very large number of associations annually (between 350 and 400), but had produced an average programme of only 50 homes per association, so the HC recognised that there was little opportunity to achieve economies of scale (cost reductions from increasing the scale of production). As a result, from 2003-04, the HC introduced a more selective approach to funding housing association development, targeting 56 per cent of their ADP on just 42 'partner' associations, which had to enter into a partnership agreement. The HC also set up a new Challenge Fund of £300 million to pilot new construction techniques through these partner organisations (HC, 2003). By 2004-05, they were pursuing the partnership approach to capital funding much more vigorously, and introduced a new framework for funding these 'investment partners'. In order to expand competition and increase capacity, private developers were also invited to apply for partner status.

As well as the schemes having to meet the HC's Scheme Development Standards (see Chapter 5), the bid had to include Housing Quality Indicators (HQIs), and associations have to match – or better – minimum 'scores' for unit size and unit layout. This was intended to ensure that costs (in terms of SHG) were not driven down at the expense of housing quality standards. This approach has since been further refined, and the current *National Affordable Housing Programme 2008-11* (Housing Corporation, 2008) identifies a number of different routes into bidding for SHG:

1. routes to bid for funding

• Investment partner route
The current National Affordable Housing Programme for 2008-11 focuses subsidy largely on housing associations and private developers which have achieved 'investment partner' status. This involves successfully demonstrating, through a pre-qualification process:

1. good standing with the HC
2. the technical capacity to deliver
3. the financial capacity to handle large grants.

(Housing and Communities Agency/Housing Corporation, 2007, p47.)

Small associations are unlikely to be able to meet these criteria, so are being forced to form partnerships with larger associations, to get their projects included within a larger bid, or even to merge with larger associations, if they want to continue to be eligible for SHG. It should also be noted that council housing ALMOs (which have achieved at least 2 stars from their inspection) are also now eligible to apply for investment partner status, and in 2008, three successfully gained a share of SHG from the National Affordable Housing Programme for 2008-11.

• Partnership plus
This is available only to top performers in the investment partner category, and only as a pilot from April 2008. It is planned that these 'plus' partners will have greater freedoms and flexibilities in the use of SHG, but will be expected to 'stretch their financial capacity' to 'minimise grant' (Housing and Communities Agency/Housing Corporation, 2007, p44).

• Specialist provision route
This is for specific CLG priorities, which are currently (2008-09):

- Rural provision
- Black and minority ethnic provision
- Supported housing
- Environmental innovation (achieving the *Code for Sustainable Homes* (CSH) at level 5 and above – see Chapter 5)
- The 'temporary to settled' initiative in London
- Community Land Trusts.

2. Efficiency targets

In order to continue to encourage financial efficiencies and increase the numbers of 'homes per £' (of grant), the Housing and Communities Agency has devised efficiency targets by English region, depending on what they assess to be the scope for further efficiencies. Achieving the targets will form part of any subsequent review of performance for further grant allocations.

3. Bid assessment

This is undertaken at regional level, and bids are assessed against four criteria:

- Value for money (subsidy per home)
- Quality, judged against the Design and Quality Standards
- Deliverability (especially planning status)
- Policy fit with national, regional and local strategies.

Whereas, at one time, there were strict cost limits on development costs, now:

> *It will be for associations to determine the cost of development. We believe that this is the right place for this responsibility, as associations need to live with the long term consequences of development costs* (Housing Corporation, 2003, p8).

(ii) Affordable Housing Investment Programme (AHIP) in Scotland

The Scottish Government recently (from 2008) introduced a three year programme, worth £1.5 billion, which allocates annual HAG funds to each region in Scotland. The AHIP allocations for 2008-09 are shown in Table 4.3.

Bids for funding remain largely on a project-by-project basis, and Registered Social Landlords must complete a *HAG Financial Appraisal*, which is assessed by the funder – though, in the case of the major cities of Edinburgh and Glasgow, this responsibility has been devolved to the respective local authorities. The system assumes a 'private finance factor', which calculates the amount of private finance expected to be obtained by the RSL, and HAG is made available to fund the remainder of scheme costs. This has generally resulted in much more generous HAG payments (as a proportion of costs) than is common now in the rest of the UK – for example, in 2007-08, the private finance factor was 18.1369 (multiplied by net rental income).

However, from 2008-09, the Scottish Government announced that it expects the numbers of homes to be delivered from HAG funding to increase over the three year period to 2011, so that levels of HAG per home will be declining. According to a report in *Inside Housing* (6 June 2008, p7), this will increase RSL's borrowing per scheme by about one-third, and the Scottish Federation of Housing Associations claims that this will inevitably lead to increased rents.

Table 4.3: AHIP allocations in Scotland, 2008-09

Region	£ million
Highlands and Islands	38.9
Argyll and Clyde	63.0
Grampian	29.9
Tayside and Forth Valley	32.0
South and West Scotland	59.5
Lothian, Borders and Fife	33.1
Glasgow	83.0
Edinburgh	36.1

Source: Scottish Government, 2008.

(iii) The capital subsidy system in Wales

As in the English system, the Welsh Assembly Government (WAG) has increasingly focused its SHG funding on fewer RSLs which are delivering larger programmes, though it has retained local authorities as key players in the process.

The main features include:

- *Agreed Programme Developers* (APDs), which are similar to the Housing Corporation's 'investment partners', but are normally consortia or groups of several RSLs and/or developers. This is intended to deliver greater efficiencies and economies of scale.
- The criteria to qualify as an APD include:
  – the expertise and track record to deliver large programmes
  – financial capacity.
- Strategic priorities for investment are determined by the WAG, and local authorities bid for resources for up to 3 years under each priority
- The LAs then agree detailed programmes of schemes with the APDs.

(iv) The capital subsidy system in Northern Ireland

The Northern Ireland Department for Social Development regulates and funds NI housing associations, but these remain relatively less significant in terms of housing provision in NI than elsewhere in the UK. This is due partly to the fact that the Northern Ireland Housing Executive retained a provider/development role throughout the 1990s, which was largely denied local authorities elsewhere. However, the focus for provision has, since the late 1990s, switched more firmly to housing associations, though there have been no attempts to move properties out of NIHE management as there have been in other parts of the UK (through LSVTs, for example, or ALMOs).

c) Private finance

As capital subsidy from the public sector declined during the 1990s, housing associations needed to access increasing proportions of private funding. This forced housing associations to adopt a much more private-sector 'business-like' approach to their activities. Private lenders view associations as they would any private company seeking finance from them, and seek always to minimise any risk that they could lose money. This means that they want detailed financial information about the company, including details of rent levels, voids, arrears and other housing assets. Private lenders always scrutinise the *business plan* prepared by a housing association. Business plans set out the present state of the organisation, indicate plans for the future, and, most importantly, show (with careful financial analysis) how those plans can be achieved. Planned schemes must, of course, be consistent with the agreed business plan.

As the dependence of housing associations on private finance increased, there were some concerns that design and construction standards were falling, as there was a temptation to 'cut corners' in an attempt to curtail costs and borrowing. So, the funding bodies devised various approaches to maintain quality; for example, the Housing Corporation introduced 'Scheme Development Standards'. In England, where grant rates fell fastest, there was also a large reduction in rehabilitation work, simply because this is inherently more at risk of cost increases, as new and unforeseen problems emerge. New build is less risky.

Private financial institutions, in general, adopt a very cautious approach to lending funds. They prefer to have a large amount of *security*, to guarantee that they will get their money back whatever happens. Small associations, with few assets, can offer little extra security; furthermore, they might be considered more at risk of failure – going bankrupt. This resulted in a certain amount of merger activity in the 1990s between housing associations who were keen to expand their asset bases, and hence, perceived security. More recently, changes in the public funders' approaches to allocating public subsidy (see above), with the focus increasingly on larger associations able to deliver larger programmes (and hence assumed to be able to achieve efficiencies and lower unit costs), has had a similar impact, with smaller associations often becoming part of larger mergers or new 'group structures'. However, the 2008 'credit crunch' in financial markets is promising to have an even more significant and far reaching impact on HAs.

The credit crunch

As identified in Section 1.4, the recent 'credit crunch' has impacted negatively on some housing associations. It affected both housing associations' abilities to borrow finance for new schemes, as well as on the potential cost of that finance (the rate of interest which must be paid). Some are finding that favourable re-financing deals are more difficult to secure (see Section 4.5).

Most importantly, the fact that households now face significant difficulties in securing loans – and especially loans which don't require a large deposit – is impacting on the sale of all new housing. This is compounded by the economic downturn and impending recession, so as unemployment rises, households are deterred from taking on new debts.

The result is that private developers are unable to sell new homes, so they are abandoning future plans. From the housing association perspective, this is impacting especially where there are section 106 agreements (agreements made under section 106 of the 1990 Town and Country Planning Act in England and Wales – or section 75 in Scotland – which permit the planning authority to require some community benefits to be provided as a condition of planning approval). So, these may, for example, require some cross-subsidy for affordable homes from the private market sale properties. However, if the market sale properties are not built, then neither is the affordable housing.

In addition, the housing associations themselves are finding it more difficult to sell properties that they themselves have built for market sale or shared ownership on cross-tenure developments. Hence, the credit crunch and recession are impacting on the sale of all new housing association ownership products (see Section 5), as fewer (and smaller) loans are available, and there is considerable market uncertainty, with fears of large price falls. This situation is deterring many households from house purchase of all kinds. Any inability to sell market sale, or shared ownership properties, threatens to seriously damage the achievement of housing association plans and cause considerable disruption to their cash flows (see Section 4).

In an effort to help to sustain private housing demand at this time, and to reassure private house builders, the Housing Corporation initially allocated at least £200 million from the National Affordable Housing Programme for 2008-09 for housing associations to purchase unsold, new properties from private developers. This scheme is not without its critics, however, as (unlike housing association new build) private housing does not yet have to meet level 3 of the Code for Sustainable Homes (see Chapter 5), so is likely to be of inferior quality to the new homes built by housing associations themselves.

3. Revenue finance for affordable housing

3.1: Sources of revenue finance

Revenue finance relates to the day-to-day, operational activities of social housing orgnisations. As both local authorities and housing associations undertake similar management functions in relation to their housing stock, they have much in common in their main sources of revenue finance. The main common elements are identified in Figure 4.5, and then key differences are subsequently explored.

Figure 4.5: The main elements in social housing organisations' revenue accounts

Expenditure :
- Debt interest payments.
- Maintenance costs, which cover day-to-day repairs and planned maintenance programmes (such as re-painting), but substantial improvements would be capital expenditure.
- Management costs, such as the costs of paying employees, office expenses, staff training, and so on.

Income:
- Rents and charges to tenants.
- Interest received – from invested reserves (in the case of HAs) or paid to councils for right to buy mortgages and other loans.
- (For some LAs only) Housing Revenue Account Subsidy.

Rents and rent setting

Prior to the 1988 Housing Act, housing associations' tenancies were subject to rent control legislation – sometimes called 'fair rents' – so their rent levels were set by a central government rent officer. After the 1988 Housing Act, when new tenancies became 'assured' tenancies, housing associations were free to set their own rents. This was essential if housing associations were to be able to secure borrowing from private financial institutions, which would want to be assured that housing associations had control over their main source of income. Nevertheless, the public sector retained some influence through the SHG subsidy system, because, if proposed rents were viewed as excessive, this could affect the housing associations ability to secure capital subsidy from the funding bodies.

Similarly, although local authorities could, in theory, determine their own rent levels throughout this period, in practice, the government was able to exert a huge influence through the revenue subsidy system by setting 'guideline' rents.

Rent restructuring

During the 1990s, in England and Wales particularly, a widening gap had developed between housing association and council rents, with higher rents in the housing association sector primarily as a result of rapidly declining SHG rates, and hence an increasing need for associations to borrow larger proportions of scheme costs to fund new development. The government was concerned about this growing disparity between rents in the affordable housing sectors and, as a result, rent restructuring was introduced from April 2002 for councils and housing associations in England and Wales.

Rent restructuring for local authorities was intended to:

- Encourage more efficient use of housing assets (by ensuring an adequate return on investment, much like the private sector).

- Increase the transparency of local authorities' Housing Revenue Account, to present 'more fairly' the financial position of the local authority.
- Assist authorities to plan their housing strategy.
- Bring accounting procedures into line with the private sector and housing associations
- Achieve consistency with central government and other local authority accounting practices (ODPM, 2002b).

This necessitated a number of other changes for local authorities, which are explored in subsequent sections.

The implication was that many council rents would have to rise relative to housing association rents, so housing association rents would (in general) be held back while council rents rose. The long lead-in time (over 10 years – though this has since been extended) was intended to permit gradual changes, with no annual increases exceeding RPI + 0.5% + £2 per week for council properties, and maximum increases of RPI + 0.5% for HA tenants. (The RPI – retail price index – is a measure of the annual rate of inflation.)

For the first time, there was now a government-set formula to determine rents, called the *formula rent*, which for each property reflects:

- Its condition and location, and 'other qualities that tenants value' (Chapter 2, p1)
- local earnings
- property size

(ODPM, 2003).

It is assumed that *property values* reflect the relative attractiveness to tenants of different properties in different localities, so this is taken as a proxy for 'other qualities which tenants value'. Property valuations are based on existing use value (EUV) – in effect, just like private house valuations – as at January 1999. This value normally remains the same during the whole period of restructuring, unless there have been substantial major capital works which have radically affected the value of the property (ODPM, 2003).

The *formula rent* is weighted:

- 70 per cent for earnings (which also takes into account the property size) Calculated from:
    average LA rent
    (national (English/Welsh) average council rent at April 2000)
    x relative county earnings
    (average manual earnings in the county divided by national average manual earnings)

x bedroom weight
(based on numbers of bedrooms).

- 30 per cent for property values
  Calculated from:
  average LA rent
  x relative property value
  (individual value divided by national average value of council properties, at January 1999 prices).

It was intended that the rent for each council and housing association property would move towards the formula rent in roughly 10 equal steps over the decade. For council tenants, there was also an annual *rent cap* (maximum amount of rent increase) to protect tenants from excessive increases in high property value areas. To permit an element of discretion, local authorities and housing associations (in consultation with tenants) were permitted to take some account of local factors, to vary rents for particular properties by up to 5% + or – compared to the formula rent. By 2008, for RSLs, the average gap between the average actual rent and the target rent was £2.70, down from £3.01 in 2007 (CRMI, 2008).

However, the government was concerned that the unexpectedly large increase in the RPI in September 2008 (to 5%) could have resulted in proposed rent increases that would be unaffordable. A cap of 7% on rent increases has been proposed from 2009-10, and convergence is now not anticipated until 2024-25.

Of course, this rent restructuring policy, intended to align housing association and local authorities rents, severely constrained associations' abilities to determine their own rent levels. This has had a significant impact on some housing associations, particularly those with a higher proportion of recent schemes or recent purchases (such as LSVT organisations), with higher costs, and hence, higher loans. As a result, a number have had to redraft their business plans, to take account of lower than anticipated future rents. As shown in Table 4.4, this appears to have had a significant impact on rent levels relative to earnings.

Table 4.4: Housing association assured rents as a % of earnings

Region	1990	1995	2000	2005	2007
England	10.9	14.2	12.8	11.9	12.1
Scotland	10.5	11.5	12.1	10.9	11.0
N.Ireland	–	10.3	10.9	10.1	10.3
Wales	13.2	14.0	12.3 (1999)	N/A	N/A

Source: Wilcox, 2008.

Research for the Housing Corporation by Kiddle and Banks in 2002 identified that smaller properties were likely to suffer the largest increases under rent restructuring, since two-thirds were currently below their average target (formula) rents. This indicated that smaller households, such as single people and couples, would be hardest hit by rent restructuring. There were also concerns that, as rents were relatively low for larger properties, this would deter associations from building homes with 3+ bedrooms in future, as their higher costs were not adequately reflected in higher rents. It was recognised that this could be especially disadvantageous for some ethnic minority households. As a result, the bedroom weightings were revised from 2006-07 (see Table 4.5), to significantly increase the relative bedroom weighting for larger properties.

Table 4.5: Formula rent bedroom weightings (for rent restructuring)

No of bedrooms	up to 2005-06	from 2006-07
1	0.9	0.9
2	1.0	1.0
3	1.05	1.1
4	1.1	1.2
5	1.1	1.3
6 or more	1.1	1.4

Source: Housing Corporation, 2005.

3.2: Local authority revenue accounts and revenue subsidy

Unlike housing associations, which have only one revenue account (the income and expnditure account, which is like the Housing Revenue Account for local authorities), there are two main revenue accounts for local authorites. As they have many expenses which do not relate to their own housing stock, these have to be separately accounted for in the General Fund Account. Accounting for council house spending occurs through the Housing Revenue Account.

In contrast to housing associations – whose main form of subsidy is capital, via SHG or HAG – the main way by which councils receive subsidy from central government is through their revenue systems. These subsidies are intended to ensure that councils are able to afford to deliver roughly equivalent services to all UK residents, whatever their local income levels. The main council revenue accounts, and their subsidies, are explored next.

a) The General Fund Account

The General Fund Account is the main revenue account for the whole council, paying for expenditure on schools, libraries, cleansing, leisure centres etc., as well as funding general housing services which are provided for private sector residents of a local authority (such as advice centres and help for the homeless). Though expenditure is on a wide range of non-housing and private housing services, the General Fund is also responsible for the payment of housing benefit to all tenants in all tenures.

Revenue *income* is obtained from a variety of sources:

- local taxes (the council tax)
- a share of national business rates (with the rate set by central government, collected from businesses by local authorities, and redistributed by the central government)
- some government grants and
- interest on any unused capital receipts.

The General Fund revenue support grant (RSG)

This is the central government revenue subsidy to councils' general (non-council housing) expenditure. The government first calculates:

Total Assumed Spending, which is the amount that the government believes is needed to permit each council to deliver equal service provision from the General Fund, having regard to the needs in the area. This comprises:

- *Aggregate External Finance* (AEF), which is the amount paid to councils from government grants (including the revenue support grant) and business rates; and
- Assumed income from *council tax* (the local authority determined local taxation).

The revenue support grant (RSG) is the most significant element of AEF, and is tied to a spending assessment called the *formula spending share* (FSS), which effectively shares out the grant funds available depending on assessed local needs.

This means that most General Fund income is not under the control of local authorities because, not only is RSG determined by the central government, so also effectively is the council tax (because if this is increased beyond the levels assumed by government, the revenue support grant will simply be reduced) and business rates. Only the level of charges, such as rents for temporary accommodation, remains under their direct control. Furthermore, within the General Fund, housing services have to compete with all other types of council provision. Increased expenditure on one element generally demands reduced expenditure elsewhere.

b) The Housing Revenue Account (HRA)

This is the main account for council housing revenue income and expenditure, and the main elements are shown in Figure 4.5. In addition, many councils will make Revenue contributions to capital outlays (RCCOs), or contributions from current revenue (CFCRs) in Scotland, which is revenue income used to help fund capital projects.

At one time, housing benefit for council tenants – called rent rebates – was accounted for in the HRA, but, from April 2004, these were transferred to the General Fund (from which RSL and private landlord tenants' housing benefit have always been paid). The HRA is now paid the value of the housing benefit payments for council tenants from the General Fund, and subsidy for it is paid into the General Fund in the same way as subsidy for housing benefit for other tenants (housing association and private).

In England and Wales only, the HRA is paid a *Major Repairs Allowance (MRA)*, which was introduced from 2001-02 in England and from 2004-05 in Wales. It '*...represents the estimated long term average amount of capital spending required to maintain a local authority's stock in its current condition*' (ODPM, 2002a). The calculation of the MRA is based on the proportions of different house types, and their ages, in an authority's stock. These figures are adjusted regionally, by a *regional adjustment factor*, to ensure that higher-cost regions (such as the south-east of England) get relatively more than low-cost areas (such as the north-east) (ODPM, 2002a). This sum is paid to the HRA as part of the central government's HRA Subsidy and then transferred to the *Housing Repairs Account*.

In England only, there is also a different system of accounting for the value of the council's housing, called *resource accounting*. The value of councils' housing stock has always been recorded in the capital account as its *historic value* – i.e. what it cost to produce at the time it was built. However, beginning in 2001-02, English councils were required to introduce resource accounting, which required that the *current value* of the stock was recorded (as housing associations and private landlords do). The stock is valued according to its *existing use value for social housing* (EUV-SH) – that is, its value allowing for the fact that it has secure tenants, which is lower than a vacant, free-market valuation. Note that this is a different valuation to that required by rent restructuring (see above), because the 'for social housing' (-SH) element reduces the EUV valuation (ODPM, 2002b).

The desire to 'encourage a more efficient use of housing assets' means that the stock must now achieve a return on the capital invested (a 'capital charge', to indicate what the asset is 'costing' annually), as well as a depreciation allowance to reflect wear and tear. This 'cost' is charged to the housing revenue account, the HRA.

The *Asset Management Revenue Account* (AMRA) was created for debt repayments by English councils only. As indicated above, the 'capital charge' and depreciation are charged to the HRA (based on the stock's capital value, under resource accounting arrangements) and transferred into the AMRA. This account is then used to pay any actual debt interest charges and repayment of capital borrowed. Since this sum is likely to be much less than the capital charge (since the historic cost of the housing is much less than its current value), the government requires any excess to be paid to the CLG, which helps to fund other types of housing subsidy (and offset the cost of the MRA).

Housing Revenue Account Subsidy (in England and Wales)

Housing Revenue Account subsidy from central government was originally intended to help to provide councils with a 'level playing field' in the provision of services to council tenants. It was recognised that, for various reasons, some councils would necessarily incur higher costs (e.g. due to higher costs for building and land, resulting in higher loan costs), or may receive less income, than others. So, it was fair that central government took a role in redistributing some income to councils. However, in recent years, most councils have ceased to qualify for positive subsidy, as their 'notional' incomes have risen above their 'notional' allowances, which is explained below. This means that many are now in so-called 'negative' subsidy, meaning that the government takes money from them. Just how this extraordinary situation arises is explained below.

The main features of the current HRA Subsidy system are:

- The HRA is 'ring fenced' to prevent contributions from the General Fund.
- Local authorities are allocated specific annual allowances for management and maintenance costs (see Figure 4.6).
- The calculation of subsidy depends on the notional balance in a notional Housing Revenue Account for each local authority, not the actual HRA balance.
- The level of subsidy is set to cover the difference between notional income and notional expenditure.

There is no allowance for arrears; the government assumes that all the rent is gathered, which is intended to place some pressure on councils to ensure that rents are collected efficiently. Voids are assumed at 2 per cent. Average rents will, of course, have to be higher to cover any sums lost through arrears or voids greater than 2 per cent. The government also does not allow for any extra spending on capital projects outside the Supported Capital Expenditure (SCE) system. So, if the local authority decides to use rental income to make revenue contributions to capital spending (RCCOs in England and Wales) / capital from current revenue (CFCRs in Scotland), then rents have to rise to cover that extra spending.

Negative subsidy

As indicated above, if there is a projected deficit in the HRA, then the HRA Subsidy funds the shortfall. But, if there is a notional surplus – which now applies in the majority of councils – then the subsidy is negative. This means that the *government takes the surplus and uses it to help to subsidise other deficit councils.*

Figure 4.6: Notional expenditure calculation for HRA subsidy

a) Management allowance
An allowance is made for management costs, taking into account the characteristics of the authority's stock, and is specifically intended to squeeze costs to encourage greater efficiency. If a local authority decides to spend more than its notional allowance on management, then rents will have to be higher than the notional average rent to balance the Housing Revenue Account.

b) Maintenance allowance (per property)
This is the notional amount that the local authority needs, based on indices of need and regional cost variations. In England and Wales, there is now also the major repairs allowance (see below).

c) Loan interest charges
In England and Wales, this is now a 'capital charge' and 'depreciation allowance', rather than the actual cost of the interest and loan repayments (see resource accounting and the asset management revenue account, below).

d) Additional allowances may be made from time to time to support the introduction of new government policies, as necessary.

Opting out of the HRA Subsidy system?

Partly as a result of concerns about the growing levels of negative subsidy, and also partly as a response to the desire of ALMOs (see Section 1) to establish themselves on a more secure, long-term financial basis, the government initiated a pilot study in autumn 2006, to explore the possible benefits and costs of councils being able to opt out of the HRA Subsidy system. This involved six English councils, and focused on determining, over a 30 year business planning period:

a) the likely shortfall in necessary revenue resources (for those councils with anticipated deficits on their HRAs), or
b) the likely operating surplus of those councils which would normally receive negative subsidy, and so be contributing to the national pot.

This permitted the calculation of the necessary 'settlement price' – a one-off payment, up front – aimed at leaving the councils in the same position, financially, as if they had remained in the HRA subsidy system.

A number of different models were tested to cover a variety of scenarios (for example, councils with high or low outstanding debts). The government was, understandably, concerned about the possible loss of control over council borrowing as a result of councils leaving the HRA Subsidy system; this risk arises because of prudential borrowing, as councils which left the HRA Subsidy system would presumably no longer get an SCE allocation, but could borrow through the prudential route (see above). However, the study found that council's business plans, '*...would not depend on a significant increase in overall borrowing and that, in many cases, there would be an opportunity to repay debt, debt that is currently only serviced with interest support through the subsidy system*' (CLG, 2008a, p7).

The study also identified a number of possible long-term benefits for councils which opted out of the HRA Subsidy system. It would:

- Assist long-term planning by freeing them from '*the unpredictability of a complex system of national resource redistribution*' (p7).
- Enhance local decision-making through greater freedom to prioritise.
- Enable more effective asset management, including the reuse and redevelopment of land.
- Improve access to private finance.
- Deliver greater efficiency, through the capacity to develop longer-term partnering arrangements (e.g. with developers).

Following the publication of the report on the pilot study in March 2008 (CLG, 2008a), the government announced a wider-ranging review of the HRA Subsidy system, to be carried out jointly by officers from HM Treasury and CLG, and published in July 2009. In the meantime, the 2008 Housing and Regeneration Act enabled councils potentially to opt out of the subsidy system in return for a one-off payment depending on their current subsidy situation. As this book went to press, the review's main outcome seemed likely to be that the HRA Subsidy system would be phased out over the coming years by redistributing the historic debt; readers are advised to check the latest situation.

Housing Support Grant (in Scotland)

In Scotland, the HRA subsidy is called *Housing Support Grant*. However, by 2002, hardly any councils in Scotland (only the Western Isles and Shetlands) qualified for Housing Support Grant, so it has become largely irrelevant. In addition, revenue (rent)-funded capital investment (capital from current revenue – CFCRs) has become relatively more important there than in England and Wales, since the constraints on the use of capital receipts (i.e. 75 per cent to repay debt) were introduced in Scotland from 1996.

3.3: Housing association revenue

The main revenue account for housing associations is the income and expenditure account, with key elements as identified earlier in Figure 4.5. This does not receive any form of government revenue subsidy, so there are no 'notional' accounts compiled by the government. However, whereas the HRA is not permitted to carry any surpluses, housing associations are encouraged to generate and maintain surpluses (called reserves) in case of any unforeseen events. However, part of the justification for various governments efforts to reduce capital grant support levels is not just to encourage greater efficiencies and value for money; it is also to encourage better use of housing association reserves, which, in some cases, are thought to be excessively high merely for 'contingency' purposes.

Another significant difference to local authorities is that housing associations are required by their funders and regulators to build and maintain a *major repairs fund*, to which they contribute (from revenue) to build up sufficient funds to pay for all future major capital replacement works (such as new roofs, windows, etc.). This is intended to ensure that they undertake adequate planning, as their stock ages, for major works in future.

As explored in Section 3.1, housing association rents are subject to rent restructuring, and this has left many feeling especially vulnerable in the face of changing market conditions – especially the 'credit crunch', which could cause capital financing costs to rise considerably (see Section 2.3). This suggests that, whilst future revenue costs (in the form of loan interest payments) may be rising, incomes (in the form of rents) will, at best, be fairly static for some years, until restructuring is complete. This is unlikely to produce a situation in which housing associations will feel happy to run down their revenue reserves to fund new capital development.

As will be apparent from the above discussion, effective management of financial resources is of key importance for all housing associations, and this major issue is explored in the next section.

4. Planning and controlling finances: the role of financial management

Housing organisations, just like any private firm or individual, have to plan how they will obtain and spend their financial resources. Someone, or group, such as the management committee, must take decisions about *priorities* for expenditure, and must plan to ensure that income will be sufficient to cover this. They must also carefully monitor and control income and spending on a regular basis, to ensure that it remains within budgets, or that staff can take steps to correct any potential deviances. Budgets may also need to be amended in the light of new and unexpected events – in other words, finances need to be actively managed.

Section 2 identified the ways that affordable housing organisations secure capital finance; however, having obtained these funds (or the prospect of them), they have to plan how they will be spent, on *what*, and *when*. Similarly, for revenue finance, they must determine income levels (principally from rents) and plan their revenue spending accordingly. This means that they have to prepare *budgets*, for both capital and revenue spending, which set out planned income and expenditure.

4.1: Budgets

The treasurer or finance manager/director will compile capital and revenue budgets for the whole organisation, which identify broad categories of expenditure and income, approved by the relevant committee. These may then be devolved to a lower level in the organisation, for further division into specific activities or localities.

The time period covered by the budget depends partly on its purpose. Generally, revenue budgets are *annual*, covering the organisation's *financial year* (April 2009 – March 2010, for example). Capital budgets may cover a longer period, of say two to five years, to reflect the timescale of a specific capital project; for example, the development of a new, large housing estate will take much longer than the implementation of a new computer system.

The main budgets may be specified in a number of ways. For example:

- **By department.**
  For a local authority, the council's budget will usually be allocated to particular *departments*, such as housing, social services, environmental services, etc.

- **By location.**
  A large organisation may need budgets for each *location*, such as a budget for each area office. Many local authorities have *decentralised* budgets, so that smaller units (the neighbourhood office, or the estate) are responsible for the allocation of their own budgets, within the overall limits defined by the centre.

- **By function.**
  This focuses on the *nature* of the income or expenditure, known as *line-items*. For example, in a revenue budget, line items might include employees (salaries, wages, pensions, etc.), office expenses (stationery, telephones, etc.), staff travel/transport costs, repairs and maintenance.

A well-used concept in relation to budgets is *cost centres*, which refers to logical groupings of budgets, which often relate either to particular functions (such as repairs) or localities.

The process of budget preparation

There are a number of possible approaches to preparing a budget.

(i) Incremental budgeting

For revenue budgets, this is a fairly common approach, which concentrates attention on the *reasons for change*, but its essential assumption is that service provision will continue as before.

It takes the *current* budget as the starting point, and concentrates on the *elements that need to change* in the budget. For example:

- costs may be rising due to inflation, or falling because prices (e.g. for maintenance) have become more competitive;
- employees may be entitled to increments, increasing the salary costs;
- there may be a need for new/additional services (e.g. for *community care provision*, or tenant involvement initiatives);
- income may be falling, for example due to reduced revenue grants.

Each line-item in the budget is adjusted for these changes. Of course, if income is static or falling, and costs are rising, then further adjustments will have to be made. Some elements may need to be reduced – for example, it may be decided to close a hostel, or to make some staff *redundant* (in which case, redundancy costs will have to be taken into account).

(ii) Planning Programming Budgeting Systems (PPBS)

This approach is particularly relevant for capital budgeting, because it focuses on the objectives of the organisation, and identifies alternative ways of meeting these objectives. For example, the objective of providing 200 new dwellings may be met through a number of different possible programmes. The costs of each of the programme elements are identified, and compared to their possible benefits – the expected output. This enables the organisation to allocate capital resources between different programmes effectively. However, in practice, it is a difficult approach to implement, firstly because the objectives of organisations are usually complex and difficult to define precisely, and secondly, because the outputs from services (such as housing) may be difficult to measure.

(iii) Zero-based budgeting

This approach starts with the assumption that *nothing is essential*. Each element of cost is identified and compared to the benefits that it provides. This is useful where alternative levels of provision are possible for each function, since it makes explicit the benefits and costs of each alternative. Alternatives are identified as decision packages, and are assessed against stated criteria – for example, the need for the activity (is it a statutory requirement?), its political acceptability, and its contribution to the organisation's objectives. The decision packages are then ranked in priority order, and resources allocated to agreed budget levels (i.e. the anticipated capital or revenue funds).

The advantage of this approach is that it focuses attention on *value for money*, and develops a questioning attitude in the organisation – is this activity *really* necessary? However, it is also very time consuming, and may require a large amount of *subjective* assessments, permitting decision-makers to favour 'pet' interests.

Budgetary control

Having *set* the budgets – i.e. set out anticipated income and expenditure, and ensured that they balance (are equal) – the budget manager(s) must ensure that each budget is monitored regularly. Responsibility will vary, depending on the 'level' at which the budget is set. For example, the treasurer/finance director is responsible for the whole of a local authority's budget, and must maintain regular checks to ensure that overall spending is constrained within budget limits. A number of local authorities operate decentralised budgets, which permit particular managers (on an estate or in an area office) to control their own budgets. These will have to be monitored regularly, not just by the managers responsible, but also by their managers.

If it seems that a budget is danger of becoming overspent, then urgent action must be taken to adjust planned expenditure so that it remains on target; if this is not possible (for example, if storm damage has resulted in much higher than expected expenditure on repairs), then the 'higher' level of management control needs to be alerted, so that other budgets can be adjusted.

Perverse incentives?

While budgets must be monitored with the intention of ensuring there is no overspend, the goal is not necessarily to spend less than the amount allocated; particularly in the case of capital projects (with credit allocations from the government), anything unspent is 'lost'. Similarly, an area manager who spends less than the revenue budget allocation may find the office budget cut in the next year, particularly if the incremental approach to budgeting is adopted.

Far from ensuring that money is spent sensibly, this will provide a perverse incentive to spend any excess money urgently, and possibly wastefully, before the end of the budget period. Any system of budgeting that penalises saving in this way will virtually guarantee waste.

Financial controls

These are procedures for the effective monitoring and control of incomes and expenditures. For example, all expenditure should be authorised by the budget holder (or delegated person), following strictly defined procdures. These procedures might include, for example:

- a form to complete, in advance, to request expenditure;
- a defined process for ordering goods and services for the organisation;
- accurate recording of the receipt of all sources of income (such as cash and cheques).

These controls are crucial to ensure adequate accountability for all spending (which is essential for any organisation which is wholly or partially funded from public funds) as well as to reduce the risk of fraud by employees.

4.2: Management accounts

Management accounts provide information about actual income and expenditure compared to planned income and expenditure. They are prepared, as their name suggests, to enable management to actively monitor the financial state of the organisation. In a social housing context, these accounts will be monitored by the board of directors or housing committee.

Where variations from budget are identified, the management accounts will provide an explanation of the reasons for the deviations, and will indicate the steps which are being (or have been) taken to correct any over or underspend. This information is often provided monthly, or at least quarterly. It is usual also for management accounts to make comparisons with previous income and spending periods, so that the third quarter of this financial year, for example, may be compared to the same quarter last year. This enables management to pick up on any worrying trends over time and take steps to address them.

4.3: Cash flow forecasts

It may not be sufficient simply to monitor overall spending to ensure that it remains within budget: particularly in the case of a housing association, budgets may need to be monitored to ensure that *at any one time* it does not spend more than the resources available – the *cash flow* into the organisation must be monitored.

If there are expected to be insufficient receipts to cover payments in a particular time period, the organisation will need to decide whether it can:

- delay some payments, until the cash flow situation improves;
- obtain temporary finance to cover the shortfall; this is much easier for a local authority;
- permanently reduce some planned spending.

For capital projects, it is particularly important that an RSL monitors its cash flow, because the amounts involved are potentially very large. Usually, they will undertake a cash flow analysis, which sets out anticipated payments and receipts in each time period (e.g. each month). The building contractor may need to receive regular payments for work completed (called interim payments, and examined in Chapter 5), but income may not be received until much later, since HAG/SHG is paid at much less regular stages, called tranches.

Having completed the cash flow analysis, the association may find it has to delay some activity – such as the start date for a particular project – in order to ensure that sufficient funds remain in the capital account each month; or, it may arrange additional, temporary borrowing. Any association which fails to do this risks bankruptcy, if it tries to spend more than the resources it currently has available.

This contrasts with the situation for a local authority housing department, which does not have to concern itself in the same way with 'day-to-day' sources of funding for expenditure. The treasurer/finance director is responsible for monitoring the cash flow for the whole authority, and has access to short-term borrowing to accommodate any short-term deficiencies. The main concern is that, over the financial year, the budget for the whole authority is balanced.

4.4: Annual accounts and financial statements

Every organisation must produce annual accounts, which summarise key financial transactions over each financial year. These are, for most organisations, a statutory (legal) requirement, but are also needed by (if appropriate) shareholders and various other stakeholders.

The annual accounts comprise two main financial statements:

- *the income and expenditure account*, which records the main sources of incomes and expenditures over the year;
- *the balance sheet*, which is a statement of assets and liabilities and how these have changed over the year.

Assets may be:

a) fixed, which last for a long time, such as the housing stock, or
b) current, which have a much shorter life – for example, bank deposits and debtors (people and organisations which owe money to the organisation, such as tenant rent arrears).

Liabilities include both longer-term loans from financial instuitutions and shorter-term debts owed to creditors (such as suppliers, which the organisation has not yet paid for goods or services).

4.5: Treasury management

This refers to the active management of all capital and money market (revenue) transactions to minimise both costs and risks to the organisation and to maximise incomes. It requires the active identification and evaluation of financial risks, so that steps can be taken, whenever possible, to reduce and control those risks. Some risks can be insured against, but many others cannot. Especially for a housing association, excessive risk is to be avoided because of the potentially catastrophic effects for the organisation (such as insolvency – going bankrupt) should the worst happen.

Actions might vary from trying to find better rates of interest for savings, or negotatiating a better deal from the bank for an overdraft, to re-financing the whole of the organisation's debts.

Re-financing

As part of their strategies for managing their assets efficiently, it has been common for housing associations to periodically review their borrowing to see if cheaper deals can be found. This is especially likely during periods when interest rates are falling, so more expensive loans are swapped for cheaper rates. Often, this will be part of a wider deal, to cover future borrowing needs as well as switching past debts. For example, during 2008, Circle Anglia secured an £800 million re-financing deal as part of a £1.7 billion package of borrowing (*Inside Housing*, 11 April 2008, p11). However, as a result of the 'credit crunch' early in 2008 – a situation in which more limited funds were available through UK financial institutions, as a result, partly, of poor lending decisions, especially by US banks – it is predicted that favourable re-financing deals will be much harder to secure in the next year or two. Already, some lenders have indicated an unwillingness to lend to housing associations in future, and others have pared down the available funds. This is an evolving situation which will need to be monitored.

5. Financial subsidy for housing customers

5.1: Subsidy for tenants

(i) Housing benefit

Housing benefit (HB) is the main personal housing subsidy payable to tenants, whether in the social or private sectors. It is a *means-tested* subsidy, so applicants must have relatively low incomes to qualify. The present HB scheme was introduced in 1988, following a rationalisation of the means test requirements for different types of benefit. It forms part of the social security budget and is administered by local authorities on behalf of the Department for Work and Pensions (DWP).

Generally, anyone entitled to housing benefit is also likely to be entitled to council tax benefit (CTB) – a reduction in the amount of tax payable to the local authority for local services – but this is also available to low-income owner-occupiers.

As the government pursued a policy of pushing up rents in the social sector during the 1990s, housing benefit was intended to 'take the strain' for low-income households – which resulted in a rapidly rising subsidy bill. In the private sector also, the abolition of rent controls, in the form of 'fair rents' for private sector tenancies from 1989, resulted in rising numbers of tenants on housing benefit as well as large increases in the amount of benefit payable. The transfer of large numbers of council properties to associations, primarily through LSVT, has also increased the cost of HB for HA tenants. These rising costs of HB are shown clearly in Table 4.6.

The allocation of housing benefit

Housing benefit 'payments' to council tenants simply reduce (or eliminate) their weekly rent, so are commonly called rent rebates. Housing association tenants receive

Table 4.6: Housing benefit costs in GB, selected years

	£ million		
Tenure	**1990-91**	**2000-01**	**2006-07**
Council	3,368	5,258	5,368
Housing association	391	3,019	5,346
Private	1,388	2,851	4,144
Total	5,147	11,128	14,858

Source: Wilcox, 2008.

actual payments – which may be paid direct to the landlord – from the local authority, and this is recorded in the General Fund (in Wales, the Council Fund). The full cost of housing benefit payments is reimbursed by government subsidy and authorities also receive an allowance as part of their subsidy entitlement towards the costs of administering HB.

As means-tested benefit, HB is expensive to administer, partly because there are so many elements to the calculation (as shown below) and any change of circumstance such as an increase in income will require a new assessment to be made. Authorities must satisfy themselves that they have sufficient evidence to verify each aspect of the claim (e.g. income, rent payable, household size etc.). In so doing, almost all authorities comply with the DWP's security guidance which advises them that claimants should provide original documents rather than copies, which can, and does in many cases result in lengthy delays in benefit payments.

Figure 4.7: Four key elements in the assessment of housing benefit

1. The household's expenditure needs

The government determines what each household reasonably needs to spend each week on essentials (excluding housing costs), and these figures are revised annually. There are two elements to this:

(i) **Personal allowances**, which relate to the household's size and age; for example, those under 25 (unless married) are given smaller allowances, couples get more than single households, and an additional amount is paid for each dependent child.

(ii) To the personal allowances are added **premiums**, to reflect the additional expenses of some household types and members; associated with age, disability or caring responsibilities, for example, families with children.

Figure 4.7: Four key elements in the assessment of housing benefit *continued*

2. Eligible housing costs ('eligible rent')
For social sector tenancies (local authority and registred social landlords) the eligible rent is, apart from exceptional cases based on the **gross rent payable**. The gross rent includes any service charges which are related to maintaining the dwelling or any communal areas, but excludes any amount which relates to household living expenses (e.g. heating and lighting which do not relate to the communal areas), personal care or support services (which are eligible for Supporting People subsidy). If there are adults living in the claimant's home (such as grown-up children, or grandparents), they are assumed to make some contribution to the rent (even if they don't). These adults are known as **non-dependants**. The assumed contribution varies with their income but the net result is a reduction in the eligible costs and therefore the amount of benefit payable.

In the private rented sector, the eligible rent is also calculated as above, but from 1996, this was subject to an overall cap (of which there are a number of different types that can be applied). The level of the cap depended on local circumstances and was determined by the rent officer. In most cases this cap was based on the **local reference rent**, but in the case of certain single claimants who were under the age of 25 the cap was restricted to the average rent payable for a room in a shared property (which is known as the **single room rent**). For most new private sector claims from April 2008, however, this series of caps is replaced by a flat rate allowance (the 'local housing allowance') which is examined in Section 5.1(ii) below. The system of rent officer caps is retained for certain anomalous cases (e.g. board and lodging).

3. Income
Since HB is means-tested, this means that the income of the household must be assessed to determine whether it is sufficient to cover both their non-housing related needs as well as their housing costs. Income includes:

(i) Earnings, pensions, benefits and any other regular or irregular earnings.
In order to provide some incentive to claimants to take employment, there is an **income disregard** i.e. a small amount of any earnings is not taken into account.

(ii) An assumed amount of interest received on capital or savings above £6,000 even if no interest is actually received. If capital exceeds £16,000, the household is ineligible for housing benefit. Note that tax credits, introduced boost the incomes of those in low-paid employment and intended to make it more worthwhile to work, increase income and hence potentially reduce HB entitlement.

4. The taper
If households have income in excess of the expenditure deemed necessary, they are expected to contribute 65 per cent of this toward their housing costs. In other words, for each £1 of income above the maximum permitted amount, the household is assumed to pay 65 pence of towards their rent. This is known as the **taper** – the rate at which benefit is withdrawn for each £1 increase in income. The severity of the taper contributes significantly to the **poverty** and **unemployment traps** – see below.

Steps in the calculation

1. Assess income

- calculate income, from wages, benefits, tax credits, pensions, etc and add assumed income from capital;
- if the claimant's income includes earnings from employment deduct from those earnings any tax and national insurance paid and then any *disregard that applies*. The actual amount of the disregard depends on the household type (single, couple, etc.), but there are also additional earnings disregards if the claimant works at least 30 hours per week and/or, in certain cases if they incur childcare costs.

2. Assess income needs

- calculate the value of relevant *personal allowances*;
- add any relevant *premiums*.

This gives the *applicable amount* of income thought to be needed by the household.

3. Calculate excess income

- If the *applicable amount* is greater than the income, then it is deducted from it to give the excess. In any other case the excess will be zero.

4. Assess eligible housing costs

- identify the *eligible rent* including any service charges;
- deduct any *non-dependant deductions* from the eligible rent that may apply.

5. Deduct 65 per cent of excess income from eligible costs

This is the entitlement to housing benefit.

Any household with an assessed income (less non-dependant deductions) which is equal to or lower than the applicable amount will be entitled to the maximum HB – i.e. 100 per cent of their eligible costs (as set out in step 4) will be paid. Other households, with excess income, may be entitled to *partial* HB – that is they will be expected to contribute an amout equal to 65 per cent of their excess (plus any ineligible housing costs) towards their rent.

Who is ineligible?

There is a wide range of exclusions. Some of the more important are:

- those with capital in excess of £16,000 (as identified above);
- full-time students, except the disabled or those with children;
- people in residential care;
- those who do not have a 'commercial arrangement', e.g. living with a close relative;

- certain migrants and recent arrivals to the UK; this includes most people who need a visa to enter the UK such as non-EU nationals, as well as asylum seekers. However, it does not exclude foreign nationals who have a permanent right of settlement in the UK, EU nationals with a right to reside (broadly, 'workers') and those whose asylum claim has been accepted.

The claims process

There are two routes into HB:

1. For tenants in receipt of a passport benefit (income-based jobseeker's allowance, income-related employment and support allowance, the guarantee credit of state pension credit or income support).

These tenants are automatically sent their claim details from the Department for Work and Pensions (DWP) to confirm. This usually results in a two-stage process, because, the local authority often requires further information to what they receive from the DWP (the 'local authority input document'). This administrative process can result in delays in HB payments. Local authority performance indicators (see Chapter 3) include 'percentage of HB claims processed within 14 days' – but this *excludes* any delay by the DWP.

2. For tenants not in receipt of a passport benefit.
They must apply directly to the local authority. The authority is responsible for producing its own HB claim forms, and while some are very good, others may be complex and very difficult for tenants to complete.

Supporting People

In order to clarify how much of any rents and charges were for non-housing elements, the government introduced this new subsidy in 2002. In broad terms, it replaced the funding of all non-housing aspects of rent charges, which were previously covered by housing benefit. As a result, housing benefit payments now cover only the cost of the housing service (providing and maintaining the properties).

Problems of the present HB system

The housing benefit system creates a wide number of disincentives, for the administrators of the system, for claimants, and for the government. These include:

Complexity

Housing benefit entitlement is very complicated and difficult to understand, and (partly because it is means-tested, requiring checking of evidence) complex to administer. This results in delays in administration, and problems for claimants while they are waiting for their claim to be determined.

Disincentive to work

This arises because of the operation of the *poverty and unemployment* traps. When income rises, whether by taking a job (and leaving unemployment), or taking a better-paid job, the combined effects of withdrawal of benefit, tax credits and extra taxes can leave the household little better-off. Although the HB taper is 65 per cent, the overall withdrawal rate can be much greater when combined with the withdrawal of council tax benefit and working/and or child tax credits. In recent years, the numbers of claimants caught by the very highest rates of withdrawal have been considerably reduced by the introduction of tax credits. In many cases, these have been sufficient to boost the incomes of working families to such an extent that they no longer qualify for HB and as such are not subject to its very high withdrawal rate. However, there is still a residual problem for those households who qualify for both HB and tax credits and those who do not qualify for tax credits at all and so remain dependent on HB.

The effects of rising rents on work incentives

The disincentive to work provided by HB has been considerably worsened by rising levels of rent in all tenures. Table 4.7 shows that the main effect of rising rents is to considerably extend the *breadth* of the poverty trap. This arises because, for those on full HB, all of any increase in rent is paid by HB. Rising rents simply expand the amount of household costs paid by the benefit system, so that the wage that has to be earned before the household escapes the 'traps' rises with every rent increase.

Table 4.7: The poverty trap: gross weekly earnings at which housing benefit entitlement ceases (selected households and rent levels)

Household type	Rent levels			
	£60	£80	£100	£120
Single person >25	£179	£245	£291	£336
Lone parent, 2 children	£110	£199	£301	£404
Couple, 2 children	£155	£264	£366	£469

Source: Wilcox, 2008.

Disincentive to economise

Since housing benefit pays the full cost of rent increases, it has been suggested that this provides a disincentive to *economise* on housing – i.e. it encourages households to take (or remain in) accommodation which is too expensive and/or too large for their needs. In addition, the removal of rent controls in the private sector may have permitted some private landlords to charge exploitative rents, and the availability of HB has enabled tenants readily to accept these inflated rents. It was also possible for claimants to move to properties which were larger than they needed, at the luxury end of the market or in more expensive areas. This led to the introduction of a number of different rent caps set by rent officers which included the *local reference rent*, or in the case of single claimants aged under 25, the single room rent which effectively restricted the amount of HB payable for private sector claims. These local reference rents are based on the average rent for the local area, related to the appropriate property size for the household. The single room rent is based on the average rent for a single room in a shared house. However, except for certain exceptional cases these rent caps have now been replaced by the local housing allowance for new private sector claimants – see below.

The high costs of housing benefit

As can be seen from Table 4.6, housing benefit is a costly subsidy which has been growing over time, as rents in all tenures have increased.

(ii) Local housing allowance – the reform of housing benefit for private tenants

The government launched *Building Choice and Responsibility: a radical agenda for housing benefit* in October 2002 (ODPM, 2002d). Its objectives were to:

- reduce barriers to work;
- ensure that people on low incomes can afford a decent home that meets their needs;
- give tenants more choice;
- extend tenants personal responsibility for paying their rent;
- provide a better, quicker service, based on simpler, clearer rules;
- make fraud more difficult.

From 2003-04, the government introduced a pilot scheme in nine local authorities (called pathfinder authorities) for private sector tenants, in which the eligible housing costs were based on a flat rate standard local (i.e. specific to each locality) housing allowance (LHA) for each size of home, rather than the actual rent charged. The LHA amount was modelled on a slightly modified form of the local reference rent. From April 2005, a further nine local authorities (called the second wave group – 2WG) joined the pilot, covering England, Scotland and Wales. As a result, HB for nearly all new private sector claimants is based on a LHA from April 2008, and is discussed below.

In order to achieve the above objectives, key features of this revised HB system are:

- the country is divided into *broad rental market areas* (BRMA), which are 'localities' for the purposes of determining the appropriate rent level;
- a series of LHAs (one for each appropriate size of property) is set, at the median rent for each size of home in the BRMA.

This means that claimants know clearly, in advance, how much rent they are entitled to claim for their given household size in that BRMA. The determination of 'eligible rent' for claimants is also much simpler and quicker for the local authority, and if the claimant moves within the BRMA, the assessment will not change.

In October 2007, the Rent Service reviewed the definition of its localities for the purposes of identifying BRMAs, which resulted in some boundary changes. In some cases, this increased the median rents but in others, they were reduced. However, a later challenge in the House of Lords to the definition of a BRMA in Sheffield was upheld (in July 2008), resulting in the 'Neuberger Principles', which has caused the Rent Service to re-examine its definitions. Essentially, the Lords decided that a BRMA must include as few neighbourhoods as possible, to avoid the median rent being distorted by an exceptionally high or low rent area being 'added in'. The Rent Service is currently reviewing all of its BRMAs, and adjusting LHAs as necessary, but this is expected to take some time.

Initially, local housing allowances were determined for all sizes of property, but, in November 2008 (as a result of a high profile case of a family in a 7 bed property in London receiving £150,000 p.a. for rent), a national cap was introduced at the 5 bed rent level.

Local housing allowances are made according to two principles:

- Payment is normally to the tenant rather than the landlord.
  This gives tenants responsibility for rent payments, and so helps them to see more clearly how much they are paying for the housing service, but also may encourage them to exercise greater choice. For vulnerable tenants, however, the local authority may decide to pay the rent directly to the landlord.
- If tenants found a property which was cheaper than their LHA, they could keep the difference, up to a maximum of £15.
  This provided a clear incentive to economise on housing and to shop around to seek better value for money, but was withdrawn in 2009.

In the longer term, the government may extend the LHA concept to the social sector, when wider reforms such as choice-based lettings (see Chapter 5) and rent restructuring (see this chapter, Section 3) have 'created the right conditions'. Clearly, until rent restructuring is complete, a change to the LHA for social tenants could cause a significant drift from (generally higher rent) housing association properties to (lower rent) local authority tenancies. At this stage, the government has not committed itself to any particular model for the social sector and has made it clear that, before it does, it would need first to be piloted.

5.2: Subsidy for owner-occupiers

While this text is primarily about affordable housing, it is important that this is viewed in the context of the financial resources made available to other tenures. It is widely accepted that owner-occupation is the tenure of choice for most households in the UK, as numerous studies have shown that most tenants aspire to move into this tenure at some future date. As a result, succesive governments have supported a range of initiatives over many years designed to assist households into owner-occupation. The most significant (and first) of these was in the form of discounts offered under the right to buy policy, which was explored in Section 1.5(i), as this was also intended to reduce the role of local authorities in social housing provision by encouraging both tenants and their homes to leave council tenure. The right to acquire is similar to right to buy, but for housing association tenants on secure tenancies (i.e. tenancies which date from before 1989, when associations did not need to borrow privately to fund development).

(i) Shared equity schemes

Shared equity schemes have been available for many years, the most common being 'conventional' shared ownership, which involved the housing association building properties for shared ownership, and rent being paid on the housing associations share of the home. More recently, in the context of rising house prices throughout the UK, as well as the inability of many households in housing need to secure affordable housing, it has been recognised that a wider range of financial assistance to buy may be appropriate. As a result, there is now a variety of schemes to assist households who cannot afford full purchase, to buy part of the property via shared ownership with a housing association.

Some of the current (in 2009) main types offered are examined below, but as this is a rapidly developing and changing policy area, readers are advised to check the main government websites for latest details.

a) Open Market HomeBuy in England offers two variants:

MyChoiceHomeBuy

This provides, in effect, a low-interest deposit, and is currently offered by eight housing associations in England. It provides a loan of up to 50 per cent of the home's value (but usually less – as low as 15 per cent). The remainder is funded by a conventional mortgage. Interest is charged monthly on this loan; initially at only 1.75 per cent, but rising annually by RPI + 1 per cent, so that it quite quickly reaches market rates. When the home is eventually sold, the housing association must be paid for its full equity share at market value.

Ownhome

This also provides a loan for a deposit, worth between 20 per cent and 40 per cent of the property's value. It is provided by Places for People, with the Co-operative Bank providing the main mortgage for the rest of the purchase cost. More generous than MyChoiceHomebuy, no interest is payable on the equity loan for five years, then 1.75 per cent fixed rate is charged for the next five years, then finally it rises to 3.75 per cent. But like the first variant, the equity share is repaid on sale at full market value.

b) Social HomeBuy in England

This permits social housing tenants, whose landlords have agreed to take part in the scheme, to buy or part-buy their exising home. The usual right to buy/acquire discount is available, but proportionate to the portion bought; as more shares are bought, further discounts are offered. The full discount is repayable if the property is sold within five years, and when sold, it must first be offered to the social landlord. It is possible through this scheme for tenants to buy 100 per cent of their property straight away, which has the distinct advantage for local authorities that they can retain all of the purchase price, unlike under right to buy (where the government takes 75 per cent for 'pooling' and redistribution to deficit councils). However, Social Homebuy has not, as yet, proved popular and sales to date have been very low.

c) Homebuy in Wales

Under this scheme, the 'deposit' loan (usually 30 per cent but possibly up to 50 per cent) is provided by a housing association. However, it is only available in those local authority areas where the local authority has agreed it is a priority, because the loans are effectively top-sliced from the SHG allocation for that authority. When the property is sold, the full market share of the equity is repaid.

d) Homestake in Scotland

This is a 'new supply' initiative, as the homes are usually built and offered by a housing association – so, it is essentially what was formerly called *conventional shared ownership*. Buyers may purchase between 60 per cent and 80 per cent share (usually with a conventional mortgage), and the association retains ownership of the remainder. When the property is sold, the housing association gets the full market share of its equity.

e) LIFT in Scotland

This is the Low cost Initiative for First Time buyers pilot, an open market shared equity scheme which is only available in selected areas with significant affordable housing problems. The buyer takes a 60-80 per cent share, with the rest funded by SHG from an RSL. No interest or rent is payable, but the full market value of the housing association's equity share must be paid back when the property is sold.

f) Co-ownership in Northern Ireland

This is an open market, conventional shared equity scheme, operated by the Northern Ireland Co-ownership Housing Association (NICHA). Potential purchasers select an open market property, and ask the NICHA to purchase a share. Rent is paid on the housing association share, with a conventional mortgage for the rest. When the property is sold, the NICHA receives full market value for its equity share.

(ii) Tax reliefs

Unlike the shared equity schemes, which target housing need, these are general subsidies, in the sense that they are available to any household, regardless of income.

As a result, they are likely to provide relatively higher levels of subsidy to the wealthiest households in the UK; but, as they are given in the form of 'tax reliefs' (which reduce the household's tax bill rather than paying a direct income supplement), the cost is not counted by the government and so largely remains hidden.

Tax reliefs include:

- Capital gains tax exemption

When most assets are sold, any gain in value (after allowing for inflation) – the capital gain – is subject to tax. In the case of the only or main dwelling of an owner-occupier, this tax is waived. This represents a significant subsidy, and is doubtless part of the reason why housing as an asset is more attractive in the UK than many other assets, such as stocks and shares. However, since this is a tax *exemption* rather than a payment, estimates of the cost of this subsidy are difficult to make or obtain, and its value will fluctuate considerably depending on the state of private housing markets and hence the numbers and values of homes sold.

Again, it should be noted that the greater the value of the property sold, the larger is the value of this tax exemption. This suggests that it is the richest who gain most, with the poorest owner-occupiers gaining relatively little in comparison.

- Exemption from schedule A income taxation

Since owner-occupiers choose to take the benefits of the value of their properties' services 'in kind' – instead of renting the homes out, to earn rent income – they used to be charged income tax on the 'imputed' (estimated) value of those services. However, this estimate was based on the rateable value of the property, which was the basis for local taxation (the 'rates'), but which had not been revised for many years, resulting in ridiculously low rental estimates. From 1963, therefore, this tax was abolished for owner-occupiers. Again, it is very difficult to assess the value of this tax exemption, because it would involve estimating the 'rental value' of all owner-occupied homes in the UK, and then making some assessment of the likely tax liability of each individual occupier (since some may have insufficient income to be eligible to pay tax in any case, and others would be liable at the highest tax rate of 40 per cent). However, we can be certain that this represents a substantial saving for many owner-occupiers, especially for those in expensive properties – suggesting that the wealthiest potentially gain most.

(iii) Mortgage subsidy: Support for Mortgage Interest (SMI) payments

This is available only to those on a means-tested passport benefit (see Section 5) who are unable to work – whether through unemployment, sickness, disability or old age. However, because it is a mortgage subsidy, it necessarily excludes large numbers of low-income owners without a mortgage – predominantly the elderly. Claimants must have assets (excluding the house) valued at no more than £8,000. A mortgage ceiling of £150,000 was introduced in 1992, reduced to £100,000 in 1994, and from October 1995, new borrowers were ineligible for any interest payments for nine months (39 weeks). The interest paid is calculated at a standard rate set at 1.58 per cent above the Bank of England base rate (regardless of what is actually paid). Despite these limitations, low-interest rates, and unemployment remaining at very low levels during the early 2000s, SMI still cost £355 million in 2005-06 (Wilcox, 2007).

For first-time buyers, whose mortgages are likely to far exceed £100,000, this level of support is clearly inadequate. However, it is the government's belief that private insurance should be taken out to cover mortgage interest for periods out of work. Many commentators have suggested that this fails to recognise that the most vulnerable mortgagors – those with insecure employment, on temporary and part-time contracts, which are increasingly common in today's 'flexible labour markets' – find insurance difficult or too expensive to obtain. In order to support some households in this situation, the Scottish Government introduced a *Mortgage to Rent Scheme*, through which an RSL buys the property – subject to valuation limits – to rent it back to the occupiers. As yet, this is not available elsewhere in the UK.

As a result of the economic downturn late in 2008, and rising unemployment, the government recognised that rapidly rising numbers of households were at risk of losing their homes through repossession. In order to permit more unemployed households to retain their homes, the chancellor announced (in November 2008) that, from April 2009, unemployed claimants are eligible for SMI after only 13 weeks, and the maximum mortgage allowable is to rise to £200,000. It is, as yet, unclear whether this is to be a permanent change or merely short term, for the duration of the economic recession.

(iv) Improvement grants

These means-tested grants are available for essential repairs to properties, to help to bring them up to acceptable standards. They include assistance with the provision of essential sanitary facilities, adequate heating, and hygienic kitchen facilities, and are available to low-income landlords as well as owner-occupiers. However, in practice, many local authorities operate a lengthy waiting list. It is, therefore, unlikely that this present system adequately addresses the problem of poor house condition in the private sector, especially in the light of expanded numbers of low-income owners (partly as a result of government policies such as the right to buy).

6. Conclusion

Changes to the financial regimes for different affordable housing providers have been used to encourage changed roles, in line with government policies. Local authorities have built very few new houses in the last two decades and have been required to work in partnership with housing associations to secure new developments. However, there were some substantial changes to the financial regimes for local authorities during the early 2000s, which promise to return greater financial control to councils, and possibly permit renewed housing development. The UK government is currently reviewing the Housing Revenue Account Subsidy system, to see whether councils could move to a new, self-financing revenue regime.

Although housing associations have taken over the main role in providing affordable housing, they do not provide anything like the quantities produced by local authorities in their heyday. This is partly as a result of the need to undertake private borrowing and bear increased risks. The recent 'credit crunch' in 2007-08 and the subsequent economic recession is threatening housing associations' abilities to deliver their planned development programmes, of both afforadable rented and homes for shared ownership.

Subsidy for tenants remains focused on the provision of means-tested housing benefit. There are a number of problems arising from this subsidy, including disincentives to economise on housing (there is no incentive to move to a smaller property as HB pays all the rent regardless) and work disincentives (it is not worth seeking work as they are likely to be scarcely any better-off – though these disincentives have been reduced for many households by the introduction of tax credits). Private sector tenants now receive a revised form of HB, the local housing allowance, which provides a fixed rate rent allowance, depending on locality and household size. This simplifies assessment, makes entitlement clearer for claimants, and promotes incentives to shop around. It is likely to be extended, in some form, to social tenants once rent restructuring has been completed.

There is currently a policy emphasis on encouraging part-ownership for those households which cannot afford the full cost of buying a home, and each government in the countries of the UK offers its own versions of shared equity schemes. However, as a result of limited mortage availability, falling house prices and the economic recession, by late 2008, there were growing problems for housing associations in finding buyers for their ownership products.

There remain also a number favourable tax reliefs for owner-occupiers, but very little help is available to subsidise their day-to-day revenue costs. For those mortgaged owners who become unemployed, however, the help available to pay their mortgage interest is rising from April 2009, and will be paid much sooner than before.

References and further reading

Ambrosi, M. (2003) 'Discounts Cut to Size', *Inside Housing*, 24 January, p1, London.

Bazlinton, C. (2008) 'Trouble at the Top', *Inside Housing*, 20 June, pp49-52, London.

Centre for Research and Market Intelligence (CRMI) (2008) *Autumn, Statistics special – the move to target rents*, Housing Corporation, London.

Chartered Institute of Housing (with National Federation of ALMOS and HouseMark) (2005) *ALMOs – a new future for council housing,* CIH, *Coventry.*

Chartered Institute of Housing/Housing Corporation (2008) *Who lives in Affordable Housing?*, CIH, Coventry.

Communities Scotland (2007) *Helping You to become a Home Owner – Homestake*, Communities Scotland, Edinburgh.

Communities Scotland (2007) *HAG Financial Appraisal*, Communities Scotland, Edinburgh.

Communities Scotland (2008) *LIFT*, Communities Scotland, Edinburgh.

Department for Communities and Local Government (2006a) *Local Authority Housing Finance: a guide to the new arrangements*, CLG, London, (re-issued version of ODPM, 2002c).

Department for Communities and Local Government (2006b) *Housing Needs Formula used to determine regional shares, 2006-07 and 2007-08*, CLG, London.

Department for Communities and Local Government (2008a) *Self financing of Council Housing Services: summary of findings of a modelling exercise*, CLG, London.

Department for Communities and Local Government (2008b) *Non HRA PFI – cost of new build social rented housing*, CLG, London.

Department for Communities and Local Government (May 2008) *Housing and Planning Statistics: Key facts*, CLG, London.

Department of the Environment, Transport and the Regions (1998) *Handling of Rent Rebates under Resource Accounting*, Consultation Paper, DETR, London.

Department for Work and Pensions (2002) *Building Choice and Responsibility: a radical agenda for housing benefit*, DWP, London.

Department for Work and Pensions (2006) *15 Months On: an interim evaluation of running the LHA in the nine Pathfinder areas*, DWP, London.

Department for Work and Pensions (2006) *Living with the LHA: claimants experiences after 15 months of the LHA in the nine Pathfinder areas*, DWP, London.

Evans, R. (2002) '£100 million fund will prop up Glasgow transfer', *Inside Housing*, 20 December p3, London.

Garnett D. and Perry, J. (2005) *Housing Finance*, CIH, Coventry.

The Guardian, 25 November 2008, 'Pre-budget report: Economy', p4, and 'Housing', p6.

The Guardian, 4 December 2008.

Hilditch, M. (2008) 'Swift Abolition of HRA on the Cards', *Inside Housing*, 15 May, London.

Homes and Communities Agency/Housing Corporation (2007) *National Affordable Housing Programme 2008-11*, Prospectus, Housing Corporation, London.

Housing Corporation (2003) *Re-inventing Investment*, Housing Corporation, London.

Housing Corporation (2005) *Rents, Rent Differentials and Service Charge for housing associations*, Housing Corporation, London.

Housing Corporation (2007) *Design and Quality Standards*, Housing Corporation, London.

Housing Corporation (2008) *National Affordable Housing Programme 2008-11 bid round*, Housing Corporation, London.

Inside Housing, 2008, 11 April, 'Thumbs up to transfer', p5, London.

Inside Housing, 2008, 11 April, 'Landlords the losers as refinancing trend dies out', p11, London.

Inside Housing, 2008, 11 April, 'Slow Progress', pp16-17, London.

Inside Housing, 2008, 25 April, 'Onwards and upwards', pp27-30, London.

Inside Housing, 2008, 6 June, 'Scots Revamp Grant rules Despite Protests', p7, London.

Jones, C. (2002) in Ambrosi, M. (2002) 'Right to Buy Owners are now the Landlords', *Inside Housing*, 13 December, p3, London.

Kiddle, C. and Banks, D. (2002) *Sector Study 20*, Housing Corporation, London.

Office of the Deputy Prime Minister (2000) *Decent Homes Standard*, ODPM, London.

Office of the Deputy Prime Minister (2002a) *Housing Revenue Account Manual*, p5, ODPM, London.

Office of the Deputy Prime Minister (2002b) *Guidance on Stock Valuation for Resource Accounting*, ODPM, London.

Office of the Deputy Prime Minister (2002c) *Local Authority Housing Finance – A Guide to the New Arrangements*, ODPM London.

Office of the Deputy Prime Minister (2002d) *Building Choice and Responsibility: a radical agenda for housing benefit*, OPDM, London.

Office of the Deputy Prime Minister (2003) *A Guide to Social Rent Reforms in the Local Authority Sector*, ODPM, London.

Stevenson, F. with Williams, N. (2007) *Sustainable Housing Design Guide for Scotland*, Communities Scotland, Edinburgh.

Welsh Assembly Government, Housing Directorate (2004) *New Proposals for Social Housing Grant Programme Distribution and Delivery*, WAG, Cardiff.

Wilcox, S. (2007) *UK Housing Review 2007-08*, CIH/BSA, Coventry and London.

Wilcox, S. (2008) *UK Housing Review 2008-09*, CIH/BSA, Coventry and London.

CHAPTER 5: How is affordable housing developed?

1. Introduction: the context of affordable housing development

Housing development may involve the provision of new dwellings, or the refurbishment/rehabilitation of existing buildings. The ability of affordable housing organisations to engage in development work is partly dependent on the policies of the central government, since subsidy is usually required to produce 'affordable' rents.

As identified in earlier chapters, the emphasis of government policy since the 1980s has been on local authorities as *enablers* of affordable housing development, rather than as providers. Housing associations were encouraged (by the 1988 Housing Act) to take over the main role of developing and refurbishing affordable housing from local authorities, initially via a large expansion in subsidy via Housing Association Grant (HAG) from the government. However, subsidy quickly declined, and housing associations were encouraged to depend more on private finance, mainly borrowed from banks and building societies.

With the introduction of 'prudential borrowing' rules for councils in England (see Chapter 4) from 2004, followed by the 2007 Housing green paper, it has become possible for some English local authorities, as well as a few high performing ALMOs, to build limited quantities of new housing. Nevertheless, this is not likely to result in any significant new build by local authorities, and housing associations seem likely to remain the main providers of *new* social housing in all parts of Britain – though still in much smaller quantities than their local authority predecessors, as Tables 5.1 and 5.2 show.

Table 5.1: Housing completions by local authorities (the Housing Executive in Northern Ireland)

	1970	1980	1990	2000	2007
England	118,943	67,337	13,873	87	345
Wales	6,513	3,493	610	17	0
Scotland	31,570	6,167	1,046	95	28
N. Ireland	7,692	2,507	1,299	77	0

Source: Wilcox, 2008.

Table 5.2: Housing completions by housing associations

	1970	1980	1990	2000	2007
England	8,176	19,299	13,821	16,681	22,014
Wales	73	917	1,685	958	405
Scotland	244	881	1,963	3,440	3,330
N. Ireland	18	325	442	915	606

Source: Wilcox, 2008.

This chapter aims first to describe the main features of the process of developing or rehabilitating affordable housing schemes, whether by a housing association or a local authority. Traditionally, this involved the housing organisation leading the process of development as the client organisation, and assembling (or using 'in-house') specialist consultants to advise and produce the design. The contracting company, the builders, are often only employed after this stage. The chapter aims to provide an overview of the process, to promote an awareness of its essential features, so that the potential advantages of, as well as possible problems generated by, this traditional approach can be better understood. A number of alternative 'short cut' approaches are also compared, including the 'partnering' approach first advocated in the Egan Report, *Rethinking Construction* (1998). The repair and maintenance of social housing, which involves revenue rather than capital spending (see Chapter 4 for an explanation of this distinction), is examined in Chapter 6.

It should also be recognised that it is possible for housing organisations to acquire additional properties in other ways, such as by buying existing properties on the open market from a private developer, or from a local authority (e.g. via a LSVT), or by leasing (a form of long-term renting) from private sector landlords. Indeed, as a result of the 'credit crunch' in 2008, when private developers found that they could not sell recently constructed homes, the government made available £200 million from the National Affordable Housing Programme in England (see Chapter 4) to enable housing associations to buy new market-sale properties. This was partly to ensure that new properties continued to be added to the affordable housing stock, despite the decline in new build by developers in this more risky financial climate, but also to limit the possibility of large-scale discounting by developers, which could have provoked a more dramatic decline in average private house prices and further destabilised a fragile housing market. However, not all associations view this as an appropriate way to acquire new affordable housing, as the housing association will not have been able to influence the design quality of these pre-constructed homes (see disadvantages of 'package deals' later in Section 6.1(b). Also, these private sector properties will not have been built to the current sustainability standards for affordable housing, under the Code for Sustainable Homes (see Section 5.2, on design standards), so will not be as environmentally sustainable as purpose-built affordable housing.

The housing development process includes all the activities, which are necessary to achieve the construction of a new housing scheme or the refurbishment of existing dwellings. The stage with which everyone is familiar, when construction work actually begins on site, occurs only relatively late in a lengthy process. Many separate issues first have to be resolved by the housing organisation, and most of these decisions will require the advice and assistance of a number of other parties, with different skills and areas of expertise. The next section identifies and briefly describes the main people with important roles in the traditional approach to the process. Their specific responsibilities at each stage will become clear in later sections, as the process itself is examined.

2. The main parties in the traditional development process

Most of these are employed by, or contracted by, the housing organisation, and so work directly for it, but a number of other (often statutory) roles have importance for successful housing development.

2.1: Parties employed or controlled by the housing organisation

The *client* requires the development, initiates the process and pays for the design and construction.

This may be a person or organisation. The client must ensure that everyone involved in the scheme's design and construction is very clear about the requirements for the scheme, by setting them out in a number of clearly defined ways – which are examined as the process unfolds. One or two people, sometimes employed in a separate development section and known as the client's representatives usually represent housing organisations in this role.

The client employs a number of professionals to direct and manage the development process. Some large affordable housing organisations may have a number of their own 'in-house' consultants, able to provide all, or most of, the specialised roles. Many others will undertake insufficient development work for it to be worthwhile to employ specialist skills internally, so they will need to employ external specialists.

The *consultant* generally designs the development and oversees its construction.

This person (or persons) is most often an *architect*, who has detailed knowledge of both house and estate design, so can advise on the best solutions to development problems and issues. When the development is a rehabilitation project, a *building surveyor* will usually be involved with the architect, or may replace the architect in the consulting role. This is because building surveyors have detailed knowledge of existing buildings – both of their design, and of the sorts of problems which arise from this. Building surveyors are also employed by affordable housing organisations to inspect property which needs repair, so will often work with housing managers engaged in maintenance work. This is examined in Chapter 6 on managing affordable housing.

The *quantity surveyor* (QS) is the client's cost consultant, responsible for costing the design initially, as well as assessing the value of work completed as the building progresses.

The QS costs the designs prepared by the main consultant, ensures that *value for money* is being obtained, and later, values the construction work as it progresses in order to permit payments to be made to the contractor. Although the QS will have to work closely with the architect, they must be appointed separately by the client, because the QS checks that the architect's design is within the organisation's cost limits and/or offers good value for money. For rehabilitation projects, the building surveyor will usually also undertake the QS role.

Other *consultants* may be necessary for some projects.

For example, where there are difficult site conditions, such as old mine workings, a *civil or structural engineer* may be engaged to undertake detailed examination of the site and advise on the design of the buildings' foundations. This professional can also advise on buildings which have special structural requirements, such as high rise flats. *Electrical, mechanical or building services' engineers* may be needed when there are additional requirements, such as lifts or communal heating systems; *landscape architects* specialise in the external areas of an estate; and *highways' engineers* can resolve complex road layout or access difficulties. Generally, the main consultant will advise when any of these are necessary.

The *contractor* is the organisation which undertakes the construction work.

Sometimes, in the case of a local authority, the contractor appointed will be the in-house 'direct works' section, but in most circumstances, an outside contractor – a construction company – will be engaged. It is important that the client and consultant maintain good communications with the contractor, in order to ensure that the work is of the right quality and is completed on time.

The *site agent* is the contractor's main representative on site, and oversees the day-to-day operation of the building work.

The site agent supervises and co-ordinates the work of all of the different skill workers, such as bricklayers, joiners, plumbers, electricians etc., to ensure that work progresses in the most efficient way.

***Sub-contractors* may be engaged to undertake some aspects of the work under the direction of the main contractor.**

The client may 'nominate' these, which means specifically identify them and require their use. This would generally only occur where highly specialised skills are required, which are not widely available. Alternatively, and most commonly, the contractors themselves may engage sub-contractors, because they have greater expertise in some field. In either case, they all operate under the direction of the lead contractor.

The *clerk of works* closely supervises the construction work on behalf of the client.

Once the construction work is underway, it is overseen by the consultant, but seldom on a day-to-day basis. For this reason, most projects will have a clerk of works, who is employed on the site to work closely with the consultant to ensure that what is built is exactly what is required by the architect's design. This role is particularly important for a refurbishment project, because, very often, new and unforeseen problems emerge once the work begins. A poor standard of work may result, unless closely monitored.

The *dutyholders* share responsibility for meeting all requirements relating to health and safety matters for a scheme, and there must be a designated *CDM co-ordinator* and *principal contractor*.

These roles, required by the Construction (Design and Management) Regulations 2007 (CDM) – which were first introduced from 31 March 1995 – are an attempt to reduce unacceptably high accident and fatality rates on construction sites. The 'dutyholders' include Clients, Consultants and Contractors, whose duties are to ensure that there are adequate health and safety controls at all stages of the development process. The client must appoint a *CDM co-ordinator* to advise on all projects, and the designated *principal contractor* must plan, manage and co-ordinate health and safety during construction, on all projects which last more than 30 days or involve 500 person days of construction work. However, the 'dutyholders' include everyone involved on the site, including sub-contractors and the workers themselves, who are required to be aware of risks and to co-operate to reduce them.

***Solicitors* are employed to advise on legal aspects and draw up contracts.**

In general, a solicitor will be needed to complete the purchase of a site or buildings, and to draw up any contracts, which specify the conditions under which the client is employing the different parties. This helps to ensure that the client has *legal redress* – can go to court for compensation – in the event of a party failing to perform adequately.

2.2: Roles outside the direct control of the housing organisation

In addition to the parties employed directly by the housing organisation, there are a number of other people whose roles are important to development. Most are public sector employees with specific statutory responsibilities – i.e. they have some obligations by law for aspects of the development process. The role of the Health and Safety Executive has already been identified, in overseeing matters affecting the safety of the public and employees whilst construction work is continuing.

Development control, exercised by the *planning authorities*, is intended to ensure that the quality of the physical environment is maintained and protected from inappropriate developments, and that new buildings, or significant changes to existing buildings, fit in with the local area.

The planning authorities are, in general, local authorities. The planning process is overseen by the government, and an important function of the planning system is to ensure that there is an adequate supply of land for housing (as well as other uses), together with the necessary supporting infrastructure.

The planning authorities are required to create spatial plans, which broadly set out where development may take place (and where it may not, such as in *green belts*) and proposed land uses (e.g. commercial, residential, industrial, or recreational) in their areas. Since devolved governments were created in different parts of the UK, although the broad principles and aims remain similar, these spatial plans and processes are now rather different in detail in each country, so, some key features of each are next examined.

Regional Spatial Strategies and Local Development Frameworks in England

The Planning and Compulsory Purchase Act 2004 provides the framework for English spatial planning, and Planning Policy Statement 12 (CLG, 2008a) provides the most recent guidance on the government's requirements. As might be anticipated, this places particular emphasis on the creation and continuance of sustainable communities.

The Regional Assemblies in England produce *Regional Spatial Strategies (RSS)* – (called the *Spatial Development Strategy* in London, and produced by the Mayor's office) – and, in the light of the regional strategy, the district or county planning authorities develop *Local Development Frameworks (LDFs)*, which indicate how these requirements are to be met. There are a number of components to LDFs, though some elements are optional, and these are briefly examined in Figure 5.1.

Local Development Plans in Wales

The Welsh Assembly Government set out its land use policies in *Planning Policy Wales* (PPW) in 2002, and this is supplemented by Technical Advice Notes (TANs). The

Figure 5.1: Components of Local Development Frameworks in England

1. **Development Plan Documents** (DPDs), which comprise:
(i) *a core strategy*, which sets out the overall vision and objectives;
(ii) *site specific allocations*, which indicates the allocation of land for different uses;
(iii) *an adopted proposals map*, which illustrates (ii) on a map of the area;
(iv) *area action plans*, which are optional and are for areas where large changes are planned, such as regeneration projects;
(v) *other development plan documents*, which are also optional, and which can expand on the detail for particular themes (such as housing).

2. **Local Development Scheme**, which is, in effect, a project/action plan for the creation of the planning documents and which indicates the status of the policies.

3. **Statement of Community Involvement**, which indicates the plans for public consultation (with communities and other stakeholders) on the draft plans.

4. **Annual Monitoring Report**, which assesses the progress and effectiveness of the plans and indicates any planned adjustments, and is submitted annually to the government.

5. **Supplementary Planning Documents**, which are optional and can add details to policies, such as design guides or issue-based documents.

6. **Local Development Orders** (which extend permitted rights) and **Simplified Planning Zones** (which simplify the planning approval process to encourage development in selected areas) may also optionally be added.

These separate elements are updated as necessary.

Sources: Planning Policy Statement 12, CLG, 2008a.
Guide to Local Development Frameworks, accessed from: www.planningportal.gov.uk

local planning authorities must create Local Development Plans (LDPs) in several stages, which are explored in Figure 5.2.

Structure plans and Local plans in Scotland

The planning system in Scotland has two key elements, both of which must be developed in consultation with local communities and other stakeholders:

(i) Structure plan

This may be prepared by one or more councils, and it takes a strategic (long-term) view of the developments that are needed in that area. This will identify priorities and, in broad terms, where these developments should be located, and must be approved by the Scottish Government.

(ii) Local plan

This provides more detailed policies and proposals for specific localities, and must conform to the broad priorities in the structure plan.

Figure 5.2: Stages in Local Development Planning in Wales

1. Pre-deposit stage
including:
– A delivery agreement, which includes a timetable for producing the plans and a community involvement scheme.
– A sustainability appraisal report, to indicate the factual basis for the plan – Pre-deposit local development plan documents, indicating the proposed overall strategy and objectives.

2. Deposit stage
The Deposit Local Development Plan is created following a six week consultation period, and is the full draft of the LDP. Comments (called 'representations') are invited from stakeholders, and a further consultation period begins.

3. Examination stage
Once the consultation phase is complete, the plans and representations are examined by an inspector (of the Welsh Assembly Government Planning Inspectorate), and an 'inspector's report' is produced. The local planning authority is required to make all changes recommended in this report.

4. Adoption stage
Once the plans has been amended to reflect the inspector's recommendations, it is published as the Adopted Local Development Plan.

5. Monitoring and review
An annual monitoring report is sent to the Welsh Assembly Government, and, at least every four years, there is a major review of the LDP, which begins the whole process again (at pre-deposit stage).

Source: Planning Policy Wales, 2002, and PPW Companion Guide, 2006, accessed from: www.wales.gov.uk

Spatial planning in Northern Ireland

The Regional Development Strategy (RDS) provides the planning guidelines for development plans up to 2025. It includes a Spatial Development Strategy and related Strategic Planning Guidelines. As in England, this is supplemented by Planning Policy Statements (PPSs).

Development Plans are devised by the Planning Service, an agency of the Department of the Environment, and apply the RDS at local or area level. These require the involvement of local communities, and the plans are monitored regularly, and updated as necessary, by the Planning Service.

***Planning officers* are generally responsible for drawing up the spatial plans and recommending whether planning applications, relating to the types and location of buildings and the use of land, should be approved.**

In most cases (see planning systems, above), a committee of the local authority is responsible for granting approval for development, but this is advised by its professional officers. A development scheme is likely to attract *planning consent* if it conforms to the local spatial plans. This is intended to ensure that:

- The interests of other occupiers in the locality are protected. So, planning approval is needed for the construction of new buildings, most changes of the use of a building (e.g. from a residential use to an estate office), and for some extensions. Neighbours have the opportunity to object to any plans, before the council considers them.
- The visual appearance and environmental quality of an area is protected.

This may result in special conditions being attached to the consent, such as a requirement to use particular types of building materials, in keeping with other properties in the locality. Some sites may have specific planning requirements; for example, old trees may be protected by *tree preservation orders*, and the plans will have to include measures to protect these trees during construction work. Some buildings are *listed*, as being of special architectural interest. There are strict limitations on the extent to which such buildings can be altered by construction activity. In rural areas, where it may be difficult for local people to access housing, local authorities may require, as a condition of planning consent, that only those who live or work in the area may rent or buy. In England, it is possible to negotiate a section 106 (of the Planning and Compulsory Purchase Act, 2004) agreement, which can require additional benefits for the local community as a condition of granting planning permission – for example, a proportion of affordable housing alongside market sale developments, or the provision of various social infrastructure projects.

In addition to controlling the location and types of construction work, local authorities have a duty to oversee standards of construction. These are governed by the *building regulations*.

***Building inspectors* are responsible for checking that standards of construction conform to the *building regulations*.**

The building regulations control the quality and standards of building construction in the UK, primarily to ensure that buildings are safely constructed, but also to promote government policies, such as high levels of insulation for energy efficiency purposes. Building regulations' approval must be obtained before any work can commence. These requirements are revised on a fairly regular basis, and the government introduced a new *Code for Sustainable Homes* (CLG, 2006), which will be incorporated into the English and Welsh regulations. This is examined later in Section 5.2.

In addition to the initial approval of the development plans, a local authority building inspector (or other authorised person, such as a representative of the National House Builders Council) must check the progress of construction at various stages, to ensure compliance with the regulations, before the next stage can commence.

Other public sector officers, such as the fire service or police, may also provide advice.

The need for their services will vary depending on the nature of the development project. For example, properties which are intended for multiple occupation, such as flats, need to be approved by the fire service, which will consider issues such as access and escape routes. This is to ensure that there are adequate, safe exits in the event of fire, and that suitable measures are taken to deter the spread of fire, such as fire-resistant doors to hallways. The police may advise on security measures, such as door and window locks or alarms, under the *Secured by Design* scheme, as well as on the use of video surveillance (CCTV) equipment.

3. The main stages in the traditional process

There are a number of different stages in the traditional process of developing a housing scheme. These can be classified in a variety of ways, but it is useful to conceive of three main, (largely) sequential phases. The boxes provide a brief summary of what takes place at each stage, and subsequent sections examine each stage in some detail.

Stage 1: Initiating the development
The first stage includes all of the activities which need to be undertaken before there is a firm decision to go ahead with the project. This involves a consideration of the need for housing in the locality, whether the development is likely to be *sustainable*, and identifying exactly *what is required* of the development. Next, (for new build only), identifying and assessing potential sites and then establishing the feasibility (in cost terms) of schemes. The consulting architect (or building surveyor) always becomes involved during this phase, but, in addition, key housing managers, social services, the police, employment services, health authority etc., may provide advice in any sustainability assessment. It is also necessary, at this stage, to ensure that adequate funding is available, whether wholly borrowed from financial institutions, or partly from public subsidy and/or the organisation's financial reserves.

Stage 2: Detailed design
This includes all of the activities which contribute to the final detailed plans for the project, generally produced by the consultant and guided by a briefing from the client. This stage will determine whether the organisation achieves the sort of new development or refurbishment that it requires, because the outcome is the final design which will be constructed. Of course, sustainability – whether environmental, social or economic – needs to be at the core of the design, to ensure that all developments produce sustainable homes in sustainable communities.

Stage 3: Constructing the development
This final stage is concerned with getting the project built. The client must first appoint a contractor to undertake the work, and there are several possible approaches to this. The consultant oversees the process of constructing the properties, with close supervision provided on site by the clerk of works.

There are some approaches which provide 'short cuts' through the traditional development process, by assigning some or all of the design stage to the contractor, and these are explored at the beginning of Stage 3. More recent partnering approaches are also examined. However, the key tasks in achieving a housing development remain basically the same; it is a question more of who is responsible for, and involved in undertaking, these tasks, at each stage.

4. Stage 1: Initiating development

This is a critical stage, because key decisions will be taken which will have important implications for the success (or otherwise) of the outcomes. This stage will determine whether any development is undertaken at all, and if so, the type and location. Key questions are, therefore:

1. What type of development is needed?
2. For new schemes, how can we identify a suitable site?
3. Is the development likely to be sustainable?
4. Will planning permission be given for the development?
5. Is the development feasible?
6. Can the development be financed?
7. How do we consult with the local community?
8. How do we acquire the site?

Subsequent sections address each of these key questions in turn.

4.1: Type of development needed

The affordable housing organisation should have clear ideas about the sorts of housing needs which it wants to develop housing for. These local needs are identified in each local authority's housing strategy, which have titles which vary in different parts of the UK:

- the Housing Strategy and Housing Investment Programme (HIP) in England;
- the Strategic Housing Investment Plan (SHIP) in Scotland;
- the Housing Strategy and Operational Programme in Wales;
- the Annual Housing Strategy (of the NIHE) in Northern Ireland.

These include data from housing associations in the area, and involve a systematic and comprehensive needs assessment, as well as an assessment of the local housing market. This helps to ensure that the organisation can be confident, before continuing with any development plans, that a need – and hence likely demand – exists. In addition, public subsidy for development – such as Housing Association Grant (HAG) and Social Housing Grant (SHG), explored in Chapter 4 – may be contingent on targeting specific key objectives in that locality, so care should be taken to conform with the relevant funding bodies' stated priorities.

In the past, local authorities built predominantly for general (family) needs, so they produced largely two and three bedroom houses. Due mainly to land constraints, most urban authorities also built flats, and, during the late fifties and sixties, many were encouraged (though the government's subsidy policies) to build high-rise homes for families (with very mixed success). Since local authorities concentrated largely on housing families, a number of housing associations were started with the aim of meeting more specialised needs, such as homes for the elderly, or for young single people. This resulted in a much higher proportion of flats being constructed in the housing association sector. Nowadays, housing associations have largely taken over the role of producing new homes for general needs, as well as continuing to provide homes for other needs groups. Meanwhile, substantial numbers of (largely) houses have been lost from the LA sector through right to buy. In addition, the *large scale voluntary transfer* (LSVT) of some local authority properties to housing associations has added significant numbers of houses to housing association stock. The proportions of houses in the housing association sector have increased significantly as a result, while the relative proportions of houses in the LA sector have been falling, so that, as Table 5.3 shows, the property profiles in both sectors are now quite similar.

Table 5.3: Property types in social tenures, Great Britain, 2006
(Percentages of households)

	Local authority	Housing association
Houses:		
Detached	1	1
Semi-detached	24	19
Terraced	28	34
All houses	54	54
Flats:		
Purpose-built	45	41
Converted	1	5
All flats	46	46

Source: Wilcox, 2008.

Recent government planning guidance, in recognising that the availability of land is a key constraint in many areas, has emphasised the need to increase the housing density (homes per hectare) of new developments, which has resulted in relatively more flats being constructed.

Of course, if there are existing properties which are to be refurbished, these will often have existing tenants, who will wish to return to their refurbished homes. In this event, there is a specific need to consult the current tenant about the proposed refurbishment. If, however, the properties are empty, then a decision will have to be taken about the need which they will meet, because this will affect the design requirements.

4.2: Identifying a suitable site

For a new build scheme, having identified the type of development needed and where, the process then moves to identifying an appropriate site; clearly, for rehabilitation projects, the site already exists. Sites for new build may be either *greenfield*, meaning a site that has not previously been built on; or *brownfield*, which is a site that has been built on before and may still have buildings which require demolition. In an attempt both to conserve open space and to encourage the revitalisation of (mainly) urban areas, the government has set targets for the proportions of new developments which must occupy brownfield sites. However, in general, brownfield sites are more expensive to build on, so tend to be less desired for development.

(i) Finding a site

There are many different possible sources of information about sites. The main ones include:

- Individual landowners, who may be a particularly important source in rural areas, where the local authority may be prepared to grant *exceptional* planning permission for a social housing scheme on a greenfield site.
- Estate agents, who sell development sites on behalf of owners in most areas.
- Development or construction companies, who may have land which is surplus to their requirements. This is most common when the market for speculative, owner-occupied dwellings is slow, so the contractors may be unwilling to risk building on their own account. In return for making the land available, however, they will often require that the contract to construct the properties is placed with them.
- Local authorities, who will have identified possible development sites in their area as part of their local spatial plans, examined earlier (in Section 2). It is increasingly common for local authorities to make land available to housing associations at low (or zero) prices in return for *nomination rights* over a

certain percentage of lettings, often 50 per cent to 100 per cent. This is the right to nominate new tenants for the scheme from their own waiting list. Some local authorities may have assembled information about development sites as a *land bank*.

- Other housing organisations, who may have been offered a site unsuited to their own requirements, but who think it may be suitable for other housing uses.
- Other public sector organisations, such as health trusts and education authorities, who may have unused sites where facilities have been closed down. In England, English Partnerships, which had (until reorganised into the Homes and Communities Agency in December 2008), responsibility for assembling land for redevelopment, recently signalled a willingness to make available smaller parcels of land to suit smaller organisations (*Inside Housing*, 11 April, 2008).

(ii) Initial site appraisal

Someone in the organisation, such as a development manager, needs to make an initial assessment of the physical suitability of each potential site. Key factors should be considered systematically, so that nothing of importance is overlooked. This approach also permits alternative sites to be compared more easily.

The initial assessment looks at the site from both the perspective of its potential to provide affordable development and the needs of the customers who will be housed. The ODPM's *Housing Quality Indicators* (2003) indicate key physical factors likely to affect housing quality as experienced by residents, and so these should form part of the assessment of a potential site. These may include:

- **Location**
  Consideration of the availability of support services (e.g. GP surgery, community facilities); retail provision; schools; play and leisure facilities; public transport; 'liabilities', meaning negative impacts such as derelict sites nearby or polluted water and noise (e.g. near major road). The significance of each of these elements may, of course, vary, depending on the need to be met (e.g. elderly or families).

- **Visual impact, layout and landscaping, open space**
  The overall likely impact of the development, in relationship to the character of the area; likely relationship of buildings to each other, such as aspects and views; landscaping of public areas, such as trees and other planting; private spaces.

- **Routes and movement**
  This includes connections with other roads within the neighbourhood; pedestrian access; the need for traffic calming; lighting requirements, etc.

A detailed *site survey* may also be necessary if there is any possibility of underlying physical problems, such as previous landfill, contamination or mine-workings, which may involve bore-hole drillings (to check samples below the surface) and soil testing.

Practical issues need also to be considered, such as:

- **Availability of utility services**
  These include electricity supplies, telephones, gas, water, and sewers. It can be expensive to provide new sources of supply, but services are more likely to be readily available in urban locations. This partly explains why development costs on rural sites tend to be higher.

- **Special conditions affecting the site**
  The landowners may wish to specify the type of development which can be constructed, or there may be existing controls affecting land use, such as covenants, which restrict rights.

- **Value for money of the site**
  The issue here is whether the asking price is 'fair'. This will depend partly on current market conditions – are sites in high demand? – as well as the particular features, locality, etc. of the site. This is likely to present particular problems in some very high demand areas (such as parts of the south of England for example), where the organisation may be competing with many private developers. High land prices will drive up the cost per housing unit and

Figure 5.3: A good site for development with services already available

may, therefore, cause the proposed development to seem poor value for money.

- **Affordability of the rents**
  Even if the site is available at a fair price, it is critical to estimate the rent levels which will be necessary to cover anticipated costs. This a key issue for housing associations, since rents need to conform to formula rent levels under the current rent restructuring policy (see Chapter 4).

4.3: Assessing the sustainability of the development

A sustainable development is one which '*...meets the needs of the present without compromising the ability of future generations to meet their own needs*' (ODPM, 2001, p1). Hence, it is not only about meeting all of the needs (whether environmental, social or economic) of its potential residents, it is also about minimising its impact on the wider society and future generations, by minimising energy use, using renewable resources, minimising carbon emissions, and recycling materials. All of these aspects must be 'built in' at the design stage. The issue of global warming is an increasing concern across the world and the UK government has targets to reduce carbon emissions from all development activity over the coming years. This is explored in some detail in Section 5.2 on environmental sustainability.

More narrowly, at this stage, the housing organisation needs to be concerned about whether households want to live in this location and whether they will continue over time to view it as a 'good' place to live. Many housing associations and local authorities are experiencing problems of low demand and anti-social behaviour, with socially and economically excluded tenants who exhibit high levels of benefit dependency. As a result, there may be whole areas and estates which have become so stigmatised that no-one wants to live there. The housing organisation must ensure that it will not be wasting money either building a new scheme, or to refurbish an estate which will continue to remain unpopular; and, in this latter event, demolition and/or other options (such as selling to the private sector) may have to be considered.

There has been considerable research over recent years into indicators of local social and economic sustainability and how housing providers can prevent or reduce social exclusion and safeguard future sustainability. Suggested indicators of sustainability (EIUA, 2002, p13) include:

a) Current demand – including indicators such as voids, waiting lists and sales in the locality.
b) Anticipated long-term demand – influenced by factors such as household formation trends and demographic change.
c) Crime and anti-social behaviour.

d) Reputation – including current residents' satisfaction surveys and rejections of offers.
e) Social exclusion indicators – including current rent arrears in the locality, unemployment, educational achievement, mortality and morbidity ratios, and benefit dependency.
f) Accessibility, to services, employment, transport.
g) Quality of the environment – including derelict land, boarded up properties, pollution etc.
h) Housing quality, including stock condition, repair costs, quality indicators.
i) Social cohesion, such as attendance at community meetings, 'community spirit', electoral turnout.
j) Community mix (demographic, social and ethnic).

Assessments of sustainability inevitably will involve many people beyond simply the designers, as only a few of these indicators relate purely to physical (development) issues. Housing managers, therefore, are likely to be at the heart of assessing the likely sustainability of any proposed new development or refurbishment, based on their knowledge of this estate (for refurbishment) or other estates in the locality, the wider area, local facilities, etc.

All of these issues are important because, as the Communities Scotland *Sustainable Housing Design Guide* (Stevenson with Williams, 2007) points out, sustainable development benefits housing (p14) by:

- reducing fuel poverty;
- providing healthier, more comfortable homes;
- increasing the real incomes of poorer tenants;
- enabling more cohesive, mixed communities;
- reducing the need to travel;
- ensuring lower long-term maintenance and management costs;
- proving more flexible housing;
- providing better value for money in the long term.

So, it will crucially affect the well-being of the residents and the long term health of the community.

4.4: Planning permission

All new housing developments require planning permission and some refurbishment schemes may also require permission if there will be external, physical changes. Applications for planning permission are considered in the context of the local spatial plans (see planning processes in each country of the UK in Section 2, earlier), so the likelihood of obtaining consent must be checked with the planning officers of the local planning authority.

Some minor works, such as small extensions to properties, may not require planning permission, and the range of these 'permitted developments' was extended in England from 1 October 2008 for houses (but not flats). These are summarised in Figure 5.4. According to the government, these changes were designed to exempt up to 80,000 households per annum (from around 330,000 applications typically submitted) from having to apply for planning permission (Conradi, 14 September 2008).

Figure 5.4: Types of development that do not require planning permission in England

At the side or back of a house:

- *Single storey extensions* of up to 4 metres depth on detached houses.
- *Single and two storey extensions* of up to 3 metres depth on any type of house.
- *Single storey garages or outbuildings*, provided they are not forward of the house's principal front elevation and don't cover more than half of the original garden.
- *Loft conversions* of up to 40 cubic metres in a terraced house or up to 50 in a semi- or detached house.
- *Roof or wall-mounted solar panels*, provided they are not installed above the ridgeline and do not project more than 200mm from the roof or wall surface.
- *Paving a front garden*, provided that the new driveway uses permeable/porous surfacing to allow water to drain through.
- *A porch* of an area of no more than 3 square metres, and no more than 3 metres above ground level.
- *A conservatory*, with similar limitations to those applying to outhouses.

Source: www.planningportal.gov.uk

Where a new driveway or paving is planned which is not permeable, then planning permission is required; this is intended to prevent future flooding problems, currently caused by rainwater being unable to flow away. Listed buildings will still require planning permission for almost all changes, and there are added limitations where the property is in a conservation area, National Park, World Heritage Site or Area of Outstanding Natural Beauty.

Changing the use of the property

In addition to the general exemptions provided by development orders, the planning acts define 'use classes', and a change of use will require planning consent in most cases. So, if, for example, a housing association wishes to convert a former warehouse into several flats, or the housing department wishes to convert an estate dwelling into a 'neighbourhood office', it will have to obtain approval, as it will involve a change of use.

Planning stages

Planning applications are usually granted in two stages: *outline* and *detailed*. At this stage, the organisation need only be concerned that outline consent is (or will be) available – though, in practice, many housing associations will opt to obtain both stages at the start, which minimises delays.

Outline applications require:

a. a brief description of the proposed development, and
b. a site plan, to identify the land.

This permits the planning authority to check that the proposed development conforms to the spatial plans for the area. Outline planning consents are generally granted, subject to further approval of specific items. These are called *reserved matters*. Reserved matters may deal with:

- siting
- design
- external appearance
- means of access
- landscaping.

The local authority will generally have some standard requirements relating to, for example, car parking requirements and the provision of play areas. If the client wishes, information about these reserved matters can be included at the outline stage.

Full (detailed) planning permission requires:

detailed information about the design, layout, etc. of the development, so this will usually be obtained when the detailed design has been prepared. Hence, this application will usually occur only after the initial appraisal stage has been completed and the 'go-ahead' for the project has been agreed.

For full planning permission to be granted, the planning authorities will be concerned that the design 'fits' in its physical context, does not cause unreasonable problems for surrounding properties, will not create traffic dangers, etc. Occupiers of neighbouring properties will be advised about the proposal and given the opportunity to object if they have concerns about any aspect, and these objections are drawn to the attention of the planning authority which must take the decision about the granting of permission.

What if approval is denied?

If planning permission is refused, the applicant has the right to appeal to the Secretary of State (in England and Wales), or the equivalent in Scotland and Northern Ireland. The appeal may be granted or refused. In recent years, in view of widespread housing shortages in the UK, the government has taken a more relaxed approach to development control, and appeals have had a greater chance of success.

If all elements in the initial site appraisal are acceptable, the next stage is to appoint a consultant to undertake a full *feasibility study*.

4.5: Feasibility study

a) Selecting and appointing a consultant

The consultant must be reliable and responsive to the client's needs. For this reason, the client organisation should undertake some checks on any new consultant, to determine whether:

- they have previous experience of similar types of project;
- past projects were completed on time, within cost budgets and to the client's satisfaction;
- their past designs are liked by the client.

Some clients will have in-house consultants (e.g. the architect's department of a local authority), but they should nevertheless meet the standards required of external consultants.

A formal *letter of appointment* – in effect, a binding contract – is not normally offered until the consultant has shown that the project is feasible and is worthwhile. At this stage, therefore, the consultant generally receives only a *letter of intent* (to appoint once feasibility is demonstrated) from the client organisation.

Once the organisation decides to proceed with the scheme, the consultant will receive a letter of appointment (agreed with the organisation's solicitor) which:

- defines the roles of client, consultant and any other relevant professionals;
- identifies the conditions of the appointment;
- specifies the fees and expenses payable;
- requires indemnity insurance, to cover the client in the event of any design failures.

This is an important document, because it effectively defines the service, which the client expects of the consultant.

b) Undertaking the feasibility study

The consultant will begin by sketching out possible estate layouts for different property types, suitable for the desired type of scheme, and identify possible construction methods. From these initial ideas, they will generally select one for further consideration. This will be the scheme which appears to meet the client's requirements best, within the client's budget.

In addition to the importance of site features and location (discussed above), the ODPM's housing quality indicators (2003) suggest standards in relation to:

- unit size/facilities (e.g. number of WCs needed);
- unit layout (adequate circulation and activity space);
- noise control, light quality (e.g. windows with open views) and services (sockets, TV points, etc.);
- accessibility, especially for the elderly and disabled (see Lifetime Homes, Section 5);
- energy and sustainability (e.g. the Code for Sustainable Homes – see Section 5) and SAP ratings – of energy efficiency).

On the basis of this initial draft design, the feasibility of the scheme will then be assessed. In general, a project is considered feasible if:

- **The estimated costs** suggest that it is likely that it can be constructed within budget constraints.

The consultant will draw up more detailed drawings from the initial sketch, to show broad design details. These enable the quantity surveyor to estimate:

- construction costs;
- the cost of site acquisition (for new build);
- fees for professionals, such as consultants and solicitors (to undertake the legal work), known as on-costs;
- fees for statutory requirements, such as building regulations' approval and planning consents;
- interest charges on any money which will have to be borrowed during the construction phase, in order to make regular stage payments to the contractor as work progresses.

Affordable housing organisations should also consider likely future maintenance costs, and may wish to build an allowance for these into the costings; for housing associations, this is particularly important, since rents will have to cover these future costs too.

- **The rent levels** which are necessary to cover scheme costs are viewed as affordable and acceptable (e.g. in the light of rent restructuring – see Chapter 4).

These will be much more certain than the estimates produced at the initial feasibility stage, since the costs are known with much greater certainty. These levels must not only conform to current rent policies, but the organisation must also feel confident that the properties can be let successfully at these rent levels.

- **Assessed levels of risk** are acceptable.

> *All projects contain risks that may affect cost, quality and/or time. Risk management is the identification and statistical analysis of these risks, followed by the formulation of an action plan to control them throughout the life of a project* (Communities Scotland, 2002, p50).

Projects to rehabilitate existing buildings may be especially risky, because structural problems may only become apparent when work begins. It is this element of higher risk that has resulted in reduced rehabilitation by housing associations; public subsidy (HAG and SHG) is fixed at the outset, so all of the risk of cost increases is borne by the housing association (see Chapter 4).

There is also the possibility that the properties cannot be let (or sold, for low-cost or shared ownership projects) once completed, so these risks must be taken into account. The demand for homes to buy is affected greatly by general economic conditions, such as interest rates and levels of unemployment, none of which are under the control of affordable housing organisations. Additional risks may arise due to events affecting the financial institutions, such as the 'credit crunch' of 2008 (see Chapter 4), which affected the availability of mortgages and bank lending. As housing association tenants must cover the organisation's costs via rents, increased voids or unsold properties mean higher rents for the other tenants.

Different organisations will be able to tolerate different levels of risk. Local authorities and very large housing associations will generally have more scope to absorb higher costs than small housing associations, for which the level of reserves to deal with possible cost increases will be crucial. The number of schemes in progress will also affect acceptable risk levels, because if the worst happened and *all* went wrong, this could create real problems.

A number of **approaches to risk assessment** are possible, but two of the more common methods are:

Sensitivity analysis
This approach attempts to identify, and quantify, particularly high-risk elements in the costs – such as the risk that interest rates will increase during the construction period, resulting in higher loan repayments. The financial calculations relating to the scheme are re-worked – usually using a computer programme – making different assumptions about these risky factors. So, for example, loan repayments may be calculated assuming interest rates of 4 per cent, 6 per cent and 8 per cent; voids may be assumed to be 3 per cent, 5 per cent or 10 per cent; or, completion time may be varied. It is then possible to see the extent to which the viability of the project is affected by these changes – in essence, how sensitive the project is to changes in specific aspects. If it became clear that, with very few changes to the assumptions, the project would cease to be feasible, then this would suggest that it was a very high-risk undertaking.

Classifying risks

This is a simpler approach, which involves grading (from 1 to 5) the:

a. likelihood of risk, and

b. the impact of the risk.

Communities Scotland's (2002) suggested grading is shown in Table 5.4. Risks to be graded may include:

- cost increases;
- problems with the contractor;
- late completion dates;
- letting difficulties.

Table 5.4: Classifying risks

	Likelihood of risk		**Impact of risk**
5	Highly probable	5	Catastrophic
4	Very likely	4	Critical
3	As likely as not	3	Serious
2	Could happen	2	Marginal
1	Improbable	1	Insignificant

Source: Communities Scotland, 2002, p52.

The overall rating of the risks can be seen from the total score, as shown in Table 5.5. If the project goes ahead, the risks identified need to be actively managed and controlled, as far as possible.

Table 5.5: Quantifying risks

	Impact				
Likelihood	Insignificant	Marginal	Serious	Critical	Catastrophic
Improbable	2	3	4	5	6
Could happen	3	4	5	6	7
As likely as not	4	5	6	7	8
Very likely	5	6	7	8	9
Highly probable	6	7	8	9	10

Source: Communities Scotland, 2002, p52.

c) The feasibility report

All of this information is set out in a feasibility report, for the consideration of the development manager, management committee, or whoever is responsible for taking decisions about development. The assumptions made for the calculations – such as interest rates, construction period, completion date, etc. – must be clearly identified. A decision is then made about whether to go ahead with the project.

Once the decision to proceed has been taken, the next step (for new build) is to acquire the site – though not before outline planning consent has been obtained, as examined in the last section. (In reality, unless this was thought likely to be granted, the scheme would not have progressed to feasibility study stage.)

4.6: Financing the development

It is critical that any proposals can be funded. The organisation may have secured SHG or HAG from the statutory funder (see Chapter 4), but will still need to ensure that the remainder can be financed by borrowing from a financial institution and/or from the organisation's financial reserves. Following the 'credit crunch' in 2008 (see Chapter 4), the availability of bank lending became much more problematic for many housing associations, so this element became more critical (and potentially more difficult) than previously.

As part of their financial assessment, the organisation will produce a *cash flow projection*, to show the likely timings of the stages of the development when major costs will arise, identify when grant will be payable, and hence when major borrowing will need to take place. An organisation that cannot pay its costs in any one period (unless it is a local authority) risks being declared bankrupt, so accurate cash flow projections are vital to the financial health of the organisation. As new information becomes available or there are changes in any key factors, the cash flow projection will need to be revised to reflect these changes.

4.7: Community consultation and involvement

Existing residents must always be involved in refurbishment plans, because they will have clear views on what works/doesn't work and what is needed. If resident ' buy-in' is secured, then residents are much more likely to be satisfied with any improvements/changes and pleased with the outcomes. It is usual to involve them, not just in the 'big' decisions (about what is to be demolished, for example, or revised estate layouts), but also in more detailed issues, such as room configurations and kitchen and bathroom designs.

It also makes sense to involve the wider local community in all decisions about new development, because, arguably, they are the local 'experts' on the locality, and may have strong views on what is needed. It is they who will have to live in the vicinity of any new housing and, hopefully, welcome the new residents. If there is unresolved hostility to the new scheme, this will not provide a sound foundation for the future integration of any new inhabitants into a sustainable community.

There a number of approaches to involving the community, which may include some or all of:

- Open meetings
- Questionnaires and/or surveys
- Focus groups
- Exhibitions (of plans, models, etc.)
- Meetings with specific community groups, such as faith groups and residents' or tenants' associations.

What is important is that real efforts are made to involve everyone, particularly traditionally 'hard to reach' groups such as young people and ethnic minorities. For example, it may be possible to put on an exhibition at the local school, and elicit pupils' views (through focus groups or group meetings) about what they would like to see in the area.

4.8: Site acquisition

This, of course, is required only when the housing organisation does not already own the site.

a) Agreeing the price

The cost of the site may be a substantial part of total costs, so it is important to obtain value for money. Before the sale price is agreed with the vendor, affordable housing providers must obtain a valuation from an independent valuer, such as (in the case of local authorities) the district valuer for HM Revenue and Customs. In any event, it is a sensible precaution against potential corruption.

It is usual to obtain an initial, informal valuation, to use as a guide for negotiation purposes. If the vendor's price remains above the valuation price, it may be possible to discuss this with the valuer, before the formal valuation is undertaken.

b) Purchasing the site

Before any money is paid, the client's solicitors must ensure that the vendor does actually own the land – in legal terms, has the *title* to the land. If the title is not registered (at a registry set up by the government), this will involve checking back through all previous purchases in the *title deeds* to ensure that the title (ownership) was properly transferred. In England and Wales, this is transferred by a *conveyance*, in Scotland by a *feu charter* or *disposition*.

If the title has been registered – at the *Land Registry* in England and Wales, or the *Register of Sasines* or *Land Register of Scotland*, then checking ownership is quite simple.

For housing associations purchasing leasehold sites in England and Wales, the statutory funders will generally require minimum lease expiry terms as a condition of receiving SHG/HAG funds. This is because the leaseholder regains ownership of the land once the lease expires. Minimum expiry times are generally shorter for rehabilitation schemes than for new build, reflecting the different life-expectancies of the two types of development.

The solicitors will then draw up a contract, and this is *completed* when payment is made and ownership is transferred in the *deeds*, which confer a *title* to the land. After this, the housing organisation is free to begin construction work on the site.

5. Stage 2: Detailed design

The next step is to determine the detailed design requirements, so that the briefing (from which the consultants will design the detailed scheme) can be prepared. This will be influenced by current ideas about what constitutes good housing design. Design issues apply both to dwelling design and to external (or 'urban') design issues – the physical context of the dwellings. According to the ODPM (2001):

> *...urban design should be taken to mean the relationship between different buildings; the relationship between buildings and streets, squares, parks, waterways and other spaces which make up the public domain; the nature and quality of the public domain itself; the relationship of one part of a village, town or city with other parts; and the patterns of movement and activity which are thereby established: in short, the complex relationships between all elements of built and unbuilt space* (p3).

These issues will be considered particularly important by the planning officers, who will advise on planning approval (see Section 2, earlier).

5.1: What is 'good' design?

Dwelling design is a somewhat controversial topic, because few designers can agree, objectively, about what makes a good design. However, it can be argued that if the design 'works' for its inhabitants, so that they feel that it gives them the main things that they want from a home, then it is, subjectively, a good design. Good dwelling designs seem to fulfil two key, human requirements in that they are:

1. Functional

Homes need to provide adequate shelter, comfort and security for their inhabitants. Both dwelling and estate design can affect these functional matters.

Figure 5.5: Recent designs seek to cluster homes together, with good visibility over any public spaces

Figure 5.6: Indefensible spaces create problems – in this case litter

Arguably, security issues have become more significant over recent years for residents, resulting in increased demand for measures perceived to improve security, such as CCTV schemes.

2. Symbolic and aesthetic
Homes are also seen as a physical expression of their inhabitants, so they can 'confer' social values such as status, a sense of worth and success, and 'respectability'. Most people prefer to live in a 'nice' home, which is aesthetically pleasing to them, and to gain a sense of well-being from this. It is not only house *types* and *styles* which are important, but *locality*.

Affordable housing providers in the past may sometimes have undervalued the symbolic requirements of dwellings, focusing exclusively on the functional aspects of the design; for example, the tower blocks built from the late 1950s may have been functionally good (though many weren't, with problems of damp penetration and poor security, for example), but symbolically, they offered little to residents. The importance of the 'image' projected by the home is perhaps most clearly demonstrated by the actions of tenants freed from landlord constraints when they purchase under the right to buy policy; almost inevitably, the external, 'public' appearance of the property is changed, with a new front door, for example, or a porch.

However, of growing prominence in the design of new housing development is the environmental sustainability agenda, which we turn to next.

5.2: Environmental sustainability

As the world has become increasingly concerned about the likely impact of global warming on future generations, the UK government has expressed its clear commitment to reducing carbon emissions from homes. As a result, a number of policies and approaches are being pursued to improve the environmental sustainability of new housing developments in the UK, which are explored next.

Ecohomes

The UK's Building Research Establishment (BRE) explored methods for assessing the environmental sustainability of construction methods and materials, and developed the Building Research Establishment Environmental Assessment Method (BREEAM) for homes, called Ecohomes. The Ecohomes rating permits all housing developments – both new build and refurbishment – to be rated for sustainability, and the BRE claims that this approach, '*...balances environmental performance with the need for a high quality of life and a safe and healthy internal environment*' (BRE, 2006). The Ecohomes rating applies to all housing in the UK, except for new homes in England, where Ecohomes has been superseded by the Code for Sustainable Homes.

The Code for Sustainable Homes

In April 2007, the *Code for Sustainable Homes* (CLG, 2006) replaced Ecohomes for the assessment of *new* housing in England, but Ecohomes continues to be used for refurbished housing in England and for all housing in Scotland and Wales. The design principles in the Code relate to nine environmental impact categories with differing weightings, as shown in Figure 5.7. The Code uses a sustainability rating of six levels, with one star representing minimum standards, and six stars indicating a carbon neutral home. In England, it is now mandatory for all new affordable housing developments to achieve level 3 of the Code.

Figure 5.7: Categories of environmental impact in the Code for Sustainable Homes

	Category	Weighting %
1	Energy and carbon dioxide emissions	36.4
2	Water	9.0
3	Minerals	7.2
4	Surface water run-off	2.2
5	Waste	6.4
6	Pollution	2.8
7	Health and well-being	14.0
8	Management	10.0
9	Ecology	12.0

Source: CLG, *Code for Sustainable Homes*, 2006.

CLG (2006, pp8-9) argues that there are a number of key benefits arising from adherence to the Code, for:

i) The environment:
- reduced greenhouse gas emissions
- better adaptation to climate change
- reduced impact on the environment overall.

ii) Home builders:
- a mark of quality
- regulatory certainty
- flexibility.

iii) Affordable housing providers:
- lower running costs
- improved comfort and satisfaction
- raised sustainability credentials.

iv) Consumers:

- assisting choice
- reducing environmental 'footprint'
- lower running costs
- improved well-being.

In its policy statement, *Building a Greener Future* (CLG, 2007a), the government set a target that all new homes be zero carbon by 2016; zero carbon means that, '*...over a year, the net carbon emissions from all energy use in the home (is) zero*' (CLG, 2007a, p4). The government is committed to progressively tightening the building regulations (in 2010, 2013, and 2016) to incorporate the code, which means that it will also gradually become mandatory for all private developments.

Energy Performance Certificates (EPCs)

The Code operates alongside a system of Energy Performance Certificates (see Figure 5.8), introduced in June 2007 under the Energy Performance of Buildings Directive (EPBD), which currently requires that all new homes, when sold, rented or leased, have an Energy Performance Certificate. This gives a rating, rather like the ratings for the energy efficiency of domestic appliances such as washing machines, with which most readers will be familiar.

EPCs can only be issued by accredited domestic energy assessors (DEAs), and it is, as yet, unclear whether most affordable housing organisations will train their own DEAs or contract the work out. The difficulty is that, once the initial assessments are completed, there will be only limited need for further assessments, following major refurbishment work for example.

Home Information Packs

The requirement to produce a Home Information Pack (HIP) whenever a home is bought or sold was introduced in England in 2007 (CLG, 2007b). This was intended to speed up the house purchase process, by supplying potential buyers with key information about the property, such as evidence of title, the local authority search (for example, to check for planned new developments in the area), and information about the lease (where the land is not freehold). However, to support government sustainability policies, it must also contain:

- an Energy Performance Certificate (see above), by which the government hopes to encourage greater efforts to energy efficiency in existing homes, and,
- *for new homes only*, a Certificate showing the Code for Sustainable Homes rating or a nil-rated certificate (which draws attention to homes which have not met any level of the Code).

Eco-towns in England

In July 2007, the government published its *Eco-Towns Prospectus* (CLG, 2007c), which invited councils and other organisations to bid to develop the first zero-carbon, *exemplar* new towns in England – the first new towns to built in England since the 1960s. According to the prospectus, these new towns are each to provide up to 20,000 new homes, in new communities that are to be sustainable in every sense; so, not only must the new homes be zero carbon, the homes and towns must also exhibit good design, have good public transport links, and promote employment and community involvement. They are to include 30-50 per cent affordable homes.

In April 2008, a shortlist of 15 bids (from 57 proposals) was published (CLG, 2008b). Thirteen of the successful shortlisted proposals were in the south and midlands of England, with two in Yorkshire, which has led some commentators to suggest that eco-towns are really simply about securing new housing in pressurised areas rather than promoting sustainability issues. The shortlisted bidders were required to begin extensive consultations with local communities and other stakeholders, and undertake detailed Sustainability Appraisals. By November 2008, three bids had already been withdrawn, and an initial valuation had shown that only one bid was likely to meet all of the published 'eco-town' criteria. In any event, with the problems faced by the house building industry in late 2008 as a result of the economic recession and 'credit crunch', it is unclear whether these proposals will be taken forward in the near future.

When the list is further reduced the proposals will then have to attract planning permission from their local authorities. Already, there are indications that not all local authorities are supportive of the proposals in their areas, as they feel that these proposals usurp their responsibilities for planning matters (see Section 2.2, earlier).

Scottish Sustainable Communities Initiative (SSCI)

This was announced in June 2008, and, rather like the English eco-towns initiative (above), it seeks to encourage bids for the development of very low or zero-carbon communities, which are environmentally, economically and socially viable, from local authorities, developers, landowners, etc. (Scottish Government, 2008). An SSCI development should:

- contribute to meeting identified requirements in the area;
- demonstrate a level of innovation and quality of design which will lead to the creation of successful places and serve as an inspiration to future development in Scotland;
- minimise pollution;
- create opportunities to live healthier, more active and environmentally responsible lives and so influence behaviour and attitudes;
- demonstrate that the delivery of high quality sustainable forms of new development is achievable within reasonable timescales;
- incorporate provision for the evaluation of the success and benefits of the

approach and outcomes, so that future developments can benefit by learning from innovation (Scottish Government, 2008 pp6-7).

Figure 5.8: Sample Energy Performance Certificate

Energy Performance Certificate

SAP

17 Any Street,
Any Town,
County,
YY3 5XX

Dwelling type:	Detached house
Date of assessment:	02 February 2007
Date of certificate:	[dd mmmm yyyy]
Reference number:	0000-0000-0000-0000-0000
Total floor area:	166 m²

This home's performance is rated in terms of the energy use per square metre of floor area, energy efficiency based on fuel costs and environmental impact based on carbon dioxide (CO_2) emissions.

Energy Efficiency Rating

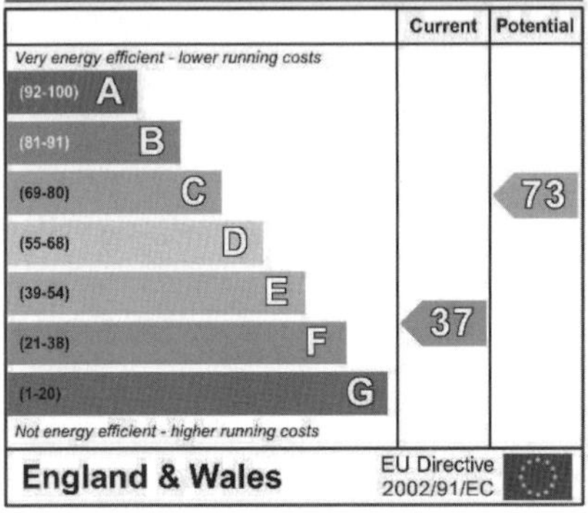

The energy efficiency rating is a measure of the overall efficiency of a home. The higher the rating the more energy efficient the home is and the lower the fuel bills will be.

Environmental Impact (CO_2) Rating

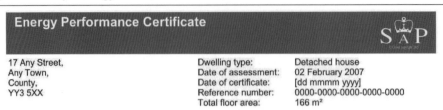

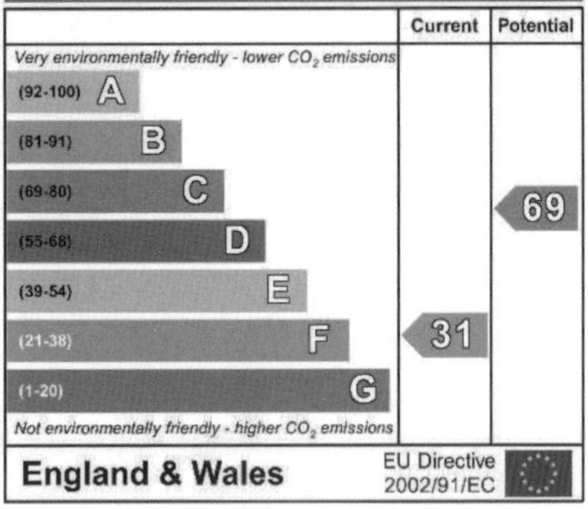

The environmental impact rating is a measure of a home's impact on the environment in terms of carbon dioxide (CO_2) emissions. The higher the rating the less impact it has on the environment.

Estimated energy use, carbon dioxide (CO_2) emissions and fuel costs of this home

	Current	Potential
Energy Use	453 kWh/m² per year	178 kWh/m² per year
Carbon dioxide emissions	13 tonnes per year	4.9 tonnes per year
Lighting	£81 per year	£65 per year
Heating	£1173 per year	£457 per year
Hot water	£219 per year	£104 per year

Based on standardised assumptions about occupancy, heating patterns and geographical location, the above table provides an indication of how much it will cost to provide lighting, heating and hot water to this home. The fuel costs only take into account the cost of fuel and not any associated service, maintenance or safety inspection. The certificate has been provided for comparative purposes only and enables one home to be compared with another. Always check the date the certificate was issued, because fuel prices can increase over time and energy saving recommendations will evolve.

To see how this home can achieve its potential rating please see the recommended measures.

energy saving recommended

Source: CLG, Sample Home Information Pack, accessed at: www.communities.gov.uk

Proposals must show:

1. How the bid contributes to meeting regional or local housing need.
2. What makes the location sustainable (e.g. access to facilities).
3. How the form and layout contributes to the highest standards of quality and sustainability.
4. How it addresses long-term sustainability.
5. How it will be delivered (e.g. will it meet planning requirements, does the proposer own the land, is finance available?).

The Scottish Government intends to support successful bids primarily through, '*...minimising the regulatory burden*' (p35), as no additional funds are being offered.

5.3: Other design standards

In addition to the requirement to achieve the government's sustainability ratings, the statutory funders have developed detailed guidance on design quality standards. For example, the Housing Corporation (now the Homes and Communities Agency) issued *Design and Quality Standards* (2007b) which identify core 'housing quality indicators' (HQIs). These relate to:

i) Internal environment
This relates to unit size, layout and services appropriate for the proposed user group, so covers aspects such a kitchen provision and layout, bathroom fittings and space standards.

ii) Sustainability
This requires employing construction methods which use products and processes that are sustainable and reduce environmental impact, reduce running costs and, '*...enhance the health and well-being of occupiers and the wider community*'. It is also expected that *Lifetime Homes* principles will be incorporated, which means ensuring that the property is adaptable to meet the changing needs of residents (such as being capable of accommodating wheelchairs and stair lifts).

iii) External environment
This covers aspects such as the promotion of mixed and integrated communities, and the balance between public and private open space.

In 2005, the Scottish Executive (now the Scottish Government) developed a sustainable development strategy for Scotland, *Choosing Our Future*. This was followed by the *Sustainable Housing Design Guide* (Stevenson with Williams), published by Communities Scotland in 2007. This identifies (p16) that a sustainable housing development has:

- Warm, dry, healthy, adaptable homes

- Environmentally friendly and energy-efficient buildings
- Access to employment, schools, shops, places of entertainment, primary health care
- Reduced the need to travel (by car) and is accessible by public transport
- A mix of tenures, incomes and age groups
- A setting which enhances the quality of life from one generation to another and integrates people into wider society so that people want to live there
- Aesthetic qualities which can be enhanced by community art.

Clearly, then, there are a variety of sustainability issues which affordable housing developers need to incorporate into their designs.

5.4: Ensuring sustainability through partnerships

The resolution of a wide range of sustainability issues will often involve the expertise of many key partners, whether individuals or organisations. Especially for refurbishment projects, there may be a need to prioritise management issues (e.g. lettings policies and tackling anti-social behaviour) as well as economic development and community involvement and development. For example, research for CLG (2006) identified increasing problems in some areas, resulting from multiple disadvantage and worklessness, which can only be tackled by holistic approaches. So, ensuring sustainability requires *partnership* approaches to development, which means involving a wide range of organisations and agencies at the outset.

According to the ODPM's (2002) Summary of Good Practice (from *Regeneration that Lasts*), factors likely to encourage effective partnership working include:

- recognition of the need for an integrated, comprehensive approach;
- commonality of purpose between the partners;
- clear leadership;
- treating all partners (including residents) equally;
- continuity of policies and, (as far as possible), personnel.

To involve a range of income groups, schemes should aim to provide mixed development, meaning that there is a mix of tenures – often, some social housing to rent, low-cost or shared ownership, and possibly some full-cost housing for sale. Such developments will usually involve partnerships with private developers, so it is critical that, by this stage of the project, all key partners are involved in the plans.

5.5: Preparing the briefing

The briefing is the document which specifies exactly what the client wants, so the more detailed the briefing, the better. Only if the designers are very clear about the client's requirements will they be able to produce a design, which fully meets them.

Naturally, the brief must incorporate all government requirements (such as appropriate rating levels of the Code for Sustainable Homes, or Ecohomes), as well as any statutory funders' design requirements (such as achieving Lifetime Homes standards – which requires that homes are capable of being adapted to suit changing physical needs, by being wheelchair accessible and capable of incorporating a stair lift, for example).

The briefing will be developed by the person(s) in the organisation responsible for the development. In an affordable housing organisation, ideally those who will have future responsibility for the development should also be consulted; managers know which design features cause management problems, and maintenance staff can advise about aspects with high maintenance costs. Indeed, organisations are encouraged to adopt a *lifetime* approach to scheme costs, so that repair implications are automatically incorporated into the scheme appraisal.

Tenants' views are also invaluable. For rehabilitation work, the people who will actually occupy the scheme can often be consulted; for new build, potential tenants may be identified for consultation, or the views of tenants on other new developments should be routinely surveyed (after a period of occupation), so that they can comment on good and bad design aspects and influence future developments.

In practice, the first version of the brief will usually develop over a period of time, as new information comes to light. This will be added to the initial brief, until, eventually, the *full brief* emerges. By the time the design is complete, the *final brief* should have been amended to include all of the information given to the consultants. This is necessary so that, when the scheme is completed, the organisation can evaluate the consultants, by checking whether the requirements of the final brief have been met. If they have, but the scheme is still felt to be unsatisfactory, then the fault lies with the client. The brief was not adequate. In this event, future briefs should be modified, to take account of the weaknesses identified in this brief.

Contents of the briefing

There are usually two key aspects:

1. The **general** requirements of the organisation, applicable to all schemes, and developed over time. Hence, this will need to incorporate all required/statutory sustainability aspects, such as the Code for Sustainable Homes or Ecohomes standards. The briefing must cover *all* aspects of design about which the organisation has clear requirements and preferences. Over time, additional knowledge derived from experience will also be incorporated into the general requirements. If the consultants have designed many schemes for the organisation, they may be familiar with their *general* requirements, but will still need detailed briefing about the specific requirements of this particular scheme. This fact is often overlooked when *in-house* architects are employed to design the scheme.

2. The **specific** requirements of the particular site or property, to meet identified needs. There are a number of possible approaches to developing specific design briefs, and they may be set out in slightly different ways. In general, they will need to cover:

i) Details about the site
These may include:

- physical aspects (location, boundaries, size, slope, aspect, soil characteristics, existing vegetation, existing buildings and whether these are to be retained, existing services and positions, etc.;
- environmental aspects such as adjacent buildings and uses, local amenities such as shops, parks, bus routes, etc.;
- legal aspects such as public *rights of way* over the land and ownership of boundaries such as fences.

Rehabilitation schemes will, obviously, impose many more constraints on the possible design, so the brief should identify these constraints fully, as well as indicating the changes desired.

ii) Cost limits for the development
Most affordable housing organisations face severe cost constraints, due partly to the need to provide affordable rents for potential tenants of the scheme, but also because of limitations on the total funds available – whether borrowed and/or from reserves.

iii) Procedural aspects
This includes statutory bodies which need to be consulted, the consents required, procedures for approval by the client, etc. In general, this will include information about the planning authority, the highway authority and public utilities (which include gas, electricity and water). If outline planning consent has been obtained, any reserved matters affecting requirements should be identified.

iv) Time limits
The *programme* sets out *target dates* for achieving each stage in the construction process, though the consultant may negotiate about these.

v) Requirements of the accommodation design
This is likely to form the bulk of the briefing and is highly detailed. It must cover both the general requirements of the organisation – accommodation features which are always wanted – and the specific, dwelling design requirements of this development. A list of common contents for this aspect of the briefing is shown in Figure 5.9.

In addition, dwellings must be designed to permit normal activities to be undertaken in the home, so designs should be checked to ensure sufficient space is allowed for circulation of people, space for furniture and removal, eating around a table, etc.

Affordable housing providers, as discussed above, are increasingly aware of the symbolic importance of design, so dwelling designs should also be attractive to an 'average' person – or, if the scheme's future tenants are known, to the actual residents.

Figure 5.9: Sample contents of a briefing for accommodation design

a) General requirements

Mainly for new build:

- type of buildings (detached, terraced, flats etc.);
- dwelling numbers, mix and sizes – this will reflect the need(s) to be met as well as desired densities (number of units per hectare);
- maximum number of storeys; higher densities may be required when land costs are very high – such as some inner city areas – and generally require more storeys.

For all schemes:

- required sustainability ratings;
- other facilities, such as car parking (and how many per unit); play areas (for general needs housing); meeting rooms (for supported housing); laundry rooms (for hostels), etc.;
- land use distribution, indicating the proportionate share for dwellings, car parking, roads and other facilities.

b) Dwelling design requirements

For new build, the organisation may prefer to use a previous standard design for each type of dwelling, because this will reduce design costs. However, whether the designs are to be *standard* or *one-off*, the same details need to be reproduced in the brief. These include:

- general design requirements, such as minimum space requirements for net floor area (which excludes garages), storage areas, plot sizes, etc.;
- room relationships, such as access to rooms from hallways, from room to room (e.g. kitchen may not open off living room), and external access requirements (to external doors, road, etc.);
- requirements for living areas, such as the type and siting of heaters and fires, radiators, TV sockets, thermostats, etc.;
- kitchen requirements, such as minimum provision and height of units, unit types, power sockets, sink position (e.g. in natural light), ventilation requirements, space for eating, laundry needs, work surfaces, etc.;
- bedrooms, such as fitted wardrobes, the position of radiators and windows, ventilation, and lighting;
- bathroom and WC, such as requirements for ventilation (e.g. extractor fan), sound insulation, a second, ground floor WC;

Figure 5.9: Sample contents of a briefing for accommodation design *continued*

- storage areas, for the storage of refuse, fuel, meters, linen, prams, bicycles, garden equipment, etc.;
- doors and windows, such as UPVC windows to reduce maintenance; windows with external panes which can be cleaned from inside; security fittings, etc.;
- provision of services, including the type of heating system, requirements for water supply, electricity and gas connections (e.g. in kitchen), etc.;
- energy efficiency requirements, indicated by SAP ratings (as required by the Sustainability Codes), including roof and wall insulation, double glazing, etc.

c) Environmental design requirements

This concerns site layout, and how the dwellings will 'fit into' their surroundings. For a rehabilitation scheme, there may be little scope for altering environmental aspects such as:

- the distribution of dwellings (such as how they are to be grouped);
- vehicle and pedestrian circulation, such as footpaths, specific vehicle access needs, and adequate access for emergency vehicles (such as fire engines);
- aesthetic and social criteria, such as dwelling orientation (what they face) and any requirements for privacy and safety;
- landscape features, like existing trees, hedges, and any preservation orders which prevent the felling of trees.

Figure 5.10: Speed reduction measures are becoming much more common to reduce traffic speed

vii) Construction standards

This section details any special requirements for the construction *methods and materials* to be used, which require expertise in construction technology and is beyond the scope of this text. As identified in Section 2.2, construction standards are

Figure 5.11: A sheltered scheme for the elderly, which makes creative use of a very large, old (protected) tree in a circular driveway

controlled by the building regulations, which ensure that only safe methods and materials are used, and approval must be obtained from the local authority. However, knowledge acquired by the organisation from previous schemes should also be incorporated, so that methods or materials that have caused problems are avoided. Additionally, there may be a desire to standardise some elements (such as door and window types, or heating systems), which will permit the holding of spare parts to be minimised, and may allow for reduced maintenance contracts to be negotiated. Since the publication of the Egan Report (1998), the government has encouraged increased use of factory produced components (such as timber or steel frames) in affordable housing construction, which would need to be specified here.

5.6: The design drawings

Once the consultants have the briefing, they can proceed to producing some drawings to show their ideas for interpreting the brief. Drawings are a physical representation of the scheme, which enable the client to see what is proposed, as well as, ultimately, the contractor to build according to the design. Nowadays, most scheme drawings are designed using a computer-aided design (CAD) system, and are commonly produced in two stages:

a) Outline drawings

The consultant must design in line with the brief, but is free to interpret these requirements as they choose. This means that, for any given briefing, a large number of possible approaches is possible. The consultant will have already produced some outline plans for the feasibility study, but ideas now need to be 'firmed-up'.

Outline plans will be sketched out, and these need to be considered by the client, to ensure that they conform to the brief. If any aspect is unsatisfactory, the consultant will need to revise as appropriate.

b) Detailed drawings

Once the client is happy with the outline scheme, the consultant proceeds to draw up detailed drawings. These are more numerous and detailed than the outline plans, and will have to be drawn carefully *to scale*. This means that a specified distance on the plan corresponds to a larger area on the ground. For example, a scale of 1:1000 means that 1 mm on the plan represents 1 metre on the site. The smaller the scale, the more closely the two distances match. All drawings will clearly indicate the scale.

A number of different drawings have to be made, in order to give a full picture of the scheme. These drawings are submitted for detailed planning consent, and are needed by the contractor so that it is clear what is to be constructed.

The main ones are:

Location plan

This places the site within its locality, showing adjoining roads, buildings, etc. It indicates the position of north with an arrow, and is usually drawn to a scale of 1:2500 or 1:1250. See Figure 5.12.

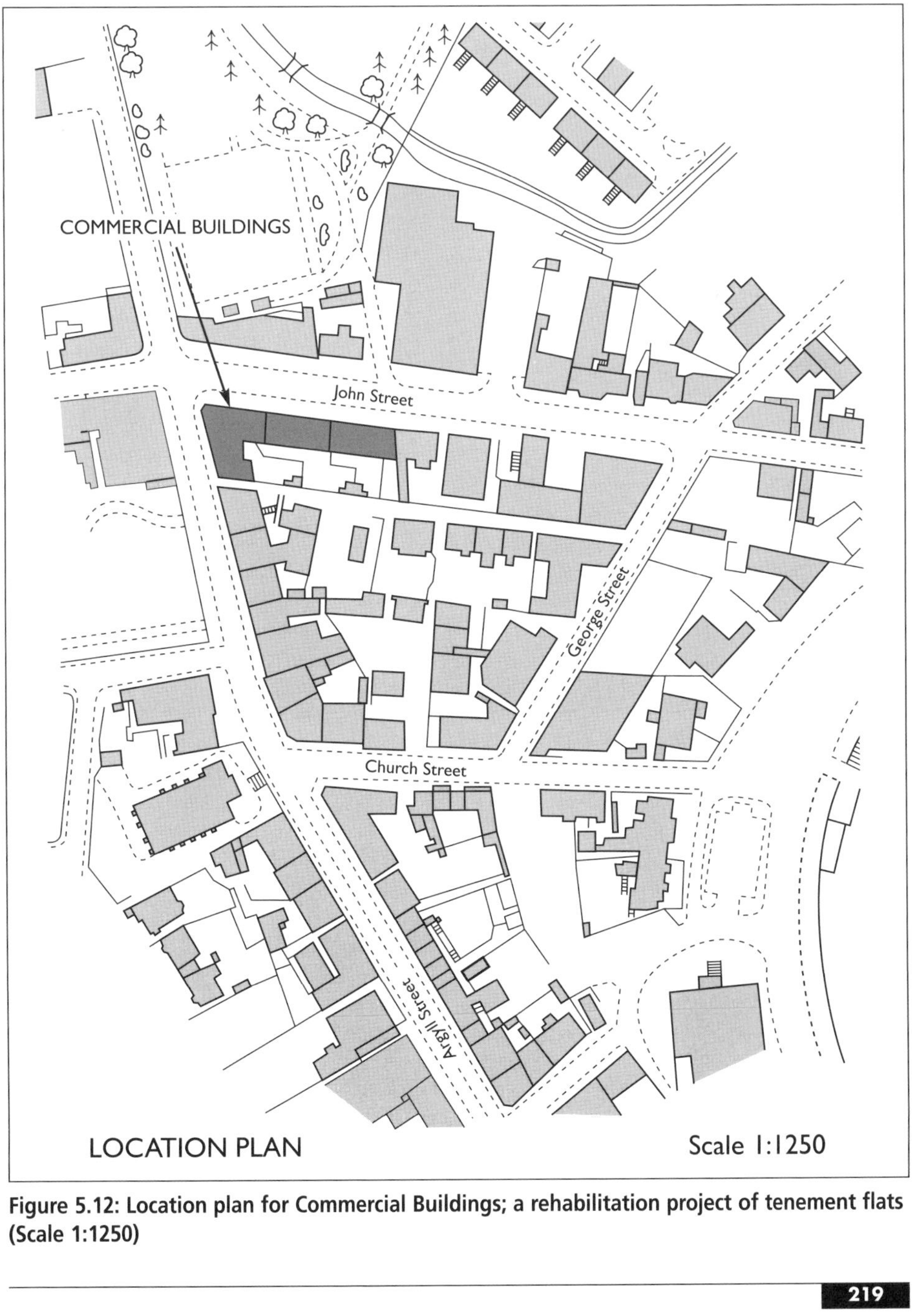

Figure 5.12: Location plan for Commercial Buildings; a rehabilitation project of tenement flats (Scale 1:1250)

Site layout plan

This shows the position of the dwellings in the site, with roads, trees, etc indicated. The scale is usually 1:500, or 1:200. See Figure 5.13.

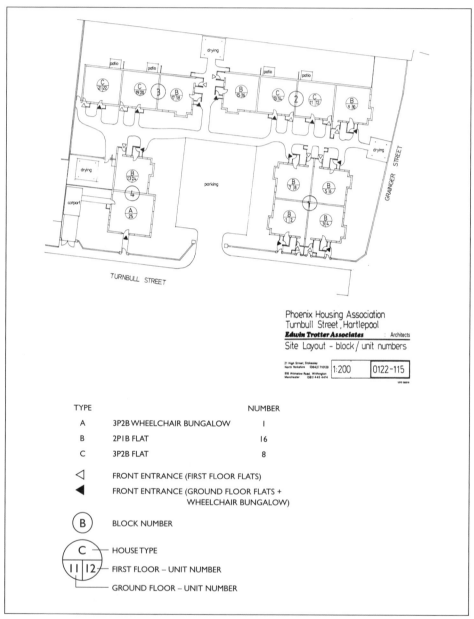

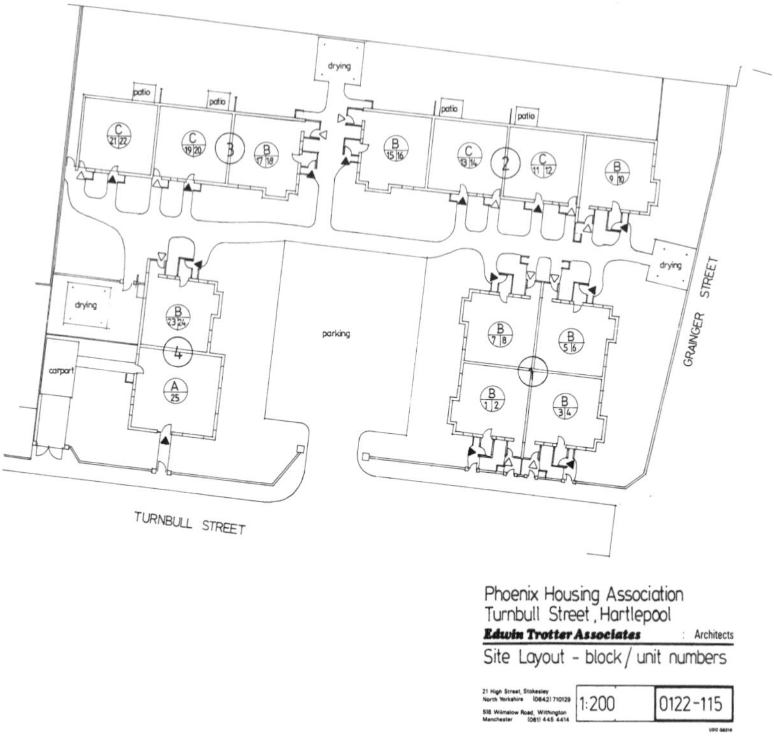

TYPE		NUMBER
A	3P2B WHEELCHAIR BUNGALOW	1
B	2P1B FLAT	16
C	3P2B FLAT	8

◁ FRONT ENTRANCE (FIRST FLOOR FLATS)

◀ FRONT ENTRANCE (GROUND FLOOR FLATS + WHEELCHAIR BUNGALOW)

(B) BLOCK NUMBER

C — HOUSE TYPE

11 | 12 — FIRST FLOOR – UNIT NUMBER

GROUND FLOOR – UNIT NUMBER

Figure 5.13: Site layout drawing for Turnbull Street, Hartlepool; a new build project of flats and bungalows (Scale 1:200)

Floor plans

These are produced for *each* floor of each dwelling type, at a scale of 1:100 or 1:50. Possible furniture layouts should be included, so that it can be seen whether the layouts are feasible. See Figures 5.14 and 5.15.

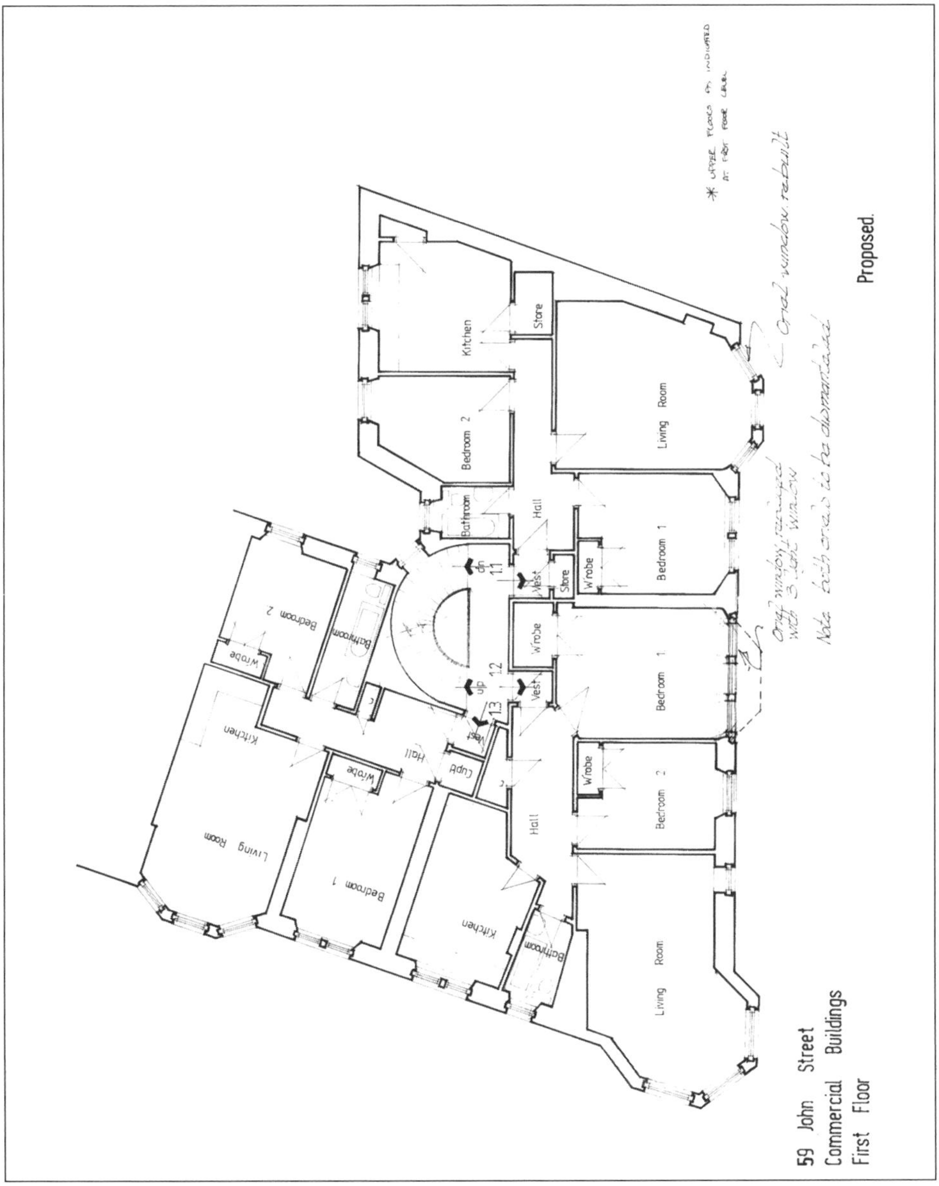

Figure 5.14: Commercial Buildings; first floor plan (Scale 1:100)

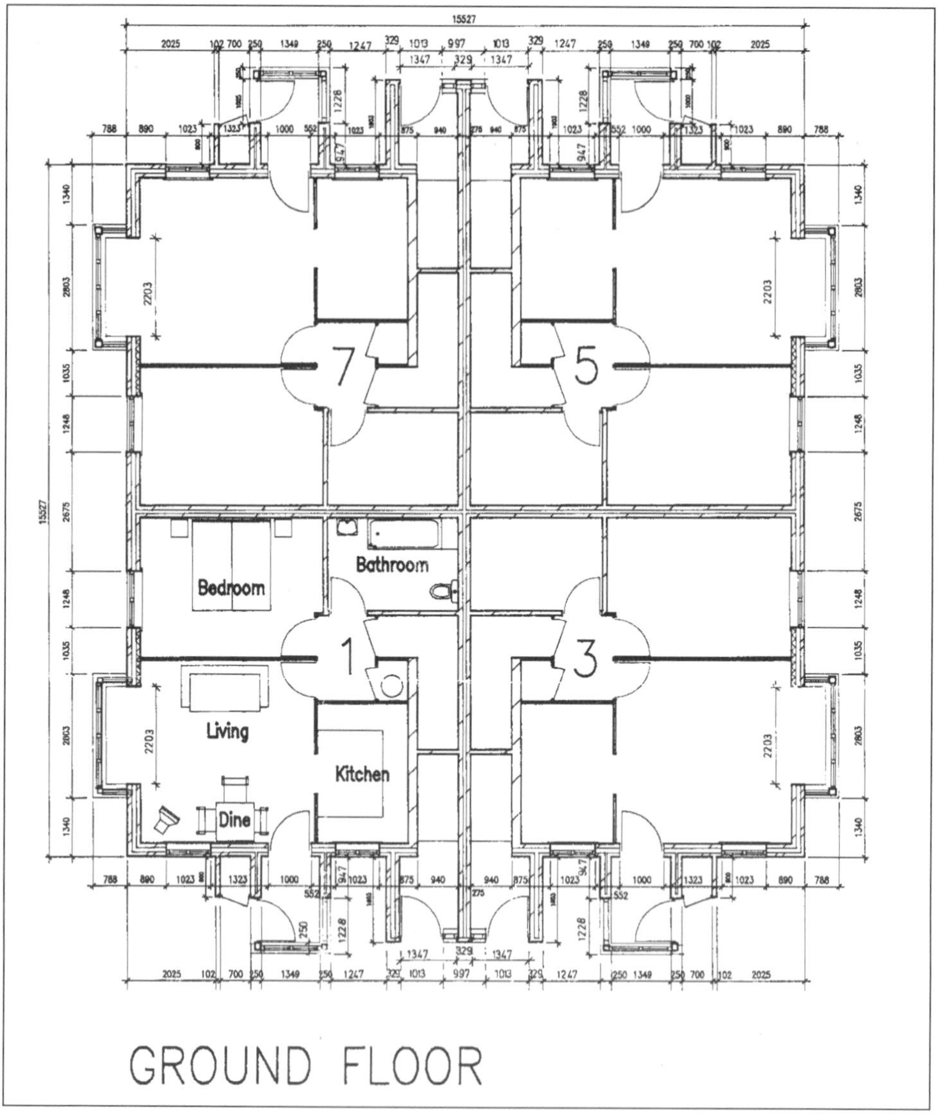

Figure 5.15: Turnbull Street; ground floor plan (Scale 1:50)

Elevations

These view the properties from various positions, such as the front, side and rear. They give an impression of what the dwellings will look like from the outside, and will generally indicate wall and roof colours. See Figures 5.16, 5.17 and 5.18.

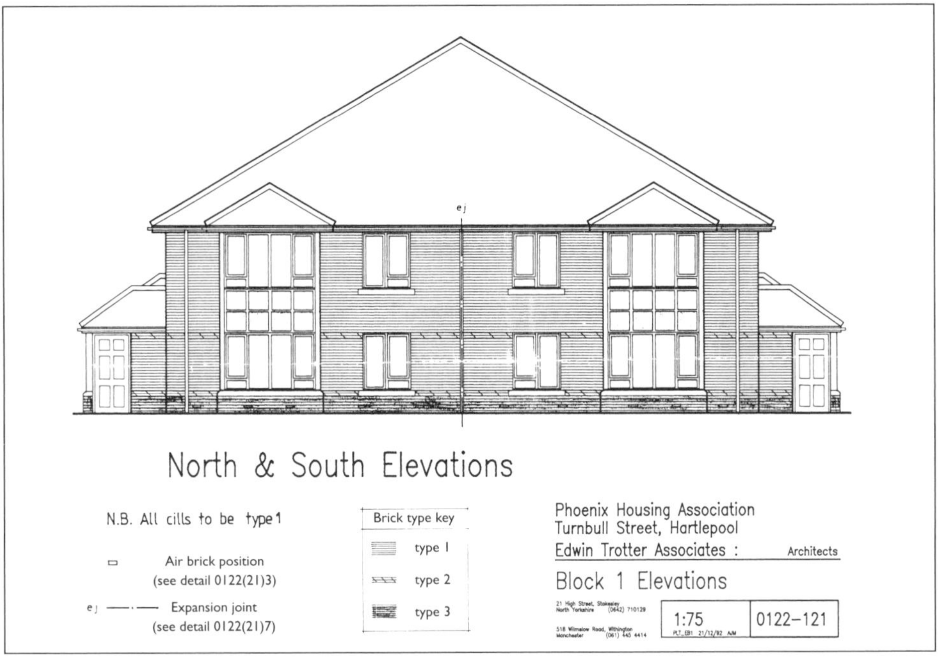

Figure 5.16: Turnbull Street elevation; North and South

Figure 5.17: Turnbull Street elevation; East and West

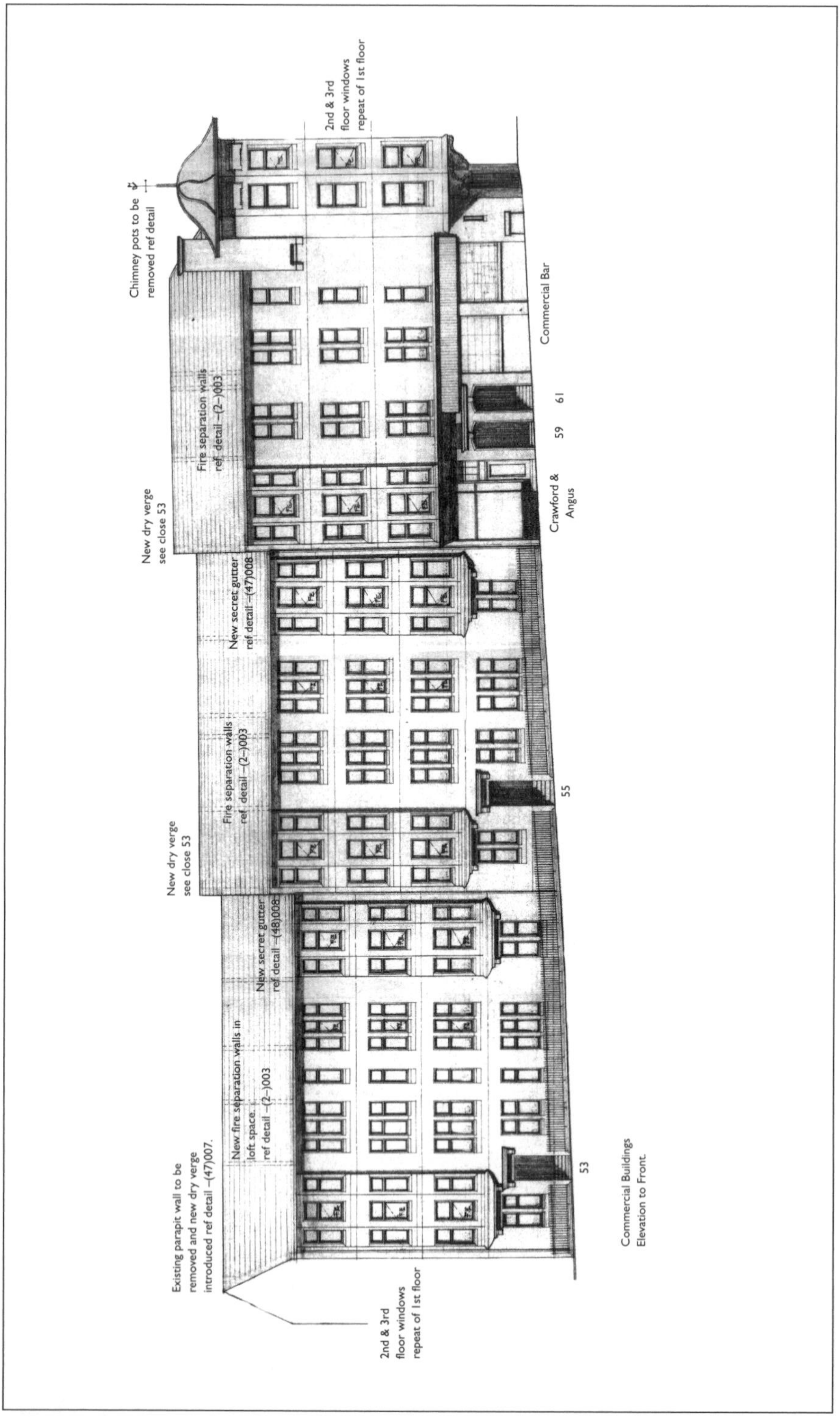

Figure 5.18: Commercial Buildings: elevation to front

c) Construction drawings

These are much more detailed drawings, which show information about methods of construction for different parts of the dwellings and the provision of services. See Figure 5.19. They have to be submitted for approval under the building regulations, and form part of the instructions to the contractor about how the scheme is to be built.

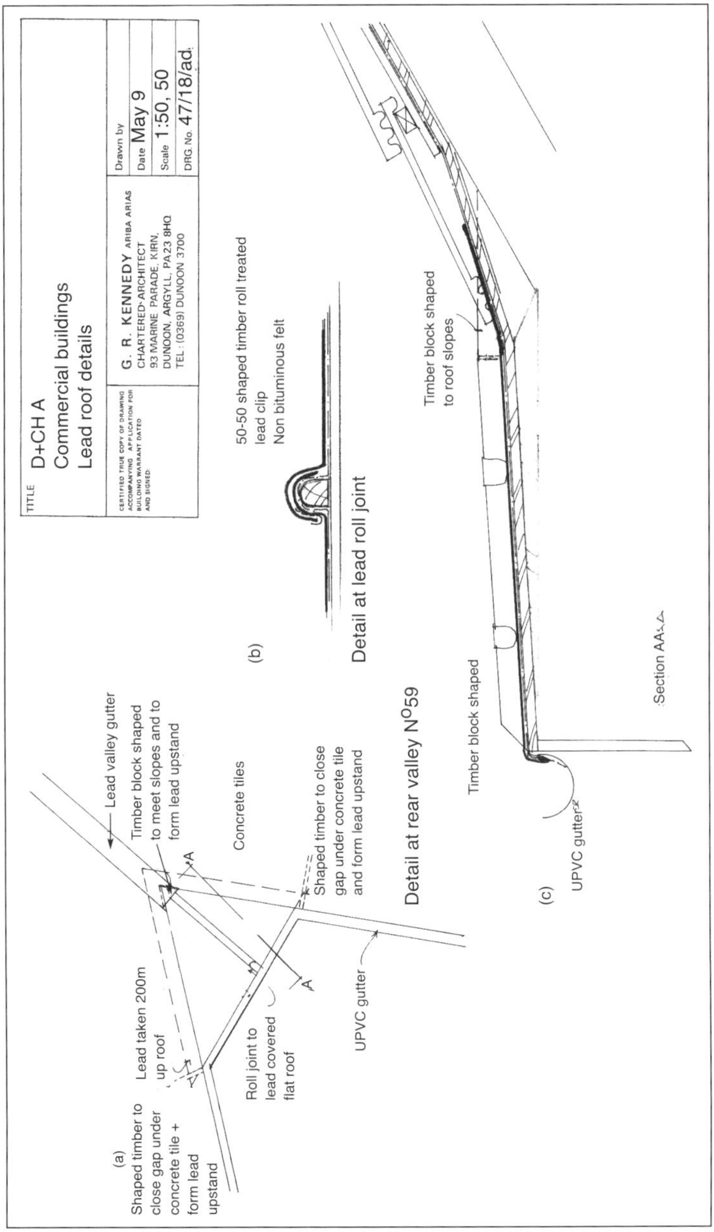

Figure 5.19a, b and c: Construction drawings showing details of roof at Commercial Buildings

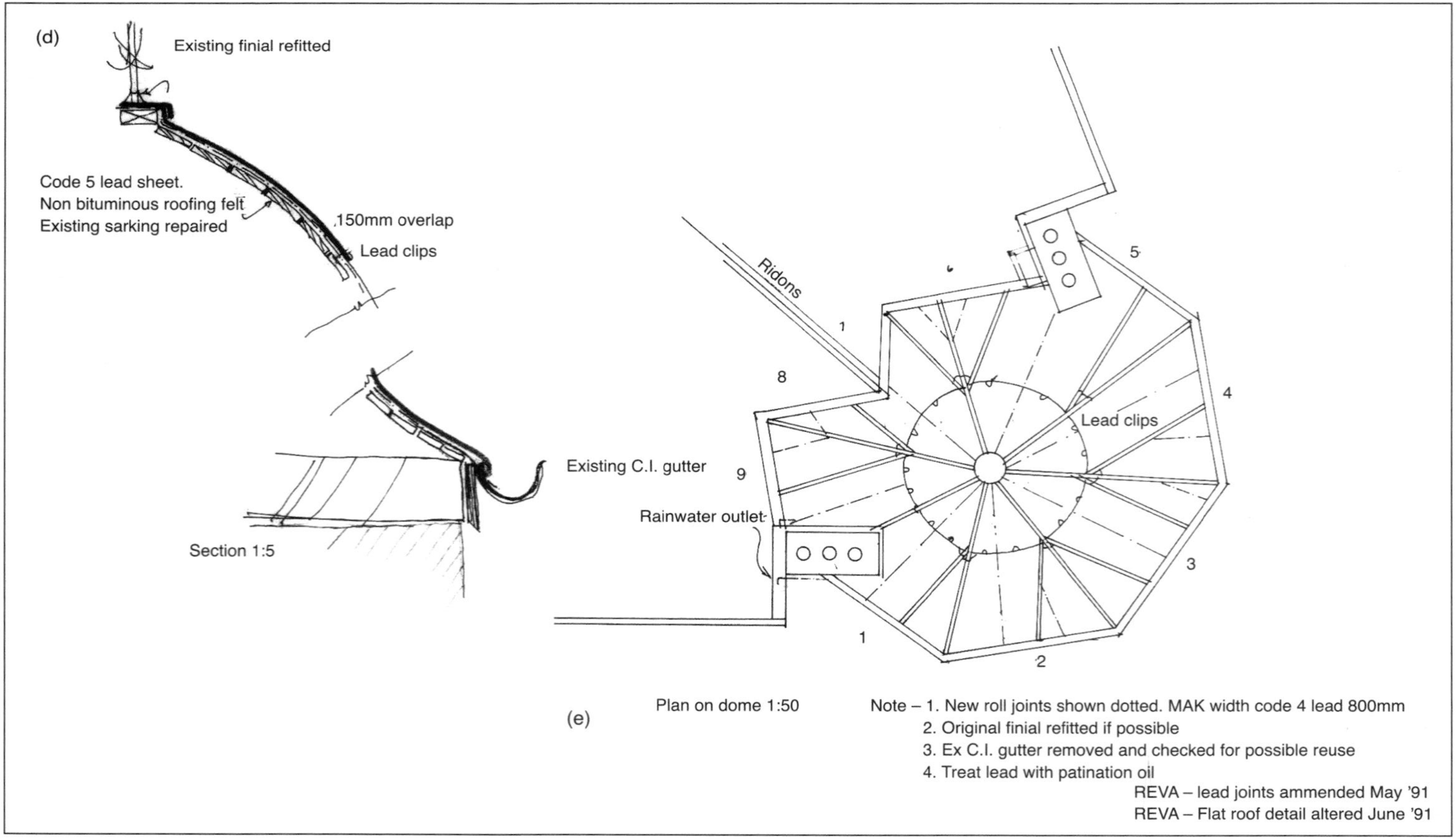

Figure 5.19d and e: Construction drawings showing details of roof at Commercial Buildings

5.7: The construction specifications

The specifications identify, in considerable detail, the construction methods and the quality of materials to be used. These are, necessarily, highly detailed and technical, and will need to match any statutory standards (such as the building regulations and the Code for Sustainable Homes or Ecohomes ratings). They are produced so that the contractor knows exactly what standards are expected for all work. Generally, they will incorporate all relevant national and European standards of performance, as determined by bodies such as the *British Standards Institute*.

6. Stage 3: Constructing the development

6.1: Selecting the contractor

a) Traditional approaches

According to Communities Scotland (2002), there are two main traditional approaches to selecting a contractor:

i) Single stage competitive tendering

This involves requesting quotations from a number of firms. However, in order to reduce the possible number of tenders (or *bids*) to manageable proportions, the consultant will generally advise on drawing up a *select list* of contractors. As it is important that there is sufficient competition to encourage keen pricing by contractors, generally, the list will consist of about six firms. Local authorities and housing associations must advertise (in the European Union as well as the UK) for firms to apply for inclusion on their select list of tenderers, whereas housing associations will generally draw up a specific list for each project. However, both must undertake a series of checks, to ensure that potential tenderers are capable of undertaking the work.

Checking potential contractors

Many organisations will ask potential contractors to complete a standard 'Organisation and Capacity' questionnaire, which covers key aspects such as:

- financial records, with information about turnover (the value of work undertaken in a year) and financial stability (assets and debts); a banker's reference is also usually required;
- details of past experience of constructing similar projects;
- references from past clients, commenting on things such as the quality of their work, their ability to complete on time, and their willingness to co-operate.

The client's quantity surveyor (QS) will usually also check whether the contractor's previous tender prices have been competitive.

Inviting tenders
When the selected firms are invited to tender, they are sent the *tender documents*, which are generally prepared by the QS. They usually comprise:

- information about the site (location, characteristics);
- the detailed design drawings;
- detailed specifications;
- information about the sort of contract which the firm will have to enter into;
- a form on which the tender price is entered;
- a *bill of quantities*, which itemises all construction activities (the quantities), for individual pricing by the tenderer.

Having received the tender documents, the contractor will be in a position to calculate the likely costs of the work, and can decide whether to put in a tender. The *closing date* and *time* for receipt of tenders must be clearly specified, and the tender must be supplied in an unmarked envelope, so that the tendering firm cannot be identified until the tenders are opened.

Selecting a tender
The sealed envelopes are opened, at the appointed time, by the consultant, client, QS and other relevant parties such as committee members. This is intended to ensure 'fair play', so that firms cannot obtain advance information about a rival's bid. The client's QS will then check the accuracy of the prices, and having assessed whether the bids are reasonable, will make a formal recommendation about which (if any) tender to accept. This need not be the lowest price, if there are suspicions that the contractor might be unable to complete the project for unrealistically low sums. If all bids are too high, the QS will need to consider how lower bids might be obtained – for example, by making alterations to the design.

Once a tender has been accepted, but before the legal contract is signed, the consultants will undertake pre-contract planning with the contracting firm (see below).

ii) Two stage selective competitive tender
When it is desirable to involve the contractor at an earlier (design) stage, the contractor is appointed on the basis of a tender that is based only on preliminary design information. Similar checking procedures to those described above will, of course, have had to be undertaken. Cost certainty will not be achieved until the second stage tender, when a firm design is available. This may be particularly appropriate when a *partnering* approach (see Section c), below) is adopted.

b) Non-traditional approaches
During the 1990s, out of a desire to achieve greater cost-certainty, it became more common for housing associations to take 'short cuts' through the development

process, with contracts that gave the contractor a greater role in relation to design. Some of these alternative approaches include:

i) Package deals

These offer the quickest way to achieve a development, because a complete scheme is purchased 'off-the-shelf' from a building company. It is paid for in one lump sum, on completion, usually to the builder's own design. This largely eliminates the role of the consultant, and can offer good value for money, but the housing organisation will have no real influence on the dwellings' designs.

ii) Design and build

Under this approach, the contractor provides the design as well as the construction work, so this also reduces the traditional consultant's role. The client can have an input into the design, by setting out precise details of the organisation's design requirements in a briefing called the *Employer's Requirements*. In this case, the client is represented on site by an *employer's agent* – usually a quantity surveyor – to oversee standards of work, rather than the consultant. Again, the price is usually fixed in advance.

iii) Develop and construct (or detail and build)

This approach is closer to the traditional approach. The consultant will produce *outline* designs, which will define very clearly what the client requires. The contractor then takes over and is responsible for turning these outline designs into *detailed* designs, which are then built. Again, an employer's agent represents the client, because the design cannot change once work commences. There is usually a fixed-price contract.

What are the advantages of these approaches?
They reduce:

- the length of the development process, which means that the client obtains a completed scheme much more quickly, and so begins to earn income sooner;
- costs; or as a minimum, offer more certainty about costs;
- the risk that the organisation will have to find additional resources to fund extra costs; this has become particularly important since HAG/SHG has been determined very early in the process, so additional costs must be met by the organisation.

What are the disadvantages?
They offer:

- less client control over the design (to varying degrees), which can:
  - reduce the possibility of standardising designs, fixtures and fittings, which can increase future maintenance costs;
  - result in a scheme which is less suitable for particular needs than developments which are specially designed;
  - eliminate the possibility of changing the design as work progresses;

- reduce possibilities to monitor and control standards of construction. This can be particularly important in rehabilitation work, where problems can easily be hidden.

c) Partnering in the construction industry

i) The background

The concept of 'partnering' in the UK construction industry was first explored by an enquiry commissioned by the DETR, chaired by Sir John Egan, and published as *Rethinking Construction* in 1998. The enquiry was set up in the belief that the UK construction industry was 'underperforming', both from a client and contractor perspective; whereas many other industries had seen huge improvements in efficiency during the 1980s and 90s, construction appeared to have made none of these gains. The Egan report dismissed notions that this was because construction was significantly different to manufacturing; on the contrary, Egan argued that:

> *Not only are many buildings, such as houses, essentially repeat products which can be continually improved, but, more importantly, the process of construction is itself repeated in its essentials from project to project. Indeed, research suggests that up to 80% of inputs into buildings are repeated* (Chapter 3, p1).

Egan identified five key *drivers for change* within the construction industry:

- committed leadership;
- customer focus;
- integrated processes and teams;
- a quality driven agenda;
- a commitment to people.

(Egan, 1998.)

These implied a significant change in the way the industry operated. The traditional approach to development, examined above in Section 6.1(a), is essentially an adversarial, 'us' and 'them' approach (client vs. contractor), with little emphasis on either the customer or quality standards. The report claimed that integration must occur around four key elements:

1. product development;
2. project implementation;
3. partnering the supply chain;
4. production of components.

In addition, it was argued that the poor safety record of the construction industry had to be addressed through better working conditions and improved management and supervisory skills. This would be assisted by greater use of standard components and processes – more factory-produced elements – where quality control is easier to achieve. This, of course, will impact on the construction techniques selected – see Section 6.4.

In contrast to traditional approaches, then, the report argued that the development process must involve building long-term relationships in the supply chain, based on clear performance targets which anticipate sustained improvements in quality and efficiency. According to Communities Scotland (2002), partnering promotes, '*...a climate of trust and agreement on mutual objectives and are applicable to most contracts, whether for development, planned or reactive maintenance*' (p34). Hence, competitive tendering, involving project-specific, one-off relationships, is inappropriate.

ii) Features of partnering

Basic features include:

1. agreed mutual objectives, which include long-term goals of sustained profitability (rather than quick profits) and 'open book' relationships;
2. a systematic approach to problem resolution, which seeks to avoid blame and disputes, and achieve 'win-win' solutions;
3. a commitment to continuous improvement, based on agreed and quantified targets, which is customer-focused.

(Communities Scotland, 2002.)

The partnering arrangement is normally agreed in a Partnering Charter. Ideally, it is a strategic (long-term) alliance, and will certainly involve the client, consultants and contractor, but, ideally, will also include others, such as manufacturers and sub-contactors, as '*...experience has shown that the benefits are significantly greater if partnering is applied throughout the supply chain*' (Communities Scotland, 2002, p35).

iii) Partnering and affordable housing organisations

The government recognised that there would be some resistance to the idea of partnering in the construction industry as a whole, so encouraged the Housing Corporation (reorganised into the Homes and Communities Agency from December 2008) to take the lead, by encouraging affordable housing providers in England to adopt Egan's principles. As a result, the Housing Corporation began to advocate 'partnering through the ADP' in 2002 and also initiated 'kick start' funding to promote the use of off-site manufacturing (OSM) techniques, targeted on a small number of suppliers of both timber and steel frame systems of construction. The Corporation argued that these pre-fabricated approaches:

- Improved supply chain relationships.
- Reduced component delivery times.

- Reduced construction times.
- Increased predictability.
- Enhanced build quality.

However, as well as requiring associations to adopt partnering approaches for their development schemes, the Corporation extended this approach to its own bidding process from 2003 (Housing Corporation, 2002). It was concerned that, by permitting small organisations to take SHG funding for very small schemes, it was not encouraging greater efficiency in affordable housing development. It pointed out that, by funding 350-400 associations annually, it was achieving an average output of only 50 homes per association. In *Re-inventing Investment*, in 2003, the Corporation argued that:

> *...the procurement of new housing in this country is too segmented, leading to competition which can be wasteful, distrustful and inefficient...*
>
> *We are confident that through selective partnering we will be able to achieve economies of scale, more efficient procurement, higher quality and increased end user satisfaction* (p4).

Hence, for 2003-04, it established a pilot Challenge Fund of £300 million, which funded a total of 50 housing associations to enter into 'partnering agreements' with the Corporation. The scheme was widened significantly from 2004-05 onwards, though there were strict criteria to be met before an association could apply for a partnering agreement. Under the three year National Affordable Housing Programme (2008-11) in England, most of the funding is made available to 'Investment Partner' organisations, which may include private developers as well as housing associations. However, for many smaller associations, their ability to develop with public subsidy has been halted, which has resulted in a number of mergers and the formation of new partnerships. These funding arrangements are explored in more detail in Chapter 4.

6.2: Pre-contract planning

Pre-contract planning ensures that no time is wasted; if various details are sorted out in advance, the contractor can get on with the actual construction work as soon as the contract is drawn up and signed. Pre-contract planning meetings will be arranged to sort out matters such as:

- *The contract commencement date*
  This may depend on the completion of site acquisition, or arrangements to decant existing tenants.

- *The contract completion date*
  Usually, the organisation will want the work to be completed as soon as possible, since faster completion means quicker letting and more rent income.

If it involves the rehabilitation of existing tenanted stock, then the decanted tenants will be able to return more quickly.

• *The programme of work*
The programme of work enables the consultant to monitor progress, and initiate appropriate steps if work falls behind.

• *The roles of the CDM co-ordinator and principal contractor*
These must be clearly agreed at the outset, so that the health and safety requirements of the CDM Regulations (2007) can be fulfilled.

• *Arrangements for informing other parties*
The building inspector must be informed about start dates, so that they can make regular inspections as work progresses. In the case of existing premises, the council tax authority should be informed, as no tax will be payable. Electricity, water and gas companies should also be contacted to take meter readings. This will ensure that the client is not liable for unauthorised use during construction work.

Anyone likely to be affected by the construction work – including local residents and businesses – must be advised about works that directly affect them. This is important not simply because it is good *public relations*; the works could interfere with a neighbour's business, with perhaps serious legal implications as a result.

• *Site security*
Building sites are regularly subject to vandalism and theft. Responsibility for secure storage for materials must be agreed, particularly in high-risk areas. Both the client and the contractor should have adequate insurance.

6.3: Agreeing the contract

A written contract ensures that all parties are clear as to what has been agreed. It reduces the possibilities of misunderstandings, and, importantly, offers the possibility of *legal action* if either party to the contract fails to deliver as agreed. The contract is drawn up by the QS, and will generally be a standard contract type, approved by the construction industry. This was, until recently, normally the JCT (Joint Contracts Tribunal) contract, but, in the context of partnering (see Section 6.1(c)) this is now considered to be confrontational, and others, such as NEC Option C, are considered more amenable to team working (Communities Scotland, 2002).

The traditional contract sets out what has been agreed, and covers:

- the **basis for payment** – the value of the contract, which will generally be for a fixed price;

Figure 5.20: Progression of traditional approach to new build house construction

- Clear the site (of existing buildings, unwanted vegetation, and top-soil).
- Dig and lay the foundations (on which the walls are constructed).
- Build the walls.
- Construct the roof.
- Fix the external joinery (such as windows and doors).

This provides a relatively secure shell for the next stages.

- Fix some internal joinery such as floors and stairs, and internal wall-partitions.
- Fix internal utilities, such as electricity cables, gas pipes, water and heating supplies.
- Complete internal finishes – plastering walls, skirtings and door casings.
- Install fixtures, such as fitted kitchen units.
- Paint internal walls and complete final finishes.

The stages in a rehabilitation project are much more variable, since the exact nature of the refurbishment will vary greatly from one scheme to another.

- the **contract period** – how long the work will take;
- the **construction design details** – what, exactly, is to be built, where.

The form of the contract may vary slightly, depending on whether it is for new build or rehabilitation, and whether there are to be *nominated sub-contractors*. These are specialist firms, which the client may want for some specialised activities (e.g. for wood treatment in rehabilitation work). In addition, the organisation itself, or its funders, may have particular requirements for adjustments to the standard forms.

If the approach to securing a contractor involves partnering, then a partnering charter is usually agreed and signed – see Section 6.1(c) above.

Once the contract is signed, the contractor can commence work on site.

6.4: The progress of construction

a) Traditional construction techniques

There are many possible approaches to constructing dwellings, which are beyond the scope of this text. However, many new, low-rise dwellings built today use traditional methods, with cavity-walls (a double wall of brick, with a space or *cavity* between to improve insulation and deter damp penetration) and tiles fixed to sloping roofs. These schemes might be expected to progress roughly as indicated below. It is, of course, the duty of the consultant to oversee the quality and progress of this work, with day-to-day monitoring by the clerk of works.

b) Non-traditional approaches to construction

As explored earlier, these approaches have become more widely used in recent years, as there is now greater use of factory-built components – often called off-site manufacturing (OSM) techniques or modern methods of construction (MMCs) – to provide faster construction at lower cost and to higher quality standards. The main, non-traditional approach in widespread use in the UK involves timber framed construction. A factory-produced, timber frame provides the main structure of the dwelling, and the walls (usually of brickwork) are constructed around the frame. Initially, this proved more popular with private (speculative) builders, because it permitted faster completion, but many more housing associations also now use it. For larger buildings, steel frames may be used.

More recently, there has been some experimentation with techniques first widely used in building 1960s tower blocks, involving the assembly of complete pre-cast (in a factory) concrete 'rooms' into a flat or house. For example, the furniture store Ikea has produced 'Bok lok' components to build homes of this type, which are relatively cheap and can be assembled ('built') much more quickly than conventional homes. However, financial institutions are notoriously conservative about construction methods and are not always keen to lend funds for the purchase of some types of non-traditional buildings.

In an attempt to stimulate innovation in the development of non-traditional approaches, as well as to demonstrate the lower costs available from modern methods of construction, the government in 2005 launched a high profile competition to build a house for a maximum cost of £60,000, called *The Design for Manufacture competition*. This was operated by English Partnerships – now part of the Homes and Communities Agency – on behalf of the Office of the Deputy Prime Minister (now, CLG). Eventually, 10 winners were selected (with the help of industry practitioners) and these were allocated sites by English Partnerships in order to build communities based on these designs. Full details can be found at: www.designformanufacture.info or through the Homes and Communities Agency website: www.homesandcommunities.co.uk

6.5: Variations to the contract: architect's instructions

Unless the development is being constructed under some sort of 'package' arrangement, the consultant may make changes to the design details as work progresses. The commonest causes of changes by the consultant are last minute economies due to unforeseen financial constraints, or changes to design details, perhaps caused by supply problems.

Additionally, external factors may force changes. The likelihood of unforeseen problems arising on site is reduced, but not eliminated by, a site survey. However, such problems are more likely in rehabilitation schemes, when many problems may become apparent only after demolition work.

All variations to the traditional contract details must be specified in *architect's instructions*, also known as *variation orders*. These are instructions issued by the consultant, which specify the alteration required (or agreed to), and, most importantly, identify the *cost* of the change. If the instruction is simply intended to clarify something, there may be no financial implication. But, where there is an added cost, the client should insist on strict limits to the amounts that can be agreed by the consultant, without *prior* approval. This is an important method by which the client can exercise tight control over costs.

Under 'partnering' arrangements, contractors are encouraged to seek cost-savings, usually via a system whereby cost-savings are shared between the parties, so that it provides a 'win-win' situation for both sides.

Extending the contract period

If the effect of an instruction is to extend the construction period, then an *extension of time certificate* must be issued. The cost implications of this depend on the cause of the delay:

- Extensions due to consultant's changes or errors will have to be paid for by the client. Clearly, if the contractor has to spend longer on site, it will increase the firm's costs – for labour, plant hire, insurance, etc.
- Extensions may be allowed for factors outside the contractor's control, for which no extra payment is made. These include bad weather, delays caused by the contractor's own sub-contractors, or strikes.
- Extensions that are the fault of the contractor result in the client being eligible for some payment in compensation. These are called *liquidated and ascertained damages*, and are deducted from any payments due to the contractor.

6.6: Monitoring information available to the client

The client will wish to monitor the progress of development, to ensure that it is satisfactory and that excessive numbers of expensive or delaying variation orders are not being issued. The main sources of information about progress include:

Site meetings

These provide a regular forum for the consultant, QS and contractor to discuss progress. The client may attend, but should certainly receive copies of the *minutes* of site meetings, which record what was discussed and agreed – including any need for architect's instructions and extensions of time.

Progress reports

The consultants will make their own, regular reports to the client, identifying progress to date and any problems. They should cover the two key elements for control: costs and time – which will be the subject of architect's instructions and extensions of time certificates. These should be identified and explained. Quality issues should be resolved as the dwellings are being built.

Site inspections

The consultant will, of course, make regular site inspections, as part of the supervisory role, and normally, a clerk of works will report to the client. However, it is also useful for the client to make occasional inspections; *not* to give instructions, which might over-rule the architect, but to check generally on quality and progress. Any problems that are noted on inspection should be taken up with the consultant.

6.7: Paying the contractor during construction

Under most contracts (though not package deals), it is usual to make payments to the contractor in *stages* as work progresses, because the firm has to pay for all materials and labour as they are used. Workers will not wait until the end of the contract to be paid! If the contractor should cease work, the client will be left with the portion of the scheme which has already been completed – it cannot be taken away – so there is little risk in making these *interim payments*.

Interim payment procedures

a) Interim certificates

The procedure for making interim payments to contractors involves the issue of *certificates* by the consultant. The quantity surveyor undertakes a valuation of the work completed, which is *certified* by the consultant. Valuations are usually undertaken at specific stages in the progress of construction; for example, when foundations are completed, when the building has reached first floor level, etc. Since the valuation relates to **all** of the work completed, the value of *previous payments* is then deducted, to calculate the payment due.

b) Retention monies

As work progresses and payments are approved, some percentage will normally be *retained*, so that the contractor is never paid *fully* for the work completed. This is intended to provide an incentive to complete the work; if **full** payments were always made, the contractor could leave the site before completing the work without losing anything.

Usually, the contractor will be keen to receive as high a payment as possible, so may contest the QS's valuation of the work. The consultant must then take the final decision about the valuation, and, in effect, arbitrate between the QS and the contractor.

If valuations include payments to *nominated* sub-contractors, the contractor will normally have to pass this payment on to the sub-contractor. For the contractor's own sub-contractors, it is the contractor's responsibility to agree their share of any payments.

c) Receipt of HAG/SHG

Housing associations may receive their public funding (if applicable) in pre-determined percentages (called *tranches*), at *key* stages in the construction process. The tranche percentages depend on the type of scheme – new build or rehabilitation, and key stages may be, for example:

(i) site acquisition;
(ii) start on site of main works;
(ii) practical completion – when the work is largely finished.

Since these stages do not correspond with normal stage payments to the contractor, which are made during the progress of construction, the client organisation must ensure that there are sufficient reserves, or access to borrowed funds (such as a bank overdraft), to make payments to the contractor prior to completion. This is why the prior preparation of an accurate *cash flow projection* (see Section 4.6) is so important.

Ending the contract

This will occur only in extreme circumstances, when, for example, the contractor is declared bankrupt, or consistently fails to deliver the standards of work required. This is known as *determining* the contract. Another contractor will have to be found very quickly to finish the work – which is why the determination of contracts is comparatively rare. Since there are complex legal requirements to determining a contract, the organisation's solicitors have to be involved at an early stage.

6.8: Agreeing completion

The client will need to ensure that the properties are substantially completed, ready for occupation, before formally accepting the work as complete. This is known as *practical completion*.

The consultant is responsible for agreeing the date of practical completion, but it is important for the client to check personally, since the consultant's perspective is different to the client's.

a) Snagging inspection

The '*snagging*' inspection is intended to identify any outstanding work for completion, and occurs about two weeks before the date for practical completion. It is undertaken by the client with the consultant and contractor. Other interested parties may also attend. When the client is an affordable housing provider, the important issue is whether the properties are ready for occupation, well built, and with everything operating properly. A systematic approach to the inspection must be adopted, if possible problems are not missed. The approach suggested by the National Federation of Housing Associations appears in Figure 5.21, and provides a

Figure 5.21: The snagging inspection checklist

It is important to have a system which can be used in a variety of circumstances rather than to wander around in an aimless fashion just saying that the colours look good. Instead, the association needs a critical and systematic review of the building. Start at the top of the building, proceeding downwards; check the internal parts of the building first, then the external parts. Check each room carefully and systematically:

- Do the windows fit properly? Are they sticking?
- Do the doors fit properly?
- Have the floorboards been fitted properly and securely?
- Has all the painting and decoration been carried out to a reasonable standard?
- Check all the services to the building, as applicable.
- Check bath, basin, toilet, to ensure they are not leaking.
- Make sure the heating system is working.
- Ensure all manholes are lifted to check that the drainage system seems to be working properly.
- Check there is a separate water stopcock for each house.
- Check that all stopcocks are properly labelled.
- Check that the interior and exterior of the building are clean.
- Check that the builders rubbish, tools, etc. have been cleared away.

Source: NFHA, 1988, pp36-7.

useful indication of the sorts of details that must be carefully examined at the snagging inspection.

b) Work to be completed

Following the snagging inspection, the client and consultant will need to agree a list of work that remains to be completed satisfactorily. This is then given to the contractor, who must ensure that this is undertaken prior to the date for practical completion.

c) Practical completion inspection

The official 'handover' of the scheme occurs at practical completion – which does not have to mean perfection. A few minor items may still need to be completed by the contractor, but the affordable housing organisation must be certain that the

Figure 5.22: Commercial Buildings on completion

Figure 5.23: Turnbull Street on completion

Figure 5.24: Close-up of Turnbull Street on completion

property is fit to be *occupied*. Outstanding items would not have to affect tenants in any significant way. For this reason, it is usual for there to be a final inspection of the properties, to ensure the client is satisfied that the work is substantially finished.

d) Handover of the development

The consultant issues a *Certificate of Practical Completion*, and the contractor hands over all items relating to the completed properties, such as keys, and operating instructions for electrical and heating equipment.

e) Management issues

Arrangements for letting or selling the completed properties must begin well in advance of completion. Rents or prices must to be determined, and the properties assessed by the valuation officer for *council tax*. Affordable housing organisations may have a *waiting list*, or a *transfer list*, from which prospective tenants may be selected. Those adopting a choice-based lettings approach (see Chapter 6) will need to ensure that the new homes are publicised and bids invited from interested households, in plenty of time for the new occupants to be identified.

If these approaches are not relevant to the type of development under construction – perhaps because the need being met is not usual for the organisation, such as shared ownership – then the organisation will need to place advertisements in the local press, to invite applications from eligible persons. Interviews may have to be arranged, and time allowed for offers to be accepted or rejected, and replacement tenants or buyers found. If the local authority has *nomination rights* to a housing association development, there must be close liaison to ensure that tenants have been selected and informed. It is important, for sustainability reasons, to ensure an appropriate tenant mix – see Section 4.3, earlier.

For rehabilitation schemes, where existing tenants will be returning, they should receive regular reports of the progress of the development, and be informed of the date when they will be able to return and the removal arrangements.

Depending on the nature of the scheme, there may be other requirements prior to completion. For example, the appointment of wardens, project workers, or caretakers; or the selection and ordering of communal furnishings and equipment.

It is important that all of these management issues are resolved in sufficient time for the new tenants to move into their dwellings at practical completion, otherwise the organisation will lose valuable rental income – or incur higher interest charges on outstanding debts, in the case of properties for sale.

7. After completion

7.1: Defects liability period

Under traditional contracts, no further outstanding payments are made to the contractor until the expiry of a *defects liability period*. Normally, the contractor remains responsible for any defects that are the result of poor materials or workmanship for a period of six months after practical completion. The consultant determines which defects are the builder's responsibility, so they should learn of all reported defects. While serious defects should be dealt with promptly by the contractor, most trivial ones can wait until the end of the defects period, so that they can all be completed together. It is expensive for a contractor to keep sending workers to rectify small problems.

The contractor has an incentive to rectify defects, because the final monies have not yet been paid. Once the defects have been rectified, the consultant issues a *Certificate of Completion of Making Good Defects*. Only then is the *final account* settled.

7.2: Final account

The contractor will usually have prepared the final account shortly after the date of practical completion. This sets out the total sums payable, less any monies already paid. It is generally prepared in conjunction with the quantity surveyor, and then checked by the consultant. This can take many months; even with a fixed-price contract, variation orders may have resulted in changes to the total contract sum, so the preparation of the final account is not always a simple matter.

7.3: Final certificate

Once the client approves the final account, the consultant issues the *final certificate*, releasing all remaining retention monies to the contractor. This will, of course, have been adjusted for any *liquidated and ascertained* damages, which may be due to the client in the event of late completion caused by the contractor.

7.4: Latent defects

Some defects may not be apparent at the end of the defects liability period. The contractor, nevertheless, remains responsible for *latent* defects, usually for a period of six years from practical completion. However, the contractor may well prove reluctant to accept responsibility, and it is expensive to pursue this through the legal system; so the client should take advice about whether this is likely to prove worthwhile.

7.5: Evaluating the development process

This vital step is sometimes overlooked by the client, but it is essential if lessons are to be learned for future projects.

- The performance of all of the parties in the development process, including the client and any partners, should be evaluated. These assessments should enable the organisation to decide whether the same people should be engaged in future, whether internal procedures and external partnership collaboration were adequate, as well as whether to adapt their approaches – including the briefing – where necessary.
- The design should be evaluated, both by the tenants and by the housing managers responsible for the scheme. This should include both house and estate design issues and will have to be undertaken at a later stage than the evaluation of the roles of the main parties, because it may take some time for design problems to become apparent. Particular attention should also be paid to elements that may have significant maintenance and repair implications, with a view to ensuring that these are not replicated in future schemes.
- Of critical importance is the sustainability of the completed development. After a little time, it is necessary to consider whether it has 'worked', not just in design terms but also in environmental, social and economic terms. Is this community 'working'/functioning well, and likely to continue to do so? Are tenants happy with their new homes? Is the performance of the homes – for example, in terms of energy efficiency – satisfactory? Performance should, of course, be checked against Code for Sustainable Homes or Ecohomes standards to ensure compliance, or to identify where problems have arisen.

Clearly, all partners will be involved in this assessment, which must include an analysis of the reasons for any less-successful elements. This is critical to enable all partners to learn from mistakes and improve future approaches.

8. Conclusion

As local authorities were increasingly encouraged to focus on their 'enabling' roles, most affordable housing development is now undertaken by housing associations. The development process necessarily involves the knowledge and skills of a range of key professionals to ensure its success. The traditional process comprises essentially three stages, consisting, firstly, of steps to initiate the development, followed by the design stage, then the construction phase. There are very specific requirements at each stage, to ensure that nothing is overlooked and that risk is minimised.

Concerns about environmental sustainability have resulted in the development of new assessments for 'green' construction designs and methods, including BREEAM's Ecohomes, and the new Code for Sustainable Homes. The Code is expected to become mandatory for all new housing developments by 2016, with changes to the building regulations planned in several stages. It is also important that the social and economic sustainability of the development is fully considered, which will usually require the involvement of a range of partners in the process, including, for example, residents, planners, the police, the education authority and the health authority. Where public subsidy is sought, new housing developments have to comply with the design standards of the relevant statutory funders.

The traditional construction process is fairly cumbersome and time consuming, and cost pressures over the last couple of decades have forced housing associations to increasingly adopt 'short cut' development procurement methods, which generally involve engaging the contractor at the (earlier) design stage in the process, in order to give greater cost certainty. Increasingly, 'partnering' approaches are adopted, which may involve the whole supply chain, and modern methods of construction (MMC) are being employed, which incorporate more factory-produced components. Partnering is a system based on mutual trust and shared objectives, and is focused on continuous improvement, for the benefit of all partners and customers. This, it is argued, produces better quality homes, at lower cost, with shorter development times, better site safety and greater customer satisfaction.

References and further reading

Building Research Establishment (2006) *Breeam Ecohomes*, BRE, Watford; available from: www.breeam.org

Communities Scotland (2002) *Building a Better Deal*, Communities Scotland, Edinburgh.

Conradi, P. *'Plump up the volume', Sunday Times, 14 September 2008, Home p4.*

Department for Communities and Local Government (2006) *The Economics of Deprived Neighbourhoods: Summary of Research*, CLG, London.

Department for Communities and Local Government (2006) *Code for Sustainable Homes: a step change in sustainable home building practice*, CLG, London.

Department for Communities and Local Government (2007a) *Building a Greener Future: policy statement*, CLG, London.

Department for Communities and Local Government (2007b) *Home Information Packs*, accessed from: www.communities.gov.uk

Department for Communities and Local Government (2007c) *Eco-towns prospectus*, CLG, London.

Department for Communities and Local Government (2008a) *Planning Policy Statement 12*, The Stationery Office (TSO), Norwich.

Department for Communities and Local Government (2008b) *Eco-towns, living a greener future – consultation paper*, CLG, London.

Department for Communities and Local Government (2008c) 3 April news release, *Eco-towns*, CLG, London.

Department for Communities and Local Government (2008d) *Greener Homes for the Future, the Code for Sustainable Homes*, CLG, London.

Department of the Environment (Northern Ireland) (not dated) *The Planning System*, accessed from: www.planningni.gov.uk

Design for Manufacture at: www.designformanufacture.info

Egan, J. (1998) *Rethinking Construction*, DETR, London.

European Institute for Urban Affairs (EIUA) (2002) *Sustainability Indicators*, The Housing Corporation, London.

Housing Corporation (2002) *Partnering Through the ADP*, Housing Corporation, London.

Housing Corporation (2003) *Re-inventing Investment*, Housing Corporation, London

Housing Corporation (2007a) *National Affordable Housing Programme 2008-11 bid round*, Housing Corporation, London.

Housing Corporation (2007b) *Design and Quality Standards*, Housing Corporation, London.

Housing Corporation (undated) *Kick Start Programme*, Housing Corporation, London.

Inside Housing 2008, 11 April, 'Agency to divvy up land as builders stay cautious', p5, London.

NFHA (1988) *Development, a Guide for Housing Associations*, NFHA, London.

Office of the Deputy Prime Minister (2001) *Planning Policy Guidance Note 1: General Policy and Principles*, ODPM, London.

Office of the Deputy Prime Minister (2002) *Regeneration That Lasts*, ODPM, London.

Office of the Deputy Prime Minister (2003) *Housing Quality Indicators*, ODPM, London.

Planning Portal at: www.planningportal.gov.uk

Scottish Executive (2005) *Choosing Our Future*, Scottish Executive, Edinburgh.

Scottish Government (2008) *Scottish Sustainable Communities Initiative*, Scottish Government, Edinburgh.

Scottish Government (undated) *Development Planning*, available from: www.scotland.gov.uk

Stevenson, F. with Williams, N. (2007) *Sustainable Housing Design Guide for Scotland*, Communities Scotland, Edinburgh.

Trotter, E. (1997) *Lifetime Homes*, JRF, York.

Welsh Assembly Government (2002) *Planning Policy Wales*, WAG, Cardiff.

Welsh Assembly Government (2006) *LDP: Planning Your Community*, WAG, Cardiff.

Wilcox, S. (2007) *UK Housing Review 2007/08*, CIH/BSA, Coventry & London.

Wilcox, S. (2008) *UK Housing Review 2008/09*, CIH/BSA, Coventry & London.

CHAPTER 6
How is affordable housing managed?

1. Introduction

The previous chapters have looked at the financing and development of affordable housing. This chapter moves on to examine the key tasks involved in managing affordable housing. It starts by attempting to define what is meant by housing management, and then considers some historical approaches to the function before looking in more detail at those key tasks which housing managers perform; such as letting houses, collecting the rent, dealing with empty properties, carrying out repairs and maintenance to the housing stock, and managing tenancies.

2. Defining housing management

In 2006 local authorities in the UK owned over 2.7 million homes with a further 2.2 million properties owned by housing associations, all of which have to be managed. (Wilcox, 2008). So what are the key tasks which have to be undertaken by housing professionals in managing these properties? The Social Exclusion Unit's Policy Action Team on Housing Management concluded that:

> *There is no single definition of the housing management task. It can vary between landlord and estate. Its nature depends on what local circumstances demand* (DETR, 1999).

Although this view is often repeated there is, however, a surprising level of agreement as to what housing management involves:

> *Most previous studies of housing management have focused mainly on 'traditional landlord functions': that is services provided primarily for tenants and funded from rental income. These functions include rent collection and arrears management, repairs and maintenance, voids and allocations, tenancy and environmental management and tenant participation* (Scott, 2001).

> *...definitions of housing management usually amount to little more than an outline of the various activities (allocation of tenancies, collection of rent, carrying out of repairs etc.) which comprise management* (Kemp and Williams, 1991).

The government's framework for assessing housing management performance under the Best Value regime provided the following definition:

management function on the authority's own housing stock
retains ownership:
ation of tenancies, including lettings to homeless households;
onse repairs;
ned maintenance; cyclical maintenance; capital works;

- *velopment and renewal;*
- *tenancy management, including tenancy sustainability and anti-social behaviour;*
- *estate management;*
- *tenant participation;*
- *leasehold management/right to buy;*
- *energy efficiency;*
- *equalities and diversity;*
- *regeneration;*
- *rent setting and collection*

(Office of the Deputy Prime Minister, 2003a.)

The Audit Commission subsequently produced a set of Key Lines of Enquiry which are used in the inspection of affordable housing landlords in England. These cover a similar list of landlord functions.

Figure 6.1: Landlord services Key Lines of Enquiry

- Access and customer care
- Diversity
- Value for money
- Stock investment and asset management
- Tenancy and estate management
- Housing income management
- Resident involvement
- Allocations and lettings
- Supported housing
- Management of leasehold and shared ownership housing
- Management of right to buy and right to acquire schemes
- Housing regeneration and neighbourhood renewal.

Source: www.audit-commission.gov.uk (2008).

This list of activities closely reflects the activities of affordable housing staff from the north of England studied in a research project into the changing nature of housing management. The study found that housing officers spent a large proportion of their time on the key housing tasks, and the proportions are shown in Table 6.1.

Table 6.1: Percentage of time spent by housing managers on key tasks

Task	Mean percentage of time spent by generic housing managers	Mean percentage of time spent by all respondents
Dealing with nuisance/anti-social behaviour	23.2%	20.3%
Lettings	22.2%	14.4%
Rent setting and collection	11.3%	11.0%
Repairs	8.0%	4.7%
Liaison with tenants' groups	6.1%	4.7%
Regeneration of estates	5.8%	4.6%
Developing strategies for under-occupation	4.0%	2.4%
Planned maintenance	2.8%	2.7%
Developing community safety strategies	1.0%	3.0%
All key tasks	**84.4%**	**67.9%**

Source: Grainger, Harding and Kirk, 2003.

As can be seen, housing management is essentially about four key tasks:

- letting houses;
- collecting the rent;
- maintaining the properties in good condition;
- managing tenancies and the environment in which tenants live.

As affordable housing management has developed in the 21st century, social landlords now find themselves managing shared equity properties and becoming increasingly involved in the practical implications of the development of mixed income new communities (MINCs).

The rest of this chapter will look at these key tasks in greater detail.

3. The historical development of housing management

Looking back often gives us pointers to the future and many of the current debates about housing management have their roots in discussions which were taking place in Victorian England. This section starts by examining the work of Octavia Hill, who is sometimes cited as the founder of modern housing management, and considers the principles which she adopted and discusses how applicable they are to contemporary housing managers.

3.1: Octavia Hill; the founder of housing management?

Housing management in itself is not intrinsically complex (although it is often demanding); the core tasks of lettings, rents, repairs and tenancy management are performed by all of those who manage housing. How then has housing management developed as a separate profession?

In the 19th century, many landlords who owned a few properties would have carried out the housing management tasks themselves, (as many private landlords do today). Others would have employed agents to carry undertake this work. These would often have been other professionals who undertook these duties as a sideline, such as surveyors, land agents or factors. In other situations the owner would have employed a middleman who would undertake repairs in exchange for a share in the rent. This system encouraged middlemen to overcrowd properties to maximise their rental income and to minimise expenditure on repairs (Power, 1987).

However, in the late 19th century a housing manager emerged who was to exert great influence on the way in which housing management was undertaken in the 20th century and whose philosophy is still discussed by housing managers today. Octavia Hill was born in 1838 to a middle class family and was persuaded between 1865 and 1866 to take on the management of a small number of dilapidated properties in the Marylebone area of London. Octavia Hill managed this housing herself and she took steps to improve what she saw were the poor housing management practices prevalent at the time. She considered that an essential element of good housing management was the necessity for close personal contact between landlord and tenants.

> *In its early days, her management, operating on a small scale, was often intensely personal; Octavia Hill's principles that people and their homes could not be dealt with separately, and that a sound landlord/tenant relationship must be based on mutual recognition and discharging of responsibilities, were put into practice by her followers* (Smith, 1989).

Only by ensuring that there was close contact on a regular basis could landlords ensure that the investment in their property was safeguarded. Such visits were an opportunity to check on the condition of the property, to ensure that tenants were not abusing the property, to collect the rent and to deal with any necessary repairs. She took a firm line on arrears and would evict those who did not pay their rent and she took a similar line against those who were guilty of persistent anti-social behaviour. The visits were also seen as a means by which tenants, who inevitably were poor and of lower class, could be educated into a better standard of behaviour. She was keen to encourage a sense of community and responsibility amongst her tenants and would also advise tenants on health and diet as a way of improving their standard of living (Power, 1987).

What echoes does this have for contemporary housing management? The emphasis on close contact between landlord and tenant is a key theme underlying local housing management. Those who argue for local offices suggest that one of the failings of centralised housing management has been that landlords have been too distant, both geographically and socially, from the tenants they house. The same idea underlies much of the support in recent years given to tenant participation and the need to work more closely with tenants.

However, it is important not to take Octavia Hill's influence too far. Octavia Hill, according to Spicker, was a '*moralistic* and *authoritarian*' landlord and this is something which most modern advocates of tenant participation and local management would want to avoid.

> *...the legacy she left to housing managers has been baneful. She founded a tradition which is inconsistent with the rights of tenants and destructive of their welfare* (Spicker, 1985).

This criticism of Octavia Hill's approach is that she failed to treat tenants with respect. It suggests that her approach was based on a belief that the working classes were inclined to get into debt, to neglect their houses and to indulge in unacceptable behaviour. This tendency could only be overcome by strict housing management, which emphasised the need to pay the rent, to reduce the overcrowding which led to immoral behaviour and to encourage communal areas to be kept clean by tenants. As Spicker goes on to say:

> *Octavia Hill's principles were misconceived at the time she formed them. Booth's research in the 1880's found that a third of the population did not have enough for the most basic sustenance – food, clothing, fuel and shelter. Landlords were 'lax' about rent collection because tenants could not pay. Debt and bad housing were the result of poverty, not indolence.*

Spicker suggests that her management practices were based on a misunderstanding of the circumstances in which tenants found themselves. It assumed that tenants would not pay; in fact tenants in many cases simply could not afford to pay. Of course, one of the effects of Hill's management style was that she would weed out the poorest tenants and only house those who could afford to pay the rents she charged.

And the problem, according to Spicker, is that the practices which she advocated are still seen today as 'good' housing management; the heavy emphasis on rent payment as a priority, preventing transfers if there are any arrears on the account, the use of Notices of Seeking Possession as a management tool, the emphasis on cleanliness, and the treatment of problem tenants by transferring them to worse estates.

3.2: The relevance of Octavia Hill to contemporary housing management

It is fairly easy to suggest that many of Octavia Hill's practices were indeed paternalistic and many would no longer be seen as acceptable today. So, why is it that her approach is still revered by many housing professionals? Perhaps it is because that whilst the motivation behind some of her practices may no longer be acceptable, the means are increasingly seen as positive housing management. In particular, her emphasis on personal contact between landlord and tenant has become adopted as good practice by contemporary housing managers and has been linked to other initiatives such as decentralisation and tenant participation. However, supporters today of a personal approach, tenant participation and decentralisation would do so from a position which accorded tenants significant rights as consumers of a service.

She has also clearly influenced the thinking of those who now advocate the social/welfare role of housing management. Many contemporary housing managers would argue that although the key tasks of management remain the collection of rents, repairs and lettings, they need increasingly to take on welfare roles with tenants; advising them on welfare benefits, working closely with social workers, the police and other agencies to overcome some of the problems faced by tenants living in housing estates.

However, some supporters of Octavia Hill also bemoan the passing of the traditional 'housing visitor' whose main role was to carry out regular inspections of tenants' properties and gardens and who would take strong action against tenants whose homes were not up to standard. They also regret the passing, in some places at least, of the housing application forms which asked housing visitors to grade the state of prospective tenants' homes as 'clean', 'satisfactory' or 'dirty'. This approach is very much in the Octavia Hill tradition, but one which is increasingly viewed as unacceptable by today's housing managers.

3.3: Developments in contemporary housing management; gold service and incentive schemes

In recent years, however, there has been an interesting innovation in housing management which has echoes back to the Octavia Hill approach. In the late 1990s, Irwell Valley Housing Association based in Salford began to develop an incentive-based approach to housing management. Under the Irwell Valley Gold Service tenants have to satisfy the following membership criteria:

- pay rent on time for at least six weeks;

- pay rent plus any arrangement to repay arrears for a period of at least 12 weeks;
- not break any other terms of their tenancy agreement (e.g. not allowing access for a gas service check).

The benefits of membership are;

- Cashback – for each week a member qualifies for membership, they receive £1 with up to £52 paid to members each year.
- A personalised membership card – the Compliments Card doubles up as a debit card onto which the Gold Service points are uploaded once a year.
- A faster repairs service (Gold Service repairs are completed in three hours for emergency, three days for urgent repairs and ten days for routine repairs).
- Access to education and training grants.
- Community Gold (where Irwell Valley will double any points pooled by a 'group' of residents).
- Community Awards – access to a pot of money to fund one-off community events.
- Back to Work fund – access to a fund for helping people back to work.
- Access to Irwell Valley contractors – for reliable contractors to complete works which are the resident responsibility.

According to Irwell Valley's website (www.irwellvalleyha.co.uk), 90 per cent of their tenants are now members of the Gold Service scheme. This model of management was developed as a way of focusing the organisation on high quality customer service and giving 'good' customers a better service. It was also designed to encourage tenants to meet the conditions of membership. The scheme has been a great success with significant reductions in arrears and empty properties as a result. The scheme, with its emphasis on firm housing management and rewarding tenants was controversial, but has increasingly been adopted by other councils and housing associations.

In 2003, the ODPM published *Incentives and Beyond: The Transferability of the Irwell Valley Gold Service to other affordable landlords*, which looked at the Gold Service scheme operated by Irwell Valley. The report indicated that the key benefit from the scheme was that tenants who complied with their tenancy agreement felt valued by the incentive scheme, but that to be really successful such schemes had to be accompanied by wider changes in the culture and service delivery of the landlord (ODPM, 2003b).

4. Letting properties

One of the key tasks of housing management is the letting of homes. Every year local authorities and housing associations let many thousands of homes; some of these are newly built or refurbished homes which are being let for the first time (new lets), but the overwhelming majority will be lettings of existing homes where the previous tenant has moved or died, creating a vacancy to be let (relets). In England, for example, there were a total of 304,900 lettings of social housing dwellings in 2006-07 as set out in the table below:

England

Table 6.2: Lettings in 2006-07 by local authorities and housing associations in England

	Total	To existing tenants	To new tenants
Local authorities	174,900	50,500	124,400
Housing associations	130,000	20,200	109,800
Total	304,900	70,700	234,200

Source: CLG Live tables: www.rsrsurvey.co.uk (2008).

Scotland

Table 6.3: Lettings in 2007-08 by local authorities and housing associations in Scotland

	Total	To existing tenants	To new tenants
Local authorities	26,877	5,247	21,570
Housing associations	24,461	n/a	n/a
Total	51,338	5,247	21,570

Source: www.scotland.gov.uk and www.scottishhousingregulator.gov.uk (2008).

Wales

Table 6.4: Lettings in 2006-07 by local authorities in Wales

	Total	To existing tenants	To new tenants
Local authorities	10,200	n/a	n/a

Source: Wilcox, 2008.

Northern Ireland

Table 6.5: Lettings in 2006-07 by the Northern Ireland Housing Executive in Northern Ireland

	Total	To existing tenants	To new tenants
NIHE	10,200	n/a	n/a

Source: Wilcox, 2008.

4.1: Who are homes let to?

As discussed in Chapter 2, demand from households for affordable rented housing is usually greater than the available supply of properties. This means that when there is a vacancy to be let, the social landlord is often faced with a number of people who wish to be considered for that vacancy. In these circumstances the social landlord needs to decide which of the competing applicants should be offered tenancies. Of course, if landlords face a situation where there is little demand they will have the problem of identifying suitable applicants to minimise rental loss and to prevent vandalism. In some parts of the country, and for particular properties, this problem of the 'difficult to let property', is a real one and poses significant challenges for housing managers. However, in most cases, social landlords are faced with the situation where they have more than one person wanting a particular home and they need to decide to whom the property should be allocated. This is often a complex issue because of the number of potential applicants who may need to be considered including:

- people whose homes have been demolished through clearance programmes;
- homeless applicants;
- key workers;
- existing tenants who wish to transfer to this type of property;
- applicants who are not already tenants who are on a common register (or 'waiting list') which may be held by the landlord for rented housing;
- refugees;
- vulnerable applicants;
- applicants wanting to obtain rented housing in another area.

Figure 6.2: Groups competing for housing

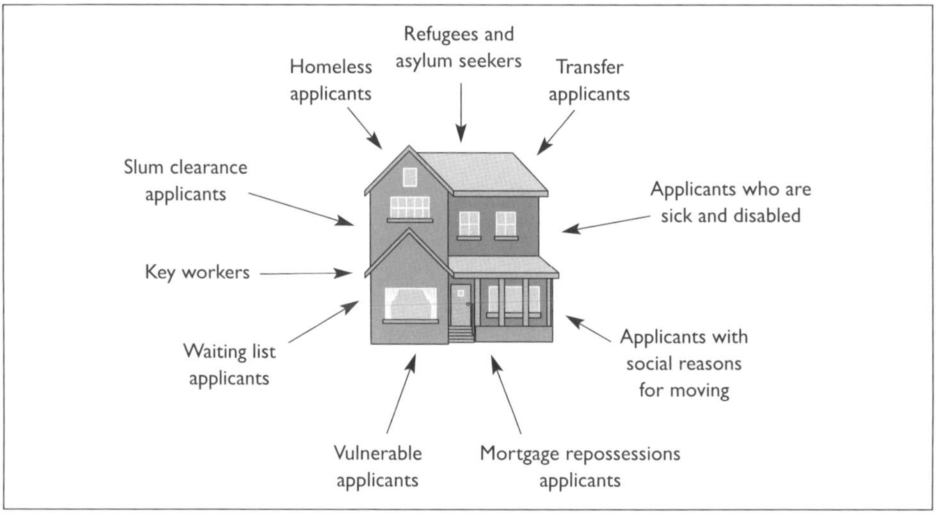

All of these people will have pressing needs; so how does the social landlord decide who should get priority for their homes?

4.2: What the law says

All social landlords have to take account of the legislation about their policies and procedures for letting their houses and this is now contained in a number of different pieces of legislation, which do not always apply equally to housing associations and local authorities.

Housing Act 1995 (Housing (Scotland) Act 1987)
All local housing authorities have a duty to consider the housing needs of their area and the need that might exist for additional accommodation.

Housing Act 1996 (as amended by the Homelessness Act 2002)
The 1996 Act set out for the first time clear procedures for local authorities in England and Wales to follow in relation to the allocation of housing. Section 159 of the act requires local authorities to allocate their housing in accordance with the act, including nominations to housing associations.

Under the terms of the Homelessness Act 2002, local authorities are no longer required to keep a *housing registe*r or waiting list but many local authorities still do. This provision was intended to pave the way for new and innovative approaches to allocations, which are considered later in this chapter.

Section 167 of the 1996 Act requires every local authority in England and Wales to establish and publish an allocation scheme which sets out clearly how they will allocate their housing. The allocation scheme must give 'reasonable preference' to the following groups:

- people occupying insanitary or overcrowded housing or otherwise living in unsatisfactory housing conditions;
- people occupying housing accommodation which is temporary or occupied on insecure terms;
- families with dependent children;
- households consisting of or including someone who is expecting a child;
- households consisting of or including someone with a particular need for settled accommodation on medical or welfare grounds;
- households whose social or economic circumstances are such that they have difficulty in securing settled accommodation.

It should be noted that homeless applicants do not come within the groups which should be given reasonable preference, although it is likely that their circumstances either prior to becoming homeless or whilst in temporary accommodation, will enable them to qualify under one or more of the above headings. These categories are broadly similar to the provisions set out in the 1985 Housing Act as to the groups which previously had to receive reasonable preference:

- to people living in unsanitary or overcrowded accommodation;
- to people with large families;
- to the statutory homeless;
- to persons living in unsatisfactory conditions;
- (Scotland only) to people living in housing below the tolerable standard.

Under section 106 of the Homelessness Act 2002, where a local authority is satisfied that an applicant (or a member of the applicant's household) is guilty of unacceptable behaviour serious enough to make him unsuitable to be a tenant of the housing authority, it can decide to treat the applicant as ineligible for an allocation. The only behaviour which can be regarded as unacceptable for these purposes is behaviour by the applicant or by a member of his or her household that would – if the applicant had been a secure tenant of the local authority at the time – have entitled the local authority to a possession order on the grounds of behaviour such as conduct likely to cause nuisance or annoyance, and use of the property for immoral or illegal purposes. The local authority will need to satisfy itself that the applicant is unsuitable to be a tenant by reason of the behaviour in question – in the circumstances at the time the application is considered. Previous unacceptable behaviour may not justify a decision to treat the applicant as ineligible where that behaviour can be shown to have improved. Local authorities who decide that applicants are ineligible because of unacceptable behaviour must give them written notification of the decision. The notification must give clear grounds for the decision, which must be based firmly on the relevant facts of the case. Applicants have the right to request a review under the allocation scheme of any decision as to eligibility, and a right to be informed of the decision of that review, and the grounds for that decision.

Earlier legislation, which is still in force, requires authorities to provide accommodation to those displaced by slum clearance programmes and they also use their 'best endeavours' to house farm workers displaced from tied accommodation.

Housing Act 1998

Under the Residents' Charter, housing associations in England must supply a copy of their lettings policy for assured tenants to the local authority and the Housing Corporation (now replaced by the Tenant Services Authority). The Regulatory Code and guidance for English housing associations also covers this issue (see Figure 6.3). The Tenant Services Authority is consulting on a new regulatory framework at the time of publication, so check their website: www.tenantservicesauthority.org

Figure 6.3: Regulatory Code (Tenant Services Authority)

- Lettings and sales policies are flexible, non-discriminatory and responsive to demand, while contributing to the need to be inclusive and the need to ensure sustainable communities.
- Associations are able to demonstrate their co-operation with local authorities in homelessness reviews, in the formulation of homelessness strategies, and in the delivery of local authorities' homelessness functions.
- When requested to do so by the local authority and to such an extent as is reasonable in the circumstances, associations provide a proportion of their stock to local authority nominations and temporary accommodation to the homeless.
- Criteria are adopted following consultation with local authorities for accepting or rejecting nominees and other applicants for housing.
- Applicants are excluded from consideration for housing only when their unacceptable behaviour is serious enough to make them unsuitable to be a tenant and only in circumstances that are not unlawfully discriminatory.
- Lettings policies:
  - are responsive to local authority housing duties;
  - take account of the need to give reasonable priority to transfer applicants including applicants from other associations;
  - are responsive to national, regional and local mobility and exchange schemes;
  - are demonstrably fair and effectively controlled.

Homelessness provisions (Housing Act 1996 (Part V11) as amended by the Homelessness Act 2002)

The law in England and Wales effectively requires local authorities to secure permanent accommodation for those applicants who were unintentionally homeless and in priority need. In assessing whether an applicant is entitled to permanent housing the applicant has to jump over a number of hurdles:

- Is the applicant homeless or threatened with homelessness?
- Is the applicant in priority need?
- Is the applicant unintentionally homeless?
- Does the applicant have a local connection with the area?

Although the definitions of a *homeless applicant, intentionality, local connection* and *priority need* were largely unchanged from the 1985 Act, the Homelessness Act 2002 extended the priority need categories so that they now include:

- a pregnant woman or a person with whom she resides or might reasonably be expected to reside;
- a person with whom dependent children reside or might reasonably be expected to reside;
- a person who is vulnerable as a result of old age, mental illness or handicap or physical disability or other special reason, or with whom such a person resides or might reasonably be expected to reside;

- a person who is homeless, or threatened with homelessness, as a result of an emergency such as flood, fire or other disaster;
- homeless 16 and 17 year olds;
- care leavers aged 18, 19 and 20;
- people who are vulnerable because of time spent in care, the armed forces, prison or custody; and
- people who are vulnerable because of violence.

There are some exceptions in the case of 16 and 17 year olds and care leavers who are owed a duty by the social services authority. However, in circumstances where the social services authority and the housing authority are one and the same, the only question is the nature of the assistance to be provided.

The Chartered Institute of Housing has published a detailed book, *Homelessness in the UK: Problems and Solutions* (Fitzpatrick *et al.*, 2009) which readers should consult for more detailed information.

Homelessness provisions in the Housing (Scotland) Act 2001 and Homelessness etc. (Scotland) Act 2003

The 2001 Act required each Scottish local authority to have a homelessness strategy, to conduct an assessment of homelessness in the area and provide free advice and temporary accommodation to homeless people. The 2003 Act went further and strengthened the rights of homeless people and was part of a co-ordinated approach to tackling and preventing homelessness. Under previous Scottish legislation, homeless people had to meet three tests in relation to homeless:

- Is the applicant in priority need?
- Is the applicant unintentionally homeless?
- Does the applicant have a local connection?

The 2003 Act began to phase out the restrictions in the priority need classification so that by 2012 all people will be encompassed by the definition and the priority need test will be redundant. However, initially priority need has been extended to include those having:

- a chronic illness;
- suffered a miscarriage or had an abortion;
- been discharged from hospital;
- left a prison or the regular armed forces.

In addition, people living or who might reasonably be expected to live with someone in priority need are included as eligible persons, along with 16-17 year olds, 18-20 year olds who run the risk of sexual or financial exploitation through misuse of drugs and alcohol, people at risk of violence or harassment because of race, colour, ethnicity or sexual orientation or a person who runs the risk of domestic violence. As can be seen this is similar to the English and Welsh amendments to the homelessness legislation, but it is clear that the Scottish Government is extending the compass of its homelessness legislation, and in particular with its extension of the definitions of priority need with the aim of abolishing the concept by 2012.

Race Relations Act 1976

The selection of tenants and the subsequent allocation of properties to successful applicants is governed by the laws on discrimination. In their Code of Practice for rented housing the Commission for Racial Equality (now replaced by the Equality and Human Rights Commission which was established in 2007) indicated that a number of research studies clearly demonstrated that ethnic minorities suffered severe discrimination in housing. This has occurred in two main ways; the first in access to housing registers, where people from minority ethnic groups may not have been accepted. The second is in the type and quality of accommodation offered to minority ethnic groups. In a number of research studies these groups were shown to have been offered poorer accommodation than whites.

The Commission for Racial Equality launched a number of investigations into the selection and allocation policies of local authorities and found discrimination to be a significant problem. For example, the Commission for Racial Equality's report into Liverpool City Council found that white people were twice as likely to get a nomination to a housing association home compared to a black applicant, four times as likely to get a new home, four times as likely to get a garden and twice as likely to get a property with central heating.

The CRE's Code of Guidance (1991) was replaced in 2006 by the Housing Code of Practice with versions produced for England, Scotland and Wales. The revised Code sets out what housing organisations have to achieve:

- set standards for achieving racial equality;
- provide practical guidance that will help organisations and individuals involved in all areas of housing to avoid unlawful racial discrimination and harassment, promote equal opportunities for all, and encourage good race relations; and
- help make sure that anyone who is considering taking a legal case, or who has concerns about the way decisions on housing matters have been made, understands the legislation, their rights, and what constitutes good practice in the field of housing.

(CRE Housing Code of Practice for England, 2006.)

Race Relations Amendment Act 2000

This act strengthens the 1976 Race Relations Act. The most important change was to place a new, enforceable duty on public authorities to promote racial equality. This requires most public bodies (including local authorities, the Tenant Services Authority, but *not* housing associations) to make the promotion of racial equality central to their work and to take the lead in promoting equality of opportunity and good race relations and preventing unlawful discrimination. In particular, they have to publish detailed Race Equality Schemes which make it clear how they meet the requirements of the act. Although the act applies in Scotland, the Scottish parliament has the power to set specific duties for Scottish public authorities.

Sex Discrimination Act 1975

This requires that landlords should not discriminate on the grounds of sex in the allocation of their property.

4.3: Types of lettings systems

All landlords need to have established a procedural system to decide who should be offered the housing that they have available to let. Under the 1996 Housing Act these procedures must be published and made available to anyone who asks for them. The scheme must give reasonable preference to those applicants set down in section 167 of the act.

Date order system

Under this system, landlords will house applicants in strict date order, making offers to those who have been registered longest on the list. Even where other systems are used, date order can still be important. For example, homeless applicants usually have priority for re-housing, but it is often the case that local authorities will aim to house first those who have been registered as homeless the longest.

Merit systems

With this system the decision as to who is allocated a particular property is based on the merits of each applicant's case. Usually the organisation will have a lettings policy and applicants are considered against the criteria set out in the policy to determine who is in the greatest need. A common problem with merit systems is that the decision to allocate a property is often based on a very subjective judgement as to which applicant is in the greatest need and therefore the most deserving to get the property. Figure 6.4 is an example of a merit system operated by a housing association.

Individual applicants are considered against these criteria and the applicant with the 'greatest need' is offered the property. However, the key problem is which criteria is given the most weight in the decision-making process and in many cases the decision may be difficult to justify given the many subjective judgements that this type of allocation system entails.

Points schemes

These exist where the applicant's circumstances are considered against a scheme where points are awarded for various indicators of housing need. For example, 10

Figure 6.4: Merit system

In considering nominations from local authorities and in selecting applicants from the association's waiting list the following matters are taken into account:

1. Size, type and location of dwelling available for re-letting and suitability to meet the applicant's housing need.

2. The applicant's housing conditions including:
   - threatened or actual homelessness
   - overcrowding or under-occupation
   - sharing facilities
   - location in relation to work, relatives, friends and services
   - state of repair of the present property and ability to influence the state of repair.

3. The applicant's ability to cope with their existing housing conditions including:
   - income
   - health
   - stress
   - previous housing history
   - the needs of dependents.

4. The availability of alternative housing including:
   - potential access to home ownership
   - ability to meet local authority residential requirements.

5. The length of time the applicant has had to tolerate unsatisfactory housing conditions.

points may be awarded to someone living in rented accommodation, but 20 points to someone living in tied accommodation. The points are totalled and the applicant with the highest points is usually awarded priority. Such schemes are relatively easy to understand and to query the points score awarded. They are of course subjective in terms of the factors considered and the weighting attached to individual points scores. An example is shown in Figure 6.5.

Group or band systems

A group system operates where applicants are initially placed into different groups (or bands) and the organisation then allocates homes to people from individual groups. It will normally use a quota which indicates that a specified proportion of allocations for each group. The groups can be few or numerous but typical schemes will include groups for:

- homeless families;
- medical cases;
- elderly;
- special needs.

Figure 6.5: Example of a points scheme used by a housing association

The housing register

The association operates a single housing register. In all cases, applicants, if they are to be accepted onto the housing register, must demonstrate that they are in housing need – the factors which the association considers are:

- Existing housing conditions.
- Ability to cope with these conditions.
- Other prospects for housing. Since our aim is to help those in greatest need, we consider the following as priority examples:
  - Homeless applicants.
  - People in overcrowded, insanitary or insecure conditions.
  - People living in accommodation lacking in standard amenities.
  - People in shared housing who would benefit from moving to a self contained property.
  - People living in under-occupied property.
  - People who would benefit from re-housing for social, emotional or medical reasons.
  - People fleeing violence.
  - People suffering harassment.

Points scheme

The factors which the association will consider and the weighting attached are set out in the points scheme:

1. **Security of tenure**

   The association will not normally award points under this heading for applicants with secure or assured tenancies.

   a) **Homeless applicant** **(30 points)**

   b) **Applicants without their own home** **(20 points)**

   People normally falling into this group are detailed below:
   - Assured shorthold tenants/licencees.
   - Residents of bed and breakfast accommodation.
   - Residents of hostels.
   - Residents of hospital, prison and other institutions.
   - Young people leaving care.
   - Applicants living in caravans.
   - Living with family/friends/carers.
   - Service tenancies and service licences, i.e. tied accommodation.
   - Sub-tenants and persons in rooms with a resident landlord.

   c) **Households Living Separately** **(25 points)**

   Applicants who could reasonably be expected to live together as a household including:
   - Couples with or without children.
   - Families with dependent relative.

Figure 6.5: Example of a points scheme used by a housing association *continued*

2. Size and type of property

In assessing overcrowding the association will take account of an unborn child where a mother is more than six months pregnant.

a) **Overcrowding (for each bedroom lacking)** **(20 points)**

We consider a separate bedroom necessary for:

Each couple living together.
A parent in a single parent family.
A single adult over 16 years.
Each child of 10 years or over who would otherwise have to share with a child of the opposite sex.

(A single bedroom is one bedspace, a double bedroom is two bedspaces)

b) **Under-occupation** **(10 points)**

For each surplus bedroom.

(One bedroom is allowed above the household's needs)

c) **People Living in flats** **(10 points)**

Families with children under 10 years living above ground floor.
Elderly people living in flats above first floor without a lift.

3. Condition of property

a) **Lack of basic facilities (for any lack of amenity)** **(40 points)**

No kitchen facilities.
No bathroom.
No inside toilet.

b) **Property in need of major repair** **(50 points)**

Property declared unfit to occupy.

4. Sharing any facilities **(10 points)**

(except for applicants living with their family)

Living room.
Kitchen facilities.
Bathroom.
Toilet.

5. Disability/medical circumstances **(30 points)**

If anyone included in the application is in poor health or has a disability which could be assisted by re-housing.

6. Social needs **(25 points)**

These points may be awarded to take account of other housing-related problems or needs including:

To move to be nearer family.
To move to be nearer work.
To move to be nearer community support.
To move to be nearer carers.
To avoid harassment/nuisance or violence.
To assist applicants with high rents/housing benefit restrictions.

Within each group, applicants can be ranked by a variety of means; merit, date order or points. If an organisation has adopted a group system it will need to decide which group should receive which proportion of lettings.

Combined systems

Most landlords will operate a variety of allocation schemes. For example, even where a landlord has a points scheme they may still use other systems within it. Some applicants may be given priority over others on the list, for instance, homeless applicants may have priority over people with very high points on the waiting list. In addition, it may be difficult to compare people on the transfer list who want a move to more suitable accommodation, with those living in unsuitable private accommodation. It is the case that many local authorities will say that they will let a certain percentage of their properties to applicants off the transfer list, and the choice of the transfer applicant will go to the person with the most points.

4.4: Nominations to housing associations

Housing associations are normally expected to offer local authorities **nominations**. This means that the housing association agrees to re-house people referred (nominated) by the local authority. The precise arrangements for nominations differ from local authority to authority. In some cases the local authority will give the association a number of possible applicants to consider and the association will make its choice. In other cases, perhaps only one applicant will be put forward for each vacancy. The association must retain the right to refuse a nomination if it feels that the applicant does not meet the association's own lettings criteria. Where local authorities give free land or other financial support to associations they will often require 100 per cent nominations to be given.

4.5: Transfers of existing tenants

Any lettings policy also has to consider the needs of existing tenants who may wish to move to a different home. This can be for a variety of reasons:

- Medical; where the current home is unsuitable (e.g. a two storey house with someone with a heart problem who has difficulty climbing stairs).
- Social; where someone may wish to move home to be nearer family, friends, school or work.
- Increased family size; where the property is no longer large enough to meet the household's requirements.
- Other reasons such as a wish to move away from an undesirable area.

In designing its lettings policies and procedures, it is essential that the landlord considers the needs of those who wish to transfer. If it does not, then these people may end up trapped in housing which is unsuitable for them. Most landlords will therefore devise a transfer policy which sets out the rules by which people may transfer and usually indicates the preference which will be given to transfer applicants above others on the waiting list. For example, if a council has a bungalow available it may consider allocating it first to an elderly tenant living alone in a three bedroom house. This means that the elderly tenant's housing needs are met and the resulting vacancy of the three bedroom house can then be let to someone off the council waiting list, such as a homeless family. (All landlords will have different views as to the preference which they give to transfer applicants, but they are required to make clear in their published policies and procedures how they deal with transfer applicants.)

4.6: Size of waiting and transfer lists

As all housing organisations have a different approach to dealing with allocations issues it is difficult to make an accurate estimate of the numbers of people on housing lists who are seeking accommodation. However, the Local Government Association has estimated that in 2006-07 around 1.6 million households (4,000,000 people) were on local authority waiting lists in England (LGA, 2007). This compares with a government estimate in 2001-02 of 700,000 households – equivalent to around three per cent of all households – containing someone who was on a waiting list for council or housing association accommodation (Mew, *et al.*, 2003, p20). In October 2008, the LGA updated its prediction and said that five million people will be on waiting lists for social housing in England by 2010 because of problems in the property market.

Figure 6.6: Number of households on local authority housing waiting lists in England 1999-2008

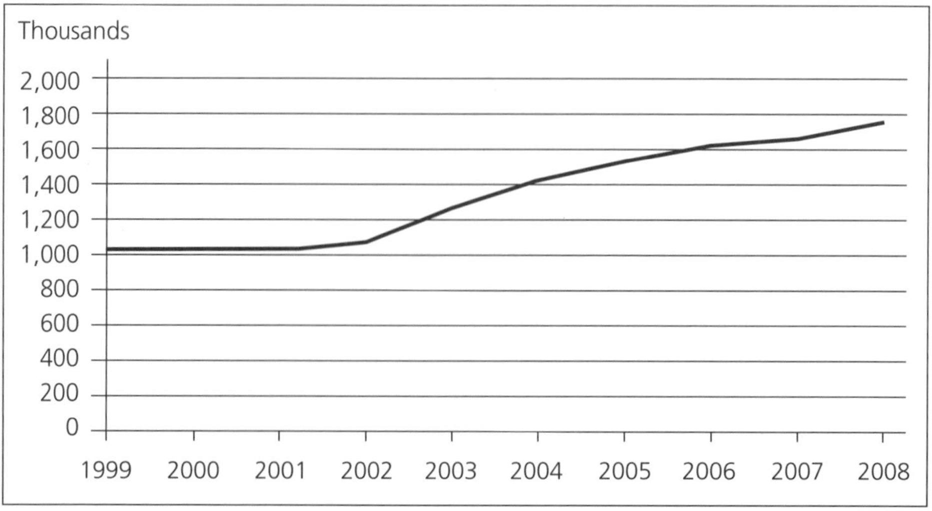

Source: CLG, 2009.

This increasing trend in the numbers of people registered on local authority waiting lists is confirmed by the government's own statistics which show that on 1 April 2008 there were a total of 1.77 million households on local authority waiting lists, an increase from the 1.67 million reported a year earlier (CLG, 2009). In explaining the increase, the government indicates that the increase since 2003 is linked to the fact that since 2003 local authorities have maintained open waiting lists and also that choice-based lettings schemes can stimulate housing demand.

4.7: Mutual exchanges

A mutual exchange is where one tenant swaps their tenancy with another tenant, usually of the same landlord but not necessarily so. The rules on such transfers are complex, but normally such transfers have to be approved, unless the tenant has rent arrears or is in breach of another term of their tenancy. It is important to recognise that a mutual exchange is technically an *assignment* of the tenancy. In other words there is not a new tenancy created, but the outgoing tenant passes on (*assigns*) their existing tenancy to the incoming tenant. This is important because it means that if a secure tenant exchanges with an assured tenant, the person who was the assured tenant now takes over an assured tenancy. The assured tenancy has fewer rights than a secure tenancy, for example, the right to buy does not apply to assured tenants, and an exchange can lead to changes in the rights of the tenants involved. Affordable housing landlords will wish to encourage such exchanges as they are a means by which tenants can move to more suitable accommodation, and they may assist the process by means of computerised exchange lists or simply by means of a display board in the housing office.

Nationally, local authority and housing association tenants can swap tenancies by means of the Homeswapper scheme (www.homeswapper.co.uk) or the Houseexchange scheme (www.houseexchange.org.uk) (also see: www.ukhomeswap.co.uk and www.council-exchange.org). There used to be a national mobility scheme called HOMESWAP, but this collapsed in the mid 2000s. Under these replacement schemes, participating tenants can advertise their homes for a mutual exchange with others who are registered. This enables a person who wishes to move to a different part of the country, usually for work or employment reasons, to do so.

4.8: Common housing registers

One issue which has recently been the subject of much debate in housing is whether local authorities and housing associations working in the same area should attempt to develop common housing registers or lettings systems. This is to deal with the all too frequent problem of a person seeking housing having to register on the waiting list of the local authority and all local housing associations to maximise their chance of re-housing. This can mean in some cases completing up to ten application forms for housing, all of which ask for very similar information. In order to resolve this problem, a number of local authorities have taken the initiative of developing common allocations polices. In some cases, this amounts to the local authorities and housing associations devising a common application form which is logged centrally and then made available to all housing providers. This saves the applicant having to complete numerous forms. In other cases, the landlords have gone further by not only having a common waiting list, but by developing a common allocations system in which all affordable housing landlords agree about the priority to be attached to every applicant, so that when a vacancy arises in any of the participant's stock, the highest priority applicant for that vacancy is selected, no matter who the landlord is. This is much more difficult to achieve as many landlords have different allocations policies and it may be difficult for a number of associations and the local authority to agree on a system.

4.9: New approaches to lettings

Increasingly, concerns have been voiced about the operation of some of these approaches to allocating affordable housing. Approaches based on waiting lists have been perceived as being time consuming and bureaucratic, typified by large application forms on which applicants are required to give lots of information before their application is even considered. Traditional approaches can be seen as being designed to meet administrative requirements as the housing professional retains all of the information to allow them to make an allocation decision; however, there have been administrative difficulties, particularly in keeping information updated. If information is out of date, time can be wasted making offers of accommodation to people who may not still be in need or whose needs may have changed since making their application. Those approaches can also be open to criticism as being closed and secretive, particularly as confidentiality requirements prevent unsuccessful applicants from being given full information about why another applicant was allocated a dwelling that they may have wanted. This can also lead to concerns that any system which cannot be easily seen to be open and fair may be failing to provide equal opportunity to all members of the community.

The government's response to such concerns was flagged in its Housing green paper, *Quality and Choice – a Decent Home for All* (DETR/DSS, 2000). Within the paper the government highlighted a desire to re-think traditional approaches to housing provision. The *Homelessness Act 2002* – which revised the legislation governing the allocation of affordable housing by local authorities – included a provision to facilitate the introduction of 'advertising schemes'. The 2002 Act also required authorities to include a statement in their allocation scheme about their position on offering choice to applicants. The revised *Code of Guidance on Allocations* (ODPM, 2002), which accompanies the legislation, clearly states the government's view that allocation policies should provide for choice wherever possible.

The Homelessness Act 2002, amended some existing legal restrictions in relation to the letting of local authority dwellings. These changes included the abolition of the requirement to operate a waiting list (housing register), and paved the way for more innovative approaches to lettings. In addition, the Housing Excellence Framework requires local authorities to have introduced, or be considering, choice-based lettings as an option for the allocation of their dwellings.

4.10: How choice-based lettings work

Choice-based lettings (CBL) are different from the traditional way of allocating housing via the waiting list. CBL allows applicants for social housing (and tenants who want to transfer) to apply for vacancies which are advertised widely in the neighbourhood (e.g. in the local newspaper or on a website).

Applicants can see the full range of available properties and can apply for any home to which they are matched (e.g. a single person would not be eligible for a three bedroom house). Priority is given to those with urgent needs, but where possible, properties are allocated on the basis of who has been waiting the longest. Authorities provide feedback that helps applicants to assess their chances of success in subsequent applications

4.11: Pilot schemes

The government funded 27 pilot schemes in 2002-03 to consider different approaches to allocating social housing in which customer choice could be made central, whilst 'need' remained a factor in the allocation of social housing. Many of these pilots were based on variations of the 'Delft' model of choice-based lettings, which developed in the Netherlands during the late 1980s and early 1990s. The pilot schemes included a mixture of 'stand alone' schemes in which the properties of one landlord alone were included in the scheme, and common approaches in which different landlords within the same geographical area signed up to a joint scheme.

In 2006 the government published research on choice-based lettings, *Monitoring the Longer-Term Impact of Choice-based Lettings* (CLG, 2006a). This research looked at the experience of 13 choice-based lettings schemes. The report noted that:

> *Choice-based lettings represents a radical departure in the traditionally rather paternalistic world of social housing. Although it implies some transfer of power to the customer, the CBL concept has caught the imagination of many housing staff. It has been embraced by numerous landlords as symbolising a commitment to modernisation* (CLG, 2006a).

The research shows that affordable housing customers welcome the choice, control and transparency of choice-based lettings (CBL). They also consider that the extra effort required to take part in CBL, by looking through vacancies and bidding for suitable vacant properties, is worth it.

Figure 6.7: Home Connections choice-based lettings scheme

Home Connections is a choice-based letting scheme initially funded by the ODPM in 2002 for £1.5 million. It was set up as a partnership of five local authorities (Camden, Barnet, Westminster, Kensington & Chelsea and Islington) and two associations (St Pancras & Humanist HA and Ujima). It developed a choice-based system with the following elements:

- all vacant properties were advertised each week on the internet and in newspapers and in public buildings, such as council offices and libraries;
- applicants registered with Home Connections could bid for each property, either in person, by post, over the internet or by an interactive voice recording telephone system;
- when bids were received each week the applicant with the highest number of points (as determined by the council lettings scheme) was offered the property.

The pilot scheme was very successful in terms of:

- increasing choice and customer satisfaction;
- reducing the time properties were empty, as only people who bid for the property would be offered it (there was a big reduction in refusal of offers);
- developing more customer-focused approaches to lettings;
- increasing access of homeless and other disadvantaged groups to housing.

Following the end of the pilot in April 2003, the partners agreed to maintain the scheme and more landlords joined the scheme.

In 2008 Home Connections in London had 17 landlords advertising their homes to let through the service.

Visit: www.homeconnections.org.uk for more information.

The 2006 report showed that there were increases in tenancy sustainment as a result of choice-based lettings, presumably because tenants are bidding for homes that they want to live in rather than being 'allocated' housing, which might not best meet their preferences. There was also evidence that applicants were changing their behaviour in relation to demand so that households with lower priority were recognising that they had to bid for properties in less demand if they were to stand a chance of being offered a home. Although the costs of setting up choice-based lettings schemes could be substantial, there were benefits in reduced void periods and lower tenancy turnover, and these were particularly marked in organisations which had suffered previously from above average turnover and below average relet performance.

The government set targets for local authorities, so that by 2010, all local authorities will have adopted a choice-based lettings system. There was also an interim target of

25 per cent of local authorities operating choice schemes by 2005. The Housing Strategy Statistical Appendix returns for 2004-05 showed that 27 per cent of local authorities had implemented CBL by 2005 with two-thirds of the rest in the process of making firm plans.

The government's local authority housing statistics for 2007-08 show that 47 per cent of local authorities in England were participating in choice-based lettings schemes on 1 April 2008, which was an increase from 36 per cent in 2007 (CLG, 2009).

Figure 6.8: Participating local authorities in choice-based letting (CBL) schemes in England, 2002-08

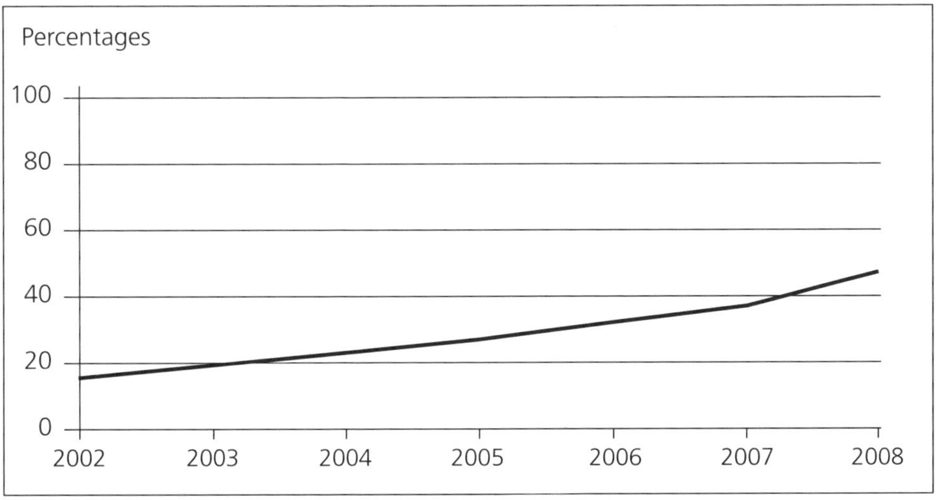

Source: CLG, 2009.

Choice models will continue to be a feature of housing policy in England in the 2000s. However, while choice-based lettings have caught the imagination of English housing policy-makers, in Scotland, a more cautious approach has been adopted with only Edinburgh City Council and Aberdeen Council having set up a choice-based allocations systems (www.choicemoves.org.uk November 2008).

5. Rents and arrears management

For all landlords, the setting and collection of rents, and the recovery of rent arrears are core housing management functions and this section considers the different approaches which housing organisations adopt.

5.1: Setting the rents

As we saw in Chapter 4, rents are the main source of revenue income for landlords and as such landlords need to establish a mechanism for setting their rents. For affordable housing organisations a number of factors need to be taken into account in deciding the system they intend to use:

- the system needs to ensure that the landlord is able to recover enough money from its tenants to meet its costs of providing and managing its homes;
- the system needs to be easily understood by tenants and staff;
- the system needs to generate affordable rents;
- the system needs to be seen as fair and equitable;
- the system needs to comply with the law and guidance from regulatory authorities (such as the Tenant Services Authority).

5.2: The law and rent setting

Following changes to government policy first flagged in the green paper *Quality and Choice for All*, (DETR/DSS, 2000) all affordable landlords in England are required to restructure their rent setting procedures to achieve convergence in their approaches over the ten year period to March 2012. This is a major change to the way in which rents are calculated and will be explored later in this section. This change does not apply elsewhere in the United Kingdom, where landlords have more freedom to set rents. It is important therefore to have an understanding of the variety of rent setting processes used by landlords.

5.3: Types of rent setting systems

This section outlines the types of rent settings systems which landlords have used in the past (but as noted above these are now being superseded, in England only, by the requirements of rent restructuring). All landlords raise income from rents to meet their costs of providing the dwelling, managing that dwelling, and carrying out repairs and maintenance. However, if a landlord owns a number of dwellings they will need to establish a system for deciding what rents to charge for what properties. For example, if a landlord owns 1,000 homes and needs to recover income of £45,000 each week to cover its costs, they need to work out what rent to charge on each property. Of course, the landlord could simply charge all properties the same rent (£45 per week in this example), but this may not be seen as reasonable if someone living in a bedsit in a tower block ends up paying exactly the same rent as someone living in a brand new four bedroom house on a new estate.

(a) Cost rents

Perhaps the simplest approach is for a landlord to charge what it costs to provide the individual dwelling. At its simplest this will involve the landlord calculating what is paid out for each property in terms of:

- loan repayments;
- management and maintenance costs;
- provisions for voids and bad debts.

They would then charge a sufficient rent to cover all of these costs. Although this appears a straightforward system it does lead to a number of problems, not least that for many landlords it may be difficult to calculate exactly what an individual property has cost. It would also lead to a number of anomalies such as rents being reduced when loans were eventually paid off, and properties built at times of lower interest rates would have a lower rent than those built when interest rates were higher. Properties which face higher maintenance costs (such as system-built properties) would have higher repairs costs and so higher rents. It would also mean that similar properties in the same area built a few years apart might have very different rents, because of interest rate changes, and this would be very difficult for landlords to explain to their tenants.

In the early days of local authority housing, this cost rent system was used by councils to set their rents but they soon found that the disadvantages of the system outweighed its benefits. They began to *pool* all of their costs to seek to recover the costs from all of their tenants in a different way, not linked to the costs involved in providing individual properties. However, cost rents are still quite common in the housing association sector, particularly for developments that have been funded since the 1988 Housing Act with the help of a private mortgage. With these developments the association will know what it has cost to provide the properties and will seek to recover the costs on a scheme by scheme basis.

If rents are not to be linked to the costs of providing an individual property then it is necessary to devise a system for charging rents on individual properties and three main systems have traditionally been used; values based, points based and formula based rents.

(b) Values based rents

Many landlords have used the value of their stock as the basis of charging rents with properties of greater values paying higher rents. Two main variants on this theme have been adopted:

- Gross values;
- Capital values.

(i) Gross values

Landlords may undertake a stock valuations on the basis of the rental income a property might generate if the landlord was responsible for the cost of repairs, insurance and maintenance and was influenced by factors such as the size of a property, its age, location and state of repair. The landlord simply adds up all the gross values of its properties and then works out the proportion of the total rent to be collected which each individual property should pay on the basis of its individual valuation using the formula:

$$\text{Rent paid for an individual property} = \frac{\text{Gross value of property}}{\text{Total gross values of stock}} \times \text{Total rent required}$$

Figure 6.9: Example of rent setting using gross values

A local authority needs to collect £18,000,000 from its 10,000 homes.

The gross value of its homes amounts to £3,500,000 as assessed by the landlord's valuer. An individual property has a gross value of £450 and its rent is calculated using the formula:

$$= \frac{\text{Gross value of property}}{\text{Total gross values of stock}} \times \text{Total rent required}$$

$$= \frac{450}{3{,}500{,}000} \times 18{,}000{,}000$$

= £2,313 per annum

= £44.48 per week

The key benefit of this system is that all properties are given a gross rateable value which reflects size, amenities, location and state of repair and as such would be easily understood by tenants. However, valuation is an inexact science, and although location and size are important factors in valuations, this does tend to lead to tenants who happen to live in more desirable areas paying significantly higher rents. But perhaps the biggest problem with using the gross valuation system is that values quickly become out of date and updating valuations is expensive.

(ii) Capital values

A similar system to the gross valuation one is to use capital values. This is where every property is given a capital valuation as if it were to be sold and the rent is related to this. In this system the tenants of a property worth £80,000 would pay twice as much rent as a property with a value of £40,000. This method obviously requires all properties to be valued and given a capital value and this is then used to calculate the rent payable on an individual property using a similar formula:

$$\text{Rent paid for an individual property} = \frac{\text{Value of property}}{\text{Total valuation of stock}} \times \text{Total rent required}$$

A main advantage of the capital value system is that valuations will normally be done by an independent valuer and most people can understand the basis on which the rent is calculated, particularly as values will usually reflect property attributes such as size, location and state of repair. But obtaining valuations may be costly as landlords will often need to commission a surveyor to carry them out and they need to be updated on a regular basis. A further problem is that once again the system leads to larger properties in more desirable areas attracting higher capital values and therefore rents. This may penalise those tenants who live in those areas or property types. Indeed, it may make large properties or properties in desirable areas unaffordable to people on low incomes and this will have implications for a landlord's policies on both affordability and equal opportunities.

(c) Points based rents

A number of landlords have set up a points system where properties are given points for individual attributes. Factors which may be relevant include:

- the number of bedrooms;
- purpose built or modernised;
- flat, house or bungalow;
- heating systems;
- garden;
- amenities;
- location;
- age of property;
- condition.

Once a list of attributes is produced it is then necessary to assign points to each of these attributes to generate an overall points score for a property. Again, the system involves the landlord totalling up all of the points in its stock and using the formula to decide individual rents as follows:

$$\text{Rent paid for an individual property} = \frac{\text{Points of property}}{\text{Total points of stock}} \times \text{Total rent required}$$

Using a points system enables differences in stock characteristics to be reflected in the different points awarded, the system does not require experts from outside the organisation to value the stock, and much of the work on identifying stock characteristics can be done in-house. It also enables those characteristics which should lead to lower rents being reflected through the scores (for example, properties in less desirable areas could be given a negative points score for the location characteristic). The system is a flexible one and can be adjusted over time, both in terms of amending the property attributes and the points attached to each one. But, if too many attributes are used, the system can be complicated to operate, and the weighting attached to individual characteristics is inevitably a subjective decision.

Each property needs to be assessed to decide the points score to be awarded and, of course, the points score may not reflect the actual costs or value of a property

(d) Formula based rents

A variation on the points system is a formula system. Here, an average rent is determined by dividing the rent to be collected by the number of properties. This average rent is then adjusted by percentages depending on the characteristics of a property. For example, if the average rent of a landlord owning 10,000 properties and collecting £40,000,000 a year is £76.92 per week then the formula system can be used in the following way to determine the rent of a three bedroom house:

Figure 6.10: Example of rent setting using a formula

For example, the formula for a three bedroom house might mean that the average rent had to be adjusted by these percentages:

3 bedroom house	+ 2.00%
Downstairs WC	+ 0.25%
No garden	– 0.05%
Full central heating	+ 0.75%
Refurbished property	– 1.00%
No car parking	– 0.05%
Unpopular location	– 1.00%
Total change required	**+ 0.90%**

Average rent £76.92 + (0.9% x £76.92) = £77.61 per week

5.4: Rent restructuring in England

As was seen in Chapter 4, the government in England introduced rent restructuring for all local housing authorities and housing associations. Rents will be restructured over a ten year period from 2002-12, so that they converge, and then similar properties in the same area will have very similar rents regardless of ownership or how the home was financed.

Under rent restructuring, rents are set according to a formula which looks at:

- size, condition and location;
- local earnings;
- property size.

The rent level by 2012 will have two elements: 30 per cent of rent should be based on relative property values, and 70 per cent of rent should be based on relative local earnings, and a bedroom factor is applied so that smaller units have lower rents. This is expressed as a formula where weekly rent is:

> 70 per cent of average rent for the housing association sector
> multiplied by relative county earnings
> multiplied by bedroom weighting
>
> plus
>
> 30 per cent of the average rent for the sector
> multiplied by relative property value

This will set the target rent for an individual unit which will increase by RPI + 0.5% each year. (Service charges should only increase by RPI.) New homes developed should use the new target rent immediately. Property values are based on 'existing use value' (i.e. the sale price on the open market). The base year used will be values at January 1999.

This new regime was introduced for both local authorities and housing associations in 2002-03. For some landlords in the higher value areas of London and the south east, this has led to potentially large rent increases. To mitigate this, the government capped rent rises to a maximum of £2 per week on top of the RPI + 0.5% increase. Similarly, in other areas target rents were lower than those being charged and reductions were also capped at £2 per week.

5.5: Housing association rents

Although English housing associations are now within the rent restructuring framework they do have some rents which are outside this regime. Housing associations have two main types of tenancies: secure tenancies and assured tenancies. Tenants of housing associations whose tenancies commenced before 15 January 1989 will normally have secure tenancies as defined by the Housing Act 1985. These tenancies are almost identical to those enjoyed by local authority tenants, except in relation to rent setting. After 15 January 1989, all new housing tenancies have been assured tenancies under the 1988 Housing Act. Assured tenancies have fewer statutory rights (for example, they do not have the right to buy). Rent restructuring applies to the majority of tenants because they are assured tenants, but not to the declining minority of secure tenants.

Secure tenancies and rents

Housing association secure tenancies have their rents set not by the housing association, but by the rent officer. The rent officer is an independent government officer who is charged with determining, amongst other things, a fair rent for housing association secure tenants. Fair rents are reviewed every two years and in determining fair rents the rent officer has to set a rent which reflects the 'age, character, location and state of repair of the property', with the aim of setting a rent which is fair to both the landlord and the tenant. In coming to a decision on the level of rent to set, the rent officer is not allowed to take into account the personal circumstances of tenant or landlord. As rents are not set by the housing association, the landlord here has no direct say over the rents which are charged for secure tenants, although landlords have to suggest what they feel the rent should be in their application to the rent officer to set the rent.

Assured tenancies

Since 1989, all new housing association lettings (both relets of previously secure tenancies or brand new lettings) have been let under assured tenancies and these properties are no longer subject to fair rents. Housing associations in the past were free to determine their own rents. In some housing association tenancies, a formula may be stipulated (for example, that rents are increased annually by the increase in the retail prices index for the previous 12 months). If the tenancy agreement does not specify the formula by which rents will be increased, then the landlord is able to set a new rent each year (but within the guidance set under the rent restructuring policy in England). This must allow the tenant to have the right to refer the proposed increase to the Rent Assessment Committee for the determination of a market rent. A Rent Assessment Committee composed of property professionals will then independently decide what a *market* rent should be for this type of property. Of course, most housing associations rents are below the average market rent in an area and if housing association tenants refer their rents to the Rent Assessment Committee for a determination they may find that their rent is increased further than that originally proposed by the housing association. In determining their assured rents, housing associations have to pay attention to the Regulatory Code published by the Tenant Services Authority (previously the Housing Corporation). The Code says that:

> *Housing associations must set rents which move towards target social rents and are on average below those in the private sector for similar properties and which reflect size, property value and local earnings.*

The Code of Guidance goes on to advise that:

> *Rents are set in accordance with the rent restructuring formula. All residents have information about their landlord's rent policy and rent levels across the association's stock and in the relevant local authority area. All residents have information about their service charges including costs that their charges cover, how charges are budgeted and increases calculated.*

The guidance prior to rent restructuring advised that associations should ensure that the rents they charged for assured tenancies are affordable for people in low paid employment, and not to discriminate in their rents between people on housing benefit and those who are not in receipt of benefit. The revised guidance no longer refers to these requirements as the rent restructuring formula effectively determines the rent which is to be set.

5.6: Collecting the rent

For both local authorities and housing associations, rents are by far the most important source of revenue. (The importance of rents for the financing of affordable housing organisations is examined in more detail in Chapter 4.) Unless landlords collect the rent due to them then they will not be able to fund their repairs service, service their mortgage loans, or pay for their housing management staff.

The amount of rent which affordable housing landlords collect is an important indicator of their financial health, and is monitored closely by the government in relation to local authorities. Similarly, in the housing association sector, rent collection and the level of arrears is monitored closely by the Tenant Services Authority (or its equivalents in Scotland, Wales and Northern Ireland). Affordable housing landlords are required to tell their tenants in their annual report how much rent they have collected each year and there are a range of performance indicators collected nationally for arrears and rent collection.

Boards of housing associations and local authority members will also wish to see regular reports from their officers about how well the organisation is doing in these areas. Auditors of local authorities and housing associations will also comment on the amount of rent which their clients collect, and particularly in the housing association sector, banks and building societies, who have lent money to housing associations, will want to receive regular reports on rent collection rates. This is because a housing association which is struggling to collect its rents may find itself in difficulty in relation to the payment of mortgages.

Within the housing association sector, the Housing Act of 1988 allowed private finance for housing associations' new development. Grant funding to associations (through what was then Housing Association Grant) was reduced significantly and housing associations were encouraged to borrow money from banks and building societies to pay for their new housing development. This has meant that most new housing association developments now carry substantial mortgages which must be repaid each year from rental income. Any shortfall in rental income may make it more difficult for the housing association to meet the loan repayments on their mortgages and because of this, housing association boards (and their regulators) now pay much closer attention to levels of rent arrears than was previously the case.

5.7: The extent of rent arrears

The level of rent arrears has always been of concern to government and other agencies involved in the regulation of local authorities and housing associations.

> *Any but the most limited and temporary arrears are damaging to the interests to all concerned; to the tenants involved, who have to manage a mounting of debt; to the landlord authorities which are deprived of resources in their housing revenue account; to the other tenants who thereby suffer higher rents or inferior service; and to ratepayers who in many cases have to bear the cost attached to meeting a larger deficit on the housing revenue accounts. This inefficiency in the use of resources also damages the case for allocation of resources to local authorities for housing* (DoE Circular 18/87).

Over the last 20 years there have been a number of influential reports on the extent of rent arrears, as outlined in Figure 6.11.

Figure 6.11: Reports on rent arrears

Audit Commission 1984 – Bringing council tenant arrears under control
This report looked at rent arrears in London, the English metropolitan district councils and 28 of the largest shire districts where the arrears problem was thought to be the worst. This report highlighted the extent of the problem of rent arrears and made a number of recommendations to local authorities as to how they should combat the increase in rent arrears which the report identified.

Audit Commission 1986 – Managing the crisis in council housing
This report indicated that many local authorities had taken on board the recommendations of the earlier report, but that in a minority of councils rent arrears were still increasing.

Audit Commission 1989 – Survey of local authority rent arrears
This report showed an increase in rent arrears in 1988-89, with the main reason for the increase in arrears being the housing benefit changes introduced in 1988. These changes had led to a reduction in housing benefit payable to some households together with changes in the rates at which benefit was withdrawn as incomes rose (the so called 'tapers').

Department of the Environment 1994 – Rent arrears in local authorities and housing associations in England
This major piece of research on rent arrears showed that arrears had increased from 1982-83 to 1991-92 from £161 million to £458 million. Arrears expressed as a percentage of the debit (the annual amount of rent collectable) rose from 4.8 per cent to 8 per cent of the debit.

Accounts Commission 2000 – Managing rent arrears – getting the balance right
This report looked at performance of councils and associations in Scotland and made a series of good practice recommendations. It set arrears targets of 3 per cent in semi-urban and rural areas and 7 per cent for city and urban areas.

Audit Commission/Housing Corporation 2003 – Rent collection and arrears management by housing associations in England
This report examined a range of data sources on the issue of rent collection and arrears management, together with in-depth studies of 12 housing associations. This research

Figure 6.11: Reports on rent arrears *continued*

identified that average rent arrears for housing associations in England rose from 4.7 per cent to 6.8 per cent of the debit between 1996-97 and 1999-2000. In addition, the report showed that in 2001-02 current housing association tenants owed £231 million, an increase of 10 per cent on the previous year.

Audit Commission 2003 – Local authority housing rent income
This report looked at the increase in local authority current rent arrears from £335 million in 1997 to £403 million in 2002, with former tenant arrears increasing by 42 per cent from £172 million to £244 million.

Audit Commission 2006 – Improving income collection
This report looked at the efficient collection of council tax, housing rent and other income by direct debit and encouraged landlords to consider how best they could increase the number of payments through the direct debit system.

At 31 March 2007, it was estimated that there were 768,985 'current tenants' and 311,885 'former tenants' in arrears in England and Welsh local authorities. The total number of local authority tenants in arrears has fallen by 52,323 since 2006, continuing the trend of recent years. Despite this decrease, the amount of arrears has increased since 2006 by £1.6 million (CIPFA, 2007, Housing Rent Arrears and Housing Benefit Statistics).

Table 6.6: Key rent arrears statistics (local authorities) as at March 2007 (England and Wales)

Current tenants' arrears	£238 million
Average arrears owed by each tenant	£310
% of tenants owing 13+ weeks	9.45%
Arrears as a % of rent roll	3.5%
Former tenants' arrears	£203 million
Former tenants' arrears as a % of rent roll	2.9%

Source: CIPFA (2007) Housing Rent Arrears and Housing Benefit Statistics.

Table 6.7 below sets out the detailed breakdown for 2006 showing arrears across different types of local authorities.

Table 6.7 clearly shows that current arrears are much higher in London boroughs and metropolitan districts. This reflects the fact that there are more tenants in these areas and these areas also tend to have higher levels of socio-economic deprivation.

Table 6.8 provides further analysis of current arrears showing that at March 2006 over 50 per cent of tenants in London Boroughs were in arrears and owed on average £400.54 each compared to the England and Wales average of 39.35 per cent of tenants in arrears owing £290.95 each.

Table 6.7: Rent arrears by types of local authorities 2006, England and Wales

	Current tenants		Former tenants		Total tenants	
	Number	Amount £'000	Number	Amount £'000	Number	Amount £'000
London boroughs	222,472	91,112	66,174	71,385	293,646	162,497
Metropolitan districts	222,077	64,871	120,176	69,825	342,253	134,696
English unitary authorities	119,964	31,698	49,959	27,450	169,923	59,148
English non-metropolitan districts	201,495	42,059	59,395	24,035	260,890	66,094
Wales	48,567	8,713	17,914	8,673	66,481	17,386
All authorities	**819,575**	**238,453**	**313,618**	**201,368**	**1,133,193**	**439,821**

Source: CIPFA, 2006.

Table 6.8: Analysis of arrears at March 2005 and 2006

	As at March 2005		As at March 2006	
	Total current Tennants in arrears %	Average amount £	Total current Tennants in arrears %	Average amount £
London boroughs	49.95	450.53	51.48	400.54
Metropolitan districts	43.51	309.58	40.37	292.11
English unitary authorities	38.18	287.72	34.57	264.23
English non-metropolitan districts	35.84	195.29	33.92	208.73
Wales	37.67	174.94	39.89	179.40
All authorities	**41.13**	**300.77**	**39.35**	**290.95**

Source: CIPFA, 2007.

5.8: Arrears over time

Comparative statistics for gross arrears show the following picture over time:

Table 6.9: Gross rent arrears (local authorities in England)

1982-83	4.8%	£161 million
1991-92	8.0%	£458 million
2001-02	5.8%	£161 million
2005-06	5.2%	£424 million

Source: Adapted from Audit Commission and CIPFA.

5.9: Housing association rent arrears

Table 6.10: Key rent arrears statistics – housing associations in England 2006

Current rent arrears at 31 March 2006	5.091%
Current arrears	£251 million

Source: Housing Corporation 2006; Performance indicators, housing corporation.

5.10: Rent arrears in Scotland

In Scotland, the Accounts Commission (similar to the Audit Commission) sets out details of Scottish councils' performance in arrears.

Table 6.11: Scottish rent arrears local authorities at 31 March 2007

Current arrears	£24.01 million
% of rent roll	6.87%

Source: Audit Scotland, 2007.

Table 6.12: Scottish housing association current arrears at 31 March 2008

Current arrears	£31.55 million
% of rent roll	4%

Source: Audit Scotland, 2007.

5.11: Collection methods

A number of methods are used by affordable landlords to collect the rent owed by tenants. Research published by the Audit Commission in 2003 (Audit Commission/Housing Corporation, 2003a), looked at the different ways in which associations collected their rent, and this showed some significant differences between landlords. All of the landlords included within the study used standing orders from those tenants with a regular income. Fifty eight per cent of landlords allowed payment by direct debit. Seventy five per cent of landlords took cash or cheques at the housing office or through a bank. The same proportion had arrangements whereby tenants could make rent payments at the post office, and an increasing number were adopting swipe card systems through which rent can be paid using the 'Allpay' or 'Pay point' facilities in shops and other locations. Only 16 per cent of landlords would accept payment by credit card.

The Audit Commission also noted a trend away from generic working towards the use of specialist officers to deal with rent arrears, particularly amongst larger associations. At the same time a Housing Corporation survey in 2000 identified that one-third of associations that had adopted a specialist approach, reported a steady decrease in arrears.

(i) Door-to-door collection

A number of research studies have shown that in the past, that door-to-door collection was the most common way in which rent was paid. The rent collector often carried out other roles in addition to receiving rent payments; such as taking repair requests or receiving transfer application forms. Door-to-door collection is usually associated with lower levels of rent arrears. This is because the collector calls on a regular, (usually weekly or fortnightly) basis, and it is more difficult for tenants to miss a rent payment. In addition, if a payment was missed it would be picked up very quickly and the arrears recovery staff could begin to take appropriate action to recover the missing payment. In recent years, the popularity of door-to-door collection has declined for a number of reasons. Door-to-door collection is labour intensive and as more and more landlords have had to review the cost of their service it has often been door-to-door collection which has been cut. As more tenants have been in receipt of full housing benefit the number of tenants paying rent themselves out of their own income has declined, which has meant that the amount of rent to be collected by a door-to-door service has fallen. And, of course, one of the most significant reasons for the decline in popularity of door-to-door collection has been the threat of robbery and assaults on door-to-door collectors.

Door-to-door collection is most cost-effective on estates where there are a large number of tenants from whom to collect the rent. This may well explain the significant difference in door-to-door collection rates between local authorities and housing associations. Housing association properties on the whole are scattered and there are very few housing association estates with a large number of properties.

(ii) Office collection

The Audit Commission research found that most landlords used some form of housing office collection. This may be the main office of the landlord, or, in some cases it will be a decentralised local housing office. In most of these offices the landlord may well have installed secure cash receiving facilities where tenants can pay their rent, usually through a computerised till which issues the tenant with a receipt for the rent paid and automatically updates the tenant's computerised rent account. For landlords, there are significant benefits in having office rent collection. It can be more cost-effective to have a cashier based in the office than rent collectors out on their patch doing rounds, cash tills can be made more secure and the use of computerised tills means that tenant's accounts can be updated immediately. For the tenant coming in to the office to pay their rent they will usually have the opportunity to raise other tenancy matters with the staff in the office. However, the main problem with office collection in terms of arrears levels is that payment of rent is at the discretion of the tenant. There is no door-to-door collector knocking on the door requesting that the rent be paid. This means that tenants may find it easier to miss a rent payment and the research evidence suggests that levels of rent arrears are higher with office collection than they are with collections on a door-to-door basis. If landlords use an office collection system it is essential that the arrears recovery procedure can quickly identify a missed payment so that appropriate action to recover the missing payment can be instigated.

There tends to be a lower level of office collection for housing association tenants as compared to their local authority counterparts. This may be explained by the fact that housing association tenancies may be spread over a large area. Many housing associations will only have one office and this may not be accessible by a majority of the association tenants. In these circumstances housing associations need to offer alternative methods of rent payment to their tenants.

(iii) Post office payments

A significant number of tenants pay their rent through the post office where the post office staff will issue a receipt for the rent paid and send the rent and data collected to the landlord. In other cases, tenants may be able to pay their rent through the Alliance and Leicester Bill Pay system, where rents are processed through the post office and payments credited to the landlord's account. The Audit Commission (2003a) research shows 75 per cent of housing associations taking rent payments through this system. Again the evidence suggests that payments by these methods are associated with higher levels of arrears and this can largely be explained by the fact that there is no external pressure on the tenant to pay the rent and it takes longer for missing payments to be identified. In recent years swipe cards have replaced the paying-in slip and other methods such as Allpay or Paypoint cards have been introduced.

(iv) Bank payment systems

Tenants can also pay their rents through a bank standing order or direct debit, transferring money from their own bank account into a landlord's account. In addition, some landlords have issued tenants with bank giro books where tenants can use these paying-in books to pay their rent into a bank nominated by the landlord. Research has shown this type of system to be more popular within the housing association sector than with local authority tenants. Some landlords have introduced on line payments to enable tenants to make payments direct from their own accounts.

(v) Rent direct

A majority of social housing tenants are now in receipt of housing benefit to assist them with their rent payments. For local authority tenants, the housing benefit is rebated from their rent (in other words it is deducted at source by their landlord). For housing association tenants, a rent allowance is paid to the tenant to assist them with meeting their rent payments and these tenants can opt to have their housing benefit payments transferred directly to their housing association landlord. Most housing associations will prefer their tenants who are in receipt of housing benefit to opt for their benefit to be paid directly to their landlord. This means that the landlord can be certain of receiving housing benefit which is due to the tenant. However, unless the tenant is in serious arrears such arrangements cannot be made compulsory.

(vi) On line

An increasing number of landlords now provide on line facilities whereby tenants can pay the rent from their own back accounts directly over the internet.

5.12: The link between collection methods and rent arrears

Over the last 20 years there has been a great deal of research into the causes of rent arrears. Key themes arising from the research include:

Figure 6.12: Factors showing a significant association with higher levels of rent arrears

- Young households (below 60 years old).
- Existence of multiple debts.
- Living in an area of above average social/economic deprivation.
- Living in London.
- Dependent children.
- Receipt of housing benefit.
- Experience of problems related to housing benefit.
- Payment at a post office.
- High rents.
- Experiencing a change in household circumstances in relation to more dependent children or a reduction in household earners.
- Unemployment and ill health.

The Survey of English Housing (CLG, 2006b) reviewed the reasons why social tenants had said they got into arrears, summarised in Table 6.13.

The Survey showed that social housing tenants have low incomes and the majority of tenants are now in receipt of some form of social security benefits. Around 60 per cent of all tenants now receive housing benefit to assist them with their rent obligations. Tenants in serious arrears tend to have larger households and thus lower disposable incomes. If income falls because of illness, debts, unemployment,

Table 6.13: Reasons why tenants said they got into arrears

	Council tenant	**HA tenant**
Problems with housing benefit	20	32
Debts	35	21
Unempoloyment	23	18
Other job-related reasons	12	10
Domestic problems	10	12
Illness	12	19
Increase in rent	4	5
Other reasons	18	21

Note: % do not add up to 100 because some people gave more than one reason.
Source: CLG, Survey of English Housing, 2006.

relationship breakdown or the birth of a baby, it is likely to lead to higher levels of rent arrears.

The Audit Commission review of local authority arrears in 2003 said that:

> *Council tenants are now more likely to be on low incomes, dependent on benefits and more vulnerable than previously. Only 31% of council tenants were in paid work (full or part time) in 2000-01, compared with around 50% 20 years ago* (Audit Commission, 2003b).

5.13: Refusal to pay

The 2003 study identified a small core of tenants with little intention of paying, particularly younger single tenants unconcerned about losing a tenancy, particularly in areas of low demand where other landlords appear prepared to offer them a new home. The study also identified a small minority of tenants withholding the rent on principle, for example where they feel they have had a poor service from the landlord or perceive the rent as being too high. A minority were also identified as 'playing' the system, prioritising other expenditure and paying enough to prevent eviction action at key points in the landlord's rent arrears recovery process.

5.14: Prevention of rent arrears

Affordable housing organisations need to give as much attention as possible to the prevention of rent arrears in the first place and there are a number of steps which affordable housing landlords can take to stop tenants getting in to rent arrears.

At the commencement of a tenancy it is essential that tenants are given proper advice and counselling about all aspects of their tenancy. Housing staff should ensure that tenants claim any housing benefit which is due to them, as well as giving them advice and assistance with claiming other welfare benefits. A number of research studies have shown that tenants who have rent arrears also have other debts and it is essential that tenants' income is maximised. In a number of housing organisations, specialist officers have been employed to assist tenants in maximising their claims for the benefits which are available.

As part of this advice, pre-tenancy counselling can be provided and it is essential also that housing officers stress to tenants the need to maintain regular rent payments, and to advise tenants on what action the landlord will take if the tenant falls into arrears. This is to generate a *payment culture*. From the organisational perspective, it is also important that landlords ensure that sufficient staff are available to deal with their rent arrears. In some cases, this may mean establishing a separate arrears team, but where arrears work is decentralised to more generic (all purpose) housing officers, it is important that the numbers of properties which they manage is small enough for them to effectively control rent arrears in their patch.

When arrears develop, it is essential that these are spotted quickly by housing staff and attention should be given to the information technology which is available to enable arrears action to be started as soon as possible.

5.15: Tackling rent arrears

Rent arrears policy and procedure

If staff are to effectively tackle rent arrears it is essential that the organisation has thought about and written down the policy and procedure it wishes to adopt for rent arrears. These procedures should reflect the good practice which a number of organisations have developed over recent years.

(i) Early action

It is important when a rent payment is missed that the tenant is contacted by the organisation to remind them of the missing payment. As soon as the payment is missed it is advisable to contact the tenant and certainly within two weeks of a missing payment a letter or a personal visit should have been actioned by the landlord. Clearly an important issue here is for the housing organisation to have an information technology system available which can identify missing payments promptly.

Home Housing Association has undertaken *payment tracking* as part of a corporate review of key business processes, to identify the value of different elements of rent collection and arrears work their staff undertake. They identified some confusion over post office payments and prioritised the improvement of rent receipts, so that tenants have more accurate information on the precise amount of rent due, and that late payments will result in their accounts showing arrears. Home HA also identified that properly submitted, completed housing benefit forms with all appropriate supporting documentation resulted in an average time for housing benefit to be posted to the rent account of 16 days. For those forms not properly completed, the average rose to 83 days. As a result of this knowledge, resources were focused more on 'front end' welfare benefit support to help tenants get their claim right first time and to prevent arrears accruing whilst the claim is being processed (Audit Commission, 2003a).

(ii) Personal contact

If there has been no response to an arrears reminder letter then it is advisable that personal contact is made by a housing officer to ascertain the reasons for the non-payment of rent and to offer the tenant any assistance which may be required to reduce the rent arrears. In some cases, this might mean helping complete a housing benefit claim, or in other cases, negotiating a suitable arrangement to reduce the arrears by instalments. It must be remembered that tenants in rent arrears may also have other debts and that they may not respond to a letter sent to them. In these circumstances a personal visit is likely to lead to greater chances of success.

(iii) Legal action

However, if letters and visits fail to achieve a reduction in arrears then the landlord will need to take legal action in the courts to recover the debt. For local authority and housing association tenants the first step is usually to serve a Notice of Intention to Seek Possession. This is a legal document which advises the tenant that if they fail to repay the arrears the landlord may take the matter to court to seek a possession order on the property.

(iv) Arrangements

When negotiating arrangements to repay arrears by instalments it is essential that these arrangements are satisfactory for both the landlord and the tenant. It might be possible for the landlord to arrange to reduce the arrears through the payment of housing benefit direct to the landlord or by the arrears direct method, through which deductions for arrears are made from income support and paid direct to the landlord.

(v) Incentives

A number of affordable landlords have introduced incentive schemes which reward the tenants for prompt payment and encourage a culture of responsibility. One of the leading schemes is the Irwell Valley Housing Association 'Gold Service' which was described earlier.

(vi) Other measures

As an alternative to seeking possession of the properties through the courts it may be possible for landlords to investigate other measures by which they might recover the debt. This can include making claims in the small claims court, or if tenants are working, seeking an attachment of earnings order, where the court can order an employer to make deductions from earnings and pay the money direct to the landlord.

(vii) Former tenants' arrears

A significant part of the total debt owing to housing associations and local authorities is not owed by current tenants but are arrears of rent owed by former tenants. The CIH suggest that less than ten per cent of former tenant arrears is recovered (CIH, 2001a).

In many cases, the landlord will not know the whereabouts of the former tenant and it may be very difficult to recover the arrears in these circumstances. However, when the landlord does know the whereabouts of the former tenant then they need to seek to recover the debt from them. Clearly, as the former tenant is no longer occupying a property owned by the landlord, the sanction of repossession is no longer available. In order to recover former tenants' debts the landlord has to use all

Figure 6.13: Key good practice points

Prevention of rent arrears
- Pre-tenancy counselling on the total financial obligations of taking up a tenancy.
- Maximising of a tenant's income through appropriate advice.
- Promoting a payment culture with tenants being made fully aware of the landlord's policies on rent collection and that eviction is the ultimate consequence of non-payment.
- Supporting tenants to submit properly completed housing benefit forms promptly, where this is necessary.
- Developing a management information system with suitable information technology support to enable a rapid response to emerging problem of arrears.
- Providing tenants with up to date information on their rent account, including differentiation between arrears due from the tenant and those due to payment of housing benefit in arrears.

Management of rent arrears cases
- The development of a management information system which gives clear and unambiguous records of the state of a tenant's rent account to enable the landlord to take early action.
- Notification within two weeks of missing payments.
- Negotiation of a workable repayment arrangement with the tenant.
- Avoid taking court action where arrears are due to housing benefit delays (although such action might be appropriate in cases where partial housing benefit is paid and the tenant's contribution is not being paid).
- Eviction should remain as a final sanction against a persistent minority of non-payers.
- Landlords should pursue former tenants for arrears where there is a realistic prospect of recovery. Specialist teams working on former tenant arrears are recommended.
- Consider introducing incentive schemes that reward tenants with clear rent accounts and those who maintain repayment agreements.
- Establishing a specialist arrears team where the arrears situation of the organisation is serious.
- The consideration of alternative recovery methods such as through the small claims court, rent direct or the attachment of earnings.

of the remedies available in the civil courts for the repayment of debt. The landlord should consider whether it may be more cost-effective to sell the debt to a debt collection agency, write it off, or attempt to pursue the debt in house. In practice, most landlords will seek to recover the debt using their own staff and only if this has failed will it be passed onto an outside agency and then written off.

5.16: Strategic and operational response

The 2003 Audit Commission report (2003b) advised that local authorities should respond to arrears at both the strategic and operational level:

Strategic response
- Having a clear corporate approach and commitment to tackling arrears.

- Establishing effective management arrangements with clear and challenging targets for staff, with good management information systems.
- Ensuring a tenant focus with flexible payment options.

Operational response

- Having an emphasis on prevention.
- Working closely with housing benefit teams.
- Having effective recovery polices and procedures.
- Maintaining a focus on former tenants who owe arrears and pursuing them more effectively.

Rent arrears are a key issue for all affordable housing landlords and with the increasing poverty of council and housing association tenants, it is likely that the recovery of rent arrears is going to be an increasingly difficult task for housing managers. In this context, it is essential that housing managers implement fair and effective recovery procedures.

6. Managing empty properties

6.1: Introduction

Letting properties is not simply about identifying applicants and then offering them the properties. It is a much longer and more complex process. All affordable housing landlords need to ensure that they keep the time that their properties are empty (their void periods) to a minimum. This is because every week a property is left empty, there is a lost week's rent with the added danger of crime and vandalism to the empty properties.

Data for the number of vacant social housing homes in England in 2007 shows around 2 per cent of the stock is vacant at any one time, although only 0.9 per cent is vacant and available to let with the other 1.1 per cent subject to major repairs, or demolition.

The situation in Scotland and Wales shows that there is a greater percentage of vacant homes in the local authority stock than in England.

Table 6.14: Vacant social housing stock in England 2007

	Local authorities	Housing associations
Total vacant homes	41,000	30,170
As % of housing stock	2.1%	2.0%
Of which, available to let	17,700	12,145
As % of housing stock	0.9%	0.8%

Sources: HSSA and BPSA returns; Housing Corporation HAR/10 and RSR (Regulatory and Statistical Return).

Table 6.15: Vacant local authority housing stock in Scotland 2007

Total vacant homes	10,600
As % of housing stock	3.1%
Of which, available to let	3,200
As % of stock	0.9%

Source: Adapted from Housing Trends in Scotland 2008.

Table 6.16: Vacant local authority housing stock in Wales 2006

Total vacant homes	16,848
As % of housing stock	10.8%
Of which, available to let	6,708
As % of stock	4.3%

Source: Adapted from Local Government Development Unit Wales website.

6.2: Voids performance

One of the key ways of traditionally measuring how well a housing organisation is performing is to look at the number of empty properties. This is usually expressed as the number of voids (empty properties) as a percentage of their stock so if a social landlord has 10,000 properties and at any one time 200 are empty then it has 2 per cent of its stock empty (or a void rate of 2 per cent).

Table 6.17 shows a somewhat confused picture. East housing association seems on the face of it to performing better. It has fewer actual empty properties at the end of March and these voids represent a much smaller percentage of its total stock. However, although this is true it does not give a full picture as to the performance of each association in minimising voids.

The other piece of data which needs to be considered is the total number of dwellings becoming empty in the year which each association needs to deal with.

Table 6.17: Void management and relets

	West housing association	East housing association
Stock	5,000	10,000
Voids at 31 March	154	100
Voids %	3.08%	1.0%
Relets in year	500	200
(Turnover %)	10%	2%

West association has to deal with 500 relets each year (10 per cent of its stock). The East association has much less work to do; it only has to deal with 200 relets each year, representing just 2 per cent of its stock. In this context, the ability of West HA to keep its voids at the year end down to 154 looks much more impressive and suggests that they are able to let each property that becomes vacant quite quickly.

The one piece of information which we now need to demonstrate that this is indeed the case is the average re-let interval (or the time that each property on average is empty before being re-let) of each property that is let. In terms of performance, this is the most important indicator as it shows how quickly empty properties are brought back into use. The relationship between the three variables can be expressed crudely as:

Voids rate = Average re-let time x turnover rate

Assume a landlord has a stock of 120 dwellings and each year 12 become vacant (at an average of one a month). If it takes on average just over 26 weeks to let each one then at the year end it will have let six of the homes that become vacant in the year, but will have six more still to be let. So it will have a voids rate of 5 per cent. Using the equation above we can demonstrate this is the case.

Voids =	5% of the stock (i.e. 6 out of 120)
Turnover =	10% of the stock (i.e. 12 out of 120)
Average re-let time =	26 weeks (0.5 of the year)

Using the formula we can demonstrate that the average re-let interval will be 26 weeks if the voids rate is 5 per cent and the turnover 10 per cent:

Average re-let interval	= Voids rate/turnover
	= 0.05/0.10
	= 0.5 year or 26 weeks

This may seem a strange calculation at first but it becomes clearer by working back with our example of West HA. It has a turnover of 10 per cent of the stock and a voids rate of 3.08 per cent. Using the formula we can calculate that it will have an average vacancy interval of 16 weeks.

Average re-let interval	= Voids%/turnover
	= 3.08%/10%
	= 0.308 year
	= 16.06 weeks

For the East HA there is a voids rate of 1 per cent (0.01). The turnover is 2 per cent (0.02) so the average vacancy interval is 26 weeks.

Average re-let interval	= Voids%/turnover
	= 1%/2%
	= 26 weeks

Clearly East HA is the worst performer in that it is taking significantly longer on average to re-let each empty property. But on the crude statistics we might have thought that it was performing well. Of course, it is not always this simple, as there may be reasons to do with poor performance to explain the high turnover rate of West HA. Nonetheless, it does seem to be able to deal more quickly with more voids than its neighbouring association. We can also look at this in the context of rent loss as a result of voids. In West HA, there are 154 voids a year on which it loses 16 weeks rent on each, so its rent loss is 2,464 rent weeks. If the average rent is £40 per week this amounts to £98,560. If it performed as badly as East HA it would take on average 26 weeks to let each void and so its rent loss would be £160,160 – a significant difference.

The Audit Commission (1986a) in their influential report on housing management argued strongly against focusing on the voids rate as a key performance indicator and they suggested that the turnover rate and the time taken to relet each property were more significant performance indicators.

In their publication, *The Challenge of Empty Housing*, Smith and Merrett (1988) produced a matrix which enables the vacancy interval to be calculated using the void rate and the turnover. Figure 6.14 shows the void rate associated with each vacancy generation rate (turnover) and average vacancy duration.

6.3: Voids management

Reasons for void properties

There are many reasons why properties are empty at any one point in time. They may be empty whilst a new tenant is being found and in some cases they may be awaiting minor repairs. In fact these two categories account for the overwhelming majority of empty properties. In other cases, however, properties are empty often for long periods because they are in need of major repair or refurbishment. Indeed, some may be awaiting demolition because they are no longer in a fit state to be lived in or because they are to be included in a major redevelopment scheme.

Of course, it is never the case that having nil voids is a sensible or achievable option. There will always be people moving home, transferring, or properties required to be empty for major repairs, however, what is important is that the period that they are left empty is minimised.

THE VACANCY MATRIX: WHAT IT IS AND HOW TO USE IT.*

Vacancy generation rate per annum (%)	Average vacancy duration (in weeks)																								
	2	4	6	8	10	12	14	16	18	20	22	24	26	28	30	32	34	36	38	40	42	44	46	48	50
1	0.04	0.08	0.12	0.15	0.19	0.23	0.27	0.31	0.35	0.38	0.42	0.46	0.50	0.54	0.58	0.62	0.65	0.69	0.73	0.77	0.81	0.85	0.88	0.92	0.96
2	0.08	0.15	0.23	0.31	0.38	0.46	0.54	0.62	0.69	0.77	0.85	0.92	1.00	1.08	1.15	1.23	1.31	1.38	1.46	1.54	1.62	1.69	1.77	1.85	1.92
3	0.12	0.23	0.35	0.46	0.58	0.69	0.81	0.92	1.04	1.15	1.27	1.38	1.50	1.62	1.73	1.85	1.96	2.08	2.19	2.31	2.42	2.54	2.65	2.77	2.88
4	0.15	0.31	0.46	0.62	0.77	0.92	1.08	1.23	1.38	1.54	1.69	1.85	2.00	2.15	2.31	2.46	2.62	2.77	2.92	3.08	3.23	3.38	3.54	3.69	3.85
5	0.19	0.38	0.58	0.77	0.96	1.15	1.35	1.54	1.73	1.92	2.12	2.31	2.50	2.69	2.88	3.08	3.27	3.46	3.65	3.85	4.04	4.23	4.42	4.62	4.81
6	0.23	0.46	0.69	0.92	1.15	1.38	1.62	1.85	2.08	2.31	2.54	2.77	3.00	3.23	3.46	3.69	3.92	4.15	4.38	4.62	4.85	5.08	5.31	5.54	5.77
7	0.27	0.54	0.81	1.08	1.35	1.62	1.88	2.15	2.42	2.69	2.96	3.23	3.50	3.77	4.04	4.31	4.58	4.85	5.12	5.38	5.65	5.92	6.19	6.46	6.73
8	0.31	0.62	0.92	1.23	1.54	1.85	2.15	2.46	2.77	3.08	3.38	3.69	4.00	4.31	4.62	4.92	5.23	5.54	5.85	6.15	6.46	6.77	7.08	7.38	7.69
9	0.35	0.69	1.04	1.38	1.73	2.08	2.42	2.77	3.12	3.46	3.81	4.15	4.50	4.85	5.19	5.54	5.86	6.23	6.58	6.92	7.27	7.62	7.96	8.31	8.65
10	0.38	0.77	1.15	1.54	1.92	2.31	2.69	3.08	3.46	3.85	4.23	4.62	5.00	5.38	5.77	6.15	6.54	6.92	7.31	7.69	8.08	8.46	8.85	9.23	9.62
11	0.42	0.85	1.27	1.69	2.12	2.54	2.96	3.38	3.81	4.23	4.65	5.08	5.50	5.92	6.35	6.77	7.19	7.62	8.04	8.46	8.88	9.31	9.73	10.15	10.58
12	0.46	0.92	1.38	1.85	2.31	2.77	3.23	3.69	4.15	4.62	5.08	5.54	6.00	6.46	6.92	7.38	7.85	8.31	8.77	9.23	9.69	10.15	10.62	11.08	11.54
13	0.50	1.00	1.50	2.00	2.50	3.00	3.50	4.00	4.50	5.00	5.50	6.00	6.50	7.00	7.50	8.00	8.50	9.00	9.50	10.00	10.50	11.00	11.50	12.00	12.50
14	0.54	1.08	1.62	2.15	2.69	3.23	3.77	4.31	4.85	5.38	5.92	6.46	7.00	7.54	8.08	8.62	9.15	9.69	10.23	10.77	11.31	11.85	12.38	12.92	13.46
15	0.58	1.15	1.73	2.31	2.88	3.46	4.04	4.62	5.19	5.77	6.35	6.92	7.50	8.08	8.65	9.23	9.81	10.38	10.96	11.54	12.12	12.69	13.27	13.85	14.42
16	0.62	1.23	1.85	2.46	3.08	3.69	4.31	4.92	5.54	6.15	6.77	7.38	8.00	8.62	9.23	9.85	10.46	11.00	11.69	12.31	12.92	13.54	14.15	14.77	15.38
17	0.65	1.31	1.96	2.62	3.27	3.92	4.58	5.23	5.85	6.54	7.19	7.85	8.50	9.15	9.81	10.46	11.12	11.77	12.42	13.08	13.73	14.58	15.04	15.69	16.35
18	0.69	1.38	2.08	2.77	3.46	4.15	4.85	5.54	6.23	6.92	7.62	8.31	9.00	9.69	10.38	11.08	11.77	12.46	13.15	13.85	14.54	15.23	15.92	16.62	17.31
19	0.73	1.46	2.19	2.92	3.65	4.38	5.12	5.85	6.58	7.31	8.04	8.77	9.05	10.23	10.96	11.69	12.42	13.15	13.88	14.62	15.35	16.08	16.81	17.54	18.27
20	0.77	1.54	2.31	3.08	3.85	4.62	5.38	6.15	6.92	7.69	8.46	9.23	10.00	10.77	11.54	12.31	13.08	13.85	14.62	15.38	16.15	16.92	17.69	18.46	19.23
21	0.81	1.62	2.42	3.23	4.04	4.85	5.65	6.46	7.27	8.08	8.88	9.69	10.50	11.31	12.12	12.92	13.73	14.54	15.35	16.15	16.96	17.77	18.58	19.38	20.19
22	0.85	1.69	2.54	3.38	4.23	5.08	5.92	6.77	7.62	8.46	9.31	10.15	11.00	11.85	12.69	13.54	14.38	15.23	16.08	16.92	17.77	18.62	19.46	20.31	21.15
23	0.88	1.77	2.65	3.54	4.42	5.31	6.19	7.08	7.96	8.85	9.73	10.62	11.50	12.38	13.27	14.15	15.04	15.92	16.81	17.69	18.58	19.46	20.35	21.23	22.12
24	0.92	1.85	2.77	3.69	4.62	5.54	6.46	7.38	8.31	9.23	10.15	11.08	12.00	12.92	13.85	14.77	15.69	16.62	17.54	18.46	19.38	20.31	21.23	22.15	23.08
25	0.96	1.92	2.88	3.85	4.81	5.77	6.73	7.69	8.65	9.62	10.58	11.54	12.50	13.46	14.42	15.38	16.35	17.31	18.27	19.23	20.19	21.15	22.12	23.08	24.04

Note: * The vacancy quotient is expressed as a percentage, e.g. the figure in the second row, thirteenth column means a one per cent vacancy quotient. Similarly the vacancy generation rate indicates the number of vacancies which appear in a stock of dwellings in any given year divided by that stock and expressed as a percentage. The vacancy generation rate is written per year and the void duration in weeks for ease of comprehension.

What it is

The matrix uses three statistics: vacancy duration, vacancy generation rate and vacancy quotient.

Vacancy duration (D): the columns refer to how long dwellings are empty on average from when they first become vacant to when they cease to be vacant and it is measured is weeks.

Vacancy generation rate (G): the rows refer to the ratio between the number of dwellings becoming void in any given year (e.g. through newbuild and turnover) as a percentage of the total stock at the start at the year.

Vacancy quotient (Q): the ratio of all vacancies to the total stock at the end at the year. This is the mass of figures appearing in the main body of the table.

As a general guide Q is equal to G multiplied by D divided by 52.

How to use it

Two examples.

First, you know Q and G are respectively 5% and 10% You want to know D. Read along the row G equals 10% until you reach 5%, then read up the column to see D equals 26 weeks.

Second, you know G and D are respectively 8% and 8 weeks, So Q equals 1.23%. How will the vacancy quotient increase if transfers policy raises G to12% but leaves D unchanged in its average value? Read along the 12% row to the 8 weeks column to see that Q will rise to 1.85%. If your total stock is 10,000 units, voids will rise as a result of the policy change from 123 up to 185.

This matrix is published by the School of Advanced Urban Studies, University of Bristol and is the creation of Stephen Merrett and Robert Smith.

Figure 6.14: The Vacancy Matrix

Source: Smith and Merrett, 1988

Improving the management of voids

Having empty properties can be an expensive business, both in terms of lost rent, but also in terms of the costs of additional repairs if empty properties are vandalised. It is important that all landlords have in place policies and procedures designed to minimise the time that properties are empty. The Audit Commission recommended that a benchmark for performance outside of London is that voids should be let within three weeks (Audit Commission, 1986b). A higher figure was suggested for London because of the difficulties of achieving the three week target in some of the most deprived parts of the country.

Identifying a void and getting four weeks notice

Most tenancy agreements specify that a tenant should give four weeks notice of their intention to end the tenancy. In most cases it is likely that the housing organisation will get much less notice. Often the first they know is when a house is broken into or when a neighbour reports that a house appears empty.

However, it makes sense to encourage tenants to give four weeks notice so that a new letting can be arranged in the meantime and any essential repairs carried out. Some organisations will make an incentive payment to any tenant who gives four weeks notice to encourage this to happen. Other organisations will also continue to charge four weeks rent as if notice had been given.

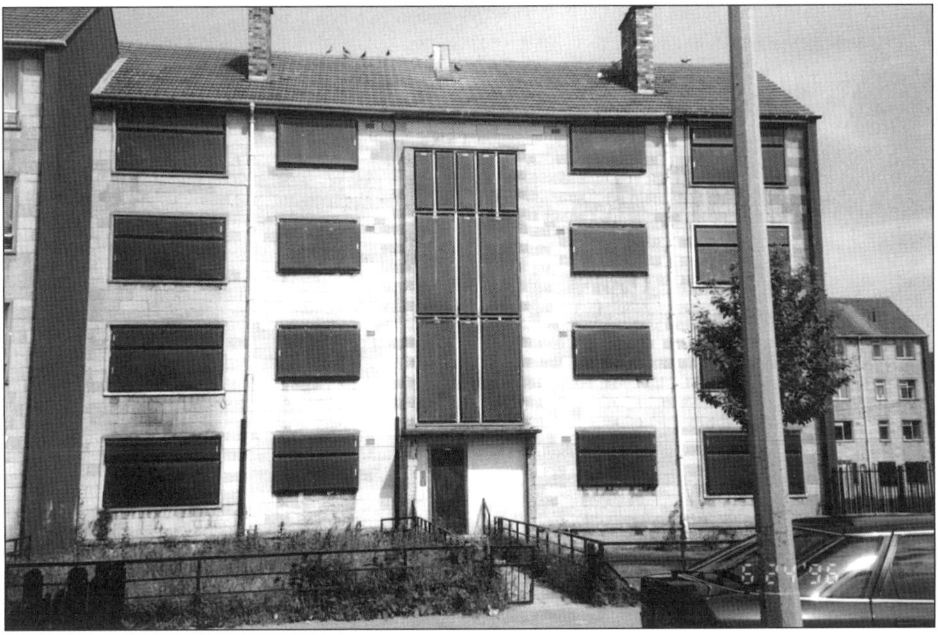

Figure 6.15: Properties boarded with Sitex security screens

Securing voids

One of the main causes of additional expenditure with empty properties is the vandalism which is caused to empty properties. In many areas, thousands of pounds worth of damage can be caused to an empty property within hours. It is essential that steps are taken to make secure those empty properties which are vulnerable to vandalism.

Many landlords will secure void properties by using plywood boards to cover the windows and doors, but these are relatively easy to remove. An alternative approach is to fix steel screens (such as Sitex – see Figure 6.15) to windows and doors. These are much more difficult to vandalise and have been shown to be successful in a number of locations.

Some housing organisations have found it necessary to put alarm systems into empty properties, whilst others have employed security guards to protect individual properties or to patrol areas where there are voids.

Pre-inspection and arranging for minor repairs

If four weeks notice is given it is possible for a housing officer to visit the property and carry out an inspection. This will:

- identify whether the property can be re-let immediately the existing tenant moves out;
- identify whether a decoration allowance should be paid to an incoming tenant if the state if the decoration is poor (or if the property should be redecorated)
- enable essential repairs to be identified;
- ensure that any costs of repair or redecoration which are to be recharged to the current tenants are agreed.

Identifying potential applicants

If the housing manager has received notice that a tenant is about to leave they can then identify in advance a new tenant for the property. The ideal situation would be for the new tenants to take up occupation on the day that the outgoing tenant leaves. In order for this to happen the organisation needs to identify who the potential tenant is, make an offer of the accommodation to that tenant, and, if the offer is accepted, make arrangements to start a new tenancy.

Whenever a void property becomes available it is necessary to identify an applicant for it. This means that the landlord's waiting list must be accurate and up to date so that time is not wasted making offers of properties to people who may already have been housed, have moved or who do not want the type of property, or the area in which it is located. It will usually involve organisations seeking to confirm on at least an annual basis that the details held on their waiting list are indeed accurate.

Offering the property

To assist in maximising the chances of take up, it is helpful if a housing officer can accompany the prospective tenants around the property which they are being offered. This enables the housing officer to establish a personal relationship with the applicant and to allow the applicant to ask any necessary questions about the property.

Cleaning of properties and repairs

Empty properties will often need at the very least to be cleaned out before prospective tenants are shown round and most voids will need some repairs doing to them. It is usually good practice only to carry out the essential repairs required before the new tenant moves in. This will save time and therefore reduce the void period. However, although this is sensible, it can sometimes mean that a prospective tenant may refuse the property because it does not appear to be in a fit state of repair. In these circumstances it may be necessary to do more than those repairs which are strictly necessary.

If only the basic repairs are to be carried out before the tenancy commences then it is essential that all of the outstanding repairs are done to the property very quickly after the new tenant moves in.

Redecoration

Most landlords will not redecorate a property when it becomes empty, although they may make an exception for the elderly. However, in some cases it may be necessary for the landlord to offer an incentive to a tenant to accept a property if the decoration is poor. This may be in the form of a cash incentive, a decoration allowance (or a rent free period of occupation), or in other cases the landlord may provide decorating materials for the incoming tenant.

Furniture

Many tenants find it difficult to furnish their new home and this has been exacerbated by the difficulty some have in accessing the Social Fund, where tenants have to borrow money through the Jobcentre Plus to purchase furniture. In some cases, tenants will accept a tenancy, move in and then very quickly give up the tenancy because they can not afford to furnish their home. There are a number of ways in which landlords have responded to this. Some have supported the establishment of furniture projects which make available a package of second-hand furniture to new tenants, whilst others have introduced furnished tenancies where the rent will include an element for furniture. This has been particularly successful for housing young single people in some areas.

Signing up

The most important stage in a new tenancy is at the start where a new tenant signs their tenancy agreement. This should be done by the member of staff who will be managing the tenancy and is an opportunity for the terms and conditions of the new tenancy to be explained in detail and answer any questions which the new tenant might have. At this stage, housing benefit claim forms can be completed so that the tenant claims whatever benefit is due to them. Arrangements should also be made for the member of staff to visit the new tenant a few weeks after they have moved in to make sure that they are settling into their new home and are not experiencing any difficulties.

Management of voids

Voids management inevitably involves a number of staff, working in different sections of the organisation. Housing management staff will be involved in receiving the terminations of tenancies, whilst technical staff may need to inspect the void and arrange any necessary repairs. At that stage, contractors may need to be brought in, and their work to be supervised. Allocations staff will also need to begin the process of identifying a new tenant and showing them round the property.

With so many staff involved in the management of voids there is a danger that things may slip and it is essential that someone has overall responsibility for void management who can chase people when a property is standing empty longer than it should. This will inevitably mean that there needs to be accurate and timely information produced about the progress of a void so that people know at what stage each void is at.

6.4: Void policies and practices

The 1993 York study of housing management of local authorities and housing associations in England (Managing Social Housing) looked at the policies and procedures relating to voids management. The study showed that:

Table 6.18: Void policies and practices in England

	Local authorities %	Housing associations %
Pre-allocation during notice period	69	82
Inspections before tenant leaves	41	60
Inspections after tenant leaves	97	93
Charging outgoing tenants for damage	71	56
Cleaning prior to re-letting	39	34
Additional security to voids usually required	12	10
Decoration incentives offered	96	86
Target periods for re-letting voids	75	65

Source: Centre for Housing Policy, York 1993; adapted from Table 10.1.

> *...in general both local authorities and housing associations had adopted good practice guidelines in the management and control of empty dwellings* (Centre for Housing Policy, 1993).

Although the implementation of good practice guidelines is important in improving voids performance, the York survey found that there was also a strong link between an organisation's voids performance and the relative level of deprivation in each area. Using a 'z score' (which is a measure of relative social deprivation) the survey found a correlation between those organisations with a low voids rate and a low z score. Organisations with a higher z score (and therefore higher levels of social deprivation) tended to have higher voids rates.

7. Repairing the stock

7.1: Introduction

Repairs and maintenance are key issues for housing managers. For almost all housing organisations repairs to their stock represents a very significant element of their revenue expenditure. For tenants, the repairs service has been shown in numerous studies to be the most important service that they receive from their landlord, and outside of paying the rent, it is the service with which tenants have most contact.

Organising an effective repairs and maintenance service involves housing management staff working closely with their technical colleagues and external contractors to ensure that the repairs service is of the highest quality. This section considers some of the key elements of providing a high quality maintenance service in affordable housing organisations.

7.2: Types of maintenance work

Repairs and maintenance work involves ensuring that the housing stock is kept in good condition. Over recent years, the rate of new house building has been falling which means that the current housing stock needs to last much longer than was originally intended. To ensure that properties remain habitable it is necessary to keep them in good state of repair and also to improve them over time to ensure that they continue to provide a good standard of accommodation.

Jobbing or responsive repairs

Most repairs will be of the jobbing or responsive nature. These will be the small, everyday repairs that most households face and include examples such as:

- leaking taps;
- faulty electric sockets;
- damaged roof tiles;

- doors and windows which need easing;
- faulty heating systems.

Cyclical repairs

These are works which can be predicted on a fairly regular basis. A good example is the external painting of woodwork and any necessary pre-painting repairs to external joinery. Most housing organisations will have a policy of repainting the outside of their homes every four or five years and where this is done the woodwork is normally inspected and any necessary pre painting repairs to joinery carried out. Another example would be the annual servicing of gas appliances, which under the Gas Safety Regulations, landlords need to do every 12 months.

Planned maintenance

There is other maintenance work which, although not on a cyclical basis, needs to be carried out on a planned basis and landlords will normally schedule this work well in advance. Examples might include re-roofing of properties, replacement of heating systems or replacement of windows. This type of work is usually organised in larger contracts and happens less frequently than cyclical repairs.

Major repairs and improvements

On occasions, landlords will want to undertake major repairs or modernisation programmes to their properties. For example, replacing electric circuits, providing new kitchens, new bathrooms and heating systems. Often these works are done when a property is not occupied and they are treated as a building contract with architects and surveyors appointed to undertake the work. These types of works are often funded by borrowing or grant and are capital rather than revenue projects. However, local authorities face restrictions in the amount of money which they can borrow to finance capital works and in some cases these works might be funded from rental income.

Some landlords will often carry out some significant works around the tenant. This means that the tenant does not have to be moved out (*decanted*), but this will only be possible if the works are such that the tenant can safely remain in occupation. Often, kitchens and bathroom and windows, for example, can be replaced with the tenant in situ although other types of major repairs or improvements may be harder to organise in this way.

7.3: Why are these definitions important?

Jobbing repairs tend to be an expensive way of undertaking essential maintenance. Indeed, the Audit Commission (1986b) in their influential report, *Improving council house maintenance*, suggested that a one-off job can cost up to 50 per cent more than the same job done as part of a planned programme. This is because as the works are not planned in advance, they can not be predicted and often they need to be done quickly. This usually means higher costs because the jobs are small, the contractor has to include travelling times to from jobs, and the landlord cannot benefit from economies by having a contractor deal with the same problems on a number of properties.

Landlords normally deal with cyclical and planned programmes in a different way to their jobbing repairs. Because they know in advance that the work needs to be done they will normally draw up a detailed specification of the works required, go out to competitive tender to a number of contractors, and achieve a cheaper price by virtue of both competition and the fact that works are usually grouped together. For example, an affordable landlord might arrange for all of the houses on an estate to be painted as part of the same contract. This will allow a contractor to have a team of painters on one estate for a number weeks and will almost certainly mean that a more competitive price can be agreed.

The landlord will also be able to closely supervise the work with a clerk of works or a surveyor and this is likely to mean that a better job will be done. (With responsive repairs it is unlikely that many jobs will be able to be supervised by the landlord whilst the works are underway.)

7.4: The law and repairs

Landlords have certain statutory obligations relating to the repairs and maintenance of their homes. These are mainly set out in the Housing Act 1985 and the Landlord and Tenant Act 1985. In addition to the statutory obligations, most landlords will also have obligations for repairs and maintenance which are set down in their tenancy agreements and are contractually binding on the landlord.

Landlord and Tenant Act 1985 (England and Wales)
Housing (Scotland) Act 1987 (Scotland)

Under section 11 of the Landlord and Tenant Act 1985 (section 113 of the Housing (Scotland) Act 1987) all landlords are required to:

- keep in repair, the structure and exterior of the dwelling (including drains, gutters, and external pipes);
- keep in repair and proper working order, installations for the supply of water, gas, electricity and sanitation (including basins, sinks, baths and sanitary conveniences, but not other fixtures, fittings and appliances for making use of the supply of water, gas or electricity);
- keep in repair and proper working order, the installations for space heating and heating water;
- in Scotland, provide and maintain the house in all respects reasonably fit for habitation.

For tenancies let after 15 January 1989 there is also a repairing obligation in relation to the common parts of buildings and installations such as communal heating systems.

This means that all landlords have clear repairing obligations for the structural and external elements such as doors, windows and roofs. In addition, they have obligations in terms of electrical installations, water supply and sanitary equipment. However, whilst many repairs are encompassed within these statutory obligations, other repairs are not. If an internal door is damaged and in need of repair this would not come within the statutory requirements. Similarly, if a kitchen unit needs replacing this is not one of the statutory obligations of the landlord.

Affordable housing landlords often carry out far more repair work than is statutorily required and in the tenancy agreement they will usually indicate the repairs for which the tenant is responsible. Landlords will typically require tenants to be responsible for items such as:

- chimney/flue sweeping;
- door furniture;
- drain/waste blockages;
- electric fuses;
- glass(door/windows);
- internal decoration;
- plugs/chains.

Defective Premises Act 1972

This act places a duty of care on landlords (in England and Wales) in respect of any building works that they carry out. Under the act, landlords and those engaged in building works (such as contractors and consultants) have a statutory duty of care to carry out works in a professional manner, to use proper materials and to ensure that the property is left in a state fit for human habitation.

Occupiers' Liability Act 1957
Occupiers' Liability (Scotland) Act 1960

This first act (in England and Wales) places a duty of care on the occupier of a dwelling in relation to all visitors to a dwelling. Although this is applicable to an occupier it can apply to a landlord insofar as they occupy part of the stock, for example in relation to lifts, communal entrances and other common parts of an estate.

A similar provision exists in Scotland under the Occupiers' Liability (Scotland) Act 1960 although in Scotland a landlord is given a specific duty of care to *any person* on their premises.

Leasehold Reform, Housing and Urban Development Act 1993
Housing (Scotland) Act 2001

Following criticisms, particularly of local authorities' performance in dealing with repairs, the government introduced a right to repair for council tenants under section

96 the 1985 Housing Act. The original scheme, which was very complex and involved the tenant being able to call in a contractor to undertake repair works where the landlord had failed to respond, was replaced with a revised scheme under the 1993 Leasehold Reform, Housing and Urban Development Act. Under the procedure for local authority tenants (introduced in 1995) a local authority in England or Wales can be instructed to issue a further repair order if the original request is not completed within a prescribed timescale. If the repair is still not completed the tenant can claim compensation of £10 plus an additional £2 for each day the repair is outstanding up to a maximum of £50.

For housing association tenants, the TSA has introduced a similar scheme, although in the housing association scheme each individual association itself can determine which repairs come within the scheme and the timescales for completion. The compensation levels (£10 plus £2 a day thereafter up to a maximum of £50) are the same as the local authority scheme.

In Scotland, the scheme applies to all tenants of local authorities and housing associations. It differs from the English and Welsh scheme in that the tenant can instruct a second contractor from the contractors' list if the landlord fails to undertake the repair. The landlord will compensate the tenant by the sum of £15 plus £3 per day the repair is outstanding up to a maximum of £100.

Environmental Protection Act 1990

This provides legal remedies for statutory nuisance where the premises are '...*in such a state as to be prejudicial to health or a nuisance*', defined as premises which are '...*injurious or likely to cause injury to health*'.

Housing (Scotland) Act 2001

This act now incorporates some common law duties into statute including a duty to inspect a house prior to the commencement of a tenancy to check that it is habitable, wind and watertight.

Gas Safety (Installations and Use) Regulations 1998

These regulations require landlords to carry out an annual safety check of gas appliances and to ensure records of such inspections are kept and made available to tenants.

Control of Asbestos Regulations 2006

These regulations require landlords to carry out regular inspections of communal areas for the presence of asbestos containing materials and to continue to monitor the condition of any asbestos found. In most cases, asbestos containing materials can remain in place if not damaged, but the condition of these materials must be regularly assessed. Contractors working in these areas need to be advised of the presence of asbestos containing materials.

7.5: Issues in repairs and maintenance for housing managers

Organising the repairs function

In the past, the repair of homes was often seen as a technical issue and housing management staff may have had little to do with repairs other than pass repair requests from the tenant to a contractor. However, in recent years it has been recognised that housing managers, if they are to deliver an effective housing service, must have greater control over repairs. This involves housing management staff setting timescales for work, passing orders to contractors, monitoring performance and paying the bills.

Because many repairs are undertaken either by contractors or another department then it is necessary for the housing department to act as a client; issuing repairs orders, monitoring the performance of contractors and checking the quality of work undertaken on its behalf by contractors. Local authority housing departments increasingly have taken over this client role.

The repair reporting aspect of the repairs service is most likely to be partly or fully decentralised to local offices. This is not surprising, since if there is a local office, tenants are most likely to make repairs requests at that location. However, in the majority of local authorities and housing associations tasks such as pre- and post-inspections of repairs and the management of external repairs contracts are most likely to be fully centralised (based in a central office), reflecting the fact that these are normally handled by specialist technical staff rather than the more generic (all purpose) housing staff at local offices.

Reporting of repairs and issuing repairs receipts

Most repairs are reported by tenants over the telephone or in person. Clearly, if there is a local office it is often housing management staff who receive repairs requests and it is essential that housing staff taking these repairs requests have some understanding of the technical issues involved. A number or training courses can be provided for non-technical staff. Some organisations have produced booklets for tenants about repairs which advise tenants of the technical terms that they should use to ensure that a repair is properly reported in the first place. In other cases, tenants have access to a repairs manual in the office and can indicate exactly what their problem is.

Good practice also suggests that tenants should be issued with a repairs receipt which will confirm the repair requested, the date of the repair request, any appointment time and the target time for completion.

Pre-inspections of repairs

For responsive repairs, most landlords will receive a repair request from a tenant in person, in writing or over the telephone. If a job is straightforward, such as a leaking

Figure 6.16: Homes for Northumberland repairs receipt

REPAIRS RECEIPT FOR INFORMATION ONLY RCPT1v10/LO62

Plain Language Commission Clear English Standard Winning Document

Homes for Northumberland

Name:

Address:

Date reported:

Priority given:

Reference No:

We have ordered the repair below and arranged an appointment for a tradesman to call on:

We have ordered the repair below which should be completed by:

Description of repair

If you can't keep your appointment please contact us as soon as possible on 01670 542424

How quickly should Homes For Northumberland complete repairs?

Priority 1 – Completed within 1 working day
Priority 2 – Completed within 3 working days
Priority 3 – Completed within 7 working days
Priority 4 – Completed within 20 working days
Priority 5 – Completed within 30 working days
Priority X – Completed within 90 working days

Right to repair scheme

If the repair is a 'qualifying repair' under the Right to Repair scheme, this will be stated in the box above. The time for completion of a repair starts from the next working day.

As you can see from the table overleaf, each qualifying repair has a set time in which we have to get it done. If your repair has not been completed by the date specified, you can ask us to get a second contractor to do the work. Unless there is a good reason why the work has not been done, we will order the work with the second contractor. You will get a copy of the repair notice we send. The second contractor will have the same time to complete the repair.

If the second contractor fails to do the work in this time without good reason (such as you did not keep an appointment), then you can get the work done yourself up to a cost of £250 and send us the bill. Please note this applies only to qualifying repairs. A full list of these jobs is shown overleaf:

Compensation for late repairs

If the second contractor we appoint does not complete the repair in time, please contact the Repairs Call Centre on (01670) 542424. Unless there is a good reason why the repair was not done, such as you did not keep an appointment, you will be entitled to £10 compensation. For every extra day you wait, you will get another £2 up to a maximum of £50. If you owe money to the Council, we will take away the amount you owe from your compensation.

tap, it may be passed by the housing officer directly to the contractor. In other cases, it may not be clear what the problem is and in those circumstances a technical officer may be sent to inspect the property and identify the problem.

Clearly, if works are inspected before an order is placed, it is more likely that clear instructions and specifications can be given to the contractor and greater control exercised over what is to be done. For example, if a tenant reports a leaking tap and the work is not pre-inspected an unscrupulous contractor may be able to go and replace the whole of the tap rather than the leaking washer.

Response times

Another key performance area which concerns both tenants and housing managers is the speed of response in dealing with repairs. All landlords should indicate target times for the completion of a repair from the time it was first reported and every organisation needs to establish systems to ensure that it can effectively monitor performance in meeting those response times. Many landlords have established response times such as:

Category of repair	Target
Dealing with emergencies	24 hours
Urgent repairs	5 days
Responsive repairs	28 days

Jobs which are outside the target time should be identified and checked to see why they are still outstanding and contractors who fail to perform can be penalised and eventually stopped from receiving any further work if they fail to improve their performance.

The government expects both local authorities and housing associations to report annually to tenants on their performance in meeting repairs and the Housing Corporation, and now the TSA, publishes league tables of performance in this key area.

Appointments for repairs

In recent years there has been an increasing trend to offer tenants appointment times for repairs to be done. In some organisations this is little more than agreeing that they will call on a particular morning or afternoon rather than a specific time. Many landlords argue that the volume of work they have makes it impossible to deal with appointments, although a number of organisations have now successfully introduced appointments systems.

Local repairs teams

Having a local repairs team is one of the ways in which a better repairs service can be delivered. A local team will know the estate and its problems and because they always work on the estate they will more likely want to do a good job the first time around. If they do not do so, they will face criticism from tenants and will also be called back to the original job to put it right. Having a locally-based team means that they can be called on more quickly to deal with problems and some costs such as travelling time can be reduced.

An alternative model is a zoned maintenance system which does not rely on an estate-based team, but is a system where a repairs team calls on an estate on a regular cycle and all non-urgent responsive repairs are packaged together for the team to deal with when they are next on the estate. This may well be appropriate where there are areas which do not have enough properties generating repair work to support an estate-based team.

Post-inspections

Where works are not regularly inspected before an order is placed, it is even more essential that landlords monitor the work that has been completed to ensure that a reasonable job has been done, that the work was carried out in a professional manner and that a reasonable price has been paid for the work. Many landlords will have a system of post-inspections where completed jobs will be inspected before an invoice is paid. This will rarely be all jobs because of the cost of inspections, but often a sample of ten per cent of jobs will be looked at. Many organisations will also have a policy that works with invoices over a certain level will always be post-inspected.

Satisfaction surveys

It is increasingly common for social landlords to assess tenants' views about the repairs service by way of a satisfaction survey. These will usually be by a pre-paid questionnaire which asks tenants a number of questions about their repair, the results of which are then collated and analysed. This might be supplemented by satisfaction surveys carried out by technical staff when carrying out post-inspections of repairs. The example shown in Figure 6.17 is used by Homes for Northumberland to check on customer satisfaction with all aspects of the repairs service.

Reducing levels of responsive maintenance and increasing planned maintenance programmes

The Audit Commission recommends that no more than ten per cent of all responsive repairs should be emergency repairs and that a target spend ratio should be set of 70:30 for planned to responsive maintenance. Given that it is more expensive to undertake responsive repairs many landlords have attempted to reduce the amount of responsive or jobbing repairs they do. This has been done by:

- Attempting to increase the amount of planned work to reduce costs and to minimise the number of responsive repairs. For example, a regular programme of roof maintenance may reduce the number of tiles that need to be replaced as one-off jobs.
- Grouping non-urgent repairs until a number of jobs have been collected to enable some economies to be gained. A contractor may be able to deal with a number of jobs in the same estate in the same day thus reducing the travelling times.
- Negotiating schedules or rates. These fix, in advance, the price for a particular job as long as an agreed volume of work is provided.

Stock condition surveys

One of the key approaches to reducing the amount of jobbing repairs has been to increase the size of planned maintenance programmes. The first step in developing a planned programme is to identify clearly what needs to be done and what the priorities are.

Figure 6.17: Repairs satisfaction questionnaire used by Homes for Northumberland

CUSTOMER SURVEY

Repairs and Maintenance Service

Property ID: Survey ID: July 2009

Customer name

Customer address

On a scale of 1 to 10 (1 being very poor and 10 being excellent), please score following statements. Please circle the score you agree with.

		Very poor		*Poor*		*Average*		*Good*		*Very good*	
1	How do you rate how easy it was for you to report your repair?	1	2	3	4	5	6	7	8	9	10
2	How do you rate the helpfulness of our staff?	1	2	3	4	5	6	7	8	9	10
3	How do you rate the advice and information given to you?	1	2	3	4	5	6	7	8	9	10
4	How do you rate the time taken to carry out your repair?	1	2	3	4	5	6	7	8	9	10
5	How do you rate the conduct of the workmen? e.g. attitude, friendliness, I.D. shown	1	2	3	4	5	6	7	8	9	10
6	How do you rate the care taken to protect your property? e.g. dustsheets and shoe protection	1	2	3	4	5	6	7	8	9	10
7	How do you rate the way your home was left after the work was finished? e.g. clean & tidy	1	2	3	4	5	6	7	8	9	10
8	How effective was the repair in meeting your needs?	1	2	3	4	5	6	7	8	9	10
9	How do you rate the overall quality of the work?	1	2	3	4	5	6	7	8	9	10
10	Overall how do you rate the service you received?	1	2	3	4	5	6	7	8	9	10

Please turn over if you wish to make any comments about the service you have received and to input your personal details.

We want to ensure that we provide services fairly, whatever a person's sex, disability, age, ethnic origin or religion. Please help us monitor and improve our service to you by providing this information. You can also make us aware of any particular needs you have when we serve you in the future.

Enquiry ID: *1*

Many housing organisations have now undertaken stock condition surveys in an attempt to quantify more precisely the amount and type of maintenance work that needs to be done. These surveys will usually be on a sample basis taking a small proportion of the stock and carrying out a detailed survey of its condition. This is then used to build up a current profile of the condition of the stock, the remedial works needed immediately, and a list of future maintenance works required. The data collected from the sample can then be aggregated to produce a profile for all of the organisation's stock.

Organisations may use their own staff to carry out a stock condition survey or may use external surveyors to undertake the work. In most cases, the surveys indicate a significant backlog of repairs that need to be tackled to bring the stock up to a reasonable condition, and from the survey organisations can draw up a list of priorities for planned maintenance. The survey can also be used to plan future programmes of work over anything up to a 25 year cycle.

The development of this approach will also need to involve the finance staff who need to advise on the likely costs of the future planned and major maintenance programmes so that they can develop strategies to ensure that these can be funded. In local authorities, this exercise will inform the housing strategy bids and their rent setting strategies, as much of this work will need to be funded from a mixture of capital borrowing and revenue income (in the form of revenue contributions to capital outlay). Similarly in housing associations, stock condition surveys and the resulting planned maintenance programmes will be used to inform (major repairs grants no longer available) the build up of major repairs provisions and sinking funds to fund future programmes.

It is also essential that a stock condition survey is not seen as a one-off exercise. All organisations should undertake a rolling programme of surveys to ensure that programmes remain up to date and priorities can be adjusted in the light of developments in the condition of the stock.

Partnering

Partnering describes an approach to maintenance and development which is characterised by the development of a longer-term relationship with a contractor, often where risks and rewards are shared between the contractor and the client, and is different to the sometimes adversarial nature of dealings between a client and contractor. This concept of partnering was a key recommendation arising from the *Rethinking Construction* report of 1998 by Sir John Egan, and is also explored in Chapter 5 (in relation to housing development).

In the repairs service, increasingly landlords are partnering with contractors to develop improved maintenance services. Key features of partnering contracts involve:

- long-term contracts;
- open book accounting;

- sharing of expertise;
- identification of cost-savings in the supply chain;
- development of a quality culture;
- sharing of IT and management information systems;
- a change in the culture from client/contractor to one of partnership and trust;
- developing good problem solving strategies;
- effective monitoring and measurement processes.

Figure 6.18: Good practice in partnering

St Pancras & Humanist Housing Association won the National Housing Award in housing management for its innovative approach to partnering. Benefits of the partnering approach with two key maintenance contactors were identified as:

- a reduction in timescales to complete the jobs;
- reduced void turn around times;
- improvements in payment processing ensuring more accurate accounting and improvements to the contractors' cash flow;
- a joint tenant compensation fund;
- simplification of procedures;
- joint training sessions;
- introduction of agreed appointment with tenants.

Source: CIH, 2001b.

8. Managing tenancies

8.1: Introduction

In the previous sections of this chapter we have looked at the traditional tasks of housing managers; collecting the rent, dealing with voids, letting properties and carrying out repairs and maintenance. However, in recent years more and more time is being spent by housing managers on other tasks such as:

- dealing with neighbour disputes;
- dealing with the results of crime and vandalism on estates;
- ensuring that common parts of estates are properly managed and maintained;
- liaison with other agencies providing services to estates, such as, police, health service, schools and community centres.

8.2: Dealing with neighbour disputes

In recent years, one of the increasingly difficult problems which housing managers have faced has been the increasing incidence of nuisance and harassment on social housing estates. This can take many forms from noisy and inconsiderate neighbours, to drug dealing from and around properties, to gangs of young people roaming the streets and terrorising whole communities, through to serious public disorder. As the problem has grown, and the expectations of tenants of the housing officer's ability to resolve the problem has increased, housing managers have had to learn new techniques to deal with anti-social behaviour and neighbour disputes.

Of course, in may cases the problems complained of are criminal matters for the police to deal with, but housing managers are increasingly called upon by tenants to take action themselves to deal more effectively with the problems. In the past, the typical reaction of a housing manager to a neighbour dispute might have been to interview the alleged perpetrator and if the case was proven, to issue a warning letter. In some cases a Notice to Quit or Notice of Seeking Possession might have been served, but very few cases ever reached the county courts for possession.

However, more recently housing managers have developed a wider range of techniques to deal with this problem. For dealing with the typical neighbour dispute, staff are often given training in interviewing and mediation skills. Indeed in some areas, such as Bolton MBC, independent mediation services have been employed in order to attempt to resolve disputes between neighbours. The Housing Ombudsman Service regularly makes use of mediation in an effort to resolve disputes between associations and tenants.

Social landlords are also making use of a wider range of legal powers to deal more effectively with the problems. As an alternative to seeking possession orders in the county court, a number of landlords have pioneered the use of county court *injunctions*, requiring anti-social tenants to stop acting in a way which is contrary to the provisions of their tenancy agreement. In some cases these injunctions have been extended to visitors to the tenant's household, and in a small number of cases have been obtained against individuals who are not tenants of the landlord, but who are causing problems on the landlord's estate. The use of injunctions requiring tenants to comply with the terms of their tenancy agreements have now been used successfully in a number of areas to deal with persistent offenders and in other cases affordable housing landlords have obtained possession orders in the courts to evict people from their homes. Under the 1996 Housing Act the courts are empowered to attach the power of arrest to injunctions if there is a threat of violence to victims. This enables the police to arrest someone immediately of there has been a breach of the injunction order.

In order to improve the chances of successful court action some landlords have taken the step of employing dedicated officers to investigate serious complaints of nuisance and harassment and to prepare the necessary statements and affidavits of court. For example, Middlesbrough Borough Council's Housing Department employs a specialist team of Housing Enforcement Officers, whose remit includes ensuring that proper statements are taken and investigation of cases are made prior to court action. The council has successfully obtained a number of injunction orders against tenants. Of course, one of the benefits of an injunction is that if the tenants breach the terms of the injunction they can be committed to prison. This is often a very powerful deterrent to people who are causing a problem on estates.

In some areas, affordable housing landlords have also employed professional witnesses. These are paid staff whose job is to witness anti-social behaviour and to provide signed statements to that effect. This initiative has been developed to overcome the reluctance of witnesses to give evidence in court proceedings because of their fears (often justified) of retaliation or intimidation.

Increasingly, in particularly problematical areas, social landlords are developing initiatives with the police to reduce the problems of anti-social behaviour. The types of initiatives which have been developed include the establishment of police stations or offices on estates, often based in the local housing office. This gives the police a direct presence on estates and also allows much closer liaison between the police and housing officers. In other areas, protocols have been agreed between the police and housing organisations about the sharing of information and the assistance which police and housing officers will give each other. Newydd Housing Association has set up a formal agreement with social services, environmental health and the police on the management of neighbour complaints.

With the development of closed circuit television (CCTV) surveillance systems, these are increasingly being placed on housing estates to increase the levels of security. Similar surveillance systems utilising alarms or miniature cameras have also been developed to put into empty properties to enable the police to deal more effectively with those causing vandalism to empty properties.

At an operational level, police crime prevention officers work very closely with housing managers on identifying ways in which the security of existing homes can be improved through the installation of alarms, door locks and security lighting, so-called target hardening initiatives – and through advice on crime prevention features to be incorporated into new housing developments. Indeed, many new housing developments which incorporate particular crime prevention features are awarded the police 'Secure by Design' certificate.

Anti-Social Behaviour Orders (ASBOs) and Acceptable Behaviour Contracts (ABCs)

The 1998 Crime and Disorder Act introduced significant new powers for landlords to tackle anti-social behaviour (Home Office, 2008). These included:

- **Anti-Social Behaviour Orders/Acceptable Behaviour Contracts**
  ASBOs can be obtained from the magistrates' court to restrict people from entering certain homes or estates in an effort to curb the anti-social behaviour of people who may or may not be tenants (and for which the eviction or injunction

route may not be applicable). These orders have been somewhat easier to obtain in the magistrates' courts and have been accompanied by the development of Acceptable Behaviour Contracts, where landlords agree acceptable forms of behaviour with tenants as a way of enforcing good behaviour. Obviously the breach of an ABC can be used in evidence in court. Following amendments to the legislation, housing associations could apply for these orders in their own right after consultation with the police and the local authority.

- **Child curfews**
  The Crime and Disorder Act introduced powers to allow curfews to be introduced where problems with children and young people roaming the streets is perceived as a significant problem.

- **Closure orders**
  These were introduced in the 2003 Anti-Social Behaviour Act and enable the police to close a property which has been involved in the production, supply or use of Class A drugs. Such orders have been used by housing organisations to remove serious drugs dealers from social housing properties.

8.3: Introductory and probationary tenancies

The use of introductory tenancies, where tenants are not given security of tenure for a period of 12 months has been widely adopted since local authorities were given the option to introduce an introductory scheme in the 1996 Housing Act. Local authority landlords adopting such a scheme must apply it to all new tenants, not only those whom they consider to be a 'risk'. Although these types of tenancies have been criticised by some landlords because they only deal with new tenants and only last for 12 months, a number of landlords undoubtedly make use of them as an additional weapon in their armoury to deal with anti-social behaviour.

Many housing associations have policies of granting assured shorthold tenancies to new tenants, to fulfil similar requirements of giving new tenants a 'probationary period', after which eviction will be relatively easy if the tenant fails to behave appropriately.

In Scotland, the 2001 Housing (Scotland) Act introduced probationary tenancies for tenants with a history of anti-social behaviour (known as short Scottish secure tenancies). In addition, a standard tenancy can be converted to a short tenancy if an Anti-Social Behaviour Order is served on a tenant or a member of the household. In addition, the right to buy is suspended where a Notice of Possession is served.

8.4: Tackling racial harassment

Racial harassment is an acute form of anti-social behaviour as well as being a criminal offence. The Race Relations Amendment Act 2000 places local authorities and other public bodies under a statutory duty to promote equality of opportunity and good race relations between different racial groups.

As a result, many landlords have reviewed and strengthened their policies and procedures for dealing with racial harassment

Advice from the government in *Tackling Racial Harassment* (DTLR, 2001) suggested the following as good practice tips:

- refer victims to effective and sensitive counselling services;
- where threats of violence are made by identifiable perpetrators use ex parte (without notice) injunctions to protect victims and witnesses;
- provide safe, good quality temporary housing for victims if required;
- arrange access to telephones for victims and interpreters if necessary;
- develop means of assessing victims' satisfaction with the process.

(DTLR, 2001.)

For more detailed advice on dealing with anti-social behaviour and community safety issues, see CIH publications (Nixon and Hunter, 2006: Anderson *et al.*, 2008 and Dearling *et al.*, 2006).

9. Performance monitoring

In recent years, there has been a growing interest in performance monitoring within most public sector organisations. There are a number of factors which are behind this increased concern for monitoring performance of housing organisations.

The increasing financial constraints on local authorities and housing associations have led all housing organisations to review how they deliver their housing services in the face of declining resources. The concern to maximise value for money has inevitably led most organisations to establish systems for setting performance targets for key areas of work, such as rent arrears, voids and repairs and monitoring the performance of the organisation against these targets.

The influence of external bodies has to be considered, such as the Audit Commission and the Tenant Services Authority, the Scottish Housing Regulator, the Scottish Government, the Welsh Assembly Government, all of whom have been powerful advocates of performance monitoring and who have been able to influence the internal working of housing organisations.

This has led to the development under the Labour government since 1997 of a significant 'inspection' culture in relation to social housing managed by both local authorities and housing associations.

Performance monitoring, the setting of performance targets and reporting on performance, and dealing with inspections are now common features of almost all housing organisations in the UK. All local housing authorities and most housing associations now publish annual reports to their tenants which include detailed performance monitoring information on their services.

The performance monitoring culture now permeates housing organisations at all levels. Councillors and boards of housing associations and ALMOs regularly receive performance information at their meetings. Senior staff of housing organisations review their key performance data on a regular basis and in most area housing offices, staff will collect information on arrears performance, voids and repairs and compare how well they are doing with their colleagues in other offices.

In almost all of the housing management tasks discussed earlier in this chapter, most housing organisations have established performance monitoring systems to check how well the organisation is performing in each of these areas. For example, most housing organisations will collect information on arrears performance, the numbers of tenants in arrears and the amount of rent collected as a percentage of the rent debits. With empty properties, almost all housing organisations will collect performance data on the numbers of empty properties, the time they are empty, and the rent lost as a result.

9.1: Tenant satisfaction

Ultimately, the test of how well any housing organisation is performing is the views of customers. The Audit Commission's Housing Inspectorate's approach to inspection is to view the service quality from the customer perspective, and in addition, both the

Table 6.19: Tenant satisfaction in housing associations at March 2008 (percentage)

	Upper quartile		Lower quartile		Upper decile		Lower decile	
	2008	2007	2008	2007	2008	2007	2008	2007
Tenant satisfaction with overal service	85.0	84.9	75.0	75.3	89.0	88.1	69.0	69.4
Tenant satisfaction with opportunities for participation	67.0	67.2	53.2	52.8	75.6	76.0	48.6	46.1
Tenant satisfaction with repairs and maintenance service	82.4	82.0	69.4	70.0	86.2	87.0	63.0	63.0

Source: Housing performance indicators, 2008, Housing Corporation.

Audit Commission and Tenant Services Authority expect housing landlords to gather data on tenant satisfaction using the same methodology. This data is usually gathered from large-scale satisfaction surveys carried out every three years. The Housing Corporation's published data on tenant satisfaction for 2006-07 showed that 79 per cent of housing association tenants were satisfied with their landlord, and that 62 per cent were satisfied with their opportunities to be involved in management.

Table 6.19 (see previous page) shows tenant satisfaction at March 2008 in English housing associations, presented in a way to show the difference between upper quartile performers who averaged 85 per cent overall service satisfaction compared to the lowest quartile at 69 per cent.

References and further reading

Accounts Commission (2004) *Housing and Social Work Performance Indicators 2002/03*, Scottish Executive, Edinburgh.

Anderson, I., Brown, A. with Nixon, J. and Hunter, C. (2008) *Tackling anti-social behaviour in Scotland*, CIH Scotland/JRF, Edinburgh and York.

Audit Commission (1984) *Bringing council tenants arrears under control*, HMSO, London.

Audit Commission (1986a) *Managing the crisis in council housing*, HMSO, London.

Audit Commission (1986b) *Improving Council House Maintenance*, HMSO, London.

Audit Commission/Housing Corporation (2003a) *Rent collection and arrears management by housing associations in England: Housing association rent income*, Audit Commission, London.

Audit Commission (2003b) *Local authority rent income*, Audit Commission, London.

Brown, T., Dearling, A., Hunt, R., Richardson, J. and Yates N. (2002) *Allocate or Let? Your Choice: Lessons from Harborough Home Search*, CIH, London.

Centre for Housing Policy, University of York (1993) *Managing Social Housing*, HMSO, London (referred to as the York Report).

Chartered Institute of Housing (2001a) *Good Practice Briefing Managing Rent Arrears*, CIH, Coventry.

Chartered Institute of Housing (2001b) *Good Practice Briefing Repairs and Maintenance*, CIH, Coventry.

Chartered Institute of Housing (2002) *Crime, Disorder and Anti Social Behaviour, Good Practice Briefing 23*, CIH, Coventry.

Chartered Institute of Public Finance (2007) *Housing Rent Arrears and Housing Benefit Statistics*, CIPFA, London.

Commission for Racial Equality (2006) *Housing Code of Practice for England*, CRE, London.

Dearling, A., Newburn, T. and Somerville, P. (2006) *Supporting safer communities: Housing, crime and neighbourhoods*, CIH, Coventry.

Department for Communities and Local Government (2006a) *Survey Monitoring the Longer-Term impact of Chioce-based Lettings*, The Stationery Office, London.

Department for Communities and Local Government (2006b) *Survey of English Housing*, The Stationery Office, London.

Department for Communities and Local Government (2009) *Local Authority Housing Statistics, England 2007/08*, The Stationery Office, London.

Department of the Environment (1987) *Rent arrears: Circular 18/87*, HMSO, London.

Department of the Environment (1994) *Rent Arrears in Local Authorities and Housing Associations*, HMSO, London.

Department of the Environment, Transport and the Regions (1999) *Report of Policy Action Team 5 on Housing Management*, DETR, London.

Department of the Environment, Transport and the Regions/Department of Social Security (2000) *Quality and Choice: A Decent home for all*, DETR, London.

Department of Transport, Local Government and the Regions (2001) *Tackling Racial Harassment; Code of Practice for Social Landlords*, HMSO, London.

Egan, J. (1998) *Rethinking Construction*, DETR, London.

Fitzpatrick, S., Quilgars, D. and Pleace, N. (2009) *Homelessness in the UK: Problems and Solutions*, CIH, Coventry.

Grainger, P., Harding, J. and Kirk, R. (2003) *Changing Organisations: Changing Roles?: The Work of the Housing Manager*, Housing & Community Research Group Discussion Paper No.2, Northumbria University, Newcastle.

Housing Corporation (2000) *Rent Arrears Standard, A guide to managing rent arrears for RSLs*, Housing Corporation, London.

Housing Corporation (2008) *Housing performance indicators*, Housing Corporation, London.

Home Office (2008) *A guide to Anti Social behaviour tools and powers*, COI, London.

Kemp, P. and Williams, P. (1991) 'Housing Management: an Historical Perspective' in Lowe, S. and Hughes, D. (eds.) *A New Century of Social Housing*, Leicester University Press, Leicester.

Local Government Association (2007) *Councils and the Housing Crisis*, LGA, London.

Nixon, J. and Hunter, C. (2006) *Tackling Anti-Social Behaviour*, CIH, Coventry.

Mew, H., *et al*. (2003) *Housing in England 2001/2: A report of the 2001/2 Survey of English Housing carried out by the National Centre for Social Research on behalf of the Office of the Deputy Prime Minister*, ODPM, London.

Office for National Statistics (2003a) *Housing Statistics 2003*, HMSO, London.

Office for National Statistics (2003b) *Social Trends 33*, HMSO, London.

Office of the Deputy Prime Minister (2002) *Code of Guidance on Allocations*, ODPM, London.

Office of the Deputy Prime Minister (2003a) *Best Value in Housing and Homelessness Framework*, ODPM, London.

Office of the Deputy Prime Minister (2003b) *Incentives and Beyond: the Transferability of the Irwell Valley Gold Service to other Social landlords*, ODPM, London.

Power, A. (1987) *Property Before People – The Management of Twentieth Century Council Housing*, Alan and Unwin, London.

Scott, S. (2001) *Good Practice in Housing Management: A Review of the Literature*, Scottish Executive, Central Research Unit, Edinburgh.

Smith, M. (1989) *Guide to Housing*, Housing Centre Trust, 3rd Edition, London.

Smith, R. and Merrett, S. (1988) *The Challenge of Empty Housing*, SAUS, Bristol.

Spicker, P. (1983) *The Allocation of Council Housing*, Shelter, London.

Spicker, P. (1985) 'Legacy of Octavia Hill', *Housing*, June 1985, Institute of Housing, London.

Thomas, A., Johnson, P. and Veale, R. (2005) *Right First time: How Housing Associations are improving their responsive repairs*, CIH, Coventry.

Wilcox, S. (2008) *UK Housing Review 2008/09*, CIH/BSA, Coventry and London.

CHAPTER 7: Meeting the challenges

Introduction

The previous chapters have explored the evolution and role of affordable housing in the United Kingdom and analysed the work which housing professionals do in relation to finance, development and housing management. Although these areas have been reviewed in separate chapters we have tried to highlight throughout this book that the task of managing affordable housing requires the integration of a wide rage of skills and knowledge. For example, the successful development of a new housing scheme requires housing managers to have a thorough grasp of development, finance and management issues in order to address all of the complex issues which have to be resolved.

As explained in the earlier chapters, affordable housing has been affected by significant changes over the last 25 years, with the result that the role of different providers has been changing substantially. This in turn has had an impact on the work of housing professionals. This final chapter looks ahead at the likely key challenges facing housing professionals and the impact these may have on their work.

Earlier in the book we documented the significant changes that took place in social housing during the 1980s and 1990s. In many ways, the challenges now faced by the sector are the product of these earlier changes and – to a great extent – the problems which they caused or left unresolved. In 1986 the Audit Commission described what they saw as the 'crisis' in social housing, a crisis characterised by poor quality housing and ineffective management. Since then there have been some very significant developments:

- the continued decline of local authority housing through stock transfers to housing associations and the impact of the right to buy;
- the introduction of the Decent Homes Standard and the development of ALMOs and PFI in response to the challenge of investing in the housing stock;
- the development of larger housing associations through mergers and stock transfer, often driven by the desire to secure additional funding to develop new housing;
- the demise of CCT and its replacement by Best Value;
- the introduction of housing inspection and the star rating system;
- the devolution of housing policy to the Scottish Government, the Welsh Assembly Government and to the Northern Ireland Assembly;
- the introduction of the Sustainable Communities Plan and the significant increase in funding for affordable housing;

- the creation of Housing Action Trusts and later, Housing Market Renewal Pathfinders to deal with regenerating areas of low demand;
- the abolition of the Housing Corporation and English Partnerships and the creation of the Tenant Services Authority and the Homes and Communities Agency;
- the impact of the 2008 credit crunch on the housing market;
- increasing levels of homelessness and repossessions.

In this last chapter of the book we want to explore six key questions:

1. **What is the future of council housing/ALMOs?**
   Is the decline in the numbers of homes owned by local authorities likely to continue through stock transfer, or, will local authority owned housing still be a significant force in social housing provision in the UK?

2. **Can housing associations undertake new development in the credit crunch and recession?**
   The impact of the 2008 credit crunch and the 2009+ recession has had a significant impact on the numbers of new homes being built. Given that most housing association new development requires a cross-subsidy from homes built for outright sale/shared ownership to help finance rented units, can the new house building targets be met if cross-subsidy is not available?

3 **What will be the impact of the new regulatory regime?**
The affordable housing regulatory regime went through a significant change with the passage of the 2008 Housing and Regeneration Act which saw the establishment of the Tenant Services Agency. What is the likely impact of this regime going to be on the affordable housing sector, particularly when local authority landlords come into the remit of the TSA in England in April 2010?

4 **What will happen to private housing markets?**
As with the affordable housing sector, the recession has had a significant impact on the private housing sector. Will prices continue to fall? How long will stagnation last? Will repossessions continue to rise? How will this impact on affordable housing demand? How long will it take before lending returns to previous levels?

5 **Can we realistically pursue the 'green' agenda in the current economic climate?**
Sustainability and the green agenda have been an increasingly important aspect of UK housing policy. Will this commitment be sustained in the current economic climate? Will level 6 of the Code for Sustainable Homes be achieved? Will private developers challenge attempts to increase their costs by further revisions to the building regulations?

6. **What will affordable housing be like in 20 years time?**
   Finally the chapter will look at the longer-term future for affordable housing in the UK. Will it become an ever increasingly 'residualised sector', or can the trends of the last 30 years be reversed?

In exploring these questions we do not intend to suggest answers, but instead we highlight the challenges faced by housing professionals over the coming years.

1. What is the future for council housing and ALMOs?

Ever since the 1980 Housing Act the future for council housing has seemed bleak. The 1980 Housing Act introduced the right to buy which has been extremely successful in transferring ownership from the council housing sector to owner-occupation. Allied to this has been the shift to a clear separation of landlord and strategic housing powers for local authorities, and as presaged in the 1988 Housing Act, the widespread adoption of stock transfer to housing associations, a limited interest in PFI, and in more recent years the development of ALMOs.

What is really striking looking back over 25 years is that the number of affordable housing dwellings has continued to fall from 7.778 million homes in 1981 to a total of just 4.805 million in 2006 (Wilcox, 2008), largely as a result of the shrinkage of the local authority sector.

Inevitably, this means that the pressure on affordable housing has intensified with more and more households registering on social housing waiting lists, and increasingly social housing has become a 'residualised' tenure for those who are unable to meet their needs in the private sector.

Whilst there is no doubt that the quality of affordable housing has improved significantly over the last 10 years (as a result of the Decent Homes Standard), it is this issue of the huge fall in the stock of social housing, and the increasing pressure from households in need which has been exercising the minds of policy-makers and politicians. The Sustainable Communities Plan and the increases in expenditure for new affordable housing, whilst welcome, are not going to close the gap between the affordable housing which can be provided and the need for it.

In these circumstances it is not surprising that there is a real and urgent debate about the purpose of social housing. In 1999, the Chartered Institute of Housing's submission (to the Institute of Public Policy Research forum on the future of social housing) argued that the aims of housing policy should be to provide:

- A housing stock reflecting modern standards of space, design, accessibility and construction.
- Sufficient houses to meet demand and allow for mobility.

- Houses at affordable costs in relation to incomes.
- Sufficient choice between buying and renting.

The report argued that, in order to achieve these aims, the UK needed a '*...sustainable housing system*', which ensures that the country:

- Has sufficient homes, so that all housing requirements can be met.
- Sustains and develops a high quality housing stock, which is built efficiently and is well-managed.
- Achieves economy and flexibility in the use of resources for housing, to support economic prosperity.
- Combats poverty and disadvantage.
- Promotes a healthy, secure and sustainable environment.
- Has choice and accountability, with systems which empower the customers.
- Sustains communities, with well-planned neighbourhoods and adequate facilities, which avoid the segregation of rich and poor.

In relation to affordable housing, the CIH argued for a '*more European approach*' which implies:

> *...a more independent non-profit sector, which operates in a more commercial way and has a wider client base, with less clear-cut divisions between tenures... but the challenge is to do this and not lose sight of social objectives.*

The Institute for Public Policy Research's report, *Housing United* published in 2000 called for affordable housing to become a '*...sector of choice rather than stay a sector of last resort*'. It should be a '*...mainstream choice, not an ever-more residualised symbol of failure*'.

Its key message was to break down the barriers between tenures, so that people can move more freely from one to the other, so there is a less rigid distinction between owning and renting, and also that affordable housing becomes – over a period of time – less physically distinct from private housing. It is not a vision that can be achieved overnight but one which – the report argues – is the right goal for affordable housing over the next 20 or 30 years. Housing professionals should be willing to commit to such a vision, and work towards it over that period, judging what they do according to whether it helps to achieve this goal or not. The alternative, according to IPPR, is an increasingly marginalised form of housing which will be less and less attractive – only a '*last resort*'.

The report argued that independent landlords of the sort being created through transfer and ALMOs were the logical future for affordable housing, and that local authorities should no longer be direct managers of housing stock. Instead, there should be various different types of '*community housing organisation*' which would run affordable housing as community-based, non-profit businesses, freed from many of the constraints which currently hamper local authorities. Ideally, there would be a single form of tenure either for affordable renting or for rented housing generally, and there would be choice between providers in a local authority area so that people could 'vote with their feet' for a better landlord or better quality house.

The National Housing Federation (NHF – the representative body in England for housing associations) also became increasingly concerned about the lack of public awareness of the significant role which housing associations play, in providing quality housing in pleasant neighbourhoods. They argued that there was:

- *Growing public prejudice against social housing and our customers.*
- *Declining satisfaction and higher aspirations among our customers.*
- *A persistent perception in government and partner organisations that we are competitive and complaining.*

(NHF 2003, p3).

As a result, from 2001-03 the NHF undertook a radical re-think of '*...what we stand for, what we do, how we do it and how we present ourselves*' (NHF, 2003, p3). This resulted in the creation of a new, national alliance of associations in England, re-branded as *iN Business for Neighbourhoods*, with the logo iN. iN made three key commitments, setting out what English HAs intended to do to make the new brand, '*...a reality, not just a promise*'.

In *Who we are* (inbiz, 2003), the NHF emphasised that housing associations were in business for their neighbourhoods, to create places where people want to live, provide a range of services as well as homes, while working in partnership with others. In other words, they are committed to addressing the three key challenges identified in the previous sections, of quality, sustainability and partnerships. These are challenges that no affordable housing provider can afford to ignore.

All of these approaches were dependent on a very significant increase in the provision of new affordable housing to create the sort of context in which these policy proposals might flourish. However, in the absence of the political will or financial capacity to deliver that massive increase in new affordable housing provision a new (and perhaps somewhat more depressing) debate has developed, which starts from a premise that social housing is a form of welfare or safety-net housing and that public policy should reflect that reality.

1.1: So, is there a future for council housing and ALMOs?

It is clear that the common thread of housing policy since the 1980s has been the continuing diminution of the role of council housing and the increasing importance of the housing association sector. For those local authorities which have been unwilling or unable to pursue stock transfer (or PFI), the creation of ALMOs has been the way in which they have been able both to increase resources for the improvement of the housing stock but also to see the separation of the strategic housing function from the day-to-day management function.

The main objective of ALMOs was to secure additional investment in their housing stock to meet the Decent Homes deadline of March 2010. As many ALMOs have now completed their investment programmes it is not surprising that a number are beginning to consider what options exist for their future. Some (such as Oldham and Stockton's ALMOs) are already considering becoming stock transfer associations. Others may simply fold and return to the control of the local authority; in other cases, the decision may be taken that ALMOs should remain as arms length management organisations.

In the autumn of 2008, a total of 22 ALMOs obtained Development Partner status, which enabled them to access funding for new developments from the Homes and Communities Agency (HCA). Indeed, in November 2008, Stockport Homes ALMO signed its social housing agreement with the HCA to become the first ALMO to receive grant with the award of £1.02 million to build 17 homes.

In February 2009, there was the first sign that government policy towards local authority housing might be changing, largely as a result of the credit crunch which was depressing the numbers of new homes being built. Ever since 1997, the government had been explicit with local authorities that there was no fourth option for local authorities which wanted to invest in their own homes and build new ones. These three options were: stock transfer, PFI or ALMOs. Indeed, in 2006-07 only 250 new homes were built in the UK by local authorities.

However, in January 2009 the housing minister announced that councils would be allowed to keep the rental income from homes they either buy, build, or bring back into use, to invest in new housing and that they would be allowed to keep the proceeds if these homes are sold to tenants through right to buy. The government said that this change was driven at least in part by need, as Margaret Beckett confirmed: '*We are determined to help keep house building going in the current climate, as the long-term need for more homes is not going to disappear*' (*Inside Housing*, 30 January 2009). It will be interesting to see whether there are further relaxations to restraints on local authority house building in future years.

Mrs Beckett also promised that councils will be able to access subsidy in the form of social housing grant (SHG). Once the preserve of housing associations, SHG is now open to private developers and to local authority owned companies. The current English housing minister, John Healey, has made SHG available to councils. The caveat here is that, welcome though SHG will be, bidding is competitive. For example, about one-third of ALMOs (the arms length companies that manage half of council housing) have qualified to receive SHG in principle, but so far only one has actually got it.

So, there are bound to be worries about how long it will take for councils to qualify for SHG in their own right, and then eventually to receive the funds. Furthermore, funding is due to decline sharply from 2010 onwards, so councils will have to move quickly.

A real shift in councils' ability to service loan charges from new schemes would occur if they could keep the rental income from their *whole* stock, not just the new units. Such a move is promised in the review of council housing finance published in July 2009. This, indeed, offers a range of potentially exciting reforms to enable council housing to become self-financing, and for councils to declare independence from a national subsidy system which stifles initiatives and is perhaps the biggest barrier of them all.

In Scotland and Wales, the pressures for stock transfer have been much stronger in Wales (particularly to community-led stock transfers) and less so in Scotland. This is because of the different housing finance regime available to Scottish local authority housing. In neither country has the development of ALMOs taken hold.

In a situation where public sector resources are limited for housing investment, it seems that the pressures for stock transfer will remain, and that over the next ten years the council housing/ALMO sector will continue to decline through both the right to buy and more importantly through stock transfer. However, the need to maintain levels of house building in the recession may lead to some relaxation to restrictions on local authorities' ability to build as presaged by the January 2009 announcement.

A further issue to consider is the ongoing investment in the housing stock. One of the great failures of local authority housing in the 1970s and 1980s was the failure to invest in the modernisation of existing homes. After all, this was the reason why the Audit Commission in their influential 1986 report referred to the '*crisis in council housing*'. It was what led to the development of stock transfer and then ALMOs as a way of ensuring homes met the Decent Homes Standard. And it has been a success with the overwhelming majority of affordable housing on track to meet the Decent Homes Standard by 2010. However, some politicians seem to have ignored the obvious point that post-2010 homes which are currently meeting the standard will require investment again in new heating systems, new windows, new bathrooms etc. and that it is essential that resources continue to be made available to local authorities and ALMOs to keep their housing stock at the required levels of investment. Again, it will be interesting to see what happens post the 2010 deadline for the Decent Homes Standard, and whether the very real improvements in affordable housing quality which have been achieved will be sustained.

2. Can housing organisations undertake new development in the credit crunch and recession?

2.1: Via housing associations?

Chapter 4 highlighted some of the ways in which the financial crisis, which emerged during 2007-08, impacted on housing association development. In particular, as Social Housing Grant (and Housing Association Grant in Scotland) had declined over previous years, associations were encouraged to focus on developing more shared ownership schemes, permitting them to recoup some of their capital expenditure from the loans acquired by the new shared owners. With the severe decline in the availability of mortgages in the UK by late 2008, especially to borrowers on lower incomes (now viewed as potentially 'sub-prime' and higher risk), sales of shared ownership homes became much more difficult. This impacted directly on associations' cash flows, as anticipated income from sales failed to materialise.

By early 2009, to limit the scale of new, unsold, empty properties, a number of associations had approached the Homes and Communities Agency (HCA) to gain approval to switch planned shared ownership schemes to affordable rental housing. This meant that their stock of homes to rent increased, but with the need for higher levels of borrowing to cover the additional capital cost of the 'lost' shared equity sales. At the same time, despite the fall in bank rate, the London Interbank Offered Rate (LIBOR) remained high, as a result of which banks were demanding higher interest charges for extended borrowing.

Prior to the 'credit crunch', a great deal of mortgage finance was made available by the banks' selling 'asset-backed' securities. Essentially, these were assets created by assembling mortgage loans into larger packages, to be sold on to other banks. This then freed up funds for banks to make further loans. The packages were rated for their riskiness by risk-assessors, with the least risky awarded three 'A's. However, increasingly, these ratings had become unreliable, with a number of so-called 'triple-As' being, essentially, all sub-prime (high-risk) packages. Hence, the banking system lost confidence in these securities, and the market for them collapsed, leaving banks much less able to make new loans.

This situation prompted the government to try to stimulate the availability of mortgage loans by:

- From April 2009, introducing a new scheme to underwrite (guarantee) triple-A rated asset-backed securities, effectively shifting the risk to the Bank of England. This was first suggested by the Crosby Review of Mortgage Finance in 2008.
- Authorising the Bank of England to buy up to £50 billion of high-quality private sector assets, such as corporate bonds (essentially, loans to large businesses) and asset-backed securities. The Housing Finance Corporation

(THFC) argues that some of these could be bonds backed by loans to housing associations (Dowler, *Inside Housing*, 23 January 2009).

- Insuring (for a charge) some risky (called 'toxic') assets held by the banks, which effectively passes on some of the risk that these assets will ultimately prove to be worthless to the Treasury.
- Ordering the Northern Rock bank – which was required to reduce its mortgage lending following nationalisation in 2008 – to resume new mortgage lending.

However, as observed by the NHF, it remains to be seen whether these new measures will result in more loans being available for shared ownership schemes in the future (Dowler, *Inside Housing*, 23 January 2009).

In addition, many housing associations have seen the value of their accumulated land banks, intended for new, future development, decline considerably in value. This will have an impact on their balance sheets at the year end, when assets must be revalued to reflect their current worth. According to Dowler (6 March 2009), these 'impairment charges' will reduce anticipated surpluses in the accounts, which will impact on the willingness of lenders to make further loans, as well as potentially increasing lending charges.

On a more positive note, however, many private developers are also struggling to sell land which they no longer wish to build on, so, for some associations, this could mean much reduced land costs for future developments. Certainly, this situation implies that the unit costs of development will be declining for some time in the near future.

In addition, as a result of the slump in private owner-occupied markets during 2008, a number of speculative housing developers are more eager to build in collaboration with housing associations. Anecdotally, it seems that many more are competing for housing association contracts to build (rather than build for private sale), and there is some evidence that tender prices (for new housing development by housing associations) have become much more competitive as a result. According to Ellery (13 February 2009), the RICS Building Cost Information Service predicts that tender prices will fall by around ten per cent during 2009 and 2010. In addition, some developers, which have already secured SHG (as HCA 'approved developers'), are soliciting partnerships with housing associations to reduce their risk. It remains to be seen whether these benefits are anything more than temporary – much depends on the how long it takes private markets to recover, and how many speculative builders go out of business during these difficult circumstances.

2.2: Via local authorities?

As Chapter 4 indicated, the issues which need to be resolved to permit local authorities to undertake new housing development are very different to those for housing associations. Some ALMOs – such as Westminster's Citywest Homes – have already secured SHG for new development (£36 million in Citywest's case), and it is anticipated that more will follow. However, much depends on whether their parent councils are able to access funding under the prudential borrowing rules (see Chapter 4).

Other councils have adopted rather different approaches. Islington, for example, embarked on the sale of commercial properties to fund £8 million of new housing development, while Barking and Dagenham council have set up a local housing company, which can bid for SHG along with housing associations (Storey, *Inside Housing*, 30 January 2009).

In 2009, the housing minister announced changes which will allow councils in England and Wales to build new homes and be allowed to keep:

- the rental income from these new homes (rather than it being considered simply as part of overall HRA rental income, to be potentially absorbed and redistributed by central government as part of HRA negative subsidy (see Chapter 4);
- any proceeds from subsequent right to buy sales of these homes (whereas, for current homes, 75 per cent of the proceeds are pooled centrally, for redistribution to councils deemed in need of additional subsidy from the government).

(Rogers, *Inside Housing*, 23 January 2009.)

While there is no suggestion of additional subsidy beyond Social Housing Grant, the review of council housing finance has now reported (see Chapter 4). There are hopes that this could permit councils to opt out of the HRA subsidy system, permitting them to keep *all* rental income. This could create substantial additional revenue funds to pay for new borrowing. However, as a result of prudential borrowing constraints, even if this were to be agreed, it is not anticipated that this will result in anything other than a fairly minor expansion in council house building – certainly not a return to the mass-building programmes of the early 1950s. And, in the present context of an economic recession and hence falling tax receipts, it is questionable whether the government will give up such a dependable source of additional funds. Readers will need to monitor future developments in relation to this.

3. What will be the impact of the new regulatory regime?

In December 2008, the new Tenant Services Authority came into being in England following the passage of the 2008 Housing and Regeneration Act. The act makes the TSA the regulator for all housing associations in England, and from April 2010 for English local authority housing.

This is a major change and creates a single regulator for all affordable housing and separates out the regulatory role from the investment role (which will now be carried out by the Homes and Communities Agency). At the very least, the new arrangements will mean that there is a renewed focus on affordable housing regulation and the new regulator has been given significantly increased powers to regulate the new registered providers.

The Housing Corporation had a more limited range of regulatory powers with which to control poorly performing associations. These included withholding development grant to some associations (but only a minority of associations were developing new homes, so this sanction was relatively weak). The main power was 'supervision' which involved the Housing Corporation placing up to three appointed board members on the board, whose role was to help steer the association out of the problems they were facing. In some cases, this might lead to the association deciding to merge with another housing association (particularly if the reason for the supervision was one of financial weakness). Indeed, the Housing Corporation's last annual report for 2007-08 reported that at the end of March 2008 there were eight associations in supervision. This compared with 51 cases in 2003-04.

Figure 7.1: Housing Corporation supervision cases

Section 1: Supervision cases summary	
Number of cases as at 1 April 2007	**17**
New cases added	4
Cases resolved	(13)
Number of cases as at March 2008	**8**

Section 2: Five-year trend					
	2003-04	2004-05	2005-06	2006-07	2007-08
Number of cases brought forward	47	51	42	23	17
New cases	25	15	8	3	4
Cases resolved	(21)	(24)	(27)	(9)	(13)
Number of cases carried forward	**51**	**42**	**23**	**17**	**8**

Source: Housing Corporation, 2008.

This relatively limited set of powers has been augmented in the new legislative framework which has now been applied to the Tenant Services Authority. The TSA now has at its disposal a much wider set of powers to regulate associations where mismanagement or service failure is identified. These include:

- enforcement notices;

- penalties and fines;
- compensation to tenants;
- establishing special inquiries;
- requiring an extraordinary audit to be undertaken;
- requiring associations to tender their housing management services;
- transferring housing management services to other organisations;
- forcing through mergers;
- appointing a special manager;
- removing board members and senior staff;
- appointing new board members.

These are significantly enhanced powers and will be used to ensure that registered providers comply with the TSAs new housing standards. These standards are being developed through a 'National Conversation' with tenants in the spring of 2009 with a view to being formalised in the autumn of 2009.

The standards will cover the following areas:

(a) criteria for allocating accommodation;
(b) terms of tenancies;
(c) levels of rent (and the rules may, in particular, include provision for minimum or maximum levels of rent, or levels of increase or decrease of rent);
(d) maintenance;
(e) procedures for addressing complaints by tenants against landlords;
(f) methods for consulting and informing tenants;
(g) methods of enabling tenants to influence or control the management of their accommodation and environment;
(h) policies and procedures required by section 218A of the Housing Act 1996 in connection with anti-social behaviour;
(i) landlords' contribution to the environmental, social and economic well-being of the areas in which their property is situated;
(j) estate management.

The regulator may also set standards for registered providers (registered providers is the new name for affordable housing landlords including for-profit private providers registered with the Tenant Services Authority in England) in matters relating to the management of their financial and other affairs (Housing and Regeneration Act 2008).

The early indications are that the TSA will be more robust in driving up standards than the Housing Corporation and will have much more of a tenant focus. Perhaps the TSA will be learning from the Audit Commission, whose robust inspection regime in housing has done much to drive up standards across the sector.

Another feature of the new regime is its emphasis on a tenant-focused service. The chair of the TSA has said that the TSA will be a more 'demanding regulator' and will seek to ensure that the TSA regulates in the interests of tenants rather than the interests of providers. This may mark a significant shift in the way in which affordable housing is regulated and may focus the work of some providers on improving services as opposed to building new homes.

The other big challenge is the extension of the regulatory regime from April 2010 to the local authority sector. This will be the first time that local authorities have been subjected to external regulation (other than through the inspection regime of the Audit Commission), and for some the intrusion of the TSA into how they manage housing will be seen as challenging, particularly with the democratic accountability of elected member for their services. It will be interesting to see how many of the enforcement powers in the 2008 Act will end up being applied to the local authority sector when the TSA becomes the 'single regulator'.

4. What will happen to private housing markets?

House prices continued to fall into the early part of 2009, with no sign of prices stabilising. As the number of borrowers with mortgage arrears grew, there were renewed efforts to try to prevent repossessions. For example, in January 2009, the Scottish Government announced the creation of a Homeowners Support Fund, to enable it to buy equity shares from mortgagees and prevent repossession. A number of banks claimed that they had also explored the creation of rescue schemes, but, when funds are in short supply anyway, this is not really seen as a feasible option.

The number and availability of mortgage products has declined considerably since the 'boom' years up to 2007, but, for low-risk borrowers, with large deposits, a range of different mortgages (such as fixed rate, tracker, and variable rate) remains available. However, as the banking system seems likely to remain fairly risk averse for the foreseeable future, this will make it much more difficult for those on low or variable incomes to secure new loans for house purchase. This is also likely to ensure continuing low levels of right to buy sales to council tenants.

The difficult situation in private markets from 2008, which was initially created by the credit crunch reducing the availability of mortgages, has since been compounded by an economic recession from the end of 2008. A recession is defined as falling national income/output for two consecutive quarters (six months). Unemployment was increasing, but so too was fear and uncertainty, which caused many potential buyers and movers to delay taking any action. So, while the demand for private homes was shrinking, the supply was being swelled by those desperate to sell (for example, to avoid repossession). By early 2009, there were growing fears that the recession could last considerably longer, and would be much deeper, than at first believed, further compounding households' reluctance to take on any new commitments. Whilst the recession continues to gather pace, it is difficult to see an early end to the slump in private, owner-occupied housing markets.

The situation in private rental markets was not significantly better. Many private landlords were enticed into private renting in the early 21st century by the lure of capital gains from rising house prices. These potentially could make up for any shortfall in income from rent (compared to their borrowing costs). However, after a year of falling prices, it has become clear that many are losing money on their investments. Private rents have fallen in many areas, partly because the supply has been increased by home owners temporarily renting out properties which they have been unable to sell. In some areas, falling rents have been compounded by the introduction of the Local Housing Allowance, which (by basing rents on Broad Rental Market Areas) has reduced the housing benefit payable in some localities.

As the numbers of empty rental properties have increased, there have been rising numbers of repossessions of buy to let properties, as landlords struggle to cover their mortgages. In such cases, any current tenants have no rights to remain and are simply evicted by the mortgagors, often with no prior warning that the landlord was in difficulties. This is likely to be putting added pressure on affordable housing providers, faced with a new range of unintentionally homeless households from repossessed private rental properties.

In the current economic climate, a return to the exceptionally high prices seen during much of the early part of the 21st century seems highly unlikely. It may be that prices will start to stabilise (i.e. cease to fall) during the latter part of 2009, though it is likely to be some years before they return to previous highs. Much will depend on the longevity of the current economic recession. On the positive side, house prices are becoming more affordable, and, arguably, are starting to return to more sustainable levels. For new builds, falling land prices should reduce future costs, though it is likely to be some time before sufficient confidence returns for new private housing development to resume on any scale.

5. Can we realistically pursue the 'green' agenda in the current economic climate?

The government target is that level 6 (i.e. zero-carbon emissions) of the Code for Sustainable Homes is achieved by all new affordable housing by 2016, with level 3 currently (in 2009) required. Nevertheless, this had already been set aside in some instances in 2008, when housing associations were encouraged to purchase unsold private housing developments that speculative builders were unable to sell – few of which would have achieved level 3. However, only £31 million (of the £200 million allocated) had been used for this purpose by the end of 2008 (Rogers, *Inside Housing,* 16 January 2009), perhaps suggesting that housing associations were less certain of the desirability of buying up these unsold private sector homes than the government.

With the effective collapse of private new build sales by late 2008, and hence virtually no new private developments being undertaken at the start of 2009, the plan to require private developers to achieve these levels of sustainability by a gradual tightening of the building regulations is also looking less likely to be achieved. Anything which adds to developers' private costs seems likely to be strongly resisted by speculative builders, as they struggle in the current climate in some cases even to sell at cost (with zero profit). In an attempt to recoup at least some of their capital investment in new build, a number have developed, in essence, new shared equity schemes to stimulate sales of recently completed developments, offering, commonly, 75 per cent equity purchase, with the remaining 25 per cent to be purchased in five years or on re-sale.

There is a suggestion that government funds should be directed to promoting the sustainability agenda via increased and extended (to more households) subsidy of various measures to make existing housing, more 'green', such as via increased home insulation and energy efficiency measures. This would have the added benefit of helping to sustain employment in parts of the housing construction industry, which saw large job-losses in late 2008 and early 2009. However, with so many competing demands on government spending, it is doubtful whether such measures can realistically be undertaken to any great extent.

Although the development of a number of new, low-carbon communities had been proposed in the UK, including the government's eco-towns (see Chapter 5), it seems inconceivable in the present context that any developer will proceed with such ambitious plans. In a situation where it is proving very difficult to sell new homes, the prospect of creating several thousand speculatively must look highly unattractive, especially when (due to low-carbon ambitions) the cost of constructing these homes will be higher.

6. What will affordable housing be like in 20 years time?

All of the above questions are linked to this final one. What will affordable housing be like in 20 years time? In reflecting on this issue we will look at the influential Hills' Review of 2006. We will also use the interesting analysis of housing policy developed in an article by Professor Cole on the future of social housing in England, published in 2007.

6.1: Hills: Ends and means: the future roles of social housing in England

The government commissioned a major independent report in July 2006 to '*...stand back and ask what role social housing can play in 21st Century housing policy*'.

Professor John Hills of the Centre for Analysis of Social Exclusion at the London School of Economics was asked to carry out the review. He was asked to consider what social housing could do to help create genuinely mixed communities. Could the way social housing was run encourage social mobility and opportunities, including in the labour market, for people to get on in their lives? And whether social housing and other support could be more responsive to changing needs and enable greater geographical mobility?

The report generated significant interest in the sector and beyond because it offered the opportunity to reflect on a more radical approach to the management of social housing. In the run up to the report there was some talk that the findings might recommend the end to tenancies for life or that social housing eligibility should be subject to regular means testing.

He argued that whilst social housing did provide a crucial role in the lives of four million households it needed to do more to improve the services which tenants received and widen choice.

Affordability:
Hills concluded that rents have remained affordable with social rents having fallen in relation to average incomes, in conrtast to owner-occupiers, who have seen a doubling of since 1996.

Quality and satisfaction:
In relation to quality, Hills concluded that the physical standard of the housing stock had improved fast in recent years, with disadvantaged households much more likely to be in 'decent homes' if they are social tenants rather than if they are private ones.

> *But trends in and levels of tenant satisfaction are disappointing: one in seven social tenants are dissatisfied with their local area and their accommodation; one in five with their landlord; and one in four with the standards of repair and maintenance. Social tenants aged under 45 are much more likely to be unhappy with their homes than older tenants, or than private tenants of the same age. Overall, space per person in housing nationally has improved, but social tenants have less space than others, and less than ten years ago.*
> (LSE, press release, 2007.)

Mixed communities:
The report found that the role of social housing had changed over the last 25 years. Not only had the sector become much smaller, it was now targeted on those in greatest need. This contrasted with a post-World War Two situation, where social housing was aimed at those with a wider range of incomes. As a result, the composition of estates has changed, with tenants now more likely be on low incomes or unemployed.

...two-thirds of social housing is still in areas originally built as council estates, and for 25 years new tenants have come mainly from those in greatest need. 70 per cent of social tenants are now in the poorest two-fifths of the population, and half of social housing is in the most deprived fifth of areas. In the areas originally built as estates in flats, more than a fifth of social tenants report drug users or dealers as a serious problem. 18 per cent of social tenants in these areas say that they feel unsafe alone even at home or outside in daylight, three times the national rate.
(LSE, press release, 2007.)

Worklessness:
On the important issue of worklessness, Hills wrote:

Low rents can help tenants get into work, because they reduce benefit traps. But more than half those of working age in social housing are without paid work, twice the national rate. Some of this reflects disadvantages such as disability or lack of qualifications, but even allowing for these, employment rates are low. This is partly because those with the greatest needs are screened into social housing, but out of private housing. But it also reflects its location in particular areas, and the 'strikingly low' rate of tenants' job-related house moves. Nationally, one in eight moves is job-related, but each year only a few thousand social tenants – out of nearly 4 million – succeed in moving within social housing (even within the same area) to get a job or to get nearer to one.
(LSE, press release, 2007.)

Mobility and the housing ladder:
Hills reported that in spring 2005 more than 50 per cent of working age occupiers of social housing were not in paid work and he concluded that the '*...likelihood of someone in social housing being employed appears significantly lower than for other tenures*'.

He suggested that there were likely to be a number of factors at play here including the way in which people in greatest need ended up in social housing, the location of social housing in deprived areas and possible dependency effects. Nationally, only a few thousand tenants move home each year for work. One reason is that it is harder to compete to buy private housing. Ten years ago, fewer than ten per cent of young first-time buyers had help from family and friends with a deposit. Now it is nearly half, and those who are helped can afford deposits that are £27,000 higher than others. The report warns that people whose parents and grand-parents are tenants will lose out, as housing wealth cascades from generation to generation of owners.

Professor Hills concluded that while social housing plays a crucial role in the lives of nearly four million households, much more needs to be done to in four key areas:

1 Increase the attention given to the existing stock and tenant population

Hills argues that whilst most of the policy debate is on the supply of new housing, greater attention should be placed on the existing housing stock and the tenant population. Looking to improve the quality of the stock and increase customer satisfaction is key. There is a need to strengthen the tenant's voice since they have restricted housing choices.

2 To support more of an income mix within existing communities

Whilst Hills does advocate ensuring that new build housing was included within more affluent estates, he argued for six new approaches:

- large-scale remodelling of estates is a high cost and therefore limited way of developing a better income mix;
- review how allocations policies sometimes contribute to polarisation and develop choice as a model;
- diversification by purchasing stock in other neighbourhoods and selling stock in existing estates;
- utilise vacant land within social housing estates to develop them for other tenures;
- offering higher quality services and better management to retain higher-income tenants in social housing;
- improve the income and employment prospects of existing residents.

3 Support the livelihoods of tenants and others in housing need

This strand looked at how the employment options for tenants might be better achieved, through:

- improving the knowledge of the benefit system might encourage more people into work, as might less rapid changes in benefit, once someone starts work;
- the linkages between employment support and housing support need to be improved – low-cost social housing should help people into work;
- landlords could employ local people at neighbourhood level;
- review allocation schemes to give more weight to job-related transfers;
- consider increasing rents to increase supply but this could cause affordability issues.

4 To offer a more varied menu of services

This involves offering tenants more than simply a standard tenancy, and looking at other intermediate options between a full tenant and owner-occupation, and the state considering offering greater incentives to tenants who leave the tenure. New tenants may be offered alternatives to social housing, whilst existing tenants might be offered a review every few years to explore other intermediate tenure options.

6.2: What future for social housing in England?

In 2007, Professor Ian Cole of Sheffield Hallam University published a paper, *What Future for Social Housing in England?* (Cole, 2007). The article attempted to summarise the different policy perspectives about the future of social housing in Britain. Since the 1949 Housing Act, Cole (p1) reports that:

> *...the sector has been riddled with legislation, labyrinthine financial arrangements, countless subsidy regimes, perennial debates about its cost, its management performance, the design and quality of its dwellings and the impact of the sector on the tenants who live in it.*

Cole identifies four perspectives on British social housing policy from:

- The market idealists
- The revisionists
- The preservationists
- The reformists.

The market idealist perspective

This approach is fundamentally 'antagonistic' to the concept of social housing and perhaps had its heyday during the Thatcher governments in the 1980s. However, in recent years there is some evidence that the view that social housing has failed as a concept is gathering some support. Cole refers to the writings of Peter King who characterises housing policy as being centralised, offering little choice and reinforcing stigma. His main policy proposal is to reduce the subsidy paid to social landlords so that there is a genuine level playing field between the social housing sector and the private rented sector.

The revisionist perspective

This approach also considers that social housing has passed its sell by date. Its proponents are said by Cole to be writers such as Dwelly and Cowans and he refers to their Smith Institute report of 2006 entitled, '*Rethinking Social Housing*'. This approach says that in 21st century Britain social housing is now the tenure '*of last resort*' and that Britain's indicators of poverty are all made worse by housing poor people in the same areas.

This approach sees social housing as a problem and that the policy emphasis should be on enabling people to escape social housing and remove barriers which make people dependent on social housing. In this revisionist role, social housing still has a purpose; as a short-term safety-net for people, but not as a long-term housing solution.

The supporters of this approach claim that the system creates a cycle of welfare dependency where poor families are locked out of economic growth and prosperity, and that a vicious circle of dependency, poverty, crime and low educational attainment develops on social housing estates.

The preservationist perspective

This approach is about defending council housing against its transfer to housing associations, or the use of ALMOs, and to support calls for more direct investment in local authority housing (the so-called fourth option). This approach is best articulated by the campaign group 'Defend Council Housing', which has had some success in opposing stock transfers and ALMO proposals in some local authority areas. Until late in 2008, the government continued to insist that there is no 'fourth option', but as we have seen in January 2009, the government had begun to suggest that councils might be able to start building again.

The reformist perspective

This approach sees a continuing need for social housing, but recognises that the system needs to be changed. The approach recognises that non-market housing can create decent homes and neighbourhoods, and points to the desperate housing conditions in some countries like the USA, where there is much greater emphasis on market solutions.

Duncan Maclennan in a submission to the Hills' Review (Maclennan, 2006a) suggested that housing associations need to have greater flexibility in what they are allowed to do, and also challenges the view that larger landlords are necessarily better or less risky than smaller ones. He argues that the success of some housing plus initiatives is often despite the regulatory regimes which have been put in place (echoing here the NHF's iN Business agenda).

The reformist approach is to restructure social housing based on what needs to be done in different localities and not according to any 'preconceived template'.

7. Conclusions

So where does this take us? Clearly the Hills' Review and Cole's interesting analysis show that there is no real consensus about the future of affordable housing in the UK. Cole suggests that Hills' response has been to propose a largely 'reformist' agenda where housing providers need to 'adapt to survive'.

The Hills' Review attracted widespread comment in the sector, not least from the implied suggestion that tenancies might not be for life. However, in reading the Hills' Review it is impossible not to be concerned at the image he portrays of affordable housing. Indeed, Hills writes (p19) of the role which social housing can play:

> *...the evidence suggests that in terms of some of the key reasons for using social housing to achieve housing policy aims, the outcomes are at present disappointing.*

The picture Hills paints is a familiar one to housing professionals. Social housing has become increasingly a polarised and residual tenure. If this is to be changed it will be necessary to address some of the issues which Hills raised, including:

- Can we provide significantly more affordable housing?
- Can we open up affordable housing to people other than those on very low incomes?
- Can we do more to attract and retain higher-income households to live in affordable housing estates?
- Can we improve the livelihoods of existing social tenants and improve their life chances?

These are important questions for policy-makers. If we fail to address the challenges posed by Hills, social housing will continue to decline and will become an even more residualised tenure than it currently is. It will require policy-makers to address not only questions of supply and quality of new and existing housing, but also to address issues of social policy, benefits policy, education and training to ensure that affordable housing can provide a decent home for people who need it into the first half of the 21st century.

Hills and Cole have expressed their views, but you too will have a view as to what the future might bring for affordable housing. What is clear, is that for the foreseeable future there will continue to be affordable housing which will need to be managed, maintained and new dwellings built for those who cannot afford to buy. What is also clear, is that affordable housing has changed significantly since the 1986 Audit Commission report on *Managing the Crisis in Council Housing*; this process of change is unlikely to slow over the next 25 years.

References and further reading

Audit Commission (1986) *Managing the Crisis in Council Housing*, HMSO, London.

Barker, K. (2004) *Review of Housing Supply: Final Report*, HM Treasury, London.

Blair, T. (2002) *The courage of our convictions; why the reform of the public services is the route to social justice*, Fabian Society, London.

Bloom, H.S., Riccio, J.A. and Verma, N. (2005) *Promoting Work in Public Housing: The Effectiveness of JOBS-Plus, Final report*, Manpower Development Research Corporation, New York.

Chartered Institute of Housing (1999) *Social Housing in the 21st Century – the key issues*, CIH, Coventry.

Cole, I. (2007) *What future for social housing in England?*, People, Place and Policy Online.

Crosby, J. (2008) *Mortgage Finance: final report and recommendations*, HM Treasury, London.

Defend Council Housing (2006) *The Case for Council Housing in 21st Century Britain*, Russell Press, Nottingham.

Department for Communities and Local Government (2006) *Strong and Prosperous Communities – The Local Government White Paper*, CLG, London.

Department for Communities and Local Government (2006) *Monitoring the Longer Term Impact of Choice-based Lettings*, CLG Housing Research Summary 231, CLG, London.

Department for Work and Pensions (2006) *A New Deal For Welfare: Empowering People To Work*, The Stationery Office, London.

Department for Work and Pensions (2006a) *Income Related Benefits: Estimates of Take-Up in 2004/2005*, DWP, London.

Department for Work and Pensions (2006b) *Households Below Average Income: An analysis of the income distribution 1994/5-2004/5*, Corporate Document Services, Leeds.

Department of the Environment, Transport and the Regions (2000) *Quality and Choice – A decent home for all*, ODPM, London.

Dowler, C. (2009) 'Bail out could revive market', *Inside Housing*, 23 January 2009, p2, London.

Dowler, C. (2009) 'Fifty associations suffer as land values plunge', *Inside Housing*, 6 March 2009, pp1-3.

Dwelly, T. and Cowans, J. (eds.) (2006) *Rethinking Social Housing*, Smith Institute, London.

Ellery, S. (2009) 'Build Prices set to fall ten per cent during two years of deflation', *Inside Housing*, 13 February 2009, p4.

Hills, J. (1991) *Unravelling Housing Finance*, Clarendon Press, Oxford.

Hills, J. (2006) *Ends and means: the future roles of social housing in England*, CASE, London.

Hill, S., Lupton, M., Moody, G., and Regan, S. (2002) *A stake worth having? The potential for equity stakes in social housing*, Chartered Institute of Housing and IPPR, London.

Hills, J. and Stewart, K. (eds.) (2005) *A More Equal Society? New Labour, poverty, inequality and exclusion*, The Policy Press, Bristol.

HM Treasury and Office of the Deputy Prime Minister (2005) *The Government's Response to Kate Barker's Review of Housing Supply*, HM Treasury, London.

Hobcraft, J.N. (2002) 'Social Exclusion and the Generations', in J. Hills, J. LeGrand and D. Piachaud (eds.) *Understanding Social Exclusion*, OUP, Oxford.

Holmans, A. (1997) *Housing Inheritance: Current trends and future prospects*, Council of Mortgage Lenders, London.

Holmes, C. (2006) *Mixed Communities: Success and sustainability*,. Joseph Rowntree Foundation, Foundations, York.

iN Business For Neighbourhoods (2003) *Who we are, what we do*, inbiz.org website, London.

Independent Commission of Inquiry into the Future of Council Housing in Birmingham (2002) *One size doesn't fit all: Community housing and flourishing neighbourhoods*, Birmingham City Council, Birmingham.

Inside Housing (2004) 'Meeting the Barker Objectives', *Inside Housing*, 24 March, London.

Institute for Public Policy Research (2000) *Housing United – report of the IPPR Forum on the Future of Social Housing*, IPPR, London.

King, P. (2006) *Choice and The End of Social Housing*, Institute of Economic Affairs, Hobart Paper 155, IEA, London.

London School of Economics (2007) John Hills' Social Housing Report, press release.

Maclennan, D. (2006a) *Looking Forward, Aiming Higher?*, paper to the JRF Housing and Neighbourhoods Committee, JRF, York.

Maclennan, D. (2006b) 'UK housing policy reform – a global perspective', in Dwelly and Cowans (eds.) *Rethinking Social Housing*, Smith Institute, London.

Martin, G. and Watkinson, J. (2003) *Rebalancing communities by mixing tenures on social housing estates*, JRF Findings, York.

McArthur A., McGregor, A. and Hastings, A. (1996) *Less than equal? Community organisations and estate regeneration partnerships*, The Policy Press, Bristol.

National Housing Federation (2003) *Action for Change*, NHF, London.

Office of the Deputy Prime Minister (2005a) *Incentives and beyond? The transferability of the Irwell Valley Gold Service to new social landlords*, ODPM, London.

Office of the Deputy Prime Minister (2005b) *Affordability Targets: Implications for housing Supply*, ODPM, London.

Palmer, G., Kenway, P. and Wilcox, S. (2006) *Housing and Neighbourhoods Monitor*, Joseph Rowntree Foundation, York.

Pensions Commission (2005) *A New Pension Settlement for the 21st Century*, TSO, London.

Quality Housing Services (2006) *Customer Satisfaction Profile*, QHS, Congleton.

Rogers, E. (2009) '£169m of housing rescue fund unused', *Inside Housing*, 16 January 2009, p13, London.

Rogers, E. (2009) 'Beckett backs council housing', *Inside Housing,* 23 January 2009, p1 and 5, London.

Social Exclusion Unit/Cabinet Office (2001) *A New Commitment to Neighbourhood Renewal: National strategy action plan*, Cabinet Office, London.

Stephens, M., Whitehead, C. and Munro, M. (2005) *Lessons from the past, challenges for the future for housing policy*, ODPM, London.

Storey, C. (2009) 'A return to the boom years?', *Inside Housing*, 30 January 2009, pp10-11, London.

Tunstall, R. and Coulter, A. (2006) *Twenty-Five Years On Twenty Estates: Turning The Tide?*, Joseph Rowntree Foundation, York.

Turley, C. and Thomas, A. (2006) *Housing Benefit and Council Tax Benefit as in-work benefits*, DWP Research Report 383, Corporate Document Services, Leeds.

Wilcox, S. (2005) *More Apparent than Real? The decline of bricks and mortar subsidies*, ENHR Conference Paper, London.

Wilcox, S. (2008) *Uk Housing Review 2008/09*, CIH/BSA, Coventry and London.

Index

Notes:

1. Acts of parliament are only included in the index in cases where there is more than one reference in the text.
2. The index covers the main text but not the Glossary or references.